The Gold Cartel

The Gold Cartel

Government Intervention in Gold, the Mega-Bubble in Paper, and What This Means for Your Future

Dimitri Speck

Translated by Heinz Blasnik

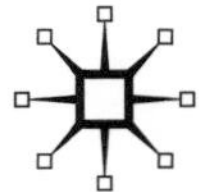

First published 2013 by
PALGRAVE MACMILLAN

Palgrave Macmillan in the UK is an imprint of Macmillan Publishers Limited, registered in England, company number 785998, of Houndmills, Basingstoke, Hampshire RG21 6XS.

Palgrave Macmillan in the US is a division of St Martin's Press LLC, 175 Fifth Avenue, New York, NY 10010.

Palgrave Macmillan is the global academic imprint of the above companies and has companies and representatives throughout the world.

Palgrave® and Macmillan® are registered trademarks in the United States, the United Kingdom, Europe and other countries.

ISBN 978–1–137–28642–0

This book is printed on paper suitable for recycling and made from fully managed and sustained forest sources. Logging, pulping and manufacturing processes are expected to conform to the environmental regulations of the country of origin.

A catalogue record for this book is available from the British Library.

A catalog record for this book is available from the Library of Congress.

‘What would happen if the Treasury sold a little gold in this market?’

Fed Chairman Alan Greenspan in May 1993

‘We can hold the price of gold very easily.’

Fed Governor Wayne Angell in July 1993

Contents

List of Figures and Tables ix

Preface xiv

Acknowledgements xix

1 Why Gold? 1

2 The Crises of the 1990s 5

3 The Strange Behaviour of Gold during Crises 8

4 The Strange Intraday Behaviour of Gold 16

5 The First Statistical Studies 19

6 Statistical Proof and Dating of Gold Interventions 23

7 Intraday Movements of the Gold Price 1986–2012 27

8 Gold is Different 34

9 Means of Gold Market Intervention I: Sales 37

10 Means of Gold Intervention II: Gold Lending 41

11 The Gold Carry Trade 44

12 Coordination of Private Banks and Central Banks 46

13 Giving the Game Away: Central Bankers are Human Beings Too 50

14 The Books are Silent 52

15 The Miraculous Gold Multiplication 56

16 How Much Gold is on Loan Worldwide? 61

17 Means of Gold Intervention III: Intervention through the Futures Market 76

18 The Gold Pool and Other Gold Market Interventions before 1993 82

19 5 August 1993, 8.27 a.m. EST: The Beginning of Systematic Gold Market Interventions 93

20 The Decisive Fed Meeting 99

21 Greenspan Ponders Gold Market Interventions 108

22 Phases of Gold Price Suppression 116

23 Shock and Awe 122

24 The Financial Market Crisis of 2008 and the Euro Crisis of 2011 131

25 Strong Dollar and Weak Mining Stocks 140

26 Interventions in the Silver Market 144

27 Swapped Bundesbank Gold and Other Mysteries 151

28 Who Intervenes? 154

29 The Mystery of 18 May 2001, 12.31 170

30 The Effects of Gold Price Suppression 180

31 The Wonderful World of Bubbles 191

32 Have Many Mini-Bubbles Created a Mega-Bubble? 199

33 Money or Credit? 221

34 Possible Scenarios for the Future 232

35 Back to Gold 262

Appendices 268

Notes 288

Index 300

List of Figures and Tables

Figures

P.1	Gold price 1970 to today, in US dollars per oz (31.1 g)	xiii
P.2	Intraday movement of the gold price on 23 April 2012	xv
1.1	Metals: ratio of worldwide stocks to production	3
3.1	Gold, US treasury notes and the DJIA 1998 (indexed)	9
3.2	DJIA, sharp declines	10
3.3	Average trend of the DJIA around significant lows	11
3.4	Average trend of US treasury notes around significant lows in the DJIA	12
3.5	Average movement of the gold price around significant lows in the DJIA	13
3.6	'Safe havens' compared	14
4.1	The gold price intraday movement on 1, 2 and 3 June 2004	17
4.2	Average intraday price movement August 1998–July 2003	17
5.1	Average intraday price movement August 1998–July 2003	20
5.2	Clawar's study	21
6.1	Gold price movements in New York vs the rest of the world	24
6.2	Price movements of gold in New York vs the rest of the world	26
7.1	Average intraday price movement February 1986–July 1993	28
7.2	Average intraday price movement August 1993–December 2012	29
7.3	Average intraday price movement in 1993, from the beginning of the year to 4 August	30
7.4	Average intraday price movement from 5 August 1993 to year end	31
7.5	Average intraday price movement in 1994	32
7.6	Average intraday price movement in 1995	33
8.1	Gold: stocks vs flows	35
8.2	Satisfying consumption from inventories	35
9.1	Gold sales by central banks	38
9.2	Influence of advance announcements of gold sales in 1999	39
10.1	Operation of the gold-lending business	42
11.1	Functioning of the gold carry trade	45
12.1	Cooperation between central banks and bullion banks out of shared interests	47

14.1 Excerpt from the balance sheet of the German Bundesbank as at 31 December 2011 53
14.2 Amount of gold lent out by the Swiss National Bank (in tons) 54
15.1 Amount of gold lent out by the Bundesbank 58
15.2 Storage facilities holding the Bundesbank's gold 59
16.1 Foreign central bank gold, the amount stored at the New York Fed 65
16.2 Foreign central bank gold holdings, total stock and stock stored in New York 67
16.3 Gold on loan worldwide, estimated on the basis of the stock stored in New York 69
16.4 Central bank gold that has entered the market worldwide 71
16.5 Gold price and global central bank gold supply 72
17.1 Intraday price movements 80
17.2 The three methods of gold price intervention 81
19.1 Gold December contract on 5 August 1993 95
19.2 Gold price from 1970, in US dollars per troy ounce (31.1g) 96
19.3 Gold 1992–96 97
20.1 Three alternative stores of value 102
20.2 Excerpt from the minutes of the FOMC meeting of 6 and 7 July 1993 103
20.3 Monetary policy-related motives for interventions against a rising gold price 106
22.1 The phases of gold price suppression 117
22.2 Gold lease rate, three months 120
23.1 Gold over three days, 27–29 July 2009 123
23.2 Gold and the euro from 23 July–2 August 2009, indexed 125
23.3 Gold: number of days per year with shock-like declines 128
23.4 Intraday movements 129
24.1 Five-Year Treasury Constant Maturity Rate 132
24.2 Gold in 2008 134
24.3 Gold in 2011 138
25.1 Gold mines and gold, 3 and 4 December 2012 142
26.1 Average intraday price movement of silver, Aug. 1998–Dec. 2012 146
26.2 Silver price 2010–12, in US dollars per troy ounce (31.1g) 147
26.3 Average intraday price movement of silver Feb. 2010–April 2011 148
26.4 Average intraday price movement of silver May 2011–July 2012 149
28.1 Excerpts from the Fed's monthly statement, January 2001 156
28.2 Excerpts from Federal Reserve bulletins compared 157

28.3 Closing prices of the front month contract at the New York COMEX for the years 1995–2002 160
28.4 Gold and share of prices in quartiles below round hundred numbers (x75–x00), smoothed 167
28.5 Gold: defence and abandonment of the $300 level 169
29.1 Gold: net positioning of commercial hedgers (proportion of total open interest) 171
29.2 Gold: share of the four largest traders of the total net short position (in percentages) 173
29.3 Intraday movement of gold from 18–20 May 2001 174
29.4 Dow Jones Industrial Average, 2000–02 178
30.1 Foreign exchange reserves of Japan and China 185
30.2 Share of foreign holders of US federal debt 186
30.3 Gold's share of total central bank reserves 187
30.4 US current account deficit 189
31.1 Conventional credit bubble 197
31.2 The inverse bubble of the gold carry trade 198
32.1 South Sea Bubble 201
32.2 US monetary aggregate M2 relative to GDP 204
32.3 USA: total debt relative to GDP 205
32.4 Market capitalisation of US corporations relative to GDP, partly estimated 207
33.1 The two facets of carriers of value 225
33.2 Investment duration of financial claims: amount relative to GDP 228
33.3 Stocks and flows 229
34.1 Germany: total debt relative to GDP 233
34.2 Canada: total debt relative to GDP 235
34.3 UK: total debt relative to GDP 249
34.4 Japan: total debt relative to GDP 251
34.5 World: total debt relative to GDP 257
34.6 Australia: total debt relative to GDP 258
34.7 The golden triangle of monetary and credit policy 260
35.1 World GDP and the global stock of gold 263
35.2 Gold 12–18 April 2013 – the 'Gold Crash' 265
A.1A Intraday charts of gold to 4 August 1993 268
A.1B Intraday charts of gold from 5 August 1993 272
A.2 Illustration: gold intraday intervention pattern (schematic) 283
A.3 Illustration: excerpt from the balance sheet of the German Bundesbank 284

Table

A.1 Interest income of the Bundesbank from gold lending (in millions of euro) 285

Figure P.1 Gold price 1970 to today, in US dollars per oz (31.1 g)

Preface

Let us look back on the financial crises of the past few years. In 2008, the bankruptcy of US investment bank Lehman Brothers triggers the biggest financial crisis in decades. Stock prices fall, many bonds no longer trade. Banks do not trust each other and interbank lending stops dead. Queues form in front of several banks and money is withdrawn in panic. With barely comprehensible speed, one terrifying news item after another is released. The total collapse of the financial system is feared. Both institutional investors and private savers transfer their investments into safe government bonds and gold. And what happens to the gold price? It falls.

Only a short time later the eurozone crisis keeps people on tenterhooks. The rescue measures enacted since the previous financial crisis have cost governments many billions. Now these governments are themselves in danger. Many have large ongoing budget deficits. More and more people have doubts about the solvency of Greece, Portugal, or even Spain. Once again, investors move their money into safe havens and buy the remaining safe bonds and gold. And what happens to the gold price during the most critical phases of the crisis? It falls.

During the crises of the 1990s, the Asian, Russian or Long-Term Capital Management (LTCM) crisis, it already appeared as though gold no longer fulfilled its typical role as a safe haven. There has to be an explanation for the fact that the gold price falls even as the markets are in the grip of panic. Sales on account of crisis-induced liquidity demand are out of the question, as the gold would actually have to be available. But in 2008, for example, both coins and bars were in short supply. This raises the question as to whether there is a 'secret player' influencing the gold price.

Rumours that central banks are intervening in the gold market have been circulating for many years. They supposedly want to avert uncontrollable price increases and it is said that they even offer part their own reserves of the precious metal for sale for this purpose. What prompts such rumours is, among other things, the extremely conspicuous manner in which the gold price tends to move in the short term. Time and again the price drops like a rock, falling within minutes by tens of dollars or more, without there

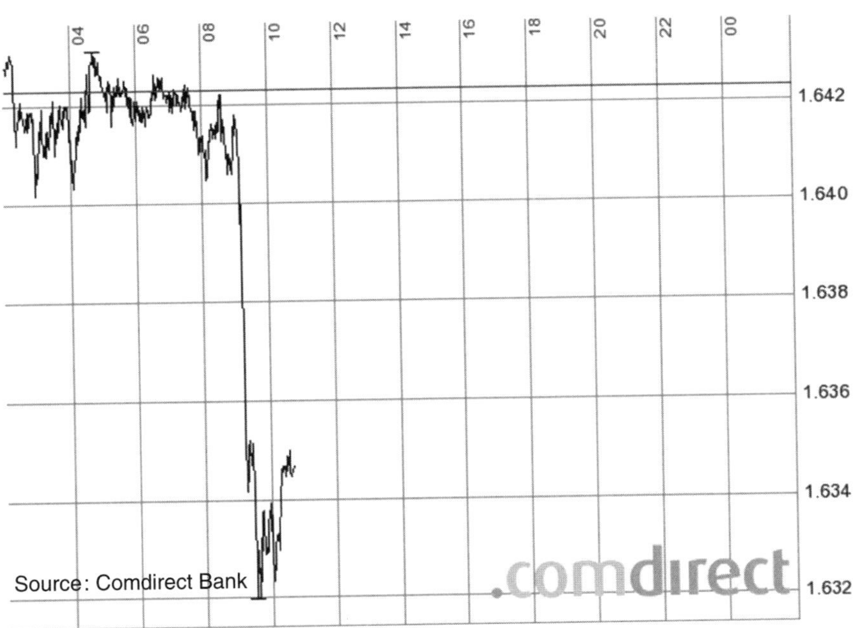

Figure P.2 Intraday movement of the gold price on 23 April 2012

being an exogenous trigger such as market-moving news. Figure P.2 shows such a price drop, similar to hundreds that have occurred both before and after.

But why should the central banks suppress the gold price? They hold a lot of gold and should be interested in a rising price, as that would produce profits for them. After all, central banks too have a duty to invest the funds that have been entrusted to them, their 'reserves', not only safely, but also profitably. Furthermore, there is the question as to whether one can carry out such activities over many years without them becoming public knowledge. Wouldn't a great many people have to be involved, which would be difficult to conceal? Moreover, investors tend to resort to countless excuses in order to blame their misfortunes on others. Isn't the theory that there are regular interventions in the gold market also an attempt to shift blame, in this case by pointing fingers at the powerful central banks?

Central banks control short-term interest rates and buy bonds in large amounts in order to support their prices. They have time and again intervened in foreign exchange markets. However, gold in amounts exceeding annual demand by an order of magnitude is stored in their vaults as well. They could, therefore, easily influence this market. Reasons for this would certainly exist, such as, for instance, the calming of markets in times of crisis. The public at large knows about interventions in, for example, the foreign exchange markets, as the central banks themselves make them public. Full disclosure of their activities is, however, not a given. Both in the foreign exchange markets as well as in the bond markets central banks have not only engaged in open interventions, but often in secret ones as well. They expect this to be more effective. These interventions do, however, leave traces in prices or on their balance sheets, which have come to the attention of market observers and researchers in the past. Many interventions that are generally known to the public today were originally performed in secret and only admitted to later.

The fact that long-running interventions leave traces has to apply to the gold market as well. There are, in particular, traces in the price itself. After all, the price is the proximate target of interventions, since they are supposed to influence it. It is therefore the primary target of investigation for the identification of interventions. In gold's case, balance sheets pose a more difficult problem. A number of balance sheet items that are mandatory for the private sector are missing in central bank balance sheets. Instead there exist hints in the form of remarks uttered by central bankers. A few of their deliberations with regard to the means and above all the motives of the effectively secret interventions in the gold market have been published.

We are following these leads. Established sources form the basis of all the essential conclusions; we touch upon market rumours only at the margins, in order to round out the picture, even though quite a few of them are probably true. The aim is to get to the bottom of the activities of the most powerful participants in the gold market, the central banks. We will see that interventions have been ongoing for many years, investigate how they work and what goals they are supposed to achieve.

However, the central banks don't act on their own, but cooperate with private institutions. Such cooperation also exists in other areas, such as for instance, in takeovers of ailing banks. Even in the case of the LIBOR scandal uncovered in 2012, in which private banks manipulated the benchmark interest rate over many years, it appeared as though a central bank had been involved, namely the Bank of England. There are many motives for such cooperation, such as the delegation of certain specific tasks. Cooperation can furthermore reduce the effort and the number of people directly involved in interventions, since not everyone taking part in an intervention is necessarily aware that they are, in fact, participating in one. Many probably simply do their work in the interest of making a profit for the bank. The private banks involved therefore not only act as agents, but incidentally pursue the same goal as the central banks on account of their profit motive.

When central banks intervene in the gold market, this affects not only the precious metals, but also other markets. They don't want to create benefits for a handful of jewellers, but specifically aim to influence these other markets. However, not only foreign exchange markets and interest rates are the actual targets of these interventions, but the financial system as a whole. Central bankers know that the credit money system depends on confidence, and they shore it also up with methods that only make sense upon a second glance.

As is the case with every bit of meddling in the markets, the following also holds true for interventions in the gold market: if one pulls a lever at one point, something moves at another, something that often wasn't necessarily intended and desired. Gold market interventions have been a formative element of the financial architecture since the 1990s. They have been one of the foundations of the large current account deficit of the USA. First and foremost, however, they have supported an exceptionally high level of indebtedness. The worldwide amount of debt in all sectors – governments, households and the corporate sector – was able to reach a record level because of them.

The finite amount of gold is diametrically opposed to the infinitely expandable amount of credit. With credit, one party's liability is concurrently always the asset of another. It is therefore impossible to simply reduce the high level of debt without doing any damage. The usual outcomes for the economy are antithetic, namely either deflation or inflation. In a deflation, borrowers default on their debt and the reciprocal credit claims are destroyed at the same time. It often coincides with severe recessions. In an inflationary period money loses its purchasing power. In an inflation, the actual problem, namely the excessive level of outstanding debt, usually remains unresolved.

The amount of outstanding debt globally is without historical precedent in peacetime. As a consequence of severing the dollar's tie to gold in the early 1970s and with the help of gold market interventions since the early 1990s, it was possible to increase the amount of outstanding credit excessively. Historically, excessively high levels of debt have always been followed by financial and then economic crises. Monetary policy measures alone won't do the trick this time either. Rather, it is to be feared that at least one generation will live through a time characterised by debt deleveraging. Gold is the obverse of credit-based money. It is no one's liability and cannot be inflated away. It is the natural antagonist of the primary object the central banks are concerned with – paper money.

DIMITRI SPECK

Acknowledgements

This book would not exist if not for a number of people who gave a helping hand directly or by doing preliminary work. Harry Clawar, Bill Murphy and Chris Powell made me aware of the topic. Frank Veneroso brought gold market interventions to the attention of the public early on, in an article published in *Forbes* magazine in 1995. My German publisher Christian Jund gave me the idea for the book's title. Palgrave Macmillan has made it possible to make the book available to an international audience. For this purpose the text not only had to be revised, but also translated, for which I want to express my sincere thanks to my translator Heinz Blasnik. Thanks also go to GATA, Philip Boggs and other sponsors of the translation. Thanks also to Pete Baker of Palgrave Macmillan, my copy-editing experts Keith Povey and Joy Tucker, along with colleagues who helped with illustrations, as well as to all suppliers of data and information (used mainly in the figures) and other supporters.

I originally published a book in Germany with the title *Geheime Gold Politik* (*Secret Gold Policy*) but this book, *The Gold Cartel,* is a completely revised new edition.

DIMITRI SPECK

Chapter 1
Why Gold?

For hundreds of years gold and silver were synonymous with the term 'money'. Most of the time payments were made directly with precious metals – for instance, with coins containing silver. However, bank notes backed by gold were often widely used as well. This was, for instance, the case in the 'gold standard', in which payment was not effected with physical gold, but the monetary unit (such as the 'dollar') was defined by a fixed weight of gold, and could be redeemed in gold on demand. It was completely outside the realm of the imaginable that it would ever be possible to pay with 'unredeemable paper money', and, historically, there were only very few temporally and locally limited episodes in which money was not backed by a commodity. Today, since the 1970s to be precise, one pays all over the world with money that is based on claims denominated in an abstract unit. It doesn't convey any rights, except the right to exchange it for other claims of the same type.

These 'dollars', 'yen' or 'euro' can only function as money because the process of their creation is based on regulations designed to limit their issuance. Historically, this system has developed because monetary systems based on gold or silver have drawbacks. The use of precious metals as money was thus frequently criticised, and they were labelled as 'barbaric relics' or 'useless metal'. Sayings like 'One cannot eat gold' are supposed to connote its alleged uselessness.

The drawbacks begin already with the production process, as gold has to be dug out of the earth with great effort. Sometimes the environment is polluted to an alarming extent in the process. The distribution of gold supplies is, moreover, regionally quite unequal, due to geographical and historical reasons. Furthermore, the supply is limited, so that the alleged 'needs' of a growing economy – or those of a government budget getting out of hand? – cannot be adequately served (whereby it is precisely this aspect that is seen as a benefit by supporters of gold).

Today, gold is no longer a means of payment. It no longer plays a role in large business transactions, in foreign trade or even in transactions between governments. It is, however, still held as a store of value. Private individuals usually hold it in the form of coins or bars (in some regions also in the form of jewellery, provided it is not trading at a large premium to its bullion value). A sizable amount of gold is also stored by the central banks, approximately 31,000 tons according to official statements. That is a multiple of the annual consumption of the metal.

The foregoing points to an important difference to other commodities, for only in silver is this store of value function otherwise found to a noteworthy extent. It is estimated that up to today approximately 170,000 tons of gold have been mined[1] and that most of it still exists in accessible form. By contrast, annual mine production amounts to approximately 2,800 tons at the time of writing, with annual consumption (industrial demand, jewellery fabrication, dentistry) amounting to perhaps 2,400 tons. Thus, the total supply of gold mined to date amounts to about 70 times the amount consumed annually. That is an extraordinarily high ratio of stocks to flows. While inventories of other commodities usually last only for months, one could stop gold production for many years and still be able to satisfy consumption demand. Of the two most important monetary functions, gold has, after all, only lost its usefulness as a medium of exchange; it has retained its function as a store of value. Figure 1.1 shows the ratio of inventories to annual production of various metals. Even though the values are only estimates, are highly variable depending on the business cycle and partly depend on definitions (is jewellery part of the stock, or is it part of what has been consumed?), they nevertheless make the extraordinary role of gold compared to other commodities plain. The chart is meant to clarify this state of affairs (only half of all the gold ever mined is assumed to be part of the available stock).

Gold is, however, also different from other investment assets. One can store value in assets like stocks or real estate as well. In contrast to gold, however, these are less liquid, often not long-lived and exposed to special risks – for instance, entrepreneurial risks. There are also differences between gold and financial capital – that is to say, credit claims, bonds and credit money. As our money is no longer backed by a commodity, it depends in the final analysis on a debtor's ability to perform. Even though the central banking system ensures that no one has to fear that his money will become worthless in the event that a specific bank draft is not honoured, this dependence is still a given – it has merely been transferred to governments. If the state no longer can or wants to fulfil its duties in this regard, money

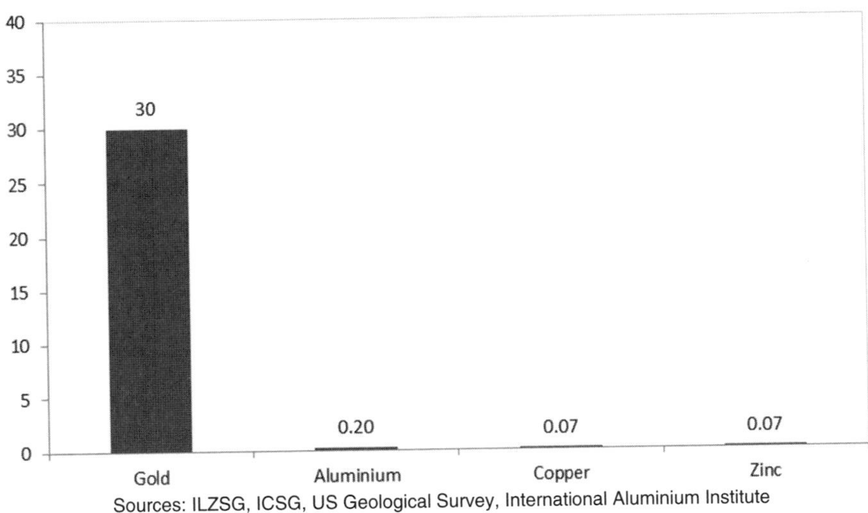

Figure 1.1 Metals: ratio of worldwide stocks to production

can become worthless at a stroke (which has happened time and again in the past).

The supply of gold can, furthermore, only be increased with great effort, namely by mining. This differentiates it from financial capital based on credit claims, which can be created on the macro-economic level by simply incurring additional debt. This procedure fosters the threat of inflation, whereby the monetary unit, the currency, loses value. By contrast to paper money, gold therefore depends neither on the volition nor capacity of a debtor, nor can it be inflated away. That makes gold unique, it makes it the ultimate store of value – and it also makes it the object of monetary and central bank policy.

Gold is a transnational money, independent of governments. It is also independent of a society's ability to maintain the purchasing power of money. It retains its real value through periods of inflation. Its value doesn't disappear even in the event that entire nations or their currencies collapse. Gold from antiquity is still worth something today, most of the national currencies that circulated only a century ago aren't. As a money transcending states, gold is in direct competition with the money which today's central banks are in charge of. When the gold price rises, investors and savers usually conclude that paper currencies are weak, that an inflation threat looms, or they fear even worse things, such as a total loss of their savings due to a banking system collapse.

Conversely, confidence is bolstered when the gold price doesn't rise. Inflation expectations are reduced when the best-known indicator of currency devaluation emits no warning signals. However, in times of tension and crisis in the financial markets, a flat gold price also has a calming effect: then it indicates that there is, after all, no sufficient reason yet to move one's funds into the ultimate safe haven. The crisis appears not to be serious. It is therefore conceivably in the interest of central banks that the gold price doesn't rise, or at least doesn't rise in uncontrollable fashion. They would have enough gold at their disposal to brake its ascent, as a multiple of annual demand is stored in their vaults. But have central banks actively arranged for the gold price not to rise in times of crisis?

Chapter 2

The Crises of the 1990s

The financial crisis of 2008 and the euro crisis are undoubtedly among the most worrisome crises of the past few decades. There were, however, also crises before these, even though their effects in most cases remained regionally contained (while still creating enormous economic problems in the regions concerned). In September 1992, the crisis of the British pound made headlines. The pound was pegged to the other European currencies through the European Monetary System (EMS). However, this led to an overvaluation of the pound relative to the strength of the UK economy. Politicians and central bankers refused to acknowledge this – at least, they didn't take any actions as a consequence (in the background there were in addition tensions in the EMS as a result of Germany's reunification and the pending European currency union). However, a number of fund managers, among them George Soros, recognised the pound's overvaluation and proceeded to bet against it to the tune of billions. They sold the pound short and eventually forced the British to abandon the defence of their currency. The pound fell and the hedge funds made big profits. Subsequently, they were accused to have been responsible for the crisis. However, after the devaluation the funds had to buy back exactly the same amount of pounds they had previously sold short. If the funds had been responsible for the crisis, then the pound would have risen back to its initial value as a result of their short covering. However, it didn't. The funds, therefore, merely provided the trigger for the pound's decline. The real reason was put in place beforehand, in the course of pegging the exchange rate. The pound was overvalued relative to the performance of the UK economy.

'The man who broke the Bank of England', as Soros was later called, could make billions in profits because he recognized a mispricing that was originally created by politicians. Above all, he showed politicians what the limits of their power were. Basic economic laws such as that of supply and demand cannot be abolished by decree. However, not all politicians drew the conclusion to henceforth act within the framework of these laws. It appears rather that the EMS crisis has given rise to the notion that it would be better to keep market interventions secret. If speculators like Soros don't notice them, they also cannot act against them. Interventions might then be successful for longer. There are two more reasons to discuss the EMS crisis at this juncture: first, as we will see further below, it happened only ten months before the interventions in the gold market began. One must therefore assume that politicians and central bankers were under the sway of the EMS crisis. In any case, they decided to execute interventions in the gold market as inconspicuously as possible. Second, Soros is of importance as he reportedly was active in the gold market as well.

In December 1994 another currency crisis followed. It is often referred to as the 'Tequila Crisis'. The Mexican peso was pegged to the US dollar and, as was the case with the UK and the pound, it was overvalued relative to the economy's fundamentals. In addition, there was a lack of political stability. The peso came under pressure and had to be devalued. An economic crisis followed on the heels of the currency crisis. The International Monetary Fund (IMF), which regarded this crisis as something new and called it 'the first financial crisis of the 21st century', helped out with billions.

Funds also came from the USA. These were provided by the Exchange Stabilization Fund (ESF). The ESF, which is administered by the government, was founded in 1934, specifically to stabilise the US dollar and the foreign exchange markets. It acts fairly autonomously and most of the time covertly. However, in the course of the peso crisis it made headlines, as it was used to circumvent Congress, which had refused to provide aid to Mexico. Many US politicians didn't regard support of other countries as a function of a US stabilisation fund.[2] The ESF is of importance with regard to gold policy, as a number of observers suspect that it is an agent in gold market interventions. It is probably the agency most likely to possess the legal authority for interventions in the foreign exchange and gold markets. More on this later.

More crises exhibiting comparable patterns followed: in 1997 the Asian crisis in Thailand, Indonesia and Malaysia, and in 1998 the Russian crisis. In each case the currencies of soft currency countries with high interest rates were pegged to a harder currency with lower interest rates. Such a pegged exchange rate leads to investment by foreigners, who believe their investments to be safe from devaluation. It also furthers the assumption of debt denominated in foreign currency by domestic debtors, as they can pay lower interest rates than previously. Both activities lead to an economic boom that is, to a large extent, driven by disproportionate credit growth. It is accompanied by a large current account deficit, an excess of imports of goods and services. These are financed with debt as well. This means that such countries consume more than they produce. It should actually be clear that such arrangements cannot last forever. In the wake of such excesses there are regularly crises forcing the economy to adapt to reality, often coupled with considerable slumps in economic activity.

In spite of that, politicians time and again adopt such currency pegs. Europe's politicians have done the same. In spite of being sufficiently forewarned by these previous examples, they have also pegged weak currencies to strong ones with the introduction of the euro (with the only difference that the common currency has made a cleansing separation more difficult). The pegging of weak currencies to a strong currency is an important backdrop of the euro crisis that has been in train since the end of 2009. Such crises due to currency pegs are usually preceded by many years of enormous capital misallocations due to too low interest rates, without which the subsequent crisis could not have developed. We will examine the market trend of the gold price during the 2008 crisis and the euro crisis in more detail later. However, does the behaviour of the gold price during crises categorically hint at interventions in the gold market?

Chapter 3

The Strange Behaviour of Gold during Crises

To begin with: gold is not a good investment. Over many decades its price remains the same, while real estate, bonds and stocks yield income or rise in price. Even in times of moderate inflation, contrary to conventional wisdom, gold often does not protect against losses in real terms. It is quite different when there are substantial risks to monetary stability. That is when gold's safe haven function comes to the fore, as it is neither dependent on a promise to pay, nor possible to inflate away. Gold, therefore, provides protection in financial crises harbouring rising default risks and when money is debased markedly. This has also been examined statistically in the context of past events.[3]

As soon as people fear for the safety and value of their investments, they flee into safe havens. In panic, they sell everything that might decline in price or lose its value entirely and invest their money in what they consider safe. We now want, first, to examine how gold behaved in the course of the Russian crisis in 1998. This crisis was one of the last major crises prior to that of 2008. One of its effects was that investors fled from the debt of not overly creditworthy borrowers. As a result of this, the US hedge fund 'Long-Term Capital Management' (LTCM) got into trouble, as it had engaged in highly leveraged bets on interest rate convergence. The threat of a collapse of the financial system loomed. The American central bank, the Federal Reserve Bank (Fed) organised what was at the time a unique rescue in order to avert a chain reaction.[4]

Between mid-July and the end of September 1998 stocks in the USA fell by approximately 20 per cent. During the same period, treasury bonds rose massively, as they were regarded as a safe haven. And what happened to the gold price? Overall, it barely moved; it even fell intermittently! It was as though gold were not a safe investment, but rather just as unsafe as the debt of a dubious borrower. The chart depicted in Figure 3.1 shows the performance of an ounce of gold in US dollar terms, of an investment in ten-year

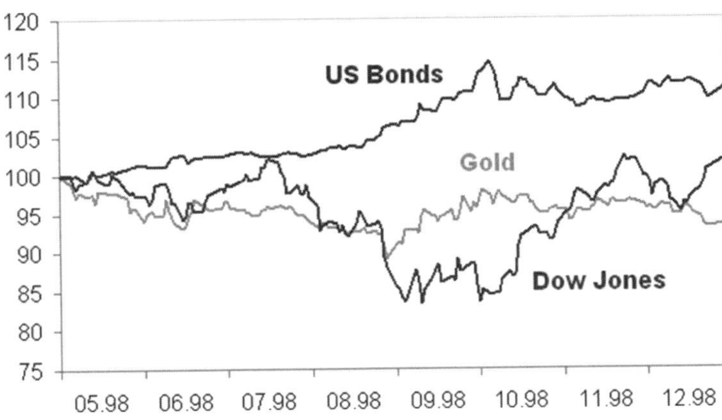

Figure 3.1 Gold, US treasury notes and the DJIA 1998 (indexed)

treasury notes and of the US stock market, represented by the Dow Jones Industrial Average during the crisis.

It is striking that gold did not benefit from the severe crisis, but, on the contrary, fell hand in hand with the stock market. Of course, gold had not become obsolete as a 'safe haven', nor should normal market phenomena like profit-taking have occurred. Why should these occur precisely at a moment when the markets were hankering for safety? One can, of course, not entirely rule out customary market-related reasons for price declines in individual cases, as sometimes, during financial crises, liquidity is needed at any price and everything is sold, including gold. That is, however, quite rare. Alternatively, the question arises whether targeted gold sales initiated by central banks were supposed to suggest calm to the markets. The crisis would be mitigated in this way; investors would be prevented from panicking even more.

In order to better estimate the price behaviour of gold in crisis situations, we now want to look at a multitude of financial crises at once, instead of only individual examples. By creating an average, we can examine the typical trend in crises and, as the case may be, detect if there are any anomalies. Financial market crises are, however, not always unambiguously identifiable by exogenous (such as political) characteristics; furthermore, they often drag on over a period of many months, while the panic in the markets takes place in the span of just a few weeks. We therefore examine not only well-known financial market crises, but more generally problematic periods in the financial markets. We identify such problematic periods by sharp price declines in the stock market, which reflects crisis sentiment quite reliably.

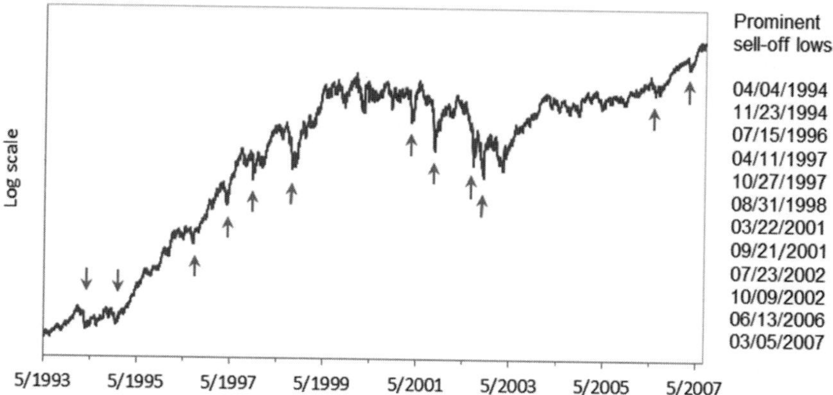

Figure 3.2 DJIA, sharp declines

We employ a manual procedure for this purpose.[5] We select the respective periods of pronounced declines manually. What is decisive for the selection is that the declines have occurred rapidly and have attained a meaningful extent relative to the preceding trend. Such declines are typically associated with uncertainty among investors, coupled with a sense of crisis and incipient panic. Figure 3.2 shows the price trend of the Dow Jones Industrial Average from 5 August 1993 to 7 September 2007. The start date coincides with the beginning of systematic interventions against a rising gold price (we will later show how the date has been arrived at), the end is chosen in such a manner that the time period since the great financial crisis is not included (we will examine this period separately).

The 12 troughs of the problematic market phases that have been chosen are highlighted on the chart. On these days, stock prices reached their lowest level in the course of the 12 pronounced declines. At these points the respective panic mood was presumably at its height as well. What triggered the declines in each particular case is not of interest; the point of the following examination, which proceeds from particular cases to the illumination of a general principle, is to show how the markets behaved on average. We therefore take a look at the mean values.

For this purpose the lowest price at the end of each decline is used as a temporal anchor. This means that we take the trend immediately before and after the low point and calculate an average of all 12 occurrences. Specifically, the average price trend of all 12 declines in the three months before and the three months after

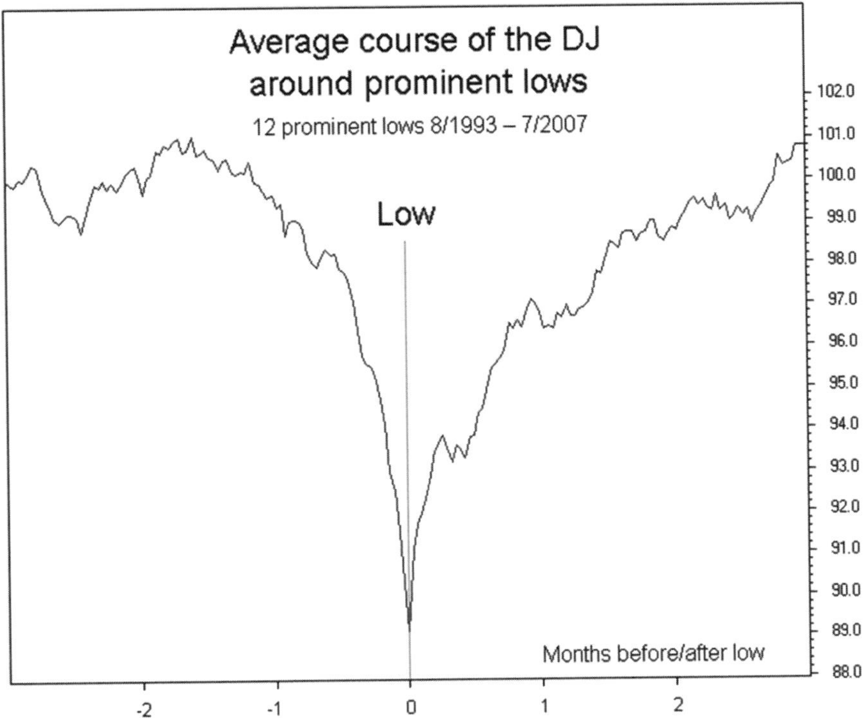

Figure 3.3 Average trend of the DJIA around significant lows

reaching the trough is determined. Figure 3.3 shows the result in detail. This is not a normal chart, but one that shows the average price trend of the Dow Jones Industrial Average in the 12 market breaks occuring over a six-month period in total. This is, therefore, how a typical market correction in the stock market evolves.

It can be seen that the market, on average, reached its peak about one and a half months before reaching its trough. Then a four-week-long period of weakness ensued, and only thereafter a marked acceleration began, about two weeks before the trough was reached. The reason for this sharp deterioration is that individual stock holders cannot limit their losses without weakening the market as a whole by their selling or hedging activities. Uncertainty and incipient panic lead to an average price decline of about 10 per cent, as market participants are unable to gauge the eventual extent of the losses in advance. They must fear that the market could fall further (which does after all occasionally happen). The chart, moreover, visualises something that has been well known in the markets for a long time: typically price declines happen much faster than the subsequent recoveries. Due to the panic that strikes when prices fall, declines happen in accelerated fashion. Recoveries, on the other hand, happen more slowly, as the fear of loss is, as a rule, greater than the fear of missing out on gains.

Next, we examine treasury bonds. As a rule they are – similar to gold – held to be a safe investment. How do treasury bonds behave during stock market declines, when a panic begins? To find this out we employ the same method as before, with only one decisive difference: as our temporal anchor we once again use the troughs of the concomitant declines of the Dow, and not those in bonds. Figure 3.4 shows the average trend of an investment in the ten-year treasury note three months before and three months after a major panic low in the stock market, not the bond market. In this way we can examine the influence of the stock market on the fixed-income markets during panic phases. The long line in the middle marks the troughs of the DJIA, the junctures at which the panic should typically also reach its apex.

We can see that treasury bonds typically begin to rise markedly about one and a half weeks prior to the significant low in the Dow. This is roughly congruent with the period during which stock prices

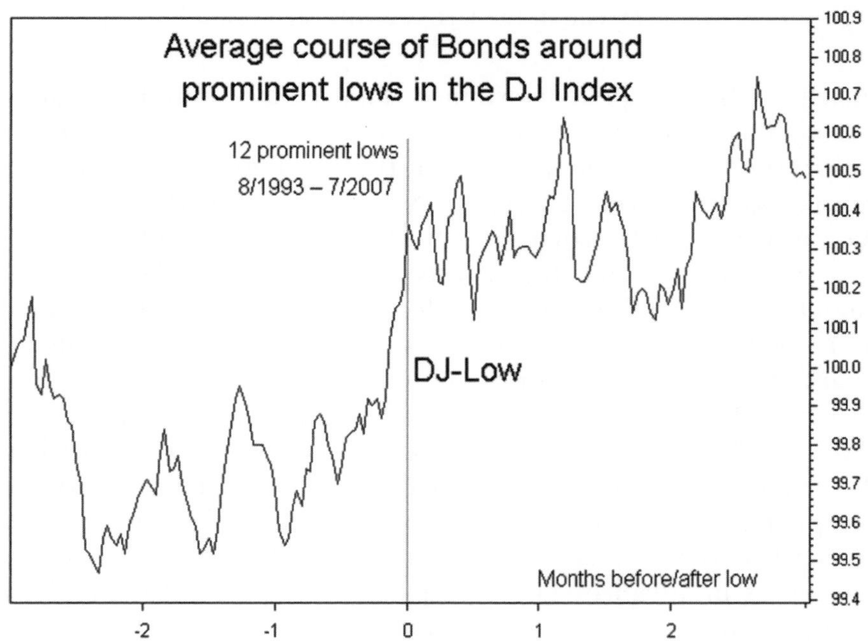

Figure 3.4 Average trend of US treasury notes around significant lows in the DJIA

fall in accelerated fashion. Bonds therefore fulfil their function as a safe destination for money as expected and rise when uncertainty grips the markets. When stocks decline fast, bonds that are regarded as safe typically rise.

Now we take a look at gold, the investment that competes with bonds during a crisis. For this purpose we once again employ the same method, whereby we analyse the average movement of the gold price around the temporal anchor set by the troughs of the respective declines in the Dow. Figure 3.5 shows the average movement of the gold price in the three months before and the three months after a significant low in the stock market. The long line in the middle once again marks the troughs in the Dow.

We can see that gold typically reaches an intermediate high about one week prior to the low in the Dow. At that time the stock market begins to enter an accelerated decline. However, now the gold price falls as well! The lowest price is reached at a later point in time than the stock market's low. The price of gold remains down for several

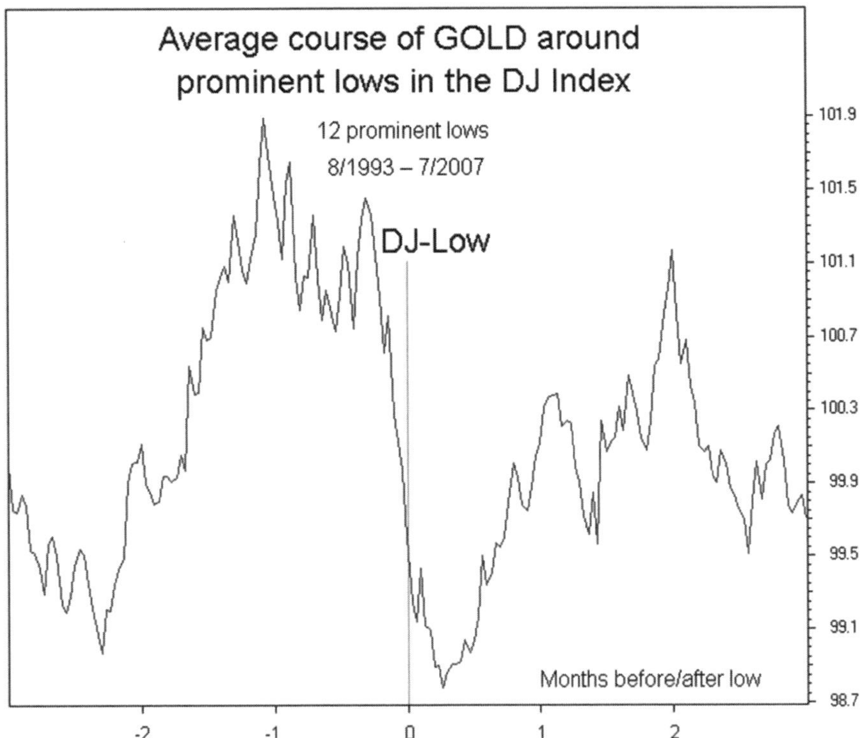

Figure 3.5 Average movement of the gold price around significant lows in the DJIA

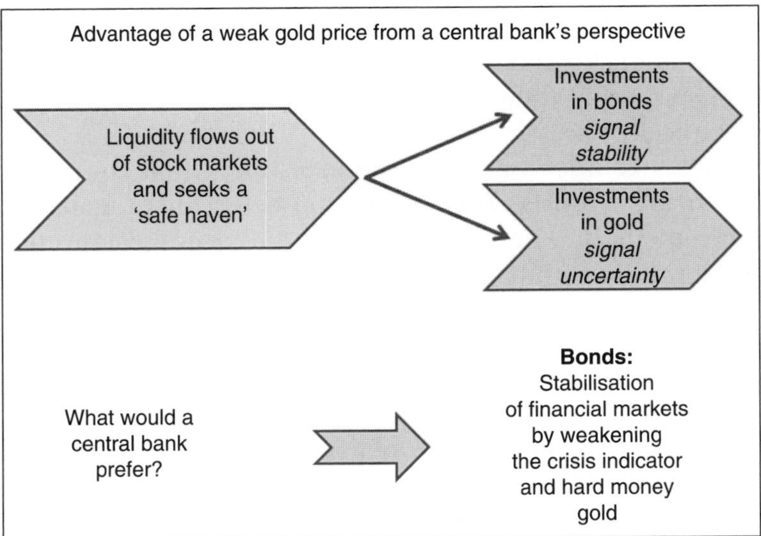

Figure 3.6 'Safe havens' compared

weeks. The decline lasts longer overall. In principle, there appears to be a connection between financial market crises and gold, as many other market observers have also recognised. Gold, however, fails to function as a safe haven, precisely in the days just prior to the stock market low, when stocks fall in accelerated fashion and uncertainty about the future is at its peak. Rather, its price moves as though gold, similar to stocks, were among the investments harbouring great risk in times of crisis.

The examination of the average of the 12 market declines confirms, therefore, what the previously discussed specific case of the Russian crisis in 1998 already suggested. The characteristics of gold have not reversed over recent years. Central banks may be interested in a low gold price, however. A falling gold price strengthens confidence in the financial markets. There are probably no more important occasions for this than financial market crises. When gold is weak, the markets are stabilised. Gold thus becomes uninteresting as a crisis investment, funds flow instead into the remaining asset classes, especially government bond markets. Subsequently they also flow back faster into the stock market. Furthermore, the impression that an uncontrollable crisis is underway is averted. Imagine by contrast that the gold price were to rise strongly in times of uncertainty. That would suggest that there are bigger, uncontrollable problems lurking. That could intensify the panic mood. The central banks, therefore, have good reasons to wish for a falling gold price, especially in difficult market periods. They are surely pleased if the gold price doesn't rise in times of incipient panic in the markets, but also not in the weeks immediately thereafter, when the markets have not yet fully calmed down (Figure 3.6). But do they, indeed, arrange for gold prices to decline?

Chapter 4

The Strange Intraday Behaviour of Gold

'Good morning, America' or 'One could set one's watch by it' – so market observers joked around the turn of the millennium whenever they watched the gold price and once again saw that it fell shortly after the open of the COMEX in New York. This happened with such unwavering regularity that many suspected it was no coincidence. Rather, they surmised that systematic interventions against gold were behind this anomaly, which typically took place at a specific time of the day, namely during the trading hours of the most important futures market. Rumours about such interventions had been making the rounds for a long time already, at least since 1995.[6] Since 1999 the Gold Anti-Trust Committee (GATA, www.gata.org), a US civil rights organisation, helped to point these interventions out. It had made it its goal to publicise them and, if possible, contribute to putting an end to them. In Figure 4.1 you can see the intraday movement of the gold price over three consecutive trading days for clarification.

The upper chart on the right shows the movements of the gold price on the three consecutive trading days beginning at midnight Eastern Standard Time (EST) of 31 May 2004. The trading hours of the COMEX are highlighted. One can clearly see how the price declines on all three days during this trading period. It was due to such price declines occurring time and again that market observers began to assume that these were not coincidental price movements. Were they right?

In order to check that, we will examine the intraday movements of the gold price over a large number of days. For this purpose, we apply the same method we have already employed in the examination of the 12 crisis-related declines in the stock market: we calculate an average of the price movements. To this end, we use one minute intraday prices[7] around the turn of the millennium, from August 1998 to July 2003. Figure 4.2, therefore, shows the average intraday movement of the gold price over a period of five years. The horizontal axis shows the time of the day (EST), the vertical axis the average

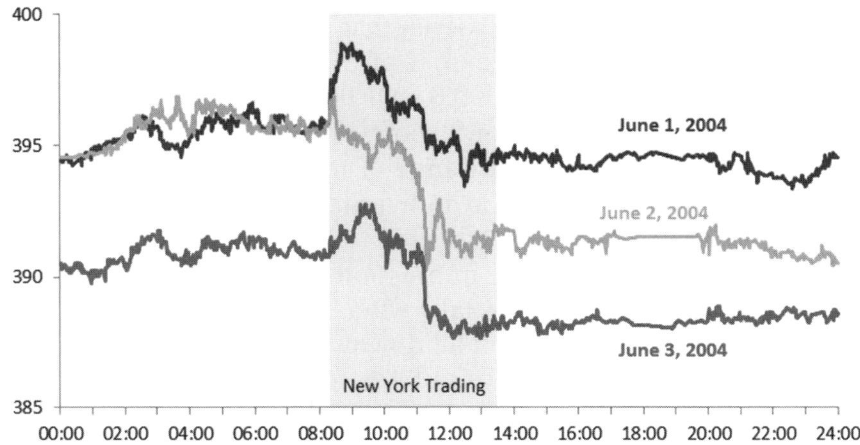

Figure 4.1 The gold price intraday movement on 1, 2 and 3 June 2004

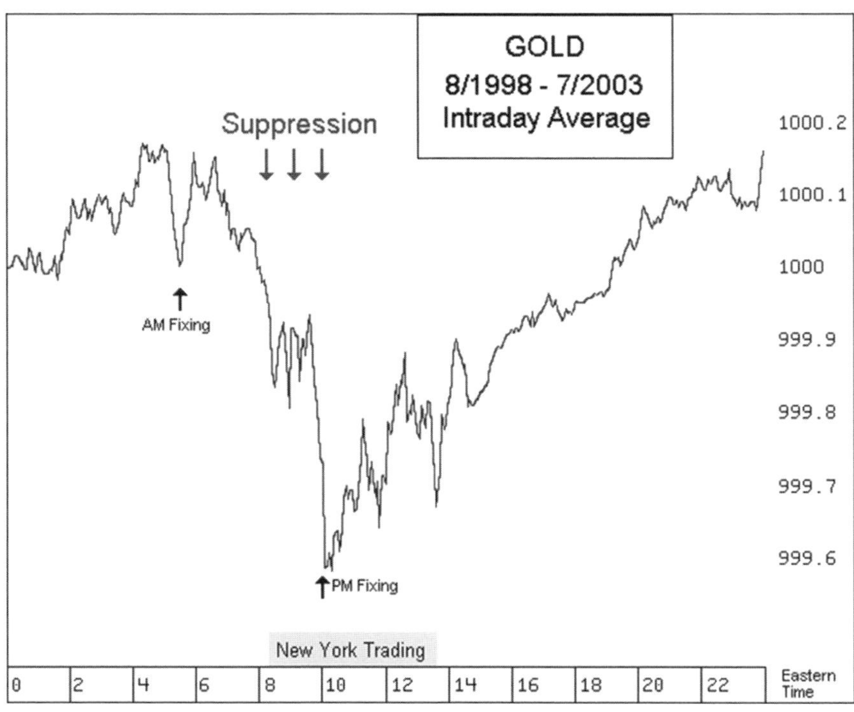

Figure 4.2 Average intraday price movement August 1998–July 2003

price level (indexed to 1,000). Given that the average includes such a large number of days, the extent of the movements is naturally rather small (ranging from 999.6 to 1,000.1, which amounts to a mere 0.05 per cent). Figure 4.2 shows the typical intraday movement of the gold price over a range of more than 1,000 days and including more than 1 million individual prices. It therefore has strong statistical significance.

The chart confirms the impression of many gold market observers: the price typically falls when the futures exchange in New York opens for trading. The downward movements occurred primarily in the first two hours of US trading. Moreover, we see that the trough of the average price movement occurs very close to the afternoon price fixing (PM fixing). The PM fixing is a kind of official world gold price, and is determined in the early afternoon in London (due to the time difference to New York, it is marked as late morning on the chart). At the less important morning fixing (AM fixing) there is, on average, also a price decline detectable, albeit a less pronounced one. A temporary sharp decline can also be seen to be focused on the closing price of the New York futures market (whereby the close of trading has been moved from 2.30 p.m. to 1.30 p.m. in the period examined above; the decline is, however, visible at both points in time). There was a tendency for the gold price to rise thereafter.

Grossly simplified, one could say that the price fell during US trading hours, while it rose during Asian and European trading hours.

There exists, therefore, a notable anomaly in the intraday movement of the gold price. This is very useful for statistical studies. A study including thousands of events is of strong statistical significance (it is more meaningful than the examination of the 12 crisis-related declines in the stock market, for instance, could be). Such a study of intraday price anomalies is suitable as statistical proof of gold market interventions. Moreover, it makes a precise dating of the beginning of the interventions possible.

Chapter 5

The First Statistical Studies

The examination of intraday anomalies has a great advantage: interventions target the price, they must therefore be visible in the price. We thus measure the intervention effect directly when we examine the price. We will later draw on other proofs as well, such as quotes from central bankers. Their evidential value is, however, usually only of an indirect nature (as a rule they don't contain official confirmation of the interventions). Only in combination with statistical proof (and the temporal and qualitative correlation won through the statistical analysis) do these quotes unfold their full significance. The proof demonstrated on the basis of price movements is not only direct, but, due to the high incidence of intraday anomalies, also significant. After all, our examination doesn't just encompass any price movement we don't like, but also shows a regularly repeated short-term pattern that lies far outside typical market behaviour and which cannot be explained otherwise.

In March of 2000, Harry Clawar published a statistical study that was devoted to these intraday anomalies.[8] He seized on the observation often remarked upon in internet forums that the efforts to keep the gold price from rising were primarily centred on New York. Beginning in September 1999, he observed the gold price closely. It appeared to him that the price had a tendency to rise after the close in New York and that it fell most of the time during New York trading hours, beginning approximately with the time of the AM fixing in London. We take a look at the extent to which his observation can be verified in the intraday chart centred around the year 2000. For this purpose we use the chart in Figure 5.1 that shows the average price movement over the 1,250 days from August 1998 to July 2003. In addition, we add lines between the points in time to which Clawar refers. One can clearly see that the market fell on average between the AM fixing and the close in New York, while it rose on average between the New York close and the AM fixing of the following day. Clawar's assumption can, therefore, be considered a rough approximation.

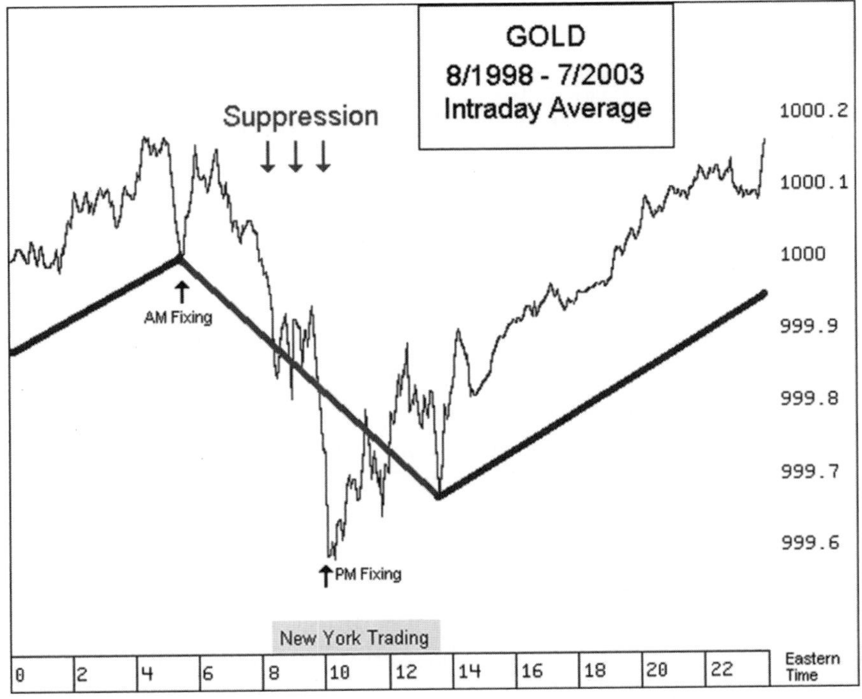

Figure 5.1 Average intraday price movement August 1998–July 2003

Clawar's original sample encompassed the period from 25 January to 3 March 2000, or 31 trading days. In this period the price fell in 69 per cent of all observations during New York trading hours as defined by these points in time, while it rose in the rest of the world 74 per cent of the time – *nota bene*, on the very same days. If the forces influencing the price were evenly distributed and not depending on the location, then both numbers would have to amount to approximately 50 per cent. During the period observed, the price of gold barely changed (by less than a dollar), whereby the cumulative gains achieved outside of New York trading hours amounted to $41, while concurrently the price fell by a cumulative $41 in New York. Clawar closes his report with the question whether there is US-led manipulation of the gold price centred in New York. Figure 5.2 shows his calculations.[9]

But why should there be intervention at a specific time of the day and not distributed evenly over the course of the entire day? We don't know the relevant motivations; Clawar, however, already provides a plausible answer, namely the location of the activity

	Spot Gold Prices 1/25/99 - 3/10/2000					
	London AM	London PM	NY Close	NY Close - London AM	London AM - Previous NY	London PM - London AM
10-Mar	$292.10	$290.25	$288.60	−$3.50	$1.40	−$1.85
9-Mar	$289.00	$290.50	$290.70	$1.70	$0.75	$1.50
8-Mar	$292.75	$291.20	$288.25	−$4.50	$1.25	−$1.55
7-Mar	$288.35	$289.75	$291.50	$3.15	$0.95	$1.40
6-Mar	$289.25	$288.80	$287.40	−$1.85	$0.95	−$0.45
3-Mar	$289.30	$288.50	$288.30	−$1.00	$2.15	−$0.80
2-Mar	$289.00	$289.90	$287.15	−$1.85	−$1.65	$0.90
1-Mar	$293.75	$292.90	$290.85	−$3.10	$2.45	−$0.85
29-Feb	$294.00	$293.85	$291.30	−$2.70	$2.30	−$0.35
28-Feb	$292.75	$292.50	$291.70	−$1.05	$0.55	−$0.25
25-Feb	$297.15	$294.00	$292.20	−$4.95	−$0.95	−$315
24-Feb	$299.90	$298.75	$298.10	−$1.80	$0.60	−$1.15
23-Feb	$305.25	$302.00	$299.30	−$5.95	$0.45	−$3.25
22-Feb	$305.40	$302.25	$304.80	−$0.60		− $3.15
21-Feb	$305.75	$305.25			−$3.05	−$0.50
18-Feb	$302.25	$303.55	$308.80	$6.55	$2.00	$1.30
17-Feb	$304.25	$306.25	$300.25	−$4.00	$2.85	$2.00
16-Feb	$300.50	$302.50	$301.40	$0.90	−$1.00	$2.00
15-Feb	$307.00	$304.25	$301.50	−$5.50	−$1.50	−$2.75
14-Feb	$308.75	$308.35	$308.50	−$0.25	−$1.45	−$0.40
11-Feb	$316.50	$311.50	$310.20	−$6.30	$1.30	−$5.00
10-Feb	$311.25	$309.00	$315.20	$3.95	$6.15	−$2.25
9-Feb	$306.00	$308.50	$305.10	−$0.90	$7.90	$2.60
8-Feb	$303.15	$296.25	$298.10	−$5.05	$0.15	−$6.90
7-Feb	$316.50	$312.70	$303.00	−$13.60	$14.30	−$3.90
4-Feb	$287.50	$293.65	$302.30	$14.80	$0.90	$6.15
3-Feb	$285.25	$285.05	$286.60	$1.35	$0.75	−$0.20
2-Feb	$283.10	$285.60	$284.50	$1.40	$0.70	$2.50
1-Feb	$283.65	$283.00	$282.40	−$1.25	$0.55	−$0.65
28-Jan	$286.15	$286.75	$283.10	−$3.05	−$0.65	$060
27-Jan	$286.50	$285.55	$286.20	$0.30	$0.90	−$0.95
26-Jan	$284.90	$285.90	$285.50	$0.70	−$0.85	$1.00
25-Jan	$288.70	$288.00	$285.75	−$2.95		− $0.70

Source: www.gold-eagle.com, Harry Clawar

Figure 5.2 Clawar's study

in New York. Interventions in market prices must be efficiently organised, just as any other activities, and one's home market lends itself to this. One knows the ropes, has contacts and it involves less effort than being engaged around the clock. It is, moreover, less costly to concentrate on price markers like the PM fixing and the close in New York, which most market participants use for orientation. Such price markers remain in one's memory and trading decisions are far more often made based on these prices than on intraday prices that have been recorded in between. Furthermore, the New York market is the most important futures market. Futures markets offer the possibility to enter into large positions with very little capital, at a fraction of the underlying nominal value. This makes it possible to reduce the financial outlay considerably. The effect of price manipulation on gold through the futures market is also not necessarily only of a short-term nature. Contrary to other commodities that are solely consumption goods, the effect on gold, which is primarily an investment asset, can even turn out to be permanent (as will be shown in more detail later). Therefore, the futures market offers the best and cheapest way to intervene in the gold market. Moreover, there are barely any drawbacks (except, perhaps, the fact that the method of acting at specific times of the day leaves statistically analysable traces behind that can be examined).

Michael Bolser adopted Clawar's idea and modified it. In December of the same year (2000), he published a study that encompasses the time period 1985 to 2000. Bolser uses the official AM and PM fixing prices as well as the closing prices at the COMEX in New York instead of actual spot prices.[10] Based on the same intraday points in time as Clawar, he not only measures the direction, but also the extent of intraday countertrend moves. He concludes that there exist conspicuous downward movements in prices since 1994 which differ from those observed up until 1993. This leads him to his conclusion regarding the first dating of the interventions, even if only exact to within one year. Since the method focuses on extreme outlier values, the number of usable events is small, even though a great number of days is examined overall. These could, for example, only relate to seven cases (depending on the extent of the price movement that is used as the extreme value). This limits the study's evidential value. It is, furthermore, not possible to achieve a dating that is precise to the day.

Chapter 6

Statistical Proof and Dating of Gold Interventions

Pinpointing a date that is precise to the day is made possible by a different enhancement to the approach. It preserves the straightforwardness of Clavar's approach – that is, it does not, as in the method employed by Bolser, target the extent of the price movements. This leaves the number of days that can be statistically evaluated equal to the total number of days examined. The method therefore encompasses – depending on the availability of suitable historical data – thousands of days, and is thus entirely adequate for attaining high statistical significance. Moreover, it makes it possible to date the beginning of the gold interventions precisely to the day.

Only one aspect had to be modified. Clawar's original approach works best during sideways movements in the gold price. If, however, the gold price were to rise by $1, for example, during New York trading hours and by $10 in the rest of the world, it would have no informative value, as prices would rise in both markets. Nevertheless, the price rise in New York is suppressed compared to that in the rest of the world in this example. The movement over the entire day must therefore be adjusted accordingly for a comprehensive study. This is done by comparing one movement relative to the other – that is, one simply deducts one price movement from the other. In other words, prices are no longer merely examined to see whether they fall in one market and rise in the other, but also how they move relative to each other. If the gold price in New York rises by a smaller amount than in the rest of the world, this is effectively the same as if it had fallen slightly New York and risen slightly in the rest of the world.[11]

In February 2001 this approach for the first time succeeded in producing statistical proof, as well as an exact dating of the beginning of the gold market interventions.[12] The differences between the local price movements were determined. The prices required for this, the 'AM fixing' and the 'New York close' were available from

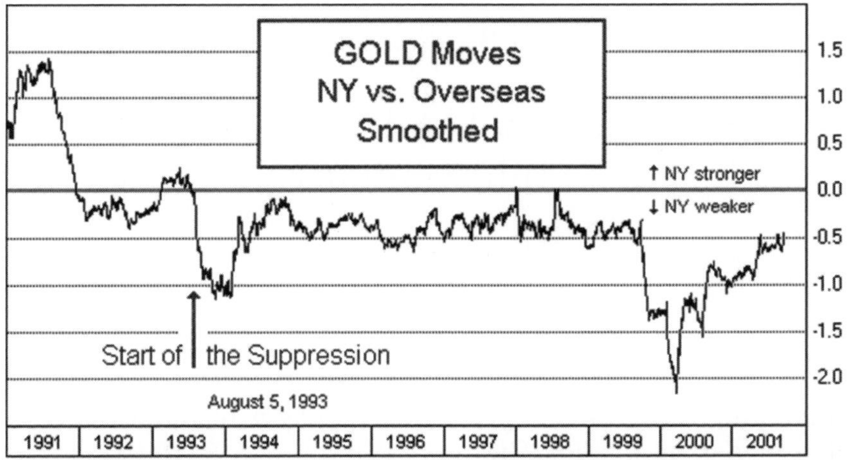

Figure 6.1 Gold price movements in New York vs the rest of the world

1991 onward.[13] When the differences were negative, it meant that the price movement in New York underperformed relative to the remaining trading hours. Figure 6.1 shows this relative price difference smoothed by a moving average (125 days). Smoothing is necessary in order to compensate for the frequent fluctuations over this long period of time. With the help of the relative intraday price movement, the figure thus makes clear at what time of the day the gold price exhibits a tendency to weaken. If the line is below the zero level, it indicates that the price has been relatively weak in New York compared to the rest of the world (and vice versa).

We can clearly see that, beginning with 5 August 1993, the gold price tended to be weaker in New York than in the rest of the world. On that day, the systematic interventions against a strong gold price began. These were predominantly executed by means of the futures market at the COMEX in New York. Ever since, the gold price has usually underperformed there relative to the remaining trading hours. This is a key date in the modern history of gold. This was the day when the systematic suppression of the sole significant competitor of paper money began. It is historically quite interesting, as it enables us to gain an understanding of the background, of how these interventions came about, which continue to this day. Without this knowledge we cannot understand the gold market interventions of today, which naturally take place against quite a different backdrop than the one that pertained back then. At the same time, 5 August 1993 is an important day for central bank and monetary policy, as it marks the beginning of an additional, and very likely the terminal, stage of the great bubble that has formed over decades in the economies of the world (more on these points later).

The study of 2001 had a number of limitations. As, at the time, only intraday data from 1998 onward were available, it was necessary to employ the AM fixing as an auxiliary data point (as Clawar did), instead of using the spot price at the open of trading in New York. Due to a lack of historical data, it was also not possible to include the New York closing price prior to 1991. Conversely, the importance of New York trading hours has been declining since the introduction of 24-hour electronic trading in the regulated futures market in 2003. Nevertheless, the method has enabled us to present statistical proof of intervention and the precise dating of the beginning of gold market interventions.

In the meantime, one-minute spot prices from February 1986 onward have become available.[14] In addition, minute-by-minute prices of the futures market at the COMEX are now available from January 1984 onward.[15] Both data sets are subsequently included in the examination of gold price anomalies. First, however, let us once again demonstrate the efficiency of the original approach employed for the 1990s by adding an enhancement. For this purpose, the chart of the gold price is shown together with the indicator of relative gold price movements. The upper line in Figure 6.2 shows the local tendency of the gold price as in the previous illustration. It is below the zero level whenever prices in New York trading are weaker than in the remaining trading hours. Since interventions against a firming gold price are predominantly executed in New York, the line is at the same time a measure of the extent of the suppression: the lower it is, the more forceful the intervention against a rising gold price. The lower line shows the gold price itself.

We can see that the intensity of the interventions at the beginning (i.e., from 5 August 1993) onward, was especially pronounced. They were also effective, as the gold price began to decline quickly, after having been in a rising trend previously. In addition, they were especially pronounced a second time, beginning in 1999 after gold had advanced by leaps and bounds as a result of the Washington Agreement on Gold (WAG). On 26 September 1999, a number of central banks signed the WAG, in which they agreed to limit their gold sales. This led to a sharp increase in the gold price in the days following the announcement, by about 20 per cent.[16] In addition,

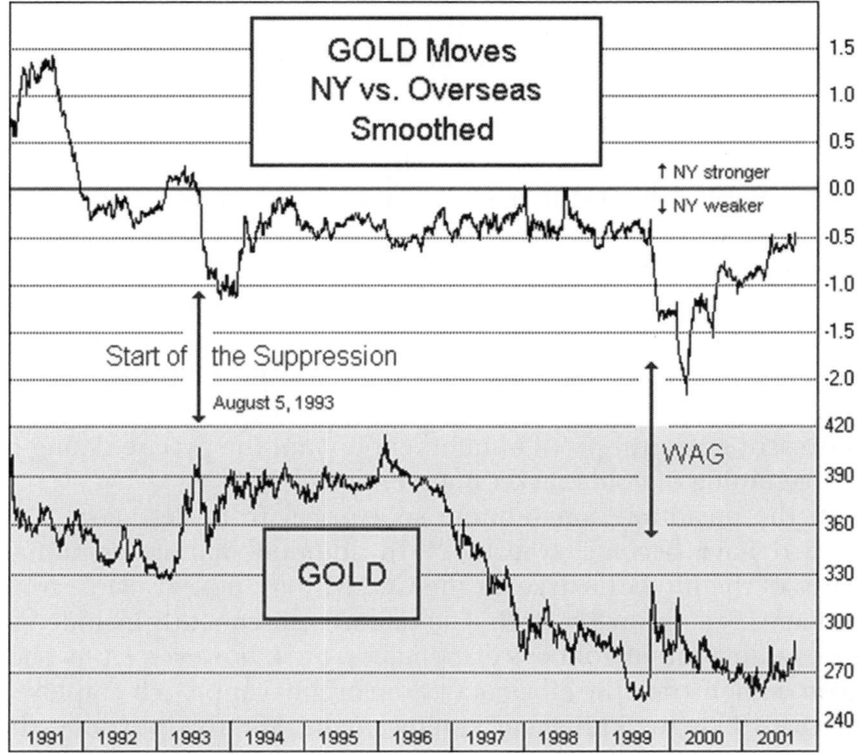

Figure 6.2 Price movements of gold in New York vs the rest of the world

the interventions were intensified after a number of smaller price increases. All in all, one can clearly discern that gold price declines generally occur in conjunction with the intraday weakness of the gold price in New York (it is probably quite difficult in this context to come up with an explanation other than interventions).

Chapter 7

Intraday Movements of the Gold Price 1986–2012

We now want to refine our examination method. Specifically, we want to not only examine price declines during US trading hours, but also any cluster of price movements, especially sharp price movements, at specific times of the day. Figure 7.1 shows the average intraday movement of the gold price before there were systematic interventions – that is, from the beginning of the available time series from 3 February 1986 to 4 August 1993, the day before the gold market interventions started. It has to be borne in mind that the New York trading hours marked on the intraday charts are only a rough approximation, as trading hours were frequently shifted.

At a first glance, the result appears to weaken the preceding analysis. After all, we can discern local tendencies in this average as well; the gold price trends slightly down in European trade in the morning, moves sideways with a slight tendency towards weakness in New York and firms up in early Asian trade. At the same time, these tendencies are not evenly distributed over the entire period. There were years when the price weakened in Europe and went sideways in New York (1988), years when it was firm in Europe and weak in the USA (1987) and times when prices rose both in Europe and the USA (in the first half of 1993). There were, apparently, no systematic interventions concentrated on mostly the same trading hours, but normal market phenomena that occasionally include local tendencies or extreme values that influence the average. We now look at the time period from when the gold market interventions began. Figure 7.2 shows the average intraday movement since 5 August 1993. In this figure there are a number of price anomalies that are sufficiently strong to be visible overall.

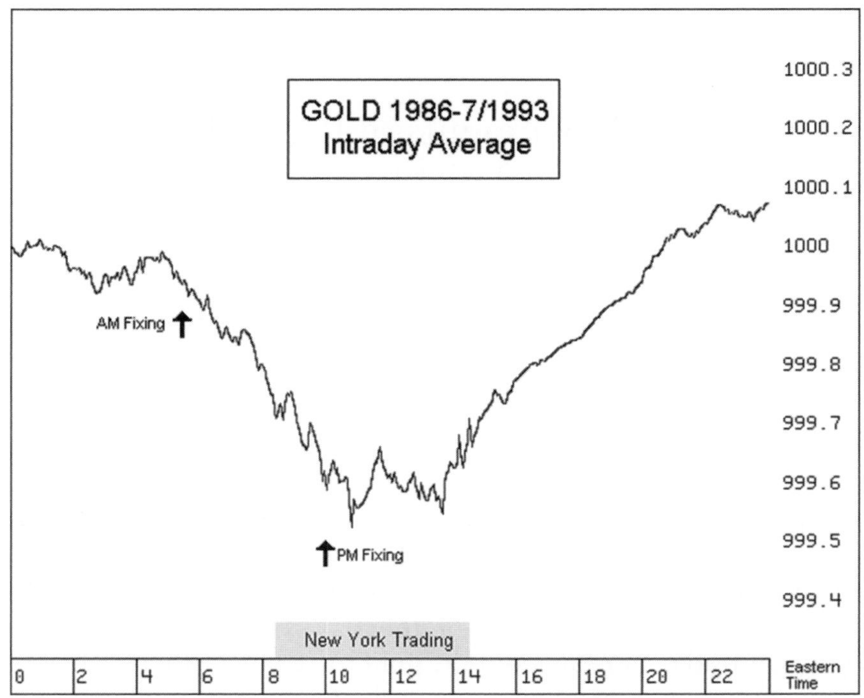

Figure 7.1 Average intraday price movement February 1986–July 1993

In contrast to the average movement prior to the beginning of the systematic interventions, we can now discern price spikes at specific points in time. The price tends to decline on average at the time of the AM fixing and at the close of the New York futures market. Especially conspicuous is, however, the price decline at the time of the PM fixing. Prior to 5 August 1993 there are no price movements that are even remotely comparable to this sharp decline at 3 p.m. London time, 10 a.m. EST. That cannot be a coincidence.

If one examines the individual years for a detailed analysis, specific key points in time are barely noticeable prior to the beginning of the systematic interventions. It is completely different in the years after the interventions began. Conspicuous moves can be discerned time and again in the intraday movements, which also crop up in the average of individual years and take place especially at specific points in time that are important from an organisational standpoint, such as the fixings or the New York close. The conspicuous moves even vary over time, but since the beginning of the interventions it is almost always possible to detect distinctive characteristics at specific points in time.

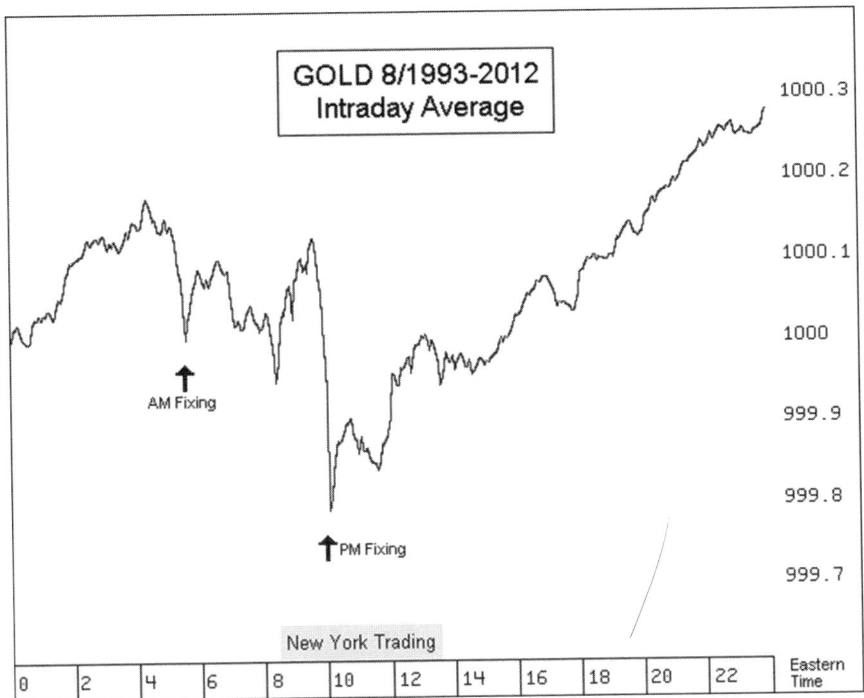

Figure 7.2 Average intraday price movement August 1993–December 2012

We take a look at a few individual years, beginning with 1993, when the systematic interventions began (see Figure 7.3). The beginning of the interventions is made clear by the comparison of the first half of 1993 with the second half, when the interventions focusing on specific times in the course of intraday trading become obvious. Until 4 August 1993 no peculiarities can be discerned.

The average between 5 August 1993, the beginning of the interventions, and the end of the year, however, clearly shows price weakness at specific points in time, especially at the close of the futures exchange at 2.35 p.m. (at the time an hour later). This can be seen in Figure 7.4.

This weakness at the close of New York trading is, however, also easily discernible in 1994 (Figure 7.5).

The intraday price weakness even moves along with the close of trading, which was shifted forward to 2 p.m. in 1995 (Figure 7.6).

When analysing market anomalies we must be aware that we are not examining physical processes of an exactly similar nature. Interventions are man-made. They haven't been executed for 19 years running in exactly the same manner every time. Naturally, there

Figure 7.3 Average intraday price movement in 1993, from the beginning of the year to 4 August

have been changes in preferences and methods with regard to the interventions. At times the interventions were focused on the open of trading at the futures exchange, such as in 1998; at times they were distributed over the entire trading day, such as in 1996; at times they were concentrated on the close of trading, such as from the beginning of the interventions on 5 August 1993 until 1995 (see Figures 7.5, 7.6 and 8.1). In 1994, and then again from 1998 onward and especially in 2008, interventions were so heavy at the time of the PM fixing that they are extremely conspicuous in the overall average (see Figure 7.3). These price declines at the PM fixing are also reminiscent of the LIBOR scandal that was uncovered in 2012, in which banks manipulated benchmark interest rates. This created fraudulent profits in numerous business lines tied to reference rates. The gold fixing is a comparable reference price, which forms the basis for further transactions.

However, not only the intervention procedures have changed, the backdrop also has not remained constant. Apart from the fact

Figure 7.4 Average intraday price movement from 5 August 1993 to year end

that the main trading hours of the futures exchange have been shifted, one must mention the introduction of electronic trading in 2003, which enables almost around-the-clock trading in futures contracts and thus makes interventions during these extended trading hours possible. There is also the varying importance of the over-the-counter derivatives market. Even the differences in daylight-saving time between countries (which hasn't been factored into our calculations) could play a role in the composition of the average. In addition, the extent of interventions in the futures market has fluctuated. In some years there was apparently not as much cause to intervene in the futures market, presumably because a large supply of physical gold was made available by the central banks.

Moreover, one must generally ask whether changes in notable peculiarities of intraday price movements are an indicator of 'natural' market behaviour or if it should not be expected that, quite on the contrary, interventionist practices are subject to change over

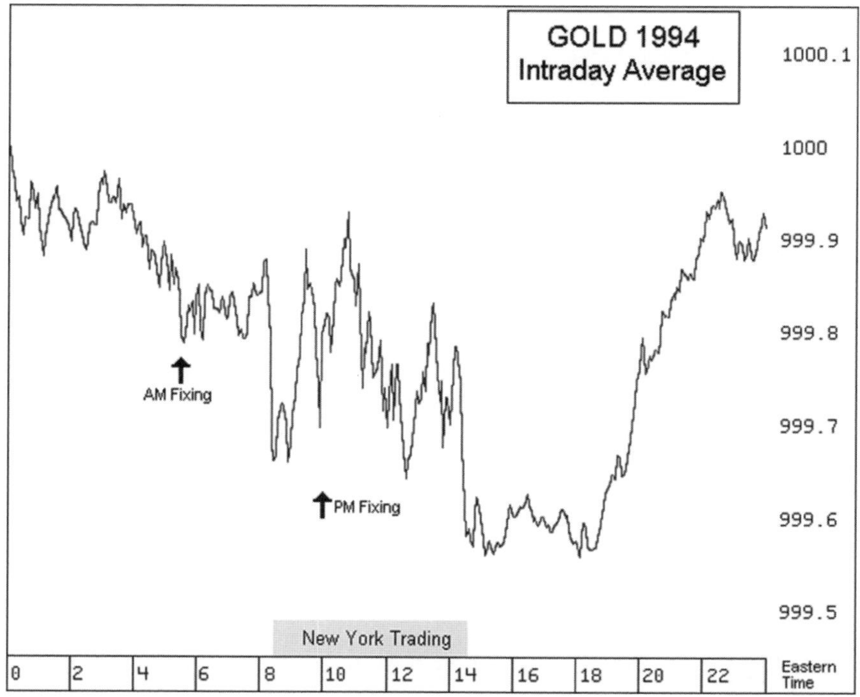

Figure 7.5 Average intraday price movement in 1994

time, and market anomalies thus change along with them. If gold mines, for instance, were to prefer selling at the PM fixing because the market is very liquid at that time of the day, and prices were to fall because of that, then the mines would do this on a regular basis and make sure that the effect on prices was economically justifiable. Then the pattern would not be weak at certain times, fail to be noticeable at all at other times and be very strong at yet other times, as is, in fact, the case. Furthermore, market participants would soon alter their behaviour if such activities were to result in an easily discernible price decline such as that seen at the PM fixing. There have been days such as 18 September 2009, when the price fell quite considerably within a few minutes around the time of the PM fixing, so that gold mines would have received $10 less per ounce sold. No normal market participant would be so clumsy to make such a mistake twice, unless he desired to influence prices (leaving aside that the other anomalies – such as the closing price – could not be explained by this).

With the expanded data set it is confirmed that the price of gold displays intraday anomalies since 5 August 1993 that did not

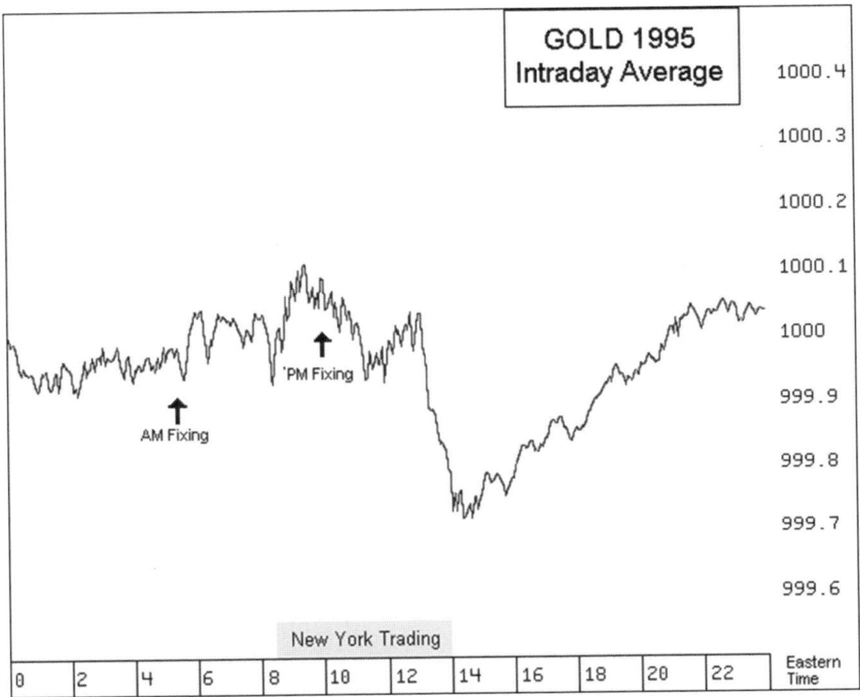

Figure 7.6 Average intraday price movement in 1995

exist previously. They are already visible in the study of the overall intraday average. Examination of the average intraday price movement in individual years buttresses this conclusion.[17] With 5 August 1993, the systematic interventions in the gold market began.

Chapter 8
Gold is Different

We already explained in Chapter 1 that gold is different from stores of value that are based on financial claims (including credit money) in terms of its ability to safeguard value, as its value is neither at risk from defaults of debtors nor from inflation. Gold is, however, also different from other commodities that are primarily or entirely consumption goods. Gold is held similarly to money, it is practically not used up. Not least due to its store of value function, a multiple of gold's annual consumption is already available in stock. Therein it is different from other goods as well. We now want to take a closer look at the magnitudes of stocks and flows that are relevant to price interventions. Figure 8.1 shows the estimates for the total amount of gold ever mined, as well as the portion thereof that is officially held in the reserves of central banks. This is contrasted with estimates of consumption and production.

This relationship is of great importance. A small fraction of the stock would suffice to satisfy demand! Conversely, a multiple of annual production would be required to increase the stock appreciably. If one were to regard gold as a mere commodity – which it undoubtedly is in the physical sense, but not economically – then one would focus one's fundamental analysis of the price on annual supply and demand. However, what is relevant for crude oil or wheat is only of secondary importance to gold. A driver who uses his car occupationally has to fill up its tank even if the price of gas doubles. However, no one has to buy gold if the price of an ounce has doubled. People buy gold on account of different considerations – for instance, in order to protect their savings for the education of their children from inflation or against the collapse of banks. Or they sell gold because they have confidence in the financial system and invest their funds at a trusted bank to earn interest. The gold price thus falls when gold is released from the stock and rises when demand for a store of value adds gold to the stock.

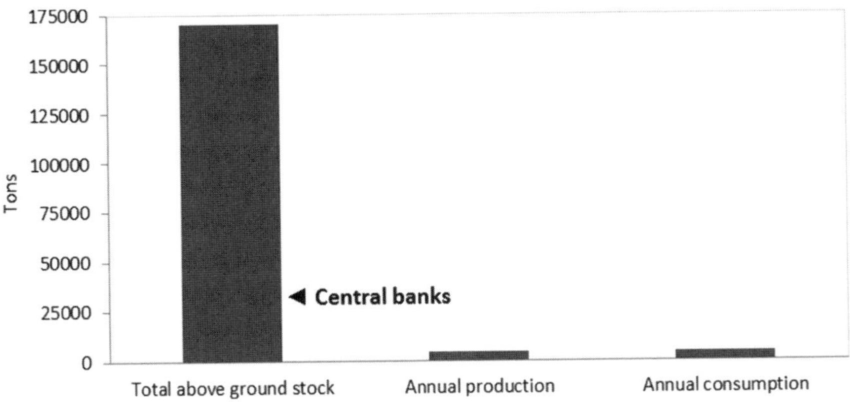

Figure 8.1 Gold: stocks vs flows

Only because the stock of gold is so large and because it functions as a store of value is it possible for financial institutions to successfully influence gold's price over many years (Figure 8.2). They can satisfy demand from the stock and can induce (potential) investors to alter their stock. No government can halve the price of gas for many years without having to fund the difference to the global market price from alternative revenue sources. It doesn't have an

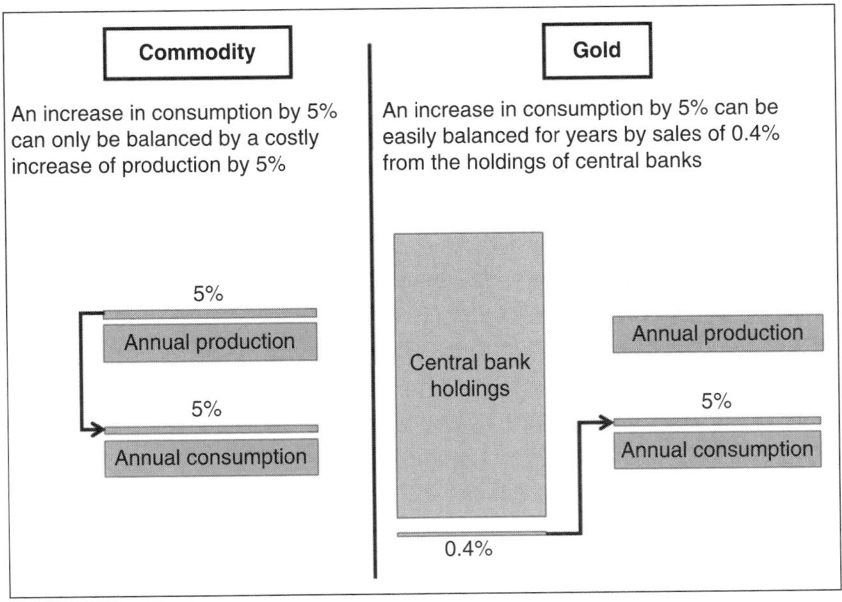

Figure 8.2 Satisfying consumption from inventories

inventory of crude oil in storage that would cover many years of demand. In the case of gold, it does! And no government can easily motivate drivers to cut their use of petrol in half. It can only laboriously prompt them to alter their behaviour through the price and definitely not by offering 'alternatives to gas investment'. With gold, it can!

Chapter 9

Means of Gold Market Intervention I: Sales

Sales are the most obvious means of impeding a price increase. Over recent decades the central banks mainly acted in the role of sellers (only fairly recently a few central banks have increased their gold reserves to an appreciable extent). Central banks used to sell up to 600 tons of gold per year. This amount must be considered in relation to annual consumption of approximately 2,400 tons. There can be no doubt that sales of this magnitude exert considerable pressure on the price. Without them it would have been decidedly higher. There are certainly a number of motives for a central bank to engage in gold sales. For instance, gold lying in a vault doesn't earn interest. Measured in currency terms (such as the US dollar), there are exchange rate risks, as gold's price can fall. It is, moreover, possible that gold is seen as making up too big a portion of reserves relative to alternative investment assets. A central bank that sells gold, therefore, does not necessarily do so because it wants to influence its price. Figure 9.1 lists the gold sales by central banks (the amounts are different from the officially reported ones, as GFMS, a research house specialising in precious metals, estimates them by including additional information).

Nevertheless, the main motive for a number of central bank sales over the better part of the past two decades was probably price intervention. However, due to a lack of official confirmation this can only be made plausible on the basis of circumstantial evidence. A central bank doesn't have to act for the purpose of price suppression of its own accord, it can also be impelled to do so. This can include lobbying by the local mining industry that uses borrowed gold to finance itself. Banks and hedge funds holding short positions can exert pressure on central banks (more on this topic later). Furthermore, a negative price trend due to intervention can induce other central banks to sell. But also negative propaganda against gold can motivate sales, such as the suggestion that gold is supposedly nowadays superfluous and generates no income, while

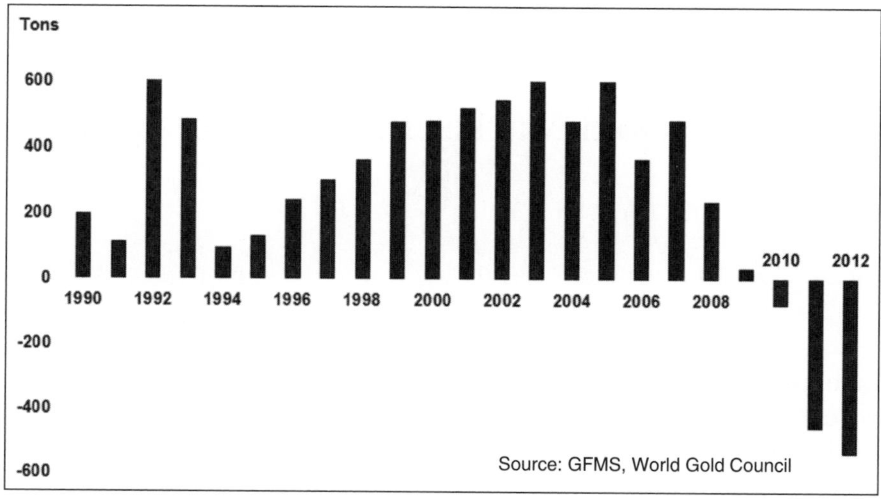

Figure 9.1 Gold sales by central banks

the remaining reserves are safe. This can go as far as the open exertion of pressure, open propaganda and defamation, such as in the case of Switzerland,[18] which was accused by politicians, organisations and the media of having acquired large amounts of gold illegitimately in World War II. A fund financed by gold sales was supposed to provide redress. It is striking that moral arguments have often been used as a pretext in cases where there was resistance among central banks and the public to gold sales. There were not only accusations of guilt such as in Switzerland's case. Conversely, such as in the case of the IMF's gold reserves, the alleged aim of financing a cancellation of the debts of poor countries was propagated (some of which protested fiercely, as their mining industry suffered from the low gold price and tens of thousands lost their jobs). Especially in the late 1990s, many politicians and journalists have, whether out of ignorance or due to other motives, excelled at disparaging gold as a central bank reserve asset with irrelevant arguments and at times disingenuous methods, and thereby pursued the interests of banks that wanted the gold price to fall.

However, we don't want to analyse individual instances of sales and the associated remarks and justifications at this juncture. It is difficult to recognise whether a politician's remarks are the result of a lack of expertise or due to a hidden ulterior motive. Quite a few politicians have probably just repeated what they have overheard and deemed to be plausible. In our communications and media society, one person quickly takes up what another has said, just because it sounds reasonable and seems to be a good idea and because it appears to help one's popularity with the media. Everyone wants to make a positive impression, even if their activities do not bode well for the future.

Still, the name of one person must be mentioned here: that of the former UK Chancellor of the Exchequer and later prime minister, Gordon Brown. In 1999 he announced gold sales in advance, which sent prices spiralling down. Of course, such advance announcements were, up until then, unusual among central banks as well, so as not to depress sales proceeds (Figure 9.2). Brown, however, announced the sales and thereby arranged for the gold price to fall and the sales proceeds along with it (the inspiration for this advance announcement may have come from a previously publicised proposal by the USA to sell IMF gold; the announcement as such was already successful in the interventionist sense, as the price turned down).

As a businessman, one wouldn't be able to hold one's own for long in this manner and most private individuals manage their affairs more cleverly as well, at least not negotiating a price that is against their interests. If there was no exogenous reason for the announcements (such as a law, but nothing is known about an exogenous reason), there are only two possible reasons left: gross clumsiness or intent – namely intent to suppress the price. Other announcements are to be seen in this context as well, especially declarations of intent

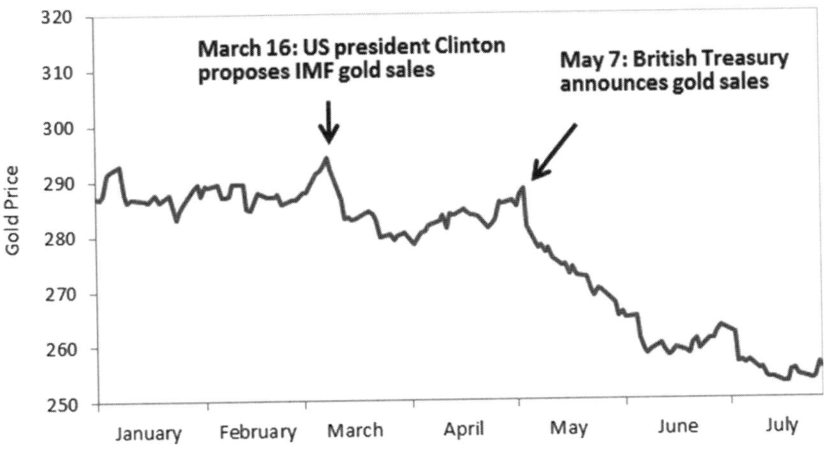

Figure 9.2 Influence of advance announcements of gold sales in 1999

to sell gold held by the IMF. With regard to this, Brown excelled as an active dispenser of advice as well, even though nothing seemed to preordain him for this role. He became active in this regard on at least four occasions over the span of a decade.[19] Clumsiness can therefore be ruled out as a reason for his advance announcement of the sale of Britain's gold.

The sale of the UK gold treasure – once by far the biggest in the world, today irrelevant – by the way, happened at just about the worst possible moment – namely near a multi-year low in the gold price (today it is thus referred to as the 'Brown Bottom'). Due to sales based on dubious motives at only a fraction of today's prices, UK taxpayers have suffered damage to the tune of tens of billions of pounds. Brown and his price-suppressing advance announcements were strongly criticised at the time, especially by the opposition in the House of Commons. Presumably due to ignorance of gold market interventions, it suspected, however, that support for the introduction of the euro was the motive, as the sales allegedly freed up funds for the buying of euros (for that purpose, however, advance announcements and the resulting price suppression would not have been necessary). Not only the opposition and large swathes of the population were against the sales, but even the Bank of England, as revealed by documents that were published later. Criticism was also voiced abroad – for instance, by the government and the unions of South Africa, where a large amount of gold is mined. Furthermore, according to a Reuters report of 6 July 1999, a number of large mining companies even enquired in a joint letter whether the true motive was the support of companies that were interested in a lower gold price due to the gold-lending business. That would also explain the advance announcements, as the UK gold sales had in this way produced extra profits for the short sellers. The circumstances surrounding the British gold sales remain mysterious, and to this day no one has apparently come close to explaining them fully.

Chapter 10

Means of Gold Intervention II: Gold Lending

Gold lending is the second instrument by which gold prices are kept low. Since the early 1980s a business has developed in the course of which a commodity – namely gold – is lent out in grand style. In so-called 'gold-leasing' transactions, gold that is 'lying around uselessly', so to speak, mainly in central bank vaults, is lent to the mines (to a smaller degree there was also lending to fabricators such as jewellers for the purpose of financing and hedging). Similar to a normal loan, the banks function as intermediaries in these transactions. These banks are called 'bullion banks' in the financial jargon. For the central banks, these banks reduce the risk of default of individual mines. Moreover, they take over detailed work such as choosing creditworthy mining companies. In exchange, these mediating banks receive a fee that is customary in business. The banks sell on behalf of the mines the borrowed gold in the market. Then the mines use the sales proceeds for investments – for instance, in new mining equipment. These investments in turn enable the mining companies to mine gold. This they use later to extinguish their gold debt with the central bank. The mines thus receive financing that is denominated in gold instead of in a currency. They must pay back gold, not dollars – in other words, they pay with what they produce. On the one hand, this hedges them against a falling gold price, but, on the other, they don't benefit from a rising gold price. Since there is no dependency on the gold price, the risk of default is more predictable, and it is therefore easier for mines to get gold loans (Figure 10.1).

Such commodity lending exists in appreciable quantity and in this form only in the gold market. Most credit is customarily denominated in money. A baker doesn't borrow bread, an oil company doesn't borrow oil, when they want to erect production facilities, but money. A precondition for the lending of gold is the already discussed large stock. Only due to the fact that gold amounting to several times annual production is stored in the vaults of central

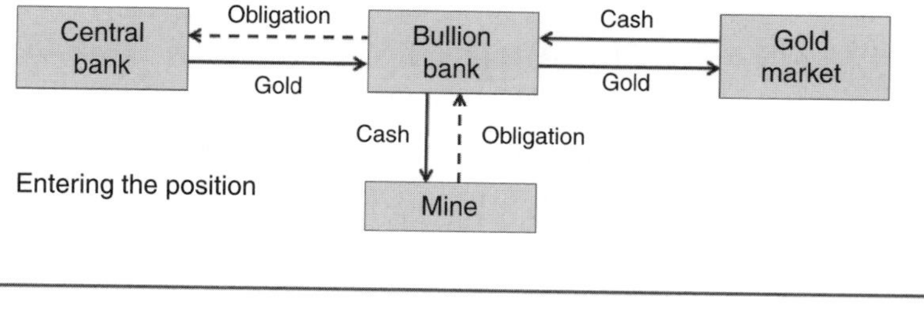

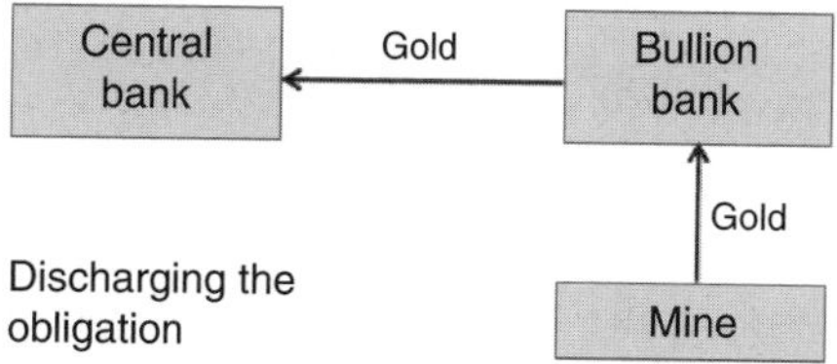

Figure 10.1 Operation of the gold-lending business

banks is it even possible for the mining companies to borrow large amounts of gold. It often happened that mining firms had amassed debts amounting to several times their annual production. Commodity loans of this type could only arise in gold and only after ending all ties of gold to currencies (which happened in 1971). A gold loan is a commodity loan and, thus, has many similarities to other types of commodity loans. There are, however, also differences to most lending businesses that involve the lending of commodities. One is that it is usually not the same gold that one has borrowed that one gives back, but different gold. That is what makes the intermittent sale on the market possible, which is, after all, intended. Such a sale, however, has the same effects as any other type of sale. It increases the supply and thus suppresses the price. Apart from central bank sales, it was therefore gold lending that made physical gold available to the market. Gold that is lent out influences the price negatively in the same manner as gold that is sold directly.

For the central banks of gold-producing countries such as Australia, the reason for lending out gold was initially the support and indirect subsidisation of the local gold industry. It was able to refinance itself cheaply, easily and independently of the gold price. Accordingly there was lobbying from the bullion banks, the gold-mining industry and associations close to them. They then tried to influence central banks globally in order to persuade them to lend out gold.

It is held that one of the main reasons for gold lending is the proceeds from the gold lease rate; the central banks receive interest for lending out gold. The gold lease rate is different from the prevalent interest rate on capital. The height of the gold lease rate is entirely independent from interest rates in the capital markets. Depending on the demand for and supply of gold loans, it can reach relatively arbitrary values. In the 1980s its average height was around 1 per cent per year, whereby maximum values of up to 3 per cent per year were reached. The reason for the low lease rate was that, at the time, only very little gold was lent out relative to the amount of gold stored at the central banks. Central banks thus had the choice of either garnering small revenues or none at all. They increasingly decided in favour of the small revenues available from gold lending. In most cases short-dated contracts were entered into. These were then usually prolonged, similar to how a private investor might simply leave a fixed-term deposit with his bank. Quite a few central banks that regarded the risk of not getting their gold back as too high, relative to the very low return of 1 per cent per annum, changed their mind when short-term spikes in the lease rate occurred. These central banks lent out their gold at 3 per cent per annum, but stuck with the lending business when lease rates fell back again to 1 per cent per annum. By the early 1990s, an estimated 50 central banks had decided to lend out gold.

At first glance it appears as though there is a free market in the gold-lending business, as the central banks are in competition with each other. However, one needs to take into account that central banks are political institutions that pursue political and monetary policy aims, not private investors that act out of self-interest. It is noteworthy that it is considered too complex and risky for private sector entities to lend out their gold at the small yield of 1 per cent per annum, in spite of the fact that they hold the bulk of the extant gold. They are, therefore, only marginally involved in this business. Since the supply of gold for lending is, thus, dominated by the central banks, the gold lease rate too is a politically fixed price. At least some central banks decide to lend out gold at low rates for political and monetary policy reasons. The subsidisation of gold mines is one reason already discussed. The mining companies are offered cheap gold loans in this way. Another reason is the financing of the profits of gold carry traders – and with this, the second group of actors in gold price suppression.

Chapter 11

The Gold Carry Trade

A carry trade is an interest differential business, which consists of borrowing money in a low-yielding currency for the sole reason of investing the proceeds in a higher-yielding one. It was, for instance, possible a few years ago to take on debt in Japanese yen at 1 per cent and receive 9 per cent by investing in New Zealand dollars. The difference of 8 per cent is the predictable profit. However, to this it must be added that at the time the loan is paid back, the then reigning exchange rate will be applied. In the above example, there will be a loss if the New Zealand dollar has fallen by about 8 per cent after a year has passed. The profit thus depends on the course of the exchange rate. It is in the carry trader's interest that the currency he has invested in rises and the currency he has borrowed in falls.

The gold carry trade is a comparable business; only the loan is denominated in gold. One therefore borrows gold from a central bank and invests it in higher-yielding instruments in order to profit from the interest rate spread. The borrowed gold must, however, first be sold in order to, for instance, invest the proceeds in fixed income instruments. While carry trades in the foreign exchange markets are also pursued by private individuals, those eligible to partake in the gold carry trade are strictly limited, as the central banks don't lend gold to everyone. In the beginning, this was open to a larger group, but the central banks became more careful and increasingly narrowed the circle of those whom they would lend gold to. In the meantime, it is mainly commercial banks that are also involved in conventional gold leasing that are active in this business, viz., the bullion banks. Figure 11.1 shows a schematic of the gold carry trade.

The gold carry trade developed for obvious reasons from the classical gold-lending business. In this, the bullion banks make a contract with a gold-mining firm regarding the future delivery of gold. They can only earn a profit in line with banking practice in these transactions, via fees or by means of a small interest spread

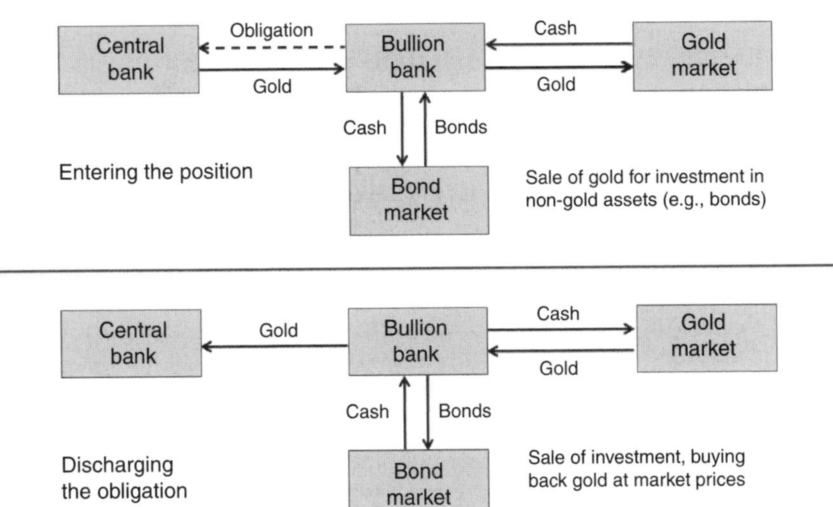

Figure 11.1 Functioning of the gold carry trade

when they transfer the loan. The central banks, however, did not make their gold lending conditional on a tie-in with lending to a mining company, as in the conventional form of gold lending. Thus, anyone with access could make use of the opportunity offered by cheap financing in the form of gold loans. A bullion bank (or another carry trader) borrows gold at a very low rate, sells it in the market and invests the proceeds in higher-yielding assets. As the difference between the gold lease rate and bond yields is usually quite high, the resulting profit is commensurately high. However, just as in any other carry trade, the bullion banks now find it in their self-interest that the gold price should fall. After all, they owe the gold, and the lower the price at which they can buy it back in the market, the bigger their profit will be. Should it rise in price, they will lose. The gold carry trade is, thus, a special type of business, the only important one of its kind, where there is an exclusive interest in falling prices (just as there is only an interest in rising prices in assets such as stocks and an interest in both rising and falling prices in the futures markets).

Chapter 12

Coordination of Private Banks and Central Banks

It is, therefore, in the carry traders' self-interest that the gold price falls. Their interest is of a commercial nature; they want to make profits. At the same time it coincides with the political interest that several central banks have in a gold price that doesn't rise (this will be discussed later). The central banks in turn could intervene in the market directly. They have already done so quite often in the foreign exchange and gold markets, both openly and covertly. However, in this instance they don't need to, or only to a limited extent. They don't need to be active in the market themselves, but can 'delegate' some of the work to the bullion banks. Those simply pursue their commercial interests when they take actions against a rising gold price.

Basically, they don't even need to be goaded into this. They do, however, require a backstop. If they take over parts of the work, such as the almost daily interventions in the futures market, it is possible that they will also require physical gold. As discussed earlier, it is possible for futures market intervention to deflect potential investors from certain investment options. It is nevertheless conceivable that the total physical demand cannot be satisfied at a low price. Then physical material is needed, either by means of sales or in the form of gold loans by central banks. The day-to-day business can, however, be entirely taken care of by the bullion banks (Figure 12.1).

Due to this alignment of interests, the suppression of the gold price is self-propelling, so to speak; it requires very little consultation. It is a process that, once initiated, can continue over many years on its own as a result of this alignment of interests. Both on the part of the central banks and on the part of the bullion banks, knowledge of the details and the backdrop is, for many participants, not necessary. It suffices that there are agreements and consultations at the highest level. The specific business on the part of the central banks appears, apart from actual interventions, to be a normal gold-lending business. On the part of bullion banks,

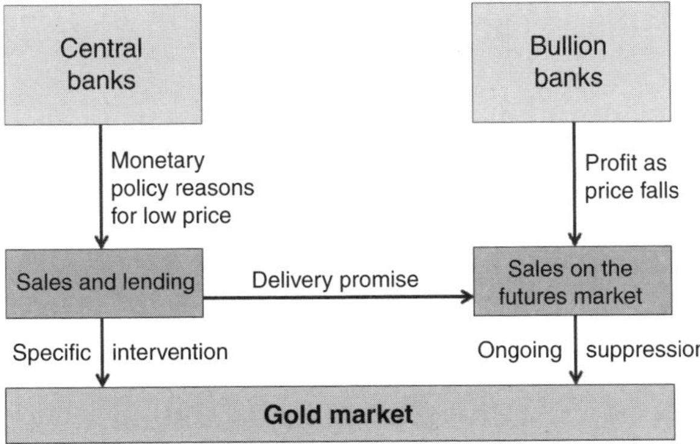

Figure 12.1 Cooperation between central banks and bullion banks out of shared interests

systematic price interventions may be conspicuous internally, but probably largely appear to be a part of the carry trade and gold-lending business. It is, therefore, not necessary for hundreds or thousands of people to be involved, which would have increased the risk that close-lipped bankers and even more close-lipped central bankers let something slip to the outside world, either on purpose or by mistake. Some of the people involved know about it, of course, but not all of them. Someone who is involved in specific business activities, even in an open market department of a central bank that deals with gold lending, need not have been apprised of the big picture. How small the number of persons can be and how limited it can be even within central banks is made clear by both a recent and a historical example. First, until recently only three people within the Swiss National Bank knew where its gold is stored.[20] Second, only four people knew the score in the 1920s, when the Bank of England even falsified data for the purpose of manipulating interest rates.[21]

What applies to the number of individuals also applies to the number of institutions. Of several dozens of bullion banks, probably only a few made use of their contacts to officialdom in a manner that went beyond usual business practice. The tight interconnections with financial institutions on a personal level have often become the target of criticism, for instance two US treasury secretaries, Robert Rubin and Hank Paulson, once were board members of US investment bank Goldman Sachs. In principle an agreement suffices for an overarching cooperation between private and official institutions (the individual gold lending contracts are of course specifically rendered in writing). Often, however, even that was probably not necessary due to the alignment of interests. Even among central banks by no means all are specifically involved. Planning the process long in advance is all in all not really necessary. It is more or less enough to pursue the common interest in a low gold price by means of changing agreements, methods and partners. There exist however specific agreements (as can for instance be determined by using analysis to ferret out certain target prices that have been agreed upon).

Cooperation between the private sector and officialdom is, however, also not without historical precedent. In the wake of the 1987 stock market crash private institutions were already mandated by the US central bank to engage in market interventions. The aim was to support the markets by buying futures contracts. This fact was well known in the marketplace at the time. It was later confirmed by government sources through Bob Woodward. Woodward became known for uncovering the Watergate scandal and was able to question highly placed government officials.[22] On 19 October 1987, the US stock market had suffered a 20 per cent decline, the biggest one-day decline in history. A seizure and breakdown of the entire financial system threatened (in 2008 a seizure could no longer be averted). The subsequently appointed 'Working Group on Financial Markets', which, among other things, was charged with 'maintaining investor confidence', was supposed to 'determine private sector solutions wherever possible'.[23] That was probably also the backdrop to the US treasury secretary conferring up to six times a day via telephone with the CEO of Goldman Sachs during the 2008 financial crisis.[24] In the LIBOR scandal, uncovered in 2012, it appears that the Bank of England, a central bank, is involved as well.[25] Cooperation between central banks and private banks in order to manipulate prices is therefore nothing special. Central banks are, after all, as their name already implies, primarily part of the banking system rather than detached government agencies.

Similar to gold lending, the gold carry trade has a negative influence on the price, since physical material increases the supply. Moreover, it ties carry traders in the form of bullion banks to the central banks by creating an alignment of their interests. Furthermore, it finances the intervention activities, as the commercial banks are able to make large profits from the interest rate differential for many years (which they have probably needed latterly, as the price has been rising for several years, which generates losses).

Aside from the daily intervention effort there is also the possibility of cooperation in terms of the carry trade itself. Although it yields a high profit due to low gold-lease rates, the profit is not safe, as the carry traders owe gold and are thus dependent on the gold price not rising. The bullion banks could, therefore, be motivated to increase their carry trades if the central banks 'guarantee' a low gold price – for instance, by means of sales or simply by increasing gold loans.

Chapter 13

Giving the Game Away: Central Bankers are Human Beings Too

In order for the cooperation between bullion banks and central banks to work, the central banks must guarantee to deliver enough gold on demand in the event of a rising price. A quote by Alan Greenspan, then chairman of the Federal Reserve, is telling in this context. He said, in 1998: 'Nor can private counterparties restrict supplies of gold, another commodity whose derivatives are often traded over-the-counter, where central banks stand ready to lease gold in increasing quantities should the price rise.'[26]

His statement did not, of course, concern systematic interventions, but a mooted regulation of interbank trading. Someone, such as a speculator, could make a malicious attempt to artificially drive the price up in order to make illegal profits. Greenspan tries to refute that anyone would be able to do so. As an example he mentions gold, and with it precisely the mechanism that is a crucial part of the systematic suppression of the gold price, which is otherwise unknown and never discussed anywhere. In spite of speaking in a different context about it, he thereby spells out quite clearly that the central banks are lending out gold in order to keep the price from rising. Greenspan doesn't say that they're already doing it, only that they are prepared to do so.

From his statement it follows, moreover, that gold lending is for the central banks – Greenspan uses the plural, 'the central banks' – already an agreed-upon means for suppressing the price of gold. Why should central banks coordinate themselves in order to avert what was, at the time, the quite improbable event of a problem in interbank trading due to a rising gold price? What are they doing about crude oil, natural gas, petrol, heating oil, platinum, palladium, silver, aluminum, nickel, zinc, copper, sugar, coffee, wheat, soybeans, corn or the much larger stock and bond markets? They have a particular solution for one commodity. This solution of increasing supplies by lending the commodity out is rather bizarre. One first has to come up with such an intervention idea. One must ask oneself why Greenspan uses gold as an example and why he names the solution of lending gold in order to influence its price. As far as this is humanly possible to judge, this means that he must already have given it his attention.

Furthermore, Greenspan mentions the occasion upon which the central banks would intervene, namely a rise in the price ('should its price rise'). This raises a further question: how could the central banks possibly determine whether a price increase is a regular one (caused by a supply shortage or rising demand) or an irregular one (caused by artificially driving the price up)? They cannot do that. If they want to avert irregular price increases, however, although they cannot differentiate them from other price increases, then they must avert every price increase. That is the logical consequence! And thus they are already (in 1998) doing it.

As an aside, it isn't even in the remit of central banks to intervene in the commodity markets – for instance, to avert problems preemptively. There is not a single law for this purpose; they do not have a mandate for it. It should also be quite difficult to find anything about this in the literature ('if the price of a commodity rises by 5 per cent within a week, the central banks should lend it out from their stock in order to avert a further increase in price'). But Greenspan doesn't think of that either as he chooses the example.

Greenspan names the example because it is perfectly useful in the context of the debate over regulations to impress on worried politicians that no additional regulations are necessary: absolutely no one can actually drive up the price of gold artificially. This is because the central banks make sure that it doesn't rise by lending out gold whenever there are rallies. Greenspan has actually spilled the beans. It was too tempting to name an example of how an unwanted price increase could be reliably averted. In spite of the different context, Greenspan's statement only makes sense if the lending of gold by central banks for the purpose of price suppression has already been employed.

Chapter 14

The Books are Silent

Transparency in public affairs is a crucial entitlement of modern societies. Accordingly, central banks regularly publish their balance sheets. The amount of gold on loan should, therefore, be reflected in their balance sheets. That would make it possible to check whether gold-lending and gold carry trades are a means of intervention. Moreover, one would know how large the amount of gold on loan actually is. But what is the reality, what exactly is published? With 8,000 tons, the USA is the largest holder of gold in the world. In the USA, the treasury department is the official holder of gold. However, neither the treasury nor the Federal Reserve publishes whether, and if so how much, gold has been lent out. In the UK the treasury is the official holder of gold as well. In the UK, no information as to the amount of gold on loan is available either. In two countries that are held to be exemplary democracies, there is utter silence on the question of gold lending. Let us look at those countries where the central banks hold the gold. One should expect in these cases that the balance sheet differentiates clearly between physically present goods and goods that have been lent out. Germany is the second-largest holder of gold, with nearly 3,400 tons. We take a look (Figure 14.1) at the relevant line item in the balance sheet of the German central bank, the Bundesbank.[27]

So Figure 14.1 shows 'gold and gold receivables'. But what are gold receivables? These are claims to gold that have been created by gold lending and related types of business. The Bundesbank holds these claims against third parties – that is, other central banks as well as bullion banks. Such a gold receivable is, however, fundamentally different from gold. It is, for instance, not certain whether the Bundesbank will get the gold back. The line item 'gold and gold receivables' is not detailed any further by the Bundesbank. It thereby ignores national accounting law, which it should actually adhere to.[28] However, it is not an isolated case internationally. Apart

Assets		
	31.12.2011 € million	31.12.2010 € million
1 Gold and gold receivables	132,874	115,403

Figure 14.1 Excerpt from the balance sheet of the German Bundesbank as at 31 December 2011

from very few exceptions, central banks don't publish, or at least don't do so systematically, how much gold they have lent out. Thus, not even a partially reliable statement on the amount of gold on loan by central banks exists.

Now, this is completely incomprehensible and there exists no cogent justification for it. It neither protects business activities (what would follow from the statement that the Fed has, say, lent out 50 tons of gold?) nor the common interests of the respective central bank or the country concerned. Even if one were not to agree with this, it would still be possible to publish the numbers with a lag. Even the time lag inherent in the annual report should be sufficient. The central banks would, moreover, have a good reason for a more transparent treatment of these issues, as rumours and estimates that a large part (up to half) of the gold held by central banks is on loan (and is thus no longer in their vaults) have been making the rounds for years. These rumours actually represent a loss of confidence. The central banks could mitigate it by simply publishing a single figure!

There is another, completely innocuous method available. Anything central banks don't want to see published they can relay to the IMF in confidence. The IMF stores such information in its confidential database and publishes a summary of it. If, for instance, a certain central bank doesn't wish to publish the composition of its foreign exchange reserves (let us say 60 per cent US dollar, 30 per cent euro and 10 per cent yen), it can report it to the IMF.[29] The IMF then summarises all the data it receives from the central banks and publishes the composition of the foreign exchange reserves of all central banks combined in its statistics. In this way the data of an individual central bank remain confidential. Researchers, the public and even the central banks themselves, however, have sound benchmark data at their disposal. This procedure has been well established for many years and most central banks take part. However, they don't do so when it comes to the amount of gold on loan.

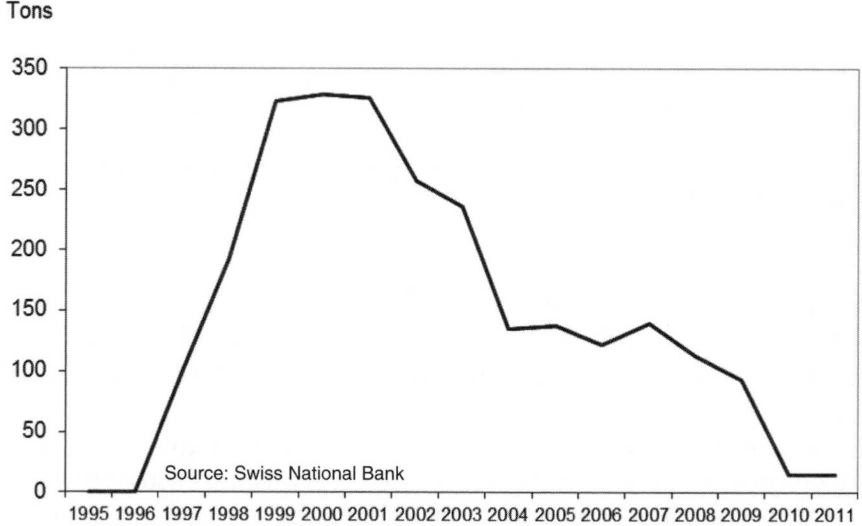

Figure 14.2 Amount of gold lent out by the Swiss National Bank (in tons)

So we have no official data. There are a few rare exceptions, namely the Bank of Portugal, which has lent out 54.9 per cent of its gold reserves (2011), the Swiss National Bank (Figure 14.2) with currently only 1.5 per cent (2011) and the Bank of International Settlements (BIS) with only 3 per cent (2012).[30] That is basically all the world of central banking has to offer in terms of transparency with regard to the gold-lending business. Only two out of a total of 70 central banks engaged in the gold-lending business at its height actually publish how much they are lending out[31] – an extremely small number! In addition, publication is also advisable from the point of view of accounting regulations (the next chapter will show a reason for this). Most central banks, however, publish no information at all about the amount of the gold they have on loan, not even with a time lag or by reporting it anonymously to the IMF. Thus, no precise information is available regarding the amount of gold on loan worldwide (as opposed to, for instance, foreign exchange reserves or gold holdings), even though this number is fundamentally of crucial importance to the gold market (as we will still see).

And what about audits? Every grocery shop controls its inventory at least once a year. In one of the most famous treasure troves in the world, Fort Knox, for example, there has not been a single proper audit in the recent past. Generally, there are no independent audits of the gold holdings of central banks or other government agencies, and only very few statements regarding quantities are published as a result of internal audits. There are no statements about the quantities held in vaults, which would allow one to draw well-founded conclusions about the amount of gold on loan. Only very recently has there been a bit of movement on the issue as a result of massive political and public pressure; the USA and Germany now want to audit part of their gold reserves.

Chapter 15

The Miraculous Gold Multiplication

What medieval alchemists were unable to do, modern central banks achieve without breaking a sweat: they multiply gold! This is not a joke, and this is how it works. The central bank of 'Lending Land' lends 100 tons to a bullion bank, which then sells them to the central bank of 'Purchasing Land'. According to established central bank practice, these 100 tons now continue to be recorded as an asset in the balance sheet of Lending Land's central bank, in the line item 'gold and gold receivables'. However, there now also 100 tons on the balance sheet of the central bank of Purchasing Land, since it has duly bought them. Et voilà! Out of 100 tons, 200 tons were created. In the balance sheets of both central banks there now 100 tons each listed under assets, which adds up to 200 tons. In this manner our hypothetical example would lead to 200 tons of reserves being declared in the statistics of the IMF, although only 100 tons exist.

Of course, the gold hasn't multiplied in reality, only on balance sheets. And, clearly, this practice is contrary to all logic. I can lend my car to my neighbour and if he drives to Chicago with it, I cannot use it to drive to New York at the same time. It is simply not possible. We cannot be in possession of the same car concurrently. There is a big difference between me having something or having lent it out. If I have lent it out, then whoever borrowed it has it at his disposal at that point in time, but not me. Moreover, there is always a residual uncertainty as to whether I will get it back.

A financial claim is not tangible property. One cannot dispose of the object of a financial claim immediately; it can, moreover, become non-performing. This has, of course, been known for a long time; receivables, therefore, have to be declared as separate line items in balance sheets. As demonstrated, anything else would be illogical and would lead to asymmetries. For instance, even the Bundesbank should have to list its receivables separately in its balance sheet. That it doesn't do that, apparently against national law, is justified by invoking 'business policy reasons'.[32] However, the gold-lending business would not be endangered if the amount of gold on loan became public retrospectively. Confidentiality would be retained as well. Moreover, the central banks of Switzerland and Portugal, which publish the amount of gold they have lent out, in effect prove that there are no business policy reasons that are at odds with publication. Business policy reasons are, therefore, a pretext. They have no basis in facts.

If the publication of the amount of gold on loan does not obstruct the national central banks in the fulfilling of their actual duties, then some sort of overriding interest must be behind the decision not to publish. That can only be the concealment of the total amount of the gold on loan globally. By not revealing the figures, the central banks implicitly admit that there is an agreement between them (albeit, perhaps, unspoken) not to publicise the amount of gold lend out by the central banks worldwide.

Also, the concealment of gold lending is most likely neither consistent with the accounting regulations of most countries nor with international accounting principles. The difference between tangible property and receivables is too important not to be enshrined in such regulations. The core principles of the IMF's accounting rules also suggest a separate listing; immediate availability is necessary, for instance, for something to qualify as a reserve asset,[33] which is, in effect and from a legal standpoint, in most cases not applicable to gold on loan. The fact that most central banks nevertheless deviate from the standards regarding this central issue is consistent with the existence of an agreement, as alleged above. If, on the other hand, a few central banks break rank from the great mass of deviationists and fulfil the standards anyway, then there should be a specific explanation for that. Portugal has had a few bad experiences (on this more later); Switzerland is 'stepping out of line' in any case; and the BIS is legally and in practice a special case (for instance, it has a few private shareholders).

Curiously enough, the Bundesbank provides more differentiated information in another part of its balance sheet. In its income statement it discloses its interest revenues from gold lending separately. This rather undermines the 'business policy reasons' cited by the Bundesbank over many years as the reason for being unable to reveal the amount on loan. If it was consistent, then it wouldn't be able to publish the revenues either. The publication of the revenues represents strong circumstantial evidence of what the agreement between the central banks is about (a concealment of the amount of gold on loan, not the revenues).

Disclosure of the revenues only, not the amounts, moreover, doesn't fundamentally dispel one suspicion: much more could, in theory, have been lent out than the revenues suggest. This may not be discernible due to missing or very low interest revenues. Thus, some market observers speculate that up to 1,700 tons of gold have been lent out – half of the Bundesbank's holdings (more on this later).

In contrast to its information policy up until the present time, shortly before completion of this book the Bundesbank, surprisingly, revealed the amount of gold lent out. Upon request, it sent a spreadsheet file which contained, among other things, columns for gold on loan, swaps and demand deposits. This, finally, gives clarity on the amount of gold lent out by the Bundesbank after years of guessing games (Figure 15.1). The amounts closely correspond to the earlier made estimates based on the published lease revenues and other reported information.[34]

Apparently, the Bundesbank has decreased its lending business with private parties in recent years, finally putting a stop to it altogether. Together with the known progression of the amount of Swiss gold loans, one can recognise initial trends in this: the amounts lent by Switzerland and the second-largest gold holder, Germany, rose until the turn of the millennium, but have decreased since then. This decrease doesn't mean that there have been no interventions in

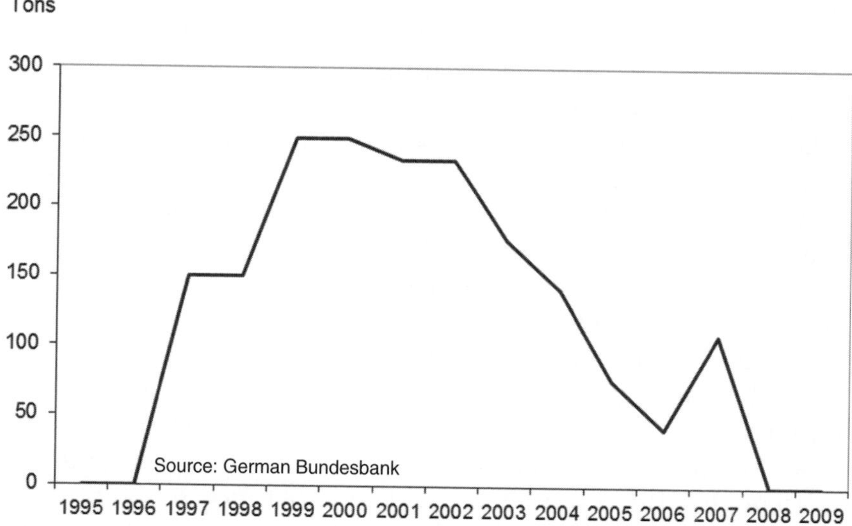

Figure 15.1 Amount of gold lent out by the Bundesbank

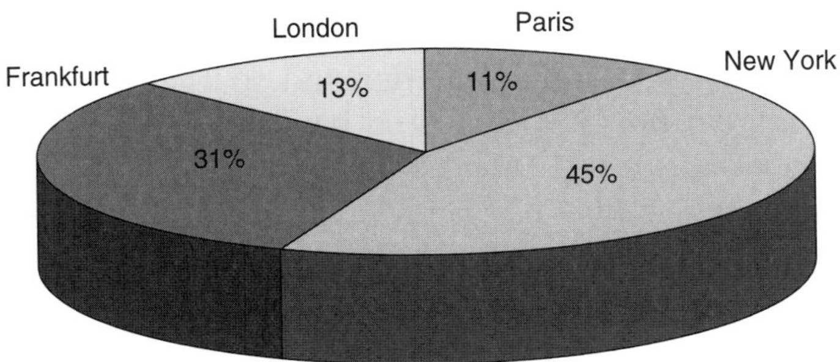

Figure 15.2 Storage facilities holding the Bundesbank's gold

the gold market since then, but only that this particular instrument is only used in certain phases, at most. However, it also might not conform to the expectation of many critical gold market observers that actually the amount of gold on loan has decreased and that this was actually possible without causing major upheaval. We will examine in the next chapter whether these trends are applicable on a worldwide basis as well.

Due to default risk, one would presume that if possible, every ton of gold would be safely stored in vaults. In spite of that, central banks lend out gold at low interest rates, fail to perform audits, or store their gold abroad. In the process, applicable national law is ignored and, upon enquiry, either pretext justifications are provided or none at all. With regard to storage localities, the Bundesbank's gold is a frequently discussed topic among market observers. Much of it is stored abroad, especially in New York. At the time of the gold standard more than 40 years ago, or during the Cold War more than 20 years ago, this made sense. As to why it still remains stored there today, the Bundesbank provides various reasons, such as transport costs or better access to foreign exchange in case of a crisis. For many decades, the Bundesbank even refused to release any public information about what amounts were stored at which storage facilities (Figure 15.2). Due to pressure from the public, as well as from several parliamentarians and the Federal Court of Auditors, the Bundesbank finally put an end to its secrecy in 2012 and published disclosures regarding the amounts held at individual storage facilities. Fortunately, the Bundesbank has recently decided in favour of more transparency with regard to gold, as is also shown by it reporting the amount on loan.

There are neither acceptable reasons for keeping the amounts on loan secret, nor for the neglect of audits, nor the storage of large amounts abroad. Many observers have, therefore, been rightly suspicious for a long time and demand a legally and factually appropriate gold policy. The central banks' policies on disclosure are pre-modern. Central bankers are not omniscient; they must face up to public and academic scrutiny. They are independent so as to allow decision-making that is not influenced by governments or other pressure groups in society, not so that they can conceal the means and results of their policies for many years. Independence does not equal non-transparency! While central banks do largely explain their other monetary policies, silence mostly reigns when it comes to gold.

Chapter 16

How Much Gold is on Loan Worldwide?

Gold sales and gold loans push the price down. The physical supply is increased to the same extent, regardless of whether a central bank sells 100 tons or lends them out. Lending is fast, the process doesn't have to be laboriously moved through committees, it finances carry traders and the public doesn't have to be informed about the amounts involved. While we are comparatively well informed about sales, there is by contrast, almost no information forthcoming from the central banks as to how much of their gold has been lent into the market. However, estimates do exist by third parties. Even if the central banks don't publish the amount of gold on loan, their business partners, who borrow the gold, may well be doing so. Furthermore, one could attempt to estimate the annual supply and demand and the amount of gold that has been lent into the market based on the difference. Both approaches are possible, but the resulting estimates unfortunately lack precision.

In contrast to central banks, many mining companies, the recipients of the revenues from the classical gold-lending business, do publish adequate information. Based on their disclosures, there are fairly reliable estimates of the amount of gold borrowed by mines and, thus, the minimum amount of gold on loan. Demand for gold loans also comes from other quarters, including, for instance, fabricators in the jewellery trade (who finance their working inventory in this manner). In addition, there are the trade, speculation and trading activities stemming from a multitude of transactions, such as the covering of claims (e.g., stemming from option trades), arbitrage (e.g., between futures and spot markets), or the balancing of shortfalls (e.g., in gold accounts). Furthermore, there is the carry trade, the borrowing of gold combined with subsequent sales and reinvestment into higher-yielding assets. In terms of the magnitude of this business, there is very imprecise disclosure or none at all on the part of borrowers. The respective estimates are often very inaccurate, as no solid basis for them appears to exist. Gold borrowed for carry trades is not disclosed separately by the financial institutions involved.[35]

The second method employs the difference between annual supply and consumption.[36] Gold that is consumed must come from somewhere. The supply on the gold market consists, essentially, of mine production, existing gold in all forms (scrap, sales of investment gold, etc.) and the sales and lending activities of central banks. Demand comes from the jewellery trade, other commercial enterprises (electronics industry, dentistry, etc.) and investment demand. If every magnitude apart from the amount of gold that is on loan were known with precision, one could calculate the latter reliably. The difference between annual supply and demand would be explained by the amount of gold lent out, since this would be the only additional gold to enter the market. The amount could be negative as well (if more gold is paid back than lent out). However, we don't know these magnitudes with enough precision to be able to make a reliable estimate of the amount of leased gold. There are already a great number of imponderables, inaccuracies and estimates regarding the basic numbers, which affect all subsequent assumptions and estimates, so that the result is at best a rough guide for the gold market. The resulting estimate of the size of the gold loans would be too imprecise. One such guide has, for many years, been provided by the specialised analysis and consulting institute GFMS (formerly Gold Fields Mineral Service, www.gfms.co.uk).

In order to understand the gold market, the 1990s are an important period, as gold lending by central banks was greatly expanded at the time. For 1995 the GFMS estimate was for global supply of nearly 3,550 tons of gold, with about 450 tons in additional loans. Demand was estimated to be 3,550 tons as well. In 1998 the well-connected financial analyst Frank Veneroso analysed and compared these data more closely in a study on gold.[37] This was based on the estimates of a mining company association, the World Gold Council (www.gold.org). These estimates, however, didn't encompass the global market in its entirety. A number of regions and types of consumption were missing. Veneroso estimated the missing numbers and added them up. Moreover, he applied a few corrections. He arrived at consumption of 4,150 tons, considerably more than estimated by GFMS. This additional consumption had to come from somewhere, which led Veneroso to assume, primarily, that there were additional gold loans from central banks.

Concurrently, Veneroso attempted to estimate the amount of gold that was already lent out. For this, he not only used the commonly known public sources, but combined them with various additional disclosures, primarily from the Bank of England. While GFMS assumed in 1995 that only 2,450 tons of gold loans were outstanding in total, he arrived at 6,500 tons, already more than twice annual production! Of that, 1,300 tons entered the market additionally in 1995 alone, also considerably more than estimated by GFMS (as Veneroso used estimates of the amounts that were made at different points in time, he could only provide rough values for the end of the year). In spite of a number of imponderables and a bias towards higher numbers, it was at least possible to conclude from his data that annual consumption was hundreds of tons higher than had been hitherto assumed, and that this gold stemmed from additional central bank gold lending. The much higher supply, of course, had to put additional pressure on the price.

Following the publication of these data, a broader swathe of the expert community became aware of the gold carry trade. That it exists at all is actually a consequence of the nature of the matter as such. If there is an opportunity to get capital cheaply, there are always likely to be market participants that will take up such a loan in order to invest it at higher yields elsewhere (similar to how many private individuals in Japan had the idea to borrow yen cheaply and invest them in foreign currencies). One must bear in mind the very low lease rates of often less than 1 per cent on the gold-lending market. However, there exist barely any authoritative reports on gold carry trades. Of these, only those about Drexel Burnham Lambert are worth mentioning. When the investment bank Drexel went bankrupt in 1990, it was unable to fulfil its gold obligations to the central banks. This was how the central bank of Portugal lost the gold it had previously lent to Drexel without collateral. However, the Greenspan quote regarding the readiness of central banks to lend out more gold in the event of a price rise only makes sense if carry traders exist.[38] In spite of the fact that they are not really taken into account in many statistics, there can be no serious doubt about the existence and significance of carry trades.[39]

Gold carry trades are, thus, a significant factor in the gold market, despite the fact that we have so little sound information about them. Some have ignored it, while others have assumed excessive amounts. There are hints that the carry trade wasn't expanded by choice. For example, there may have been lobbying of mining companies by bullion banks, urging the borrowing of gold. This leads one to conclude that the bullion banks preferred the standard banking practice of credit mediation to the carry trade.

Veneroso later brought his estimates up to date,[40] and there were additional estimates based on different methods. Worth noting here are those of Reg Howe,[41] who examined outstanding derivatives, as well as those of James Turk,[42] who analysed storage facilities. Around the turn of the millennium, figures of up to 10,000–18,000 tons of gold on loan were making the rounds, more than half of all central bank holdings. Was it possible that there was really only half as much gold stored in the vaults of central banks than they had disclosed?

All these estimates rested on dubiously reliable bases. More precise data could only be reported by the central banks themselves. Many conventional estimates even pretended that the carry trade didn't exist as a discrete phenomenon (but instead was effectively a consequence of other – speculative – activities). Some didn't see a need to adjust their numbers, even after the carry trade had been a topic of debate for years. The size of the carry trade was, conversely, often overestimated by those who did take it into account. Most of them were (rightly) also of the opinion that the gold price was being suppressed, but concluded that the central banks had lent out a large part of their gold holdings. Sometimes they expected (and perhaps hoped for) a short squeeze, a covering of the positions of borrowed gold in conjunction with the considerable price rise this would cause. At times, there appeared to be an unbridgeable gap between the two sides. That the truth could lie somewhere in the middle, not precisely, but somewhere between the two extremes, was barely considered. The amount may have been about 8,000 tons at its maximum, which were lent out around the turn of the millennium. Since then it has probably declined.

One can fairly easily make the case that the truth is, indeed, somewhere in the middle, that less than half of the gold was on loan, but also that it was more than the classical gold-lending business would have amounted to. In 2000 Howe and Elwood considered whether the amount of gold stored abroad could provide indications regarding the gold loans.[43] As it happens, many central banks, similar to the Bundesbank, don't only store gold in their own cellar, but have it dispersed all over the world. Even at the time when gold was still tied to currencies (in 1971 the final such tie between the dollar and gold was dissolved) it was general practice to keep gold accounts with other central banks or keep storage facilities in other countries in order to make gold payment transactions easier. Furthermore, security aspects played a role, especially on account of World War II and, later, socialism. In addition, the USA was a net payer of gold after World War II, but the recipients sometimes shied away from transporting it and erecting new storage facilities. For these reasons, the Federal Reserve Bank of New York, one of the regional reserve banks of the US Federal Reserve system, became one of the main storage facilities for the gold of foreign central banks. At its peak more than 70 central banks kept about one third of the global holdings of central bank-owned gold there, respectively about half of the holdings of foreign central banks excluding the USA! New York is, therefore, by far the most important storage area for central bank gold. In keeping with the US tradition of transparency and its penchant for statistics, the New York Fed publishes monthly how much gold it stores for other central banks (in allocated storage, i.e., segregated by ownership). Figure 16.1 shows the amount of foreign central bank gold stored in New York in tons.

Let us look at the time period from the beginning of the systematic interventions in 1993 until 2001, when the stock held in New York stabilised. During this time period it declined by about 3,000 tons. That is less than a third of the initial stock in 1993 (even if one uses 1980 as the beginning, the stock has only declined by less than half). But this makes it entirely implausible that up to half or more has been lent out! The vault in New York would have emptied much more in that case. After all, it must be taken into account that a part of the outflow of 3,000 tons could also have been caused by sales

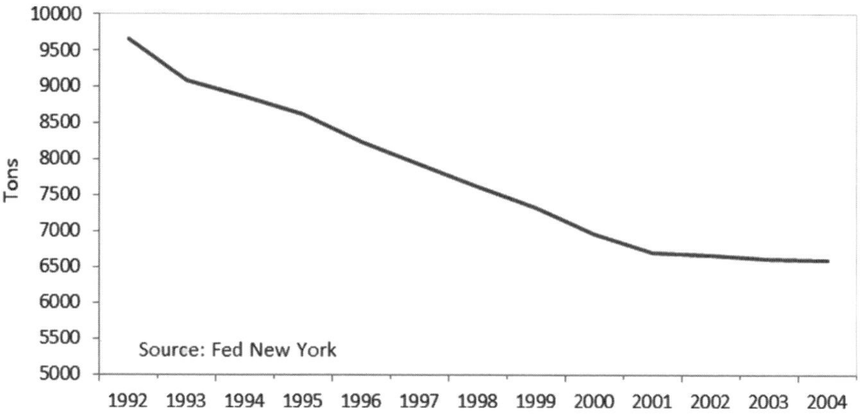

Figure 16.1 Foreign central bank gold, the amount stored at the New York Fed

(or maybe due to mere pure relocation). In addition, many central banks would probably mobilise gold in New York more readily than at many other storage facilities, so one should expect disproportional outflow from there. An outflow of about one third would not correspond with a loan quota of 50 per cent in 2001, making clear that considerably less than half of the gold holdings of central banks were lent out.

Conversely, however, the outflows of 3,000 tons also don't fit with the conventional estimates that do not take the gold carry trade into account separately. This is because, in the same time period, about 2,500 tons of gold were sold. If one only adds small loan amounts to this, then the outflow of 3,000 tons from New York appear to be too high. If about one third of the global holding of gold is stored there, one would expect a far smaller number (there is no reason to suppose that in this time period especially large amounts of gold were shifted to other storage facilities). The truth is, therefore, presumably really somewhere in the 'middle', which concurs with the conclusions arrived at so far: that there is a gold carry trade and there are systematic interventions in the gold market. However, the amount of gold on loan was not as large as some of the more extreme estimates would have us believe.

We now want to develop a method from the above considerations in order to estimate the total amount of gold on loan worldwide. For this purpose, we once again show the amount of foreign central bank gold stored in New York, this time from 1960 to 2012 (Figure 16.2). Above this we depict the total amount of gold that all foreign central banks (i.e., without the USA) have published as their total holdings.

The upper part of the figure shows the total gold holdings of all countries except the USA; below it is the amount stored in New York. In the early 1960s, the total stock increased. The USA, at the time, had a balance of payments deficit which, according to the rules of Bretton Woods, was often still balanced with gold (in the Bretton Woods Agreement the USA had pledged to other countries that it would exchange dollars for gold). At the end of the 1970s the stock fell slightly due to sales. Thereafter it stabilised, only to fall again in the 1990s due to many central bank sales.

Now to the line showing the foreign gold stored in New York. It increased in the 1960s at a less than proportional rate, as some countries like France, the gold holdings of which rose, apparently preferred to store their gold at home. In the 1980s, the line began to steadily decline at a slow pace. One reason may have been worries

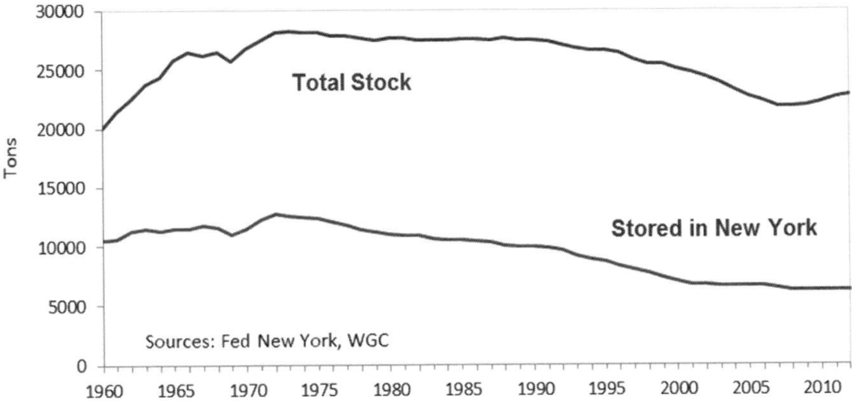

Figure 16.2 Foreign central bank gold holdings, total stock and stock stored in New York

about security after the USA had frozen Iranian assets as a result of the Iranian hostage crisis of 1979. Since 1993, the stock then began to decline even faster, and remained unchanged for several years after the turn of the millennium. We can see that there is often a certain correlation between the two curves, which is to be expected, since the lower curve represents the gold stored in New York, which is part of the total gold holdings of all countries except the USA.

The upper line, the total stock, and the lower line, the part of which that is stored in New York, are therefore closely correlated with each other. If all central banks were to disperse their gold holdings evenly at all times, then the two curves would even be in a fixed relationship – if not for gold lending. But the upper line of the total balance sheet stock of gold contains the gold that is on loan as well, since the central banks count it as part of their gold reserves, even if it consists only of receivables. Since gold that has been lent out and then sold in the market necessarily must leave the vaults, the gold that has been lent to private parties is, thus, definitely not contained in the lower line! We do, however, have the means to calculate an estimate of the total amount of gold on loan from the shape of the curves: whatever disappears from the vaults, but not from balance sheets, must be gold that has been lent out.

However, we must make two assumptions for this purpose, namely the starting point (when did gold lending begin) and regarding the progression of the lines relative to each other (since there are other storage areas than New York). There are, therefore, uncertainties, but the aim is to arrive at an estimate. As the starting date, we choose 1980, as gold reached its price peak at the time; gold lending in large amounts before that time can be ruled out. One could just as well take a later point in time as the starting point (the literature occasionally mentions 1982 as the time when gold lending began to gain in popularity); that would, however, only reduce the total loan amount by a few hundred tons.

The second assumption is more problematic. Here we assume that the two lines are progressing at a specific ratio. For one thing, it is assumed that the gold that has been sold, bought and lent from New York was in a constant relation to the gold sold, bought and lent elsewhere. Moreover, we assume that there was no transfer of gold between New York and other storage areas.

The method is easy to understand if one applies a simplification. If there were only the storage facility in New York, then the amount of gold disclosed on balance sheets less the amount on loan would be equal to the amount in storage. The calculation would then be simple and reliable. If, for instance, the amount of gold on balance sheets were to decline by 400 tons, then this would be a decrease due to sales, since the loans are not disclosed. If at the same time the amount in the vault were to decline by 500 tons, then 100 tons must have been lent out.

So we introduce a fixed ratio that results from the ratio at the starting year 1980, and uncertainties arise. The principle, however, remains. If the stock held in New York declines proportionally by more than the total amount disclosed on balance sheets (i.e., through sales), then it is assumed that the difference was due to gold loans. We must thereby assume a starting year (such as 1980) with the loan amount 'zero', since we don't know how much was on loan at a later date (such as the year 2000; this is the difference between reality and the simplified example with just one storage facility). There is, therefore, only an iterative solution (of the 'discrete differential equation'). It is accompanied by imponderables.

One of those is the amount of gold lent out by the USA. That is the 'big unknown', as there is no utilisable basis for an estimate of the amount of gold lent out by the USA – although, as the biggest holder of gold it would have the biggest lending potential. In addition, there is the fact that the USA, due to the special role of the dollar as an international reserve currency, has the greatest interest in a gold price that doesn't rise due to gold lending. Since it is likely that our estimate will tend to be too high,[44] it is assumed

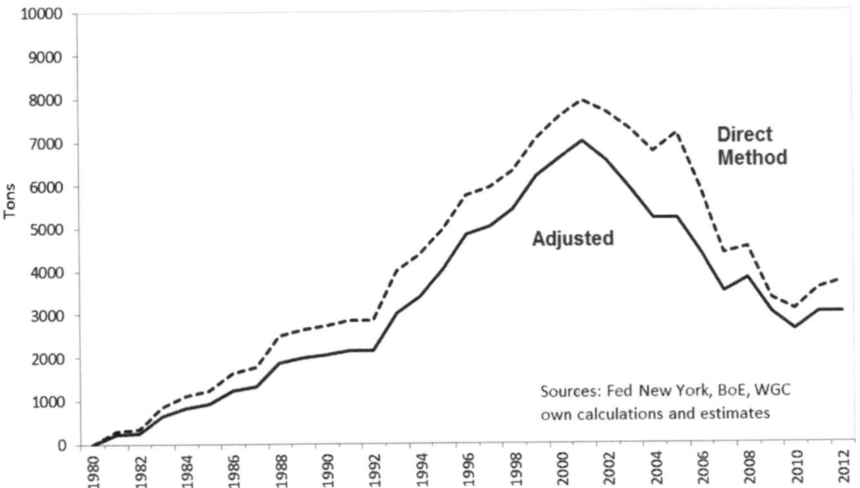

Figure 16.3 Gold on loan worldwide, estimated on the basis of the stock stored in New York

here as a simplification that this is balanced by the methodically not ascertainable amount of gold lent out by the USA. Figure 16.3 shows the worldwide gold lending activities of all central banks. The upper line shows the directly calculated amount, the lower line is corrected by a few additional factors.[45]

The progress is quite harmonious: until 1993, gold loans only increase slowly (as the business is only beginning to be established), then they rise steadily. Apart from the classical form of gold lending, the carry trade becomes visible as well, as the amount is greater than that resulting from conventional calculations that only take into account the amounts borrowed by mines. This confirms that the carry trade existed already prior to 1993. When the systematic gold interventions in August of 1993 began, some carry traders stood to lose out as a result of a rising gold price and were interested in a falling gold price – they became partners in cooperation with the central banks.

Since the beginning of the systematic interventions in 1993, an increase in the amounts lent out began. As an aside, if one looks at the monthly data in detail, gold was being removed from New York at an accelerated pace precisely beginning with the month of August when the gold market interventions started. Until 2001, the amount of gold on loan rose to nearly 8,000 tons; since then it has been falling to about 3,000 tons. The upper line lies generally above the conventional estimates, and thus illustrates that carry trades exist. At the same time it is considerably below the more extreme estimates, which assume that up to 18,000 tons of gold were lent out.

The progression also reflects the backdrop and the movements of the gold price. In the 1980s, the gold loans by central banks have contributed to gold's weakness, although one can probably only speak about intervention activities in a few cases. From the time when the systematic interventions began, the central banks have increased their gold lending, which has kept the gold price under pressure. Since the beginning of the bull market in gold in 2001, the amounts on loan have declined, as is to be expected (since the borrowers are making losses). Overall, there have been hardly any supply additions through gold loans by the central banks since then (apart from, seemingly, 2008 and 2011). This assumption of the amount lent out in recent years also fits with the picture that is suggested by the special cases of the Swiss and Portuguese national banks, which publish the amounts on loan, as well as the Bundesbank (as described in the preceding chapter).

However, one would expect a more pronounced decline. One can now revise the line created on the basis of the stock held in New York using certain parameters and considerations based on the trend. The lower line shows the amount on loan thus adjusted by external factors. While it continues to be based on the stock held in New York, it takes into account several other (likewise quite uncertain) factors. What makes it more pleasing is that it assumes a stronger decrease since the beginning of the bull market in 2001. For this, we use anchor points for 1993 (3,000 tons), for the turn of the millennium (7,000 tons) and the present (3,000 tons) as well as the starting value for 1980 with its amount of zero gold on loan. The possible error is greatest for the present.[46] Since the central banks don't publish exact figures, it is perhaps most sensible to help visualise the imprecision regarding the amounts on loan by publishing both lines. Somewhere, in a cloud determined by these lines (in and around them), the actual amounts reside.

We now expand our examination of the sales of central banks, which affect the market as well. In this manner we can examine whether the central banks, with gold holdings exceeding annual consumption by far, were actually the decisive factor influencing the price of gold. To this end, we take the amount of gold that has entered the market by means of central bank lending activities (as determined directly by our method, without the adjustment). In addition, we chart the graph of the net amount of gold

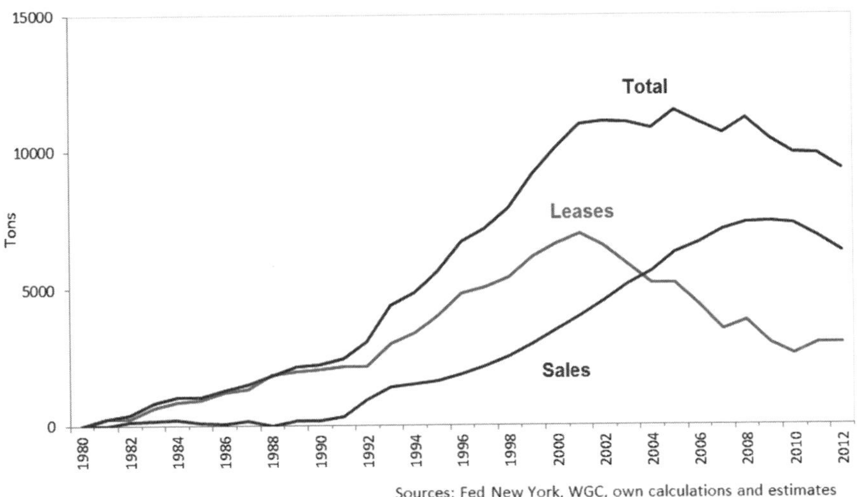

Figure 16.4 Central bank gold that has entered the market worldwide

(Figure 16.4) that has been sold by central banks since 1980 (determined by officially disclosed holdings). The third, upper line shows the sum of the two – in other words, all of the gold that has come to the market by means of gold lending and gold sales by central banks.

Until the beginning of the 1990s, sales were still immaterial relative to the later disposals. Nevertheless, individual sales have influenced the market and have likely been engaged in for this purpose. Since 1992, sales have increased. Even in the bull market since 2001 they have not declined, but continued, which is important, as the gold loans outstanding declined around the same time period. With 7,000–8,000 tons of gold on loan in the year 2000, the total amount of gold lent out reached a magnitude of several times annual production (approximately 2,500 tons). This amount is realistically not readily available on the market. In 2001, the carry traders among the borrowers were thus not in a situation in which they could conceivably close out their positions. They were, therefore, dependent on a prolongation of the contracts.

However, the borrowers were able to reduce their gold debts later by buying gold that the central banks sold, which the borrowers then used to settle their gold debts with the central banks. As the sideways move of the upper line signals (the sum of gold sales and gold loans), approximately the entire amount of gold sold by the central banks was, in effect, used to pay back gold loans to the central banks. Not to put too fine a point on it, one could say that the central banks have given the previously lent out gold back to themselves. The central banking system as a whole has, of course, lost the relevant amount of gold; in a total account the gold that was lent out was ultimately booked as sales of commensurate magnitude.

In spite of all uncertainties, the method of estimating the size of the gold loans via the stock held in New York provides guidance regarding the size as well as the progression of the gold loan amounts, and both fit with an overall picture that makes sense. Thus, the total amount of gold shown to have come to the market courtesy of central banks by means of loans and sales (the upper line in Figure 16.4) encompasses approximately the amount that actually did come to the market via the central banks and influenced gold's price negatively. We therefore want to contrast this total with the price of gold. This total of sales and gold loans influences the supply of gold and with it the price of gold (and not, as some market commentators who are unaware of the loans say, merely the sales by central banks) (Figure 16.5).

Figure 16.5 Gold price and global central bank gold supply

The upper line shows the gold price from 1980 onward, the lower line the amount of gold central banks have brought to the market directly and indirectly. One can see very clearly that the gold price tended towards weakness in the 1980s due to the altered backdrop, which the central banks promoted. In mid-1993, the price of gold attempted to rally, which was averted by an increase in disposals. Thereafter, gold moved sideways, but generally fell until 2001. This was accompanied by continuing disposals on the part of the central banks, which were the main reason for the fall in price. The entire decline, from August 1993 to 2001, was dominated by the central banks. In the course of this, their holdings not only dropped through sales, but also through gold loans in an amount that in its totality could no longer be returned without major problems. From 2001–12 the gold price rose, at its peak nearly eightfold. This was accompanied by a sideways movement in total gold disposals by central banks. The continuing sales couldn't rein in the rally, as concurrently gold loans of approximately similar size were called in, for which gold was needed. Fundamentally, there was a structural deficit that the central banks had offset for years, which was then no longer the case. The rally was partly also an adjustment of the gold price as a result of having been strongly suppressed by the central banks previously. In sum, the chart suggests that the gold price was largely determined by the size of central bank disposals. Central banks were the main factor influencing the price of gold.

It also becomes increasingly clear that the systematic interventions in the gold market have been in retreat since 2001, insofar as the central banks no longer made additional gold available; the price increase could only be delayed, no longer prevented. Only in the year 2008 and then again 2011 was gold effectively put on the market again by the central banks, presumably in order to calm the markets that were beset by uncertainty due to the financial crises. That made it possible to prevent an increase of the gold price in this critical time period, specifically above the level of $1,000 respectively $2,000 per ounce. Since 2001, gold market interventions are, therefore, becoming less frequent, especially with regard to gold loans.

In view of the fact that several years have already passed, that the gold price has gone up by multiples, that gold loans could apparently only be partially unwound and that, in addition, the vaults have been emptied by sales and loans, it appears that the activities, especially since 1993, were quite shortsighted. As happens with so many market manipulations, they come home to roost after a while. One must seriously question to what extent the institutions involved were aware that their interventions would one day produce the opposite effect. One must also ask to what extent they considered whether they would, in their totality, get the gold they had lent out back without a hitch when they entered into these positions. Moreover, it would be interesting to know whether the central banks, given that they conceal the amounts of gold on loan from the public so effectively, at least know themselves how much gold has been lent out in total.

The line showing the gold that has been sold and lent worldwide by central banks thus reveals many details. The most important one, from a long-term perspective, is that the central banking system, since 2001, has not been net disposer in the gold market, even though the sales figures alone suggest that it was still disposing of gold for many years. In reality, this process was stopped in 2001, since which time the gold price has risen. The central banks have put gold on the market since 1965. At the time they still held nearly 38,000 tons. By 2001 there were perhaps 25,000 tons left that were effectively in their vaults (i.e., having deducted gold loans). On average, they made some 370 tons per year available to the market. Overall, the central banking system has lost about a third of its gold (if one deems the gold on loan as lost). However, given that over the same time span a lot of gold has been mined, the economy has grown and with it the number of financial claims; the system should have bought gold in order to preserve its relative position. The gold it disposed of was mainly used to make jewellery, the jewellery trade being the main buyer.

From a monetary policy perspective, the sideways trend indicates that, within the institutions, the forces that are against a disposal of central bank gold have prevailed. It remains to be seen, however, to what extent this represents a new long-term trend and whether the central banks will stop the gold disposals on a sustained basis – or if they even start buying it again, as central banks have been net buyers since 2010 for the first time since 1988, lately even in sizable amounts. Moreover, it remains to be seen whether this is a reversal of the trend towards less and less precious metal backing of money, which has occurred since the 1960s.

From a medium-term perspective, the most important factor is that the process of gold market intervention since 2001 is in its first phase of retreat. This is happening in a manner similar to that often forecast by representatives of the gold price suppression thesis (and is still 'forecast' even a long time after 2001), in that the central banks (overall) relinquish the gold that has been lent out and instead engage in sales of similar magnitude. That the systematic gold market interventions have entered a new phase, or, to be more precise, are in the initial phase of their liquidation, could only be guessed at due to the rally in the gold price itself, until now. One of the main reasons why the termination process that has been underway for years hasn't really been properly perceived regards the estimates of the size of outstanding gold loans.

We assume that, as of 2001, there were about 7,000–8,000 tons of gold on loan, and, further, that since then this amount has decreased. This position lies between the conventional estimates of those who largely ignore the carry trade (who estimate a smaller amount) and the far higher estimates typical of the representatives of the gold price suppression thesis (who estimate up to twice this amount). Overall, there is a lot that argues in favour of the notion that not as much gold has been lent out as has been estimated on the part of those who have (rightly) held the view that the central banks have intervened against a rising gold price.

As a result of the smaller amount of gold on loan, less gold has been put on the market in order to lower the price than hitherto assumed. Either this smaller amount was sufficient, or there had to be yet another source of gold. If less gold than assumed is available, how is the suppression of the gold price achieved? Since there is probably no gold coming forth courtesy of actual alchemists, there have to be other ways to achieve the goal of preventing or at least slowing down a price increase. We examine how it is possible to satisfy even physical demand through other means than actual delivery of the commodity.

Chapter 17

Means of Gold Intervention III: Intervention through the Futures Market

Physical demand can ultimately only be satisfied with physical material. One fashions a wedding ring from real gold, not from futures and options. Real demand must be served in a real manner, in the event that the material is demanded in physical form. Nevertheless, one hears now and then that the demand for gold can be satisfied with derivatives or 'paper gold'. In the case of investment gold, it is occasionally, indeed, possible that the gold is not bought physically. If an investor buys an ounce via one of the many legal constructs established today – certificates, exchange traded funds (ETFs) or gold accounts, to name just three – the question whether the gold was physically bought and stored always arises. This is so because it is possible that the investor merely has a claim to an ounce and that, overall, fewer ounces were bought than claims were issued (fractional reserves). It can even be the case that he has only bought the right to participate in the price change per ounce.

In these cases, the demand is either not at all or only in part effectively placed in the market, so that the buying of such claims doesn't influence the gold price. In the gold community it has, therefore, often been discussed in recent years whether this 'paper gold' has been employed in a targeted manner in order to suppress the gold price. For one thing, it was asserted that demand had been deliberately diverted into paper gold; for another, that some constructions, contrary to their legal documentation, were backed by fewer ounces than promised, so as to keep physical demand (and with it the price) low. This topic doesn't play a role for the analysis of gold intervention here, in spite of its potential importance for investors, as the evidence for both theories is insufficient. It should also be mentioned that paper gold and fractionally reserved gold accounts have been around far longer than the systematic interventions. The fractional reserves problem is, however, still of importance in terms of its magnitude, especially in the institutional market in London.

The futures market is, nevertheless, a crucial key to understanding how gold market interventions function. As already demonstrated, the gold price falls especially often during the trading hours of the most important futures market, the COMEX in New York (today part of the CME Group). It often does so abruptly, whereby it falls without a trigger event in a very short time by noteworthy amounts. In order for these shocks to be of importance in terms of gold market intervention, it has to be possible, in principle, to influence the price of a physical good through the futures markets.

The classical futures market is a fixed contractual agreement regarding the delivery of a commodity in the future. Just as one can agree to the delivery of a car at a fixed price in a month's time with a car dealership, so the delivery of, for instance, 100 ounces of gold can be firmly agreed to in the futures market. The difference with buying a car is that it is easy and customary in the futures market to trade the contract itself. In this manner, one participates in the intermittent price movements without the commodity being physically moved.

It has become difficult to eradicate prejudice that speculators generally – and especially those trading in the futures market – are to be blamed when prices move in an unwelcome direction. When wheat, crude oil and other commodities climbed to all-time highs in 2008 and then again in 2011/12, financial investors in the futures markets (mainly pension funds) were held responsible by the media. In a similar vein, some shareholders blame the futures market for 'beating up prices' when stocks decline. Conversely, one rarely hears praise of the futures markets when agricultural prices fall or stock prices rise. Evidently, the common prejudice is emotionally ingrained. We therefore want to estimate to what extent the futures markets can actually influence the spot price of gold.

Actors in the financial markets are used to a close relationship between futures and spot markets. If one of these markets moves more forcefully than the other, the differences are removed by arbitrage. If, for instance, stock index futures rise more strongly than the spot market, then the arbitrageur buys stocks on credit, stores them and sells the futures contract short in order to deliver the shares into the futures contract when it matures. In this manner, futures and spot markets trade within a tightly limited range. It is different in the commodity markets, as – depending on the type of commodity – a number of preconditions for an unproblematic arbitrage may not be a given. Among these are, for instance, high storage costs, the perishableness of a commodity and its limited availability for borrowing (such as with crude oil that hasn't been produced yet). For these reasons it is possible for spot and futures prices in the commodity markets to develop quite differently. If wheat futures are bought, for instance, it is their price that increases, not that of spot wheat. The latter's price is still determined by the state of affairs in the physical market. At most, the futures market can affect the spot price (by tendency and in a transitory manner) due to psychological reasons (one uses the futures market as a guide) or due to the limited possibilities for arbitrage (which goes hand in hand with changes in warehouse stocks).

The fact that it is not the futures markets that drive spot prices has been shown by the commodity bull market up to 2008. At the time, there were also strong price increases in commodities for which no important futures market exists (rhodium, uranium and others). Striking examples are also provided by the closing of futures markets in the past (such as that for onions in 1958 in the USA), as prices often rose strongly thereafter as well. In the case of consumable commodities, it is ultimately supply and demand in the physical market, especially consumption and production, that determine the price, not speculators and financial investors on the futures markets. What is the situation with gold though?

While the influence of the futures markets on the markets for consumable commodities is usually grossly overestimated, it is often the other way around with gold. In reality, though, the precious metal differs from most other commodities in this respect as well. For one thing, the arbitrage between spot and futures markets works quite well, as gold doesn't perish, is easy to store and can usually be borrowed in sufficient amounts. Similar arbitrage possibilities exist to those in financial markets, which makes it possible to influence the price on the physical market directly via the futures market, even though only for a limited time period.

However, there are far more possibilities for influencing the market by other means. This is so because gold is primarily an investment metal. A multiple of annual consumption is stored in vaults and under mattresses for this purpose. However, investment decisions strongly depend on price developments. This is especially so in the case of gold, which doesn't pay any dividends or interest. Gold is ultimately only held as an investment because one expects its price to rise (whether generally or for insurance purposes – i.e., only for certain contingencies). This relationship is clear and also known in central banking circles.[47]

Gold thus becomes less interesting when its price or expectations regarding its price decline. The investor is disappointed. A potential gold investor can be dissuaded from investing in this manner. A holder of gold can, moreover, be induced to lower his stock. The mechanism of gold market interventions is specifically oriented towards this goal: investors are to be frustrated, interested parties are to be persuaded to find alternative investments more interesting. This is achieved by normal sales in the futures markets, whereby those prices that investors primarily focus on matter most (the PM fixing, closing prices). The effect is strengthened by deterring investors with the abruptness of the moves. This is accomplished by inducing sudden and extremely fast downward moves by massive sales on the futures market. If gold falls like a stone out of the blue, market participants are subjected to additional uncertainty. The speed of the losses increases one's pain; the surprising timing raises doubts about one's ability to forecast the market.

Such interventions in the futures market first push short-term-oriented investors out of the market, which strengthens the downtrend – and then medium–term-oriented ones. Later, it is possible to buy back the contracts that were sold in the course of the interventions at leisure and often at a profit. The magnitude of such profits from manipulation and the extent to which private parties to the interventions have financed them in the market, which has been slowly rising for many years, can hardly be estimated from outside. Figure 17.1 shows several such shock-like intraday moves.

Some of the examples show intraday movements below the psychologically important round level of 1,000. A rise above this level could attract more investor interest. As the price falls suddenly and massively, investors are persuaded to sell and interested parties abandon the market. The characteristic features of these moves are, therefore, that they take place during the trading hours of the futures exchange and that they are often abrupt – that is to say, prices often decline sharply within a few minutes. Furthermore, these moves often happen without any trigger such as news or moves in other markets. This unsettles investors even more, as they begin to subjectively regard their investment as more unpredictable than other investments.

The decisive point about futures market interventions in the gold market in general and the sudden sharp declines specifically is that they deter investors and interested parties from participating in the market. In contrast to other commodities, it is possible to achieve this goal in gold on a permanent basis. Since gold is not a

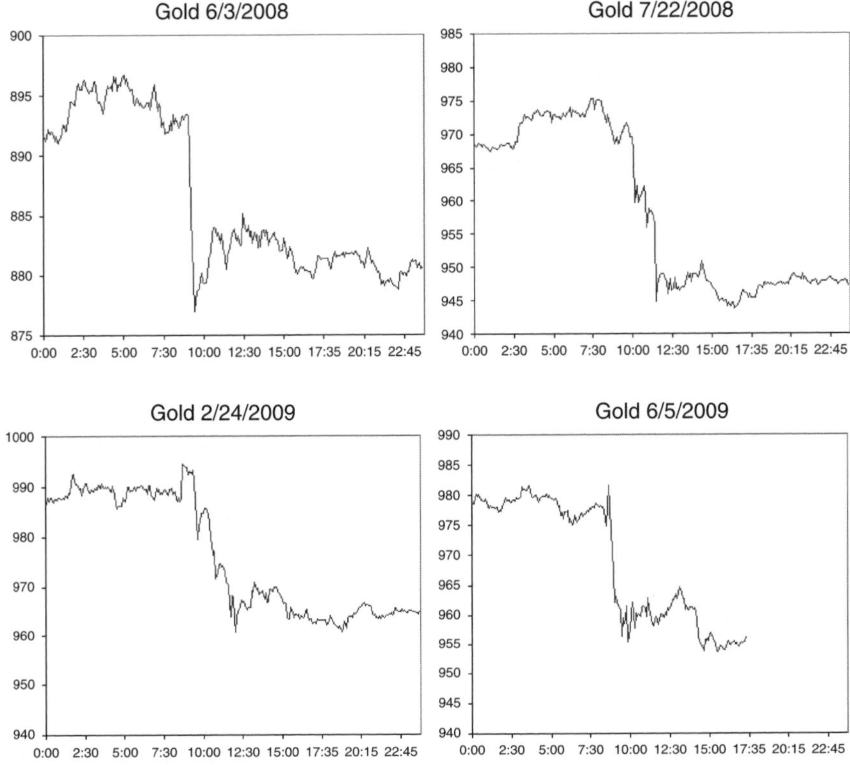

Figure 17.1 Intraday price movements

consumable commodity but serves as a store of value, it is possible for such an exertion of influence over investors to affect the price permanently, without having to place physical material in the market. The abrupt sales in the futures markets are a third important pillar of the gold market interventions, apart from sales and lending. They have an effect that is similar to that of the latter in the physical market.

Although these suspicious declines have been widely known for years and are discussed by market participants, the permanence of the effect is often underestimated, and this holds especially for its importance for the physical market. One requires less physical gold in order to influence the price. Conversely, this means that relatively little gold from lending can suffice to influence the price to the extent that has been observed. It is not necessary for half the gold held by central banks to have entered the market in order to be able to explain the developments in the gold market over recent years.

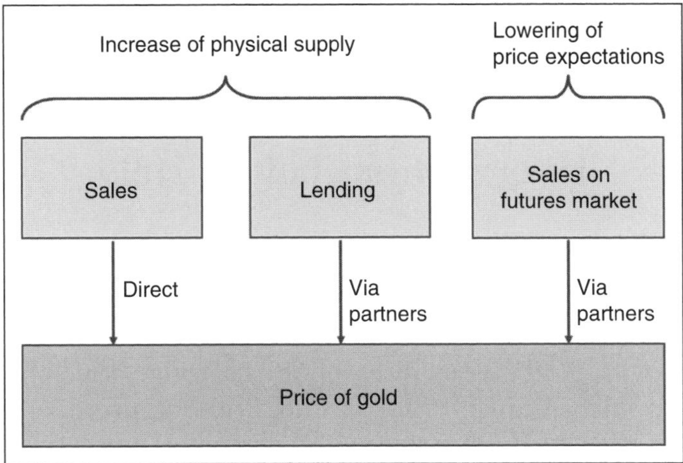

Figure 17.2 The three methods of gold price intervention

The effect of the marked intraday declines is the decisive key for an encompassing understanding of the systematic gold interventions since 5 August 1993. Because of them, less gold is required from the vaults of central banks to prevent the price from rising (or from rising fast). In the context of an investment asset like gold, there exists a mechanism to influence the spot price through the futures market that – in contrast to the situation in consumable commodities – can exert a permanent effect on the decisions of investors by influencing the investment decision process. Ultimately, it is expectations about prices that are being influenced. This can be carried out not only by the futures markets; there are also other means that can be considered (short-term activities in the spot market or media pitches, for instance).

Chapter 18

The Gold Pool and Other Gold Market Interventions before 1993

The systematic gold market interventions of today, which have been underway since August 1993, are not without precedent. There have been other gold price suppression activities in relatively recent history, which can be regarded as immediate antecedents, making the continuity of central bank policy in this area clear and highlighting their motives. What is also of importance is that the interventions took place quite openly at the time. That makes the fundamental principle obvious. But, first, a brief look at the antecedents.

After World War II, the Americans were able to establish a currency system (Bretton Woods) that resulted in the US dollar playing the main role as the world's reserve and trading currency. The USA had the largest gold reserves by far at its disposal and was the strongest economic power. The earlier precious metal standards were not reintroduced. However, the USA (and only the USA) promised to exchange its currency against gold at a fixed exchange rate on demand. For $35, one ounce of gold could be had. The dollar was supposed to be as good as gold in this way, the exchange rates between nations were largely fixed and any imbalances were supposed to be offset and minimised. The promise to deliver an ounce of gold for $35 applied solely to central banks, not private parties. Nevertheless, the gold price also often tracked this level in the free market, as the Bank of England bought and sold gold for many years at this level on retainer and on behalf of the Americans. As a result, the gold price was fixed, not unlike under a gold standard.

However, the vaults in America began to empty over the years. Although the US economy was still quite healthy in the 1960s, there was an external deficit. Americans were travelling a lot and the USA had large defence costs overseas, which later intensified with the Vietnam War. As a result, more and more gold flowed to the central banks of other countries. The Americans asked their partners to refrain from asking for gold from the US reserve system, by invoking their military costs abroad. They threatened to close bases. With socialism, an ideology was in power beyond the Iron Curtain that was striving for world domination. As they didn't want that, the West Germans (and other nations) ceased to ask for more gold from the Americans. Moreover, they were not interested (similar to the Chinese today) in seeing the reserve currency weaken considerably. As a result, they kept their reserves largely in the form of US dollars (in contrast, especially, to the French). In the early 1960s, there was already a gentlemen's agreement in place: a number of central banks refrained largely from the gold exchange and, instead, were satisfied with US treasuries.[48] In a letter of March 1967, the German central bank chief Blessing affirmed that Germany would continue not to convert dollars into gold.[49] The US administration internally already spoke about a dollar standard. It was stressed as an advantage of this solution that it would allow the USA 'to live with moderate deficits indefinitely', even though it wouldn't offer an 'unlimited printing press'.[50] At the time, the way was already paved for the excessive indebtedness that today, more than 40 years later, poses so many problems.

In parallel with these developments in the central banking system, the market has also demanded more and more gold since the late 1950s. In 1960, the pressure on the dollar became so pronounced that the Americans were forced to increasingly intervene in the gold market themselves. They wanted to better fix the price on a permanent basis. Altogether, eight countries united in 1961 and began to engage in coordinated purchases and sales in the market in order to fix the price. A part of their gold reserves was bundled in the 'gold pool', according to a key. Since there was a tendency for more gold to be demanded than was offered in the market, the gold price was effectively prevented from rising by means of sales.

Depletions were, therefore, egged on from two directions, in spite of other central banks holding partly still (e.g. from France and Spain) and from private parties. The system that contributed to stability and economic growth in the first few years after World War II began to careen out of balance. On the one hand, the money and credit supply as well as the real economy grew too fast, on the other, there were external imbalances. The hard way of debt deleveraging and reducing imbalances was eschewed. With the disposals of gold through the gold pool, the inevitable rise of the gold price could only be delayed, but not averted. In addition, tensions between the participating nations grew.

The system was based on the fact that gold flowed between the central banks. When central banks asked for less gold, that may have made political sense, but, from an economic standpoint, politicians defied the necessity of reducing imbalances. The French particularly disliked the stance of the Americans. They kept asking for gold, exited the gold pool and criticised the fact that the construction made it easier for the Americans to buy stakes in French industry. Moreover, they disliked – just as the British did earlier (and, as an aside, the Chinese do today) – the fact that a national and not an international currency played the main role in world trade and was the reserve currency. In addition, the French insured themselves against a possible decline of the dollar.

All these political skirmishes can, however, be completely disregarded compared to the market forces that stemmed from the underlying imbalances. More money and credit than goods were created, an imbalance that is difficult to correct (and which persists to this day). Moreover, there were imbalances in foreign trade. The Americans had to react. It was foreseeable that they would soon run out of gold. They faced a choice between tough cutbacks (and, as a result, a certain recession) or an upward revaluation of the gold price (as demanded by the market, which however, wouldn't have fixed the imbalances as such).

They decided to do something completely different: they cut all ties to gold. In August 1971, then US president Richard Nixon 'closed the gold window'. Even the economically most powerful nation was now merely left with a currency that depended on its will and abilities. Practically no nation had money that was tied to a commodity any more. For the first time in thousands of years of humanity's economic history, there were almost only paper money systems around the world. The consequences were felt immediately, and they were grave. The economy began to weaken, unemployment rose. The dollar, once backed by gold, lost increasingly in value against other currencies like the German mark. Prices rose worldwide. In the USA, the inflation rate threatened to reach high double-digit territory. Gold rose more than 20-fold. Near the end of the 1970s, after only a few years, confidence was almost completely destroyed. It appeared as though it would only be a question of time until the dollar was worthless and with it, arguably, other currencies as well.

That is the backdrop to the second large gold intervention of recent history, that of the 1970s. It marks a developmental stage between that of the gold pool of the 1960s and the interventions since August 1993 that are ongoing to this day. It is true that the gold pool was also used to sell gold in order to avert a price increase. However, this happened within the framework of a currency that was tied to gold. The gold price was pegged to the dollar at a fixed rate, directly in the international central banking system and indirectly relative to private parties. However, the interventions of the 1970s, which we now describe, took place against a backdrop that was, in principle, similar to that of today. Prices and currencies were not tied to the metal; paper money was exclusively used as money. The interventions of the 1970s were, therefore, very similar to those of today, with one main difference: they were conducted openly. The central banks sold gold in order to keep it from rising. Both the gold pool and the interventions of the 1970s were, by contrast to today, activities in which the public participated. They were published, there were discussions about them. There were debates and research studies. Although there were secret auxiliary agreements (for instance, in the context of the gold pool, an obligation to provide additional contributions), the facts were known in principle. They were not kept secret, unlike those since 1993. Not only are the latter not published, but measures are taken (such as keeping silent about the amount of gold on loan) to keep them secret. It is possibly that the parties responsible had the essential failure of these two previous interventions on their mind when they decided on this covert course, but the waste of the gold sales by the Netherlands shortly before that date may have contributed too.

What did the interventions of the 1970s look like? Abrupt sales in the futures markets probably didn't play a role then, as the futures market for gold had only just been introduced. There was also no increase of the physical supply by means of gold loans and the gold carry trade – the end of the tie between currency and gold was not yet established long enough for this type of business to develop to a noteworthy extent (i.e., using the now possible interest rate differential). The third method was more obvious at the time – gold interventions consisted primarily of one thing: sales. The central banks sold gold in order to limit the rise in its price. They wanted to reduce the loss of purchasing power of money in this manner, they wanted to build up confidence and they wanted to strengthen the dollar. Already, shortly after the tie between money and gold was cut for the first time, the gold price was influenced with the intention of achieving such indirect effects.

Gold had been demonetised; officially, it was now a mere commodity like any other and retained a special role at best due to historical concatenations and reasons. The central bankers nevertheless concerned themselves with this 'commodity'. They regularly sold gold in the late 1970s in order to keep its price from rising too much. After all, that would have signalled that the paper money system they administered wasn't going to work. Against this backdrop of high inflation rates and a weak dollar, an article in *Time* magazine in 1979 makes the deliberations at the time clear. The dollar was in free-fall, the Bundesbank was engaged in interventions, expending billions in order to support it. Then Fed chief Paul Volcker was tasked with stopping the panic. As *Time* magazine explains:

> Volcker... drafts plans for what could be the second massive dollar-rescue program the US has had to mount in eleven months. Among the steps under discussion: LARGER GOLD SALES. The 750,000 oz of Fort Knox bullion the US now sells monthly might be doubled, in hopes that this might help drive prices down.[51]

There were, thus, regular gold sales in order to suppress the price. The mooted plan was now to double the amounts disposed of in the ongoing sales.

Acceptance of the dollar was low: 'Central banks and private holders are reluctant to accept any more dollars, whose value declines almost daily.' The issue was the acceptance of paper money, and especially the US dollar, both among private parties and central banks. At the core was the question of competition. Gold stood against the state-issued fiat money; its weakening would strengthen paper money. That is why rising prices were to be prevented (we will find the same motivations in the current gold market interventions since 1993). However, lest the impression arise that there was unanimity among central bankers, one of Volcker's predecessors needs to be quoted. The former Fed chief of many years, William McChesney Martin, argued in the same article in favour of a contrary opinion regarding the sales, and did so vehemently. If he were still in charge, he said, the USA would sell gold only 'over his dead body'.[52] So there is no consensus, even within individual institutions.

Volcker spoke out much later, in memoirs published in 2004, weighing in personally regarding the gold sales and price suppression, saying they should have taken place in the early 1970s, as the dollar was already developing in an unfavourable manner at the time. So in the year 2004, Volcker makes the following remark with respect to the dollar weakness of 1973: 'Joint intervention in gold sales to prevent a steep rise in the price of gold, however, was not undertaken. That was a mistake.'[53] We can see here quite clearly that the central bank regarded preventing a rise in the gold price as a useful policy, with the goal of supporting the currency – the US dollar. It is, of course, an indirect means, as it is actually all about raising the dollar's value relative to other goods and other currencies. A weak gold price was supposed to achieve that. There is, thus, a continuity in gold price manipulation by central banks, which was continued after all ties to gold had been cut in 1971.

However, there were further developments later. For one thing, the central banks have cited other reasons for the sales they have conducted lately. It is no longer openly discussed that the sales were designed to limit a rise in the price of gold. Instead, gold's official demonetisation or the too high share of gold in overall reserves were put forward. With regard to the interventions of the 1970s, the motive that a rise in the gold price was to be prevented was at least occasionally mentioned. Moreover, the number of instruments employed has increased. Apart from sales, there are today, in addition, gold lending and sales on the futures market to influence prices. Cooperation with private entities in the form that exists today is new as well.

Market interventions now take place more or less continually – they are an almost daily accompaniment of gold price movements. This is why it makes sense to call the modern-day interventions since 5 August 1993 'systematic interventions'. That doesn't mean that there weren't any before. Rather, it is that, in today's interventions, sales, lending, futures market interventions and the cooperation between state-owned institutions and private banks are all coming together. Furthermore, complete secrecy is striven for. Between the simple sales of the 1970s and the modern multifaceted interventions there was a process. As already discussed, the gold-lending business came into being in the 80s. In addition, private institutions were deputised in the context of the support measures following the 1987 stock market crash. These are the two cornerstones of the transition from the simple sales of the 70s to today's complex interventionist practices involving gold lending and cooperation.

There was, therefore, a transition period between the 1970s and the beginning of the systematic interventions on 5 August 1993. At the end of the 70s, Fed chief Volcker stopped the rampant devaluation of money by putting in place radical monetary policy measures (such as interest rate hikes). The economy fell into recession. The 80s, however, were marked by low inflation rates, low interest rates and a fluctuating dollar exchange rate. Alas, indebtedness rose as well and a stock market boom began that ended in October 1987 with a market crash. That raised fears that a global economic crisis threatened and led to the already mentioned stock market support operations by private institutions on behalf of new Fed chief Alan Greenspan. The global economic crisis never showed up and, to simplify somewhat, everything continued with business as usual. As inflation declined from 1980, bond prices rose and real interest rates were positive, gold came under pressure from these factors. There were, therefore, fewer occasions for interventions, but a few still took place.

With regard to putative gold interventions in the period between 1980 and 1993, there exist no reports on the part of central banks. That doesn't mean that there haven't been any interventions, it only means that they weren't reported. In principle, one can gloss over interventions with silence, or one can make them public. That holds true for interventions in foreign exchange markets as well. Covert interventions promise more effectiveness, as one doesn't contribute to raising anyone's awareness regarding problematic situations. On the other hand, offensive announcements of interventions are supposed to discourage market participants from taking positions against the central banks. Moreover, there are also interventions that are in between these, which are enacted so blatantly that they are noticed by market participants, while certain doubts may perhaps remain.

There is no doubt, in principle, that covert interventions exist, as several have been made public by participants or central bank spokesmen in retrospect or became obvious through central bank reports. The best-known foreign exchange interventions of the years in question were the Plaza agreement, the Louvre accord, the Paris agreement (all concerning the US dollar) and alignment measures in advance of the European currency union. Foreign exchange interventions are better known and better documented[54] and are therefore useful (albeit with certain differences) as analogies for the gold market interventions. In addition, verbatim minutes of the Federal Open Market Committee (FOMC) meetings are published with a lag of five years, which provide valuable insights into the deliberations and procedures in terms of foreign exchange interventions; in the case of gold market interventions these shouldn't be very different. There were central bank sales of gold after 1980 and in several of them it seems likely that they were also motivated by a desire to influence the gold price negatively. Furthermore, there were gold price movements after the crash of 1987 that aroused the suspicion of market participants and were interpreted as interventions (the market turned precisely at the $500 level at the time and then began to fall). Finally, there are conspicuous balance sheet peculiarities that suggest activities in the gold market by the already mentioned ESF, which is tasked with interventions (more on this later).

A date deserving of a separate mention is 27 April 1987. According to one-minute price charts, the gold price lost more than $20 within four minutes at the COMEX, a shock-like decline, such as those that characterise the later systematic gold market interventions, and which wasn't repeated until their beginning on 5 August 1993. The free-fall took place at noon, when trading volume is lighter than otherwise, which would make interventions easier. What is interesting is also the backdrop. Two days after the abrupt decline in the gold price, on 29 April 1987, the Fed held a telephone conference that was recorded verbatim and has since been published.[55] According to the conference minutes, massive foreign exchange interventions were enacted. The dollar had declined massively against the yen, the trade deficit was large, the media were talking about a 'trade war', the US president commented on the topic of foreign exchange rates. The director of the operative foreign exchange desk of Fed and treasury, Cross, cites the then respectable amount of over $20 billion which central banks expended in April alone in order to support the dollar. Interestingly, the extremely abrupt decline in the gold price took place on exactly the same day that the dollar reached its low against the yen. What traders specifically noticed was that the currency followed the precious metals. The *New York Times*, for instance, wrote: 'Foreign currency traders said activities in the precious metals market were particularly significant. Typically, precious metals react to the dollar's movements, but a number of traders said the reverse was true yesterday afternoon.'[56] There are, therefore, strong indications that interventions in the foreign exchange markets at least on that day, when the foreign exchange interventions were finally successful and the dollar turned around, were accompanied by a parallel intervention in the gold market. It is neither possible to find direct proof for gold market intervention, nor to further buttress the supposition contextually. Unlike the beginning of the systematic interventions since 5 August 1993, therefore, it can not be ruled out completely, at present, that the decline was a mere technical reaction to the previous strong rally in the precious metals and not triggered by interventions.

It can, however, be reliably demonstrated that the connection between gold and the dollar, and about the implications of that, was still a feature of the thinking of the people in charge in the 1980s. For instance, Fed governor Wayne Angell asked a colleague rhetorically, in June 1988, what he intended to do if the dollar were to fall and gold were to rise.[57] Furthermore, a low gold price was probably especially welcome to the US administration under Ronald Reagan (president from 1981–89), in order to keep the gold-exporting Soviet Union from profiting from higher revenues. The period between 1980 and 1993 certainly wasn't an 'idle' one. The evolution towards the modern, systematic gold market interventions was a step-by-step process with many facets. In the course of a number of activities, such as sales and gold loans that were justified by different reasons, the intention to influence the gold price seems to have played a role as well. There were, however, probably also direct interventions with the sole aim to influence the gold price. But a systematic approach similar to that since 5 August 1993 is not yet discernible.

Before we move on to today's interventions, we want to take another look at the interventions of the 1970s. They have two further facets that enable a better understanding of interventions since 1993. In the middle of the 70s, the futures market for gold at the New York COMEX was introduced. In subsequent years, there was a lively debate over the extent to which the futures market could influence prices in the physical market. In principle the topic was the same as today, only in reverse: just as investors are now discouraged from investing by price shocks and unfavourable price developments, so the futures market, back then, dragged the physical market up with it. At the time, a great number of people made use of the leverage effect and bought gold at the COMEX. These price increases, then, induced many savers to buy bars and coins. A number of them were first motivated to engage in purchases by the price increases in the futures market. Since gold is an investment asset and not a consumable commodity, the actors in the futures market were able to influence the price in the physical market as well. In early 1980, after the price of gold had risen more than 20-fold, the CFTC (Commodity Futures Trading Commission) intervened and altered the rules in the futures market (in a highly questionable manner). That put a radical brake on the price increases of precious metals. The influence of the futures markets was subsequently debated further – perhaps not always in a sufficiently differentiated manner, but that is irrelevant for the assumption that the possibility that the futures market influences prices exists in principle. The effect in the precious metals markets at the time was still known – among experts, at least. In that sense, the situation in the futures market of the 70s and also the interventions of 1980 may have been a source of inspiration for the interventions since 1993.

The second facet of the interventions of the 1970s that could be meaningful for the interventions of today is more relevant to our notion of interventions. After all, gold is rising since the turn of the millennium. Therefore the question could arise today whether in the face of a gold price that has risen several-fold, interventions can even be said to have taken place. However, they did take place in the 1970s, when the gold price rose strongly as well. Intervention does not mean that prices don't move or only move in the direction desired by central banks. Intervention can also mean that prices rise less quickly than they would otherwise. Central banks are not omnipotent. The 1970s show that there can be prolonged interventions in the gold market that are designed to merely slow the price rise down.

Interventions show no uniform result. Prices can go sideways, they can (in order not to be too conspicuous) move sideways in a volatile manner and they can move in the desired direction (namely down, in the case of gold market interventions). They can however also merely lead to a slowdown of the price rise, even if it appears on the surface as though they were failing. Such a slowdown can even be their goal. This multitude of intervention results can be observed in the modern-day gold interventions since 1993 as well. They result in a gold price that is moving sideways (1994–95), one that declines (1997) and one where the price increase is slowed down (in the bull market since 2001). Instead of contemplating the entire time period, one therefore has to differentiate between these phases.

On the whole we now have a picture of the antecedents of today's gold market interventions. These have not occurred out of the blue, but have evolved organically from their predecessors. In addition, there are developments like the futures markets and the gold-lending business, which entered the scene in the 1970s and 80s. Now we also want to briefly look at the time immediately preceding the beginning of the modern-day interventions since 5 August 1993. At the end of 1992, there was the already mentioned EMS crisis. The

Bank of England was unable to defend the British pound. From the point of view of many central bankers and politicians, the fall of the British pound must have looked like a sign of powerlessness. Some of them didn't hold market imbalances responsible, but the fund manager George Soros, who had recognised these imbalances, took advantage of them.

As a result of the EMS crisis, gold actually started to move up. In the gold bull market in the first half of 1993, gold rose (supported by low real rates) 25 per cent within five months. Once again Soros made the papers, this time via reports that he had bought a stake in a gold mine. So much for the monetary policy-related climate of mid-1993. The EMS crisis, with the pound having been pegged prior to its outbreak, which was commonly known, was certainly no motivation for engaging in open interventions in the gold market. At that point, the private carry traders entered the game. Even though we don't know about the exact magnitude of their business and depend on estimates, we do know that they were effectively short in the market. They consequently lost money in the course of the gold rally and were interested in falling prices, just as the central banks were. A cooperation modelled on the pattern of 1987 must have suggested itself. The proximate trigger event for an intervention in the markets was, of course, a market move. On 30 July 1993 the gold price raced past the $400 level and closed at $407. It wasn't supposed to go above the $400 level. Central banks were afraid that there would, once again, be a self-feeding gold rally, similar to what happened in the 1970s. Over the following days, the gold price fell slightly (it may have been heading that way already, but there is no specific evidence for this).

Chapter 19

5 August 1993, 8.27 a.m. EST: The Beginning of Systematic Gold Market Interventions

On 5 August 1993, at 8.27 a.m. EST, something very special happened, something that the market didn't get to see very often, but which would subsequently happen over and over again, albeit in somewhat milder form. Gold fell like a stone, out of the blue, in an abrupt and, for investors, very painful move. Within seven minutes the gold price lost $13. Such a sudden and fast decline had last happened six years earlier, on the 27 April 1987, as already discussed (when there were also many hints that an intervention was taking place). Back then, a preceding rally of 14 per cent over a month was reversed. This time, the immediately preceding monthly rise was only 4 per cent. After such a moderate rally it appears unlikely that the sharp decline was merely a technical reaction.

It wasn't the upward momentum that was important this time: the important point was a specific level. Gold was pushed back below the $400 level: $400 was the level that triggered the first gold market intervention of the series of systematic interventions that persist to this day; $400 was, moreover, the point that would mark the intervention level for several years. Central banks probably chose this round number level for several reasons: for pragmatic reasons (one had to pick something), because the memory of the situation in the late 1970s was still fresh (the price of gold exploded, at the time, after it broke through $400), but also because they knew that market participants would pay more attention to a round number. If gold were to fail to take this level, it would become uninteresting to many.

Of course, the notable, sudden move down became an important topic of debate. It was inexplicable and, for market observers, atypical and unexpected. After all, they didn't know anything about an intervention. Markets often behave in an unexpected manner, but rarely to such an extent. We want to recall the sentiment and opinions by looking at press reports on the event. For instance, the next day the *Wall Street Journal* called the decline a 'blitz of selling', in order to make clear that the move was entirely unexpected and beyond all experience. 'A blitz of selling by gold investors turned into the biggest single day rout in precious metals markets since the Persian Gulf war of 1991.'[58] Market participants were quoted with phrases like 'brutal' and 'bloodbath'. They offered a variety of explanations for the sharp decline, ranging from the decision to let European currencies fluctuate in a wider band, to 'options related', 'commodity funds', 'Middle Eastern', 'Swiss' and 'Chinese' selling, to the inescapable George Soros, who, back then, often served as an excuse for inexplicable market moves. Another explanation was that 'the market just decided it'. The multitude of justifications suggests that these were guesses and is a hint that the reason for the decline was ultimately not known. The reasons also don't fit with the characteristics of the decline, which happened especially fast and on the futures market.

The German daily *Süddeutsche Zeitung* reported about the situation in the London spot market:

> When early in the afternoon at the open of COMEX in New York the price per ounce plunged 'within seconds' from $393 to $384, the traders at the Thames declared themselves 'speechless'. Such a drastic price correction hasn't been expected by anyone.[59]

The newspaper report reflects the surprise of market participants about the sudden decline of the gold price quite clearly. That gold would fall that heavily within minutes (it didn't happen within seconds) simply didn't conform to their experience in any way. In typical market trends, surprising moves always occur, but what could be behind such a sudden price decline? One could speculate about the reasons as the many voices quoted in the *Wall Street Journal* did; one can, however, also openly admit one's ignorance. Accordingly, the *Süddeutsche Zeitung* continued beneath the sub-heading 'Guessing Game': 'About the true triggers of this mini crash there were still guessing games going on yesterday.' Market participants had no explanation for the abrupt decline. It was very unusual, they simply didn't know what could have triggered such a completely atypical move. No one had given intervention a thought!

The effects of the intervention, however, were already manifesting themselves, as the first questions whether the bull market in gold was over were raised. Consequently *Süddeutsche Zeitung* titled its article 'First Doubts about Gold Bull Market'. The operation

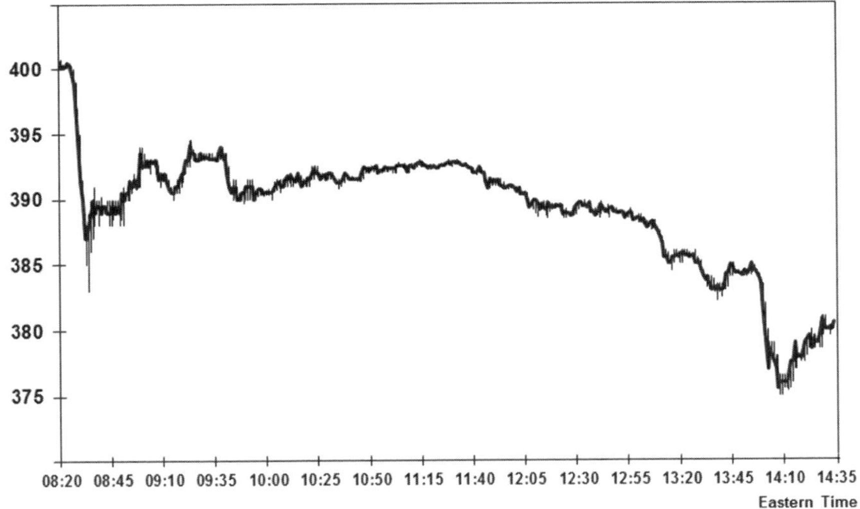

Figure 19.1 Gold December contract on 5 August 1993

had succeeded; market participants and observers were unsettled! An abrupt decline, the better part of which was over in a few minutes, was enough to sow doubts about a rally that had lasted for months! We want to take a look now at how prices moved during the day. Figure 19.1 shows the intraday movement of the most heavily traded gold futures contract at the New York COMEX.[60]

We can see that the gold price fell like a stone after the open of the trading session! Especially between 8.31 a.m. and 8.33 a.m., the price of the futures contract fell by $10 from $395 to $385. This must be the move the *Süddeutsche Zeitung* discussed (the futures contract traded about $3 above the spot price which the *Süddeutsche Zeitung* referred to). It is this type of triggerless, abrupt downward move that has become a feature of the gold market ever since and which market participants have since observed hundreds of times (examples were shown in the foreword and Chapter 17). This shock-like decline is designed to unsettle investors and interested parties to such a degree that they simply stay away from the market. It is a standard pattern of interventions in the gold market. Not every gold market intervention has this effect (there is also the 'braking manoeuvre' when prices rise), but most of the sharp declines are likely due to interventions. At the end of the 5 August 1993 session, we see the event yet again for a second time. The price of gold once again fell abruptly, even if not to the same extent as right after the open. That was supposed to hold, to put an end to the bull market.

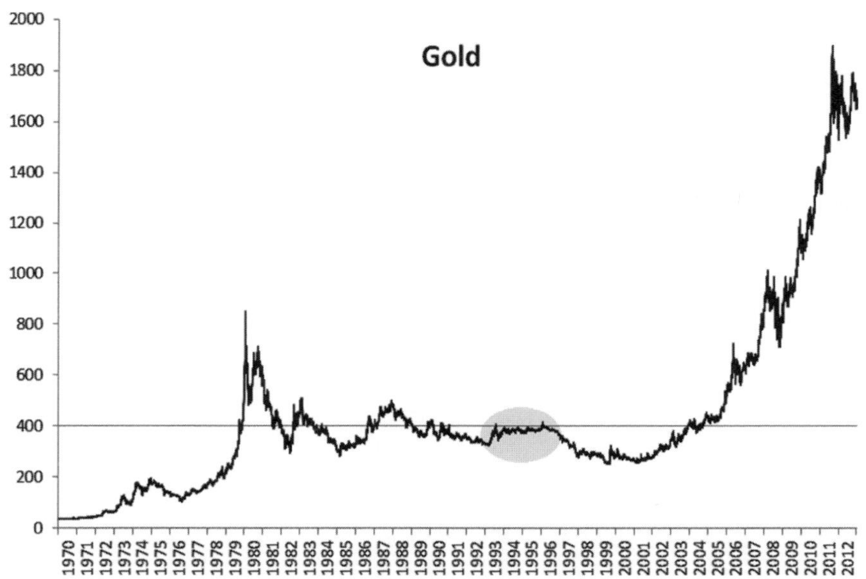

Figure 19.2 Gold price from 1970, in US dollars per troy ounce (31.1g)

It would, indeed, not merely be the start of brief correction. Rather, the interventions would keep the gold price from rising for many years. The round number 400 plays an important role in this. It marks the beginning of the gold market interventions. It was, however, also thereafter the barrier over which gold was not allowed to rise for several years. Figure 19.2 shows the gold price long term in dollars per ounce since 1970.

The initial intervention level of $400 is obvious in Figure 19.2. One can see quite clearly how the price was literally stuck just below this level from mid-1993 to late 1996. There is nothing comparable in the price chart. The price is almost moving in a straight line. This can also be shown by well-established volatility measures. For instance, the 251-day volatility declines in the mid-1990s to only about 6 per cent, while the 40-year average was calculated at 18 per cent. Although the interventions began with an especially sharp decline, the reduced volatility is explained by their goal to keep the gold price from rising above a certain level. By this sideways move in a tight channel, the $400 level is shown to be a long-term intervention level. The existence of such a level that has been used over many years is also obvious. The first time one executes interventions 'big time', an initial likely choice would be a direct manner that is geared to a fixed level. Dynamic and more complex interventions more probably follow later, as in other areas of activity.

Through these factors, the intervention level is a well established fact. First, the round number 400 results from the start of the intervention started in early August 1993. In addition the level was the barrier above which the gold price was not allowed to rise for many subsequent years, as determined by the conspicuous sideways movement on the long-term chart. The intervention barrier is uniform, at the beginning of the interventions as well as in the subsequent period. The level has thus been independently determined twice and thereby confirmed. Central banks had decided that gold shouldn't rise above $400 per ounce. But what are their motives? To find out, we look at the period concerned in detail.

Figure 19.3 shows the movement of the gold price between 1992 and 1996. One can clearly see the increase in the price of gold in the first half of 1993, which began at $330 and became the trigger for interventions against a further price rise. After the level of $400 was exceeded, the gold market interventions began on 5 August 1993 with a sharp decline, which drove drive the gold price back down to below $350. Thereafter, gold rose again to almost $400, after which it enters a sideways movement lasting several years, remaining largely below the $400 intervention level.

There is still no official confirmation of the gold market interventions and also no published minutes of the talks in which the interventions were decided upon. The interventions, however,

Figure 19.3 Gold 1992–96

didn't come out of the blue. Just as they had a prolonged antecedent with precursor activities like the gold pool, they have a more immediate prelude as well. The rise in the gold price must have been discussed before the interventions were decided upon; the rise was recognised as a problem. There was no cogent reason to conceal one's thoughts at that point. Looking at what was discussed at the last FOMC meeting prior to the interventions, we indeed find several of the main motives for the gold price suppression set forth there. Even the intention of preventing gold from rising is put into words.

Chapter 20

The Decisive Fed Meeting

Eight times a year the FOMC of the Federal Reserve Bank, which consists of 12 members, meets in order to discuss the situation and to decide on the height of its administered base interest rates. The members deliver brief expert presentations, questions are answered and debates take place. At the end a vote is held. Verbatim minutes of the meetings are recorded. After five years have passed, these minutes are made public. The systematic interventions in the gold market began on 5 August 1993. The last FOMC meeting prior to that date took place on 6 and 7 July 1993, about a month before.

We take a closer look at that meeting. The meeting was chaired by then Fed chairman Alan Greenspan. He calls upon Fed governor Wayne Angell to speak. Angell had made the topic of 'gold' his speciality. Figure 20.2 shows an excerpt of his statements, as recorded in the minutes.[61]

As Angell is called up, the main question that is in the air is whether base rates should be raised. The main function of such a tightening of monetary policy is to stabilise the purchasing power of money – that is, to counter rising prices. Their main disadvantage is that they endanger economic growth. Angell begins with his statements. He mentions high pessimism, economic growth, the lagged effect of monetary policy measures and inflation. One of his deliberations is that forecasts of future developments are difficult on account of limited knowledge about monetary magnitudes and that one should therefore include additional factors. Then he weighs the various factors that argue for a future increase in inflation rates, as well as others that argue for a future decline in inflation rates. On that occasion he reflects upon his own estimates made in the past, as well as those made by the FOMC as a whole, which were, in his opinion, not good enough. In short, it is all about how a central bank can prevent inflation and how it can recognise that inflation is threatening.

He then continues with a letter that was sent to him by a saver. Angell's remarks on the letter, according to the minutes, are as follows:

> I don't get letters too often, but here's a letter: 'My wife and I have been married 51 years. We worked very hard for every penny we earned and have been extremely frugal, saved for old age. I can't tell you how much I hate inflation for what it does to those savings. Our circumstances dictate that they be invested conservatively and all of the interest we've been getting from our investments is lower than the rate of inflation. It is taxed as income, which is not taxation but confiscation of capital.' Now, they go ahead and give me a little bit of praise regarding my position on inflation, but they finish it off and say 'Although I'm not optimistic that you will be successful, I can't thank you enough for your efforts.' Well, I guess that's about it! [Laughter].[62]

With his words, the saver has pointedly grasped the difficulties a central bank faces in fighting inflation. At the same time, Angell probably wants to remind his colleagues what their work is in his opinion ultimately about.

Angell now brings gold into the discussion and tells his colleagues:

> You know, there's a lot of loose talk around. Everybody has an opinion about gold prices. There's a lot of gold going into India and it flows into India because clearly people there want to hold gold rather than rupees, a paper currency that goes down in value. And clearly gold is going into Indonesia and into China as people there choose to hold a more reliable safeguard against these crazy paper currencies that have terrible inflation rates. But the price of gold isn't being affected by a little increase in the number of Chinese who are buying gold. The price of gold is pretty well determined by us.

Angell points out that gold is bought as an alternative to paper currencies, but opines that buyers in Asia are not the main reason for the rising price of gold. He makes clear to his colleagues that it is ultimately they, the decision-makers at the US central bank, who determine the price of gold (what he means precisely, he will explain later): 'For many things, like land prices, long-term interest rates can have a significant impact. But the major impact upon the price of gold is the opportunity cost of holding the US dollar.'

Angell points to a connection between long-term interest rates and the price of gold. The biggest influence on the gold price he sees, however, is the level of (short-term) interest rate proceeds yielded by dollar-denominated investments, which a gold holder must do without.

Angell explains his view: 'No other currency has a reserve base that causes someone to be able to say: "Well, I don't like holding my own currency." If you don't like holding your own currency, you always have the option of holding dollars instead.' When Angell spoke earlier about opportunity costs, the interest rate proceeds which one could have received alternatively, he made clear that gold and the dollar are alternative stores of value – that is, they compete with one another. Now he points out the special role of the dollar: the main competitor of other currencies is primarily the US dollar. Basically, he divides stores of value into three groups: gold, the US dollar and all other currencies.

> But we set the stage. We have a low interest rate that causes this saver out here to say he and his wife have been had. And I understand how they've been had. We're in a period in which we're going to increase some income taxes; but I'm not one who believes that people who are making more than $250,000 a year are going to cut back their consumption because their income tax rates go up. I think their saving rate is going to come down. We're in a period of being impacted by inflation expectations, and it shows up in the price of gold. We've had a 20 percent increase in the price of gold since last February's Humphrey–Hawkins meeting.

Now he brings inflation expectations into the discussion. They will still play a central role in his deliberations. In this context he points to the bull market; gold has risen by 20 per cent since the so-called Humphrey–Hawkins testimony in February (the testimony takes place twice a year in Congress). What ultimately bothers him about the gold price increase is that it indicates higher inflation expectations (something he will shortly point out).

Let us summarise his deliberations up to this point. There are three stores of value (Figure 20.1): gold, the US dollar and all other currencies. They compete with each other. The holders of weak currencies which exhibit high inflation rates can switch to gold or to the dollar. The price of gold is determined in this context by the yield that can be alternatively received by investing in US

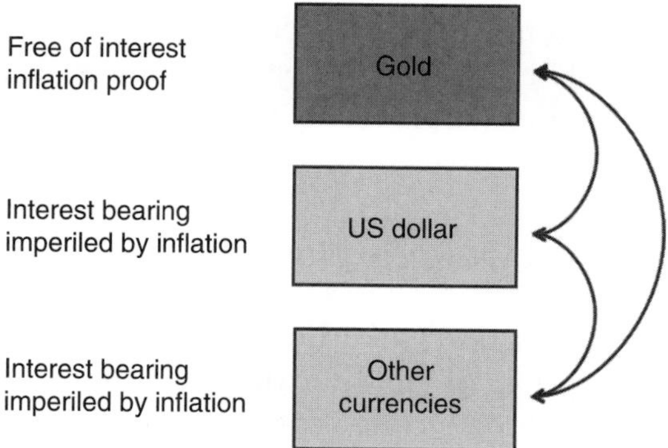

Figure 20.1 Three alternative stores of value

dollar-denominated assets. At the same time, a rising gold price also indicates that investors expect higher inflation. This was the case in early 1993, as evidenced by the rise in the gold price.

Angell continues: 'Now, [yearly] world production of gold only runs 2.3 percent of world stocks.... the value of the world's stock of gold is a measly $1.4 trillion.' The characteristic feature of gold is that its total stock is very large (relative to production). This, as we have found, is one of the preconditions for direct interventions. Angell doesn't talk about one though, and it probably hasn't crossed his mind. However, he names this precondition in direct conjunction with the wish that the gold price should not rise (which he will shortly articulate). Now it is up to him or any of the others present to connect the dots in order to get the idea about systematic interventions by means of sales and gold lending: 'Now, a lot of that is held by central banks. But we were at one time in a restraining mode, making it unprofitable for central banks to hold gold.' His statements do not aim at interventions, but go in a different direction. If the Fed were to raise its base rates (this is the decision that is specifically debated), then it would not be profitable for other central banks to hold gold, as they would get higher interest rates from their US dollar-denominated investments. He thinks politically here; the height of interest rates is supposed to influence other central banks, to tempt them to sell gold or refrain from buying gold. This would mean that other central banks would become part of the effort to weaken the gold price. Even though he doesn't go into more detail on this topic here, this would benefit US securities, as central banks keep up to two-thirds of their foreign exchange reserves in the main reserve currency, the US dollar. 'But I think this year those who have held gold have said they've got the best deal

Governor Angell:

You know, there's a lot of loose talk around. Everybody has an opinion about gold prices. There's a lot of gold going into India and it flows into India because clearly people there want to hold gold rather than rupees, a paper currency that goes down in value. And clearly gold is going into Indonesia and into China as people there choose to hold a more reliable safeguard against these crazy paper currencies that have terrible inflation rates. But the price of gold isn't being affected by a little increase in the number of Chinese who are buying gold. The price of gold is pretty well determined by us. For many things, like land prices, long-term interest rates can have a significant impact. But the major impact upon the price of gold is the opportunity cost of holding the U.S. dollar. No other currency has a reserve base that causes someone to be able to say: "Well, I don't like holding my own currency." If you don't like holding your own currency, you always have the option of holding dollars instead. But we set the stage. We have a low interest rate that causes this saver out here to say he and his wife have been had. And I understand how they've been had. We're in a period in which we're going to increase some income taxes; but I'm not one who believes that people who are making more than $250,000 a year are going to cut back their consumption because their income tax rates go up. I think their saving rate is going to come down. We're in a period of being impacted by inflation expectations, and it shows up in the price of gold. We've had a 20 percent increase in the price of gold since last February's Humphrey-Hawkins meeting. Now, [yearly] world production of gold only runs 2.3 percent of world stocks. I thought it rather dramatic--I had not thought about that with the price of gold at $390 an ounce--that the value of the world's stock of gold is a measly $1.4 trillion. Now, a lot of that is held by central banks. But we were at one time in a restraining mode, making it unprofitable for central banks to hold gold. But I think this year those who have held gold have said they've got the best deal going as the [value of the] world's gold stock has appreciated $234 billion since our February meeting. We can hold the price of gold very easily; all we have to do is to cause the opportunity cost in terms of interest rates and U.S.

Treasury bills to make it unprofitable to own gold. I don't know how much change in the fed funds rate and the Treasury bill rate it takes to do that, but I'd sure like to find out.

Figure 20.2 Excerpt from the minutes of the FOMC meeting of 6 and 7 July 1993

going as the [value of the] world's gold stock has appreciated $234 billion since our February meeting.' Gold holders, among them foreign central banks, have, up until this point, made an excellent investment with gold. When gold rises this much, it returns more than US dollar-denominated investments, which lose attractiveness. All of this bothers Angell, which he now gives voice to: 'We can hold the price of gold very easily.'

What a sentence! Here a US central banker, many years after the ties to gold have been cut and also years after the turbulent, inflation-prone and dollar weakness exhibiting 1970s, expresses his wish to keep the gold price from appreciating further. It is, after all, not the case, as is sometimes believed, that central banks are automatically interested in a rising gold price, given that they are gold holders and profit from a price rise as the value of their holdings increases. Angell had earlier enumerated the reasons for his opinion. It became clear also in his preceding statements that central banks do not necessarily hold identical interests. Angell continues as to how he imagines that the 'holding' of the gold price can be accomplished: 'All we have to do is to cause the opportunity cost in terms of interest rates and US Treasury bills to make it unprofitable to own gold.' As a means to avert the increase in the price of gold, he proposes to raise interest rates in order to make non-interest-bearing gold unattractive.

This method would, however, endanger the economic upswing. At this point in time he doesn't appear to think of direct interventions, only about hiking interest rates. As it turns out, he will lodge the only vote in favour of tighter monetary policy in order to fight inflation. Had he already thought about gold market interventions, he could have waited for a few months to see if they were effective. However, there is still nearly one month before the start of the direct interventions, and the idea about interventions is hanging in the air for those looking at his statements. In the tension between inflation and endangering the economy, leaving interest rates low and suppressing the price of gold must have seemed like the egg of Columbus, with which one fights inflation expectations without endangering the economic upswing.

Fear of inflation was what had motivated Angell to talk about gold. He pointed to a connection between long-term interest rates and the gold price (in the following meeting he underscored this further); above all, however, he saw a connection with the short-term interest rates that can be directly influenced by the Fed. Gold is in competition with the US dollar, the dollar is in competition with other currencies. A weak gold price makes it unprofitable for other central banks to hold gold. This is what caused Angell to express the wish to 'hold the gold price'. The proximate reason for this wish was the rise in the gold price in the first half of the year 1993. This, in turn, awakened fear of inflation in Angell. His thoughts revolved around the competition between alternative stores of value and inflation expectations. Based on his statements and with the help of further economic deliberations, we now want to work out the advantages of a weak gold price from the point of view of monetary policy. The aim of this is to comprehend the motives, not to discuss the drawbacks which a suppression of gold also exhibits (and which are probably greater, but only appear with a lag or at different junctures).

'Holding' the price of gold is designed to make it unprofitable to possess gold. If investors are not interested in suppressed gold, then they invest in other assets, including bonds, which lowers their yields, thus reducing the cost of debt service (especially that of the US government). However, bonds are not only supported by this competitive feature, but also by inflation expectations. When investors expect inflation to be low, they will accept lower yields. Inflation expectations, in turn, are directly connected to the price of gold, as a rising gold price is an inflation signal. Low inflation expectations lower the actual inflation rate, as no saver feels compelled to engage in premature spending in order to protect his savings from the devaluation of money. They also have a moderating influence on price and wage demands. A weak gold price, thus, fights inflation without the Fed having to raise short-term interest rates and risk a weakening of the economy. In the triptych of currencies (gold–dollar–other currencies), a weak gold price also supports the dollar. The inverse correlation between the dollar and gold is also well established empirically. A strong dollar has further consequences – among them the possibility of incurring debt in favourable conditions (since no currency devaluation has to be priced in).

There are, therefore, a sufficient number of motives that could have induced the monetary authority to engage in direct gold market intervention a month later. In the following enumeration of motives, including their functions, the stabilisation of markets in times of crisis is listed as well. While it does not feature in Angell's statements, it is nonetheless obvious. Also listed are the profits of private gold borrowers (carry traders) with their unhedged positions, as the interventions are financed that way. From the point of view of the central banks, this motive is primarily seen as a means to an end. What isn't listed are indirect effects, such as the easier financing of the US current account deficit and the associated US consumption, as there exists no evidence that such indirect effects were a decisive motive (in the late 1960s the balance of payments deficit was, however, in a comparable situation an explicitly mentioned motive, as we will still see). In principle one can assume that the decision-makers did not take all of the effects into account (Figure 20.3).

Angell wanted to 'hold gold' by raising interest rates. That is the established instrument of central bankers. He doesn't talk about direct interventions and doesn't have them in mind yet at that point in time. However, he already points in this direction. Gold

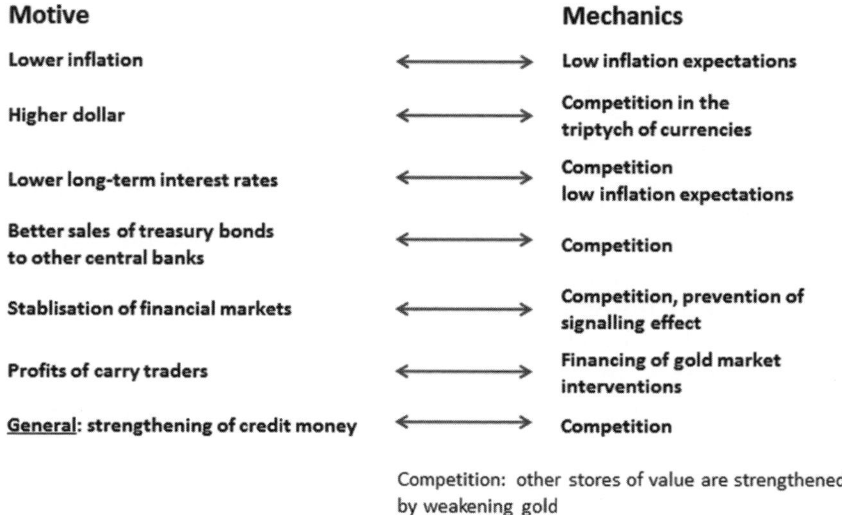

Figure 20.3 Monetary policy-related motives for interventions against a rising gold price

is stored in amounts that exceed annual production by multiples. Angell points out what the fundamental difference between gold and all other commodities is. Moreover, he mentions that a large part of the extant gold is stored in the vaults of central banks. These large gold inventories are the precondition for holding the gold price down with interventions over a long period of time. When Angell spoke about 'holding' the gold price in July 1993, he didn't mean direct interventions, but he did recognise and named their preconditions. Someone merely had to put the pieces of the puzzle together. It seemed obvious to suppress the gold price with the help of the large inventories by means of sales and especially by gold lending.

What we see here – in the statements by Wayne Angell in the minutes of the FOMC meeting of 6 and 7 July 1993 – are, of course, not the minutes of the gathering that would decide on the gold market interventions in subsequent weeks. We do, however, see a kind of prequel, which paints a picture of the first deliberations and building blocks. Important motives are explained and with the rally in the gold price in the first half of 1993 we also see the trigger event. In the next meeting the intervention level of $400 was mentioned (more on this below). Not yet mentioned were direct interventions (although the large gold inventories were one of their building blocks) and the harnessing of gold lending (which is only clearly proved by Greenspan letting it slip later). Alan Greenspan was one of those present at the Fed meeting and was probably also present when the interventions were decided upon (his function, his inadvertent blabbing and one statement, which we will quote below, suggest as much). Perhaps Angell was there as well (since it his field of expertise), perhaps yet other people (for instance, from the treasury, which administers the US gold reserves). However, FOMC meetings are not the place where systematic gold market interventions were organised. They, therefore, also don't give us any information on who organised the gold suppression and how. The circle that ultimately decided on them must have conferred in the subsequent weeks, between 6 July and 4 August 1993, and must have involved private gold borrowers – who must have had problems following the preceding gold price increase, and who possibly executed the interventions in the futures market. Central banks (the responsible financial institutions) of other countries must have been included as well. Angell made his statements on 6 July 1993; according to the minutes, there was a subsequent meeting at the UK embassy. His thoughts were perhaps developed further on that occasion; perhaps the relevant decisions were already set into motion there. Much (e.g., the modalities and size of the British sales) points to the important role of the British in the systematic gold market interventions.

Chapter 21

Greenspan Ponders Gold Market Interventions

We first want to take a look at the subsequent Fed meeting. On 6 and 7 July 1993, the meeting discussed in Chapter 20 took place; on 5 August 1993, the interventions began. Twelve days later, on 17 August 1993, the next FOMC meeting took place. Angell said: 'I recognize that the price of gold has come down from $400 to $371 and that really is a factor that parallels the move that took place in the bond market; and that has worked very, very well.'[63] That sounds like a success message. It hasn't merely worked well, not very well, but very, very well – which raises the question of what precisely it is that is supposed to have worked so well. Gold market interventions are the only thing that can be meant – after all, the method proposed by him at the previous meeting, namely to hike interest rates, had been rejected. He establishes the connection with the lowering of bond market yields that happened in parallel. In the preceding FOMC meeting Angell only mentioned this facet; here he shows that he thinks of the decline in yields, in other words rising bond prices, as an effect of the 'holding' of the gold price. It is also worth noting that Angell mentions the round number of $400 (despite the fact that gold had been above that price for several days), whereas he mentioned the $371 level precisely (even though it was a fluctuating market). The $400 level played a role several times (as evidenced by later minutes).

We want to take another look back, however, to a different Fed meeting prior to the beginning of the systematic interventions. This meeting took place on 18 May 1993, about two and a half months prior. In this meeting Angell emphasises the competition the commodity money gold represents for paper money:

> People can talk about gold's price being due to what the Chinese are buying; that's the silliest nonsense that ever was. The price of gold is largely determined by what people who do not have trust in fiat money system want to use for an escape out of any

> currency, and they want to gain security through owning gold. Now, if annual gold production and consumption amount to 2 percent of the world's stock, a change of 10 percent in the amount produced or consumed is not going to change the price very much. But attitudes about inflation will change it.[64]

Angell summarises all the items here that are influenced by a suppressed gold price (inflation, yields, dollar, etc.): ultimately it is all about credit money itself. The debtor-free and non-inflatable gold is the competitor of paper money.

In this meeting, however, Fed chief Alan Greenspan himself talks about gold market interventions. He already thinks about preventing a rise in the gold price with their help. He even talks about interventions explicitly! Furthermore, he mentions the special role and signalling effect of gold:

> I have one other issue I'd like to throw on the table. I hesitate to do it, but let me tell you some of the issues that are involved here. If we are dealing with psychology, then the thermometers one uses to measure it have an effect. I was raising the question on the side with Governor Mullins of what would happen if the Treasury sold a little gold in this market. There's an interesting question here because if the gold price broke in that context, the thermometer would not be just a measuring tool. It would basically affect the underlying psychology.[65]

Greenspan himself ponders gold market interventions only a few months before they actually began! *Note bene*, the topic is sales in order to influence prices (and not due to investment considerations). What is interesting is the line of argument: he sees gold as a thermometer, as a signalling device. That is precisely what the gold market interventions are about – to avert a signal, namely the signal that inflation might be on its way (or that the financial markets are in crisis). Greenspan wants to influence what the 'thermometer' shows. Otherwise, there is the threat that, 'should gold break out against this backdrop', it would influence psychology 'fundamentally'. Perhaps it is this is why the level of $400 concerns him.

In order to gain a better understanding of the background and methods, reports about foreign exchange interventions that were presented at the meeting are also interesting. The dollar had lost about 10 per cent against the yen since the beginning of the year.

In order to support their export sector, the Japanese had regularly intervened against a further rise in the yen, to little avail. On 27 April 1993, the Americans also began with interventions on the initiative of the treasury department. On this topic the report by the deputy director of the foreign exchange desk, Gretchen Greene, mentioned that:

> the Desk visibly bought dollars at progressively higher dollar rates. In total it purchased $200 million for the US monetary authorities, shared equally between the Federal Reserve and the Treasury, as well as for the Japanese authorities. Later, Secretary Bentsen in Congressional testimony and Under Secretary Summers in a press briefing confirmed that the United States is prepared to intervene in the foreign exchange market. Further, Summers said . . . The Administration believes that exchange rates should reflect fundamentals, and attempts to artificially influence or manipulate exchange rates are inappropriate.[66]

This passage is mainly of interest because it shows that interventions are simply not correctly presented to the public. There was an intervention, but only the willingness to intervene was presented. Moreover, there was a pretence of being against interventions. If one takes the administration at its own word, then it has just done something it deems inappropriate. It is, therefore, not surprising if the facts surrounding gold market interventions are concealed or presented falsely.

What makes this passage interesting is also the fact that these interventions in the foreign exchange markets were implemented in plain sight of market participants. They were supposed to notice them, so as to be induced to cover the positions they held in the opposite direction – that is, to be dissuaded from entering into such positions in the first place. This is also comparable to the current situation in the gold market, where the behaviour of investors is also supposed to be influenced and where market participants can also see, time and again, how a rising gold price is intervened against (even though some participants in the gold market appear to believe that there are no interventions). Greenspan expresses the effect with regard to the yen interventions as follows: 'One [approach] was to intervene moderately in the market but visibly. This clearly came as a surprise to the market; just watching the screens one could immediately see a variety of the shorts begin to cover.'[67] Furthermore, the *modus operandi* is revealed. The intervention was implemented between financial institutions, the treasury, the Fed and the Bank of Japan. For such a coordination (if a differently structured one), a lot of hints also exist in the context of gold market interventions.

Support of the dollar against the yen is, however, also an important backdrop for the gold market interventions, as one of their goals is to support the dollar. In the first half of 1993 the dollar lost markedly in value against the yen. A further decline could have been detrimental to the USA as well, especially with regard to the problem of the refinancing of debt, which the director of open market operations, William McDonough, discussed as follows:

> Let me just add a footnote. [In the period] before the intervention that Gretchen described and the Chairman commented on there's no question that the Japanese were not resisting rumors in the market reminding the United States that Japanese life insurance companies held a lot of rather long Treasuries and that if they dumped them, the price to the United States would be rather high.[68]

Support of the dollar could, therefore, contribute to preventing a sell-off in US treasury bonds, which could have become quite a problem. There were at the time definitely sales of foreign securities on the part of Japanese pension funds in order to limit losses on account of the devaluation of currencies, which weakened these currencies even further (that was not only relevant for the dollar). It is possible, however, that the Japanese were bluffing a little, in this case, in order to move the Americans to participate more actively in the interventions. In principle, the Americans have a strong self-interest in a dollar that doesn't fall too much, due to the financing of their debt and their deficit.

This brings the currency-related backdrop that pertained when the gold market interventions began into relief. It probably played a special role in their context as well. The yen was rising and the Japanese and Americans both wanted to prevent that. The situation reminds one strongly of the 1970s, when then Fed chief Paul Volcker wanted to pursue coordinated gold market interventions in order to prevent a rise of the yen. Now the yen was rising again, and once again there were deliberations within the Fed to suppress the price of gold. Then they actually did it.

It is interesting that much of what took years to be recognised externally as an effect of the gold market interventions can be proved by a quote from a central banker. The essential points were mentioned by central bankers: inflation, the dollar, or the intention to suppress the price – for almost every facet there exists a statement by a leading central banker. Of course, there are many details missing – who, when, how, where and in what amounts – but the overall picture is already reasonably clear.

Apart from the yen's strength, inflation was the second (and even more important) motive for the beginning of the systematic gold market interventions. We therefore want to look at the situation concerning this matter at the time more closely. Why did intervention begin against a rising gold price in order to fight inflation? Why were interest rates not raised, as usual? The reason is simply that the structure of data at the time suggested that the inflation was atypical, driven by inflation expectations. Inflation was too high, but the economy showed signs of weakness. The Fed feared a repetition of the 1970s scenario, of high inflation coupled with weak economic growth (stagflation). A few quotes may serve as representative examples for the deliberations in advance of the interventions.

From the minutes of the two Fed meetings before the beginning of the systematic gold market interventions, first Alan Greenspan: 'Well, this is a very crucial period for us.... I think we can rule out that the usual money and credit phenomenon is pushing inflation.'[69] Greenspan emphasises the difficult situation. He excludes credit and money as the causes for too high inflation rates. Fed governor William McTeer points to the problem: 'I don't understand this recent split in the economy with the real sector seeming to turn down and inflation seeming to pick up at the same time. It's a mystery to me.'[70] McTeer explains what the difficult situation consists of. The real economy is weak, but inflation is rising. Fed governor Lawrence Lindsay summarises the cause of the inflation: 'I think the reason that we've had the higher inflation was well argued by you, Mr Chairman. It is expectations-based.'[71] After other reasons are excluded, inflation expectations are fingered as the cause for the inflation. Fed governor David Mullins backs this up with numbers and comparisons:

> I suspect inflation is driven mostly by expectations... Since I think we have 4 percent inflation, I now see a couple of issues. The first is whether a 3 percent federal funds rate is appropriate in this environment... The last time we had a 3 percent federal funds rate was in 1963. This is not a 1963 inflation environment. When one looks around the world today, the only other 3 percent short rates observed in captivity are found in Japan.

> And their economic environment in terms of fundamentals is clearly as sluggish as ours, if not more so. But we are not in a Japanese inflation environment. Their inflation is on the order of 2 percentage points below ours... I would suggest that the result of the negative real short rates in the 1970s was not pleasant... As inflation concerns fester, I think long rates will move on up... There is no compelling evidence of any change in the outlook for growth... We have a very different inflation environment than the one we thought we were in.[72]

Inflation is at 4 per cent, the federal funds rate, however, is only at 3 per cent. It is far too low, both historically and by comparison to international rates. It is, moreover, below the inflation rate (negative real interest rate). When this happened in the 1970s, inflation rose, but the economy did not develop well. In 1993 the economy doesn't develop well either (and an interest rate hike would endanger the economy further). In addition, the height of the inflation rate was a surprise to the Fed. Furthermore, high inflation expectations weaken the bond market, investors demand higher yields. Fed governor Angell then once again brings gold into debate and speaks of its international importance:

> We clearly see in the price of gold that people are making bets out there... The cost to the world of the United States pursuing inflationary policies in the late 1960s and the 1970s is unbelievable. We're still paying the cost because many other central banks with no confidence in us think they have to be Rambo-like in beating their chests.[73]

People buy gold because they want to hedge themselves against the devaluation of money. He points to the inflationary policy of the USA in the 1970s that created worldwide damage. Other central banks still bear a grudge against the Americans because of that.

We now have clear picture of the inflation situation, which shortly thereafter led to the decision to engage in systematic gold market interventions. Inflation was extraordinarily high, but the usual explanations could be ruled out. According to the general view of the participants at the meeting, inflation was driven by inflation expectations. At the same time economic developments were disappointing. Base rates were oriented towards the weak economy, below the rate of inflation, and thus far too low to fight inflation. They were also too low historically and compared to rates internationally. A repeat of the inflation scenario of the 1970s threatened.

Rising rates should really have been necessary, but that could have brought on a recession. Only Wayne Angell, the last remaining Fed governor frequently lodging a dissenting vote, argued in favour of this hard line, in order to protect the value of money. The others voted in favour of keeping rates low. However, that meant the inflation problem still had to be dealt with. Since inflation was a result of inflation expectations, it was possible to fight the inflation by influencing inflation expectations. The 'thermometer' was gold; its higher price signalled the danger of a devaluation of money. That was how the idea to prevent a further rally came about.

The gold interventions were, thus, the key to solving this balancing act. How does one fight inflation without raising interest rates and endangering the economy that way? By suppressing the gold price and thereby signalling monetary stability to people. What wasn't considered in all this were the side effects of the therapy. Interest rates continued to be too low, which furthered credit growth and the formation of a bubble in the financial markets (which led to the highest ever recorded valuations in the US stock market in the late 1990s).

The political background must not be glossed over in this context. In 1993 the Democrat Bill Clinton had become the new president of the USA. He had promised to balance the government's budget, which had been strongly in deficit over many years under successive Republican administrations. Greenspan had personally argued in favour of lowering the budget deficit with the Clinton administration. Specifically, Clinton wanted to push through a programme to reduce the budget deficit by several hundred billion dollars. Such a reduction typically weighs on the economy. Governments, however, find it exceedingly difficult to keep their expenses in check. The programme was touch and go. Republicans were against it for opportunistic political reasons; Greenspan, although a Republican, was in favour of it for economic reasons.

A reduction of the budget deficit would not only have positive long-term effects with regard to the size of the debt. It would also have a positive effect on inflation expectations, which had been such a big topic with the Fed, as the government would incur less price-driving credit. Furthermore, long-term interest rates would fall if the government demanded less capital, which in turn would be good for economic growth and living standards. The danger was that the Democrats might change their minds. A rate hike that weakened the economy would likely have led to the plan's failure. A weak economy meant lower revenues, and higher expenses, such as for stimulus programmes. Greenspan didn't want to send the wrong signal at that juncture in the form of a rate hike. Finally, the programme, called the Omnibus Budget Reconciliation Act, was made into law on 5 August 1993 (what a coincidence!), by a very close vote of 218 to 216 votes in the House of Representatives and, on the next day, once again in a very close vote, in the Senate with 51 to 50 votes.

Chapter 22

Phases of Gold Price Suppression

We can divide the systematic gold market interventions of modern times into three clearly discernible phases: the limiting phase from mid-1993, the lowering phase from 1996 onward and the retreat phase from mid-2001 (Figure 22.1). There are hints of a new phase, of a forthcoming end to the systematic interventions. We now want to give an overview of the individual phases (specific details will be discussed still later).

Phase I began on 5 August 1993, at 8.27 a.m. EST, and lasted almost three years. During this phase, the gold price was supposed not to rise above $400. Monetary policy-related motives like the fight against rising inflation expectations were chiefly pursued. The level was a high-water mark and agreed upon between central banks. Private bullion banks played a decisive role, but the central banks devised the target. For the first phase there are still hints and motives that can be gleaned from the Fed minutes – later the topic was no longer discussed there (apparently, this was decided due to the publication of the minutes after five years). The level above which the gold price was not supposed to rise was fixed and a result of the monetary policy goal. Although the intention was noble, the activity deserves a critical appraisal. For one thing, it resulted in unintended side effects such as the expansion of credit excesses; for another, there exists no mandate for central banks or treasury departments to intervene in the gold market over many years and outside of any open political process.

Phase II began on 21 November 1996, at 10.01 a.m. EST. The goal simply to avert a price rise changed with this phase, which lasted until 2001. In this time, the gold price was pressured down to the level of $250 per ounce. In spite of a falling gold price trend, there was an upper level as well in this second phase, situated at $300 per ounce. Furthermore, there was an agreement to produce an annual closing price at $290 for the futures price at the COMEX. These levels, however, played a less important role than the $400 level in Phase I. Although the monetary policy-related effect of

Figure 22.1 The phases of gold price suppression

a gold market intervention is even stronger when the gold price falls than when it merely moves sideways, a sideways movement would have been sufficient to weaken inflation expectations and strengthen the dollar. Since inflation actually declined, one could have ended the interventions during the first phase. Instead, they were actually increased in the second phase. Why?

The reason is to be found in the teamwork between the central banks and private banks. For the bullion banks involved, the carry trade was a profitable business. They, therefore, wanted to increase it more and more. Furthermore, it was in their direct interest to see the price fall, as that increased their profits, since they owed gold. At some point they would have to persuade the central banks to engage in sales, as they could otherwise never close their positions – if they ever bothered about such remote deliberations.

The participating central banks continued with the cooperation once it was well established. Perhaps they were in a kind of prisoners' dilemma, as they had already entrusted so many tasks to the private banks. Perhaps they didn't really consider, in the beginning, what an expansion of the gold-lending business and such a low gold price would mean in the worst case. Perhaps some central bankers and politicians developed a certain hubris that they, finally, had a grip on money, credit and constant economic growth, with suppression of the gold price as a decisive building block. In any case, it was quiet on the 'front', the price of gold didn't intrude, the demonetisation of gold appeared to continue. Soon, so it appeared, gold would be a commodity like any other – and no longer a store of value that mercilessly revealed the weaknesses of credit money.

Profit was the main motive on the part of private parties in Phase II; the monetary policy motives of the central banks were a factor, but no longer the decisive one. This idea is supported by the fact that several central banks were pushed, apparently against their original intentions, to sell their gold – for example, the Swiss National Bank and the Bank of England. The means of applying pressure were in part highly questionable. Although it is known which politicians urged gold sales at the time, it is not known with certainty where the then prevailing pressure originated. It is actually difficult to imagine that the pressure came originally from central banks like the Fed. A combination of the profits of the gold carry trade in conjunction with the anti-gold spirit of the times, a few profiteers using the opportunity on the side and monetary policy hubris may explain a lot, perhaps all of it. In any case, this second phase still awaits full clarification. The pressure was too exceptional, the profits too illegitimate, the extent and duration of the gold interventions were too great, the decline in the gold price politically unnecessary and the magnitude of the gold-lending business too risky. The people of Europe, to whom the bulk of the gold that has been sold belonged, have lost a high double-digit amount in the billions in sales alone.

One of the main characteristics of the second phase were the diverging interests of bullion banks, central banks and politicians. The profit-oriented gold carry traders were interested in a low gold price. They engaged in massive lobbying and public relations efforts in order to push through more sales and gold loans by the central banks and with them a falling gold price. The central banks, meanwhile, were content with a gold price that didn't rise. In the course of Phase II, the central banks began to work against a falling gold price. Even Greenspan, who was one of the initiators of the gold market interventions, now spoke out in favour of gold. On the other hand, a number of politicians were siding with the carry traders, which led to the gold sales by the UK and Switzerland.

It is this backdrop that allows one to date the beginning of Phase II. There was no abrupt beginning, such as in Phase I, and probably also no explicit agreement. Rather there was a process, which led to the central banks selling and lending out ever more gold. This culminated in a decision: the Swiss National Bank sheltered one of the biggest gold treasures in the world in 1996. The Swiss Franc was, moreover, synonymous with sound money like no other currency. If the Swiss were to sell their gold, it would not only mean that a lot of gold was going to come to the market. It would also send a signal that gold had lost its importance as the ultimate store of value. Other central banks would find it easier to engage in sales or gold lending themselves if even the Swiss were prepared to let go of their gold. On 18 November 1996, a working group presented its results, at first only internally. It finally recommended mobilisation of the Swiss gold reserves. In a speech that received wide attention at the time, the result was made public. Fears rose gradually that the threatened sales and loans could 'flood' the world with gold. The reaction became obvious in the futures market on 21 November, as open interest, a measure of the number of outstanding bets on the price, rose markedly. Market observers made the connection with the publication of the results of the working group.[74] Well-informed circles were apparently aware that the gold price would now fall for an extended period. In advance of the expected sales and gold loans, they positioned themselves in the futures market. The beginning of the downward move that would last for many months became visible in the price charts at 10.01 a.m. EST.

Phase III began on 18 May 18 2001 at 12.31 p.m. EST. Even today (2013) interventions against gold are still in this third phase, the first stage of their termination. Gold sales and gold lending are being reversed; there is no longer any gold coming to the market from the central banks, as their sales merely approximately balance the lent out gold that has to be returned. Since this constant supply that was previously provided to the market is missing, the gold price rises for fundamental reasons. The pragmatic goal of this phase is merely to prevent too fast a rise of the gold price. The increase is tolerated because of the need to avoid loss of even more gold. The price increase, therefore, doesn't mean that no more interventions take place. It is, rather, a braking manoeuvre, in conjunction with an orderly retreat. Naturally, there are no longer any fixed upper limits and fixed price levels, as in the prior phases. However, Phase III apparently sports temporary limits (for instance, the gold price was not supposed to rise above the psychologically important round level of $1,000 during the financial market crisis of 2008 and above the $2,000 level during the euro crisis in 2011).

For carry traders the rally in the gold price generates losses on their remaining gold loan positions. This is balanced by the continual income from the interest rate differential. Moreover, interventions through the futures market continue and have even intensified. With these abrupt actions followed by short-term covering at short-term lower prices, profits of unknown magnitude result. What is worth noting is the gold lease rate in this phase. While it was at about 1 per cent on average in the two decades before, it fell, with the beginning of the bull market, to almost 0 per cent, where it remained for some years.

This raises the question as to why there are still central banks lending out gold at such an interest rate. The obvious explanation is that the central banks want to maximise the profits of the remaining gold carry traders, in order to minimise their losses due to the rally. Other reasons for the low lease rate (see Figure 22.2) are difficult to determine: for instance, the benefits in the form of interest income plus the saved storage costs could sufficient for them – this is rational, but hardly imaginable in view of the small amounts involved; they could be doing it as a mere favour to the bullion banks – but central bankers are not usually that corrupt. Practical reasons like a lack of storage capacity can also be ruled out, as other central banks like the New York Fed or the Bank of England provide vault space at low costs or for free, which is markedly safer than lending gold to private banks (storage costs at the most widely used central

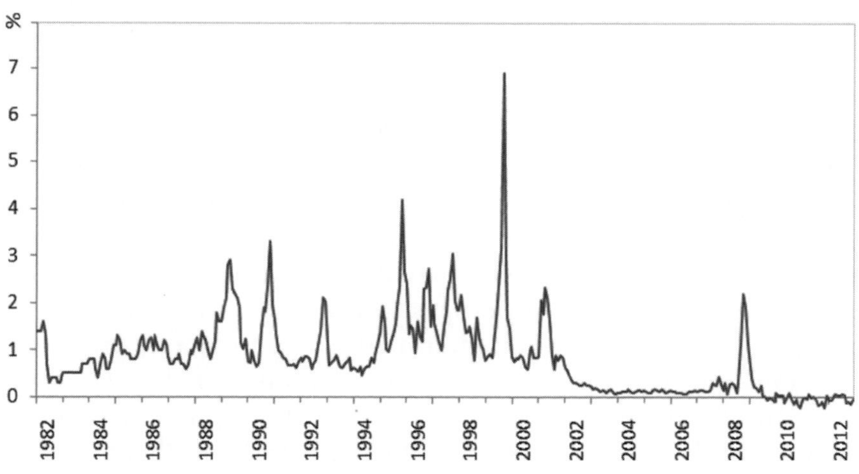

Figure 22.2 Gold lease rate, three months

bank vaults currently are between 0 and 0.03 per cent per year). Even the situation at the beginning, which the central banks got themselves into, namely that they wouldn't all get their gold back at once, doesn't explain the height of the lease rate, since they could, even then, ask for a higher interest rate (and would have had to on account of the higher risk).

Since the financial market crisis of 2008 the gold market interventions are possibly in a slow transition to a fourth phase, nearing the end of the systematic interventions. Characteristic features of the third phase are still in evidence, but there are also conspicuous differences. During the financial market crisis of 2008, the main aim was to quell panic and bring confidence back to the financial markets. Lowering inflation expectations played no role in this rather deflationary environment. The gold price was driven down considerably for the first time since the 1990s. Gold lending was once again increased. Moreover, more shock-like interventions than previously were employed.

Chapter 23

Shock and Awe

Shocks are an essential methodological feature of the gold market interventions. Not every intervention is abrupt – there are also many others, such as limiting advances in intraday trading. Nevertheless, surprising, fast price declines are among the features that characterise the interventionist practices in the gold market. The aim of this intervention method is to scare investors and interested parties off. They are supposed to refrain from entering the market. The method has been discussed several times already; now follows some supplemental information. The following example (Figure 23.1) is well suited to illustrate the effects of such shock-like movements.

We see in Figure 23.1 the movement in the gold price over three days with the sudden decline on 28 and 29 July 2009. Gold had worked higher over the preceding days to the level of $955 per ounce and it appeared to be only a question of time before it would swiftly rise to $1,000, the level that apparently had to be defended at all cost. Within little more than 24 hours, gold fell by $30, beginning with a sudden free-fall of prices, clearly discernible by the vertical line downward in the price chart.

This intervention is a good example of how an abrupt decline can influence investment decisions. The well-known and influential market newsletter writer Dennis Gartman had recommended buying gold in the days prior to the sharp decline. In view of the decline, he recommended to immediately sell again and felt compelled to issue the following statement in his market newsletter:

> we wonder very publically is it possible for us to have traded gold more poorly than we have in recent weeks and months ... There comes a time when we must say that we are out of synch with gold, and that time is now ... For now, we'll leave gold to others wiser than we.[75]

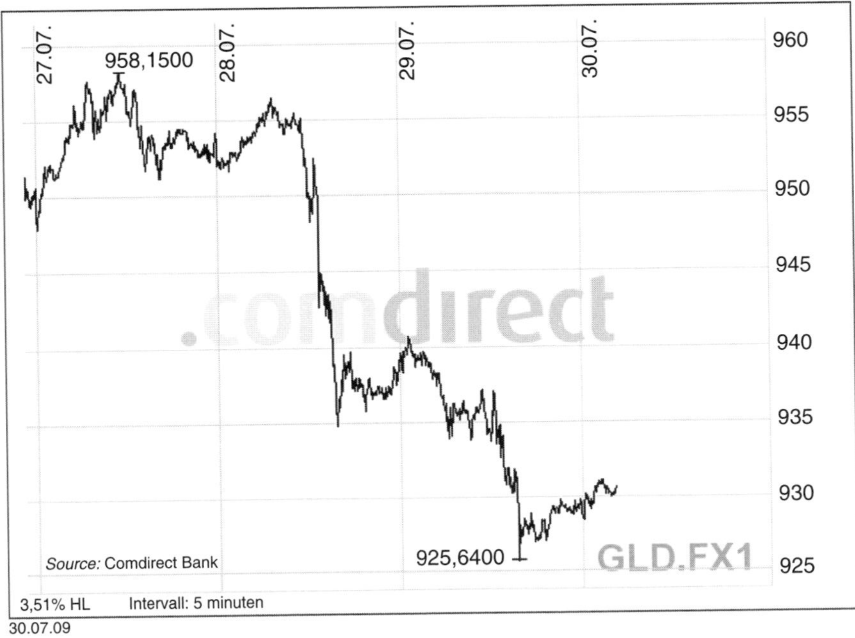

Figure 23.1 Gold over three days, 27–29 July 2009

Gartman, therefore, reacts precisely as intended by the interventionists: he capitulates. Of course, a professional like him won't turn away from the market entirely, but he is out of it for now and thereafter will likely be more cautious.

Other people let themselves get scared off completely. It is enough if, out of 100 investors on average, say 20, are scared off over time in such a manner that they stay out of the market. In that case there is now, indeed, less demand in the market and the price is influenced permanently. It is a particular characteristic of gold that futures market interventions can have a permanent effect. This is why they must be regarded as a true pillar of the interventions, apart from physical supply (by means of outright sales and loans). As a result of this strong effect, less gold has come to the market in physical form, as is typically assumed by supporters of the (in principle correct) gold intervention thesis.

The abrupt interventions against gold on 28 July 2009 began shortly before 9.30 a.m. EST, interestingly close in time to a statement issued by the chairman of the regulatory agency of the US futures markets (the Commodity Futures Trading Commission [CFTC]). In the course of the rally, which continued until 2008 in the commodity markets, it appeared that a heightened concentration of a few investors in the futures markets had formed via new financial constructions ('index investments'), which had not been accounted for by the rules heretofore. In the wake of the higher concentration on the buy side, the chairman of the regulatory body announced new rules in order to preempt conceivable maladjustments. That should, however, have been positive for the gold price (as in gold, there is a concentration on the sell side, which would have been forced to cover). Possibly, it was an additional motivation of the gold market intervention to avert an anticipative reaction in the market.

But the interventions at the end of July are even more interesting in other ways. Parallel to the decline in gold, the dollar rose. Apparently, there were also interventions in the foreign exchange markets in order to support the dollar. The backdrop to these interventions appears to have been the high amount of capital required that week. The record amount of $100 billion in US treasuries was to be auctioned. The amount was so large because of a need to finance the very big rescue packages and support measures resulting from the 2008 financial crisis.

A specific threat was that the auction might not go well, or that a higher yield would have to be offered. The auction was, indeed, a bit slow to start and, at the end of the week, considerably less than usual had been bought by foreign central banks (even though everything went smoothly in the end and the bond markets relaxed again). Reticence by central banks and other potential buyers was probably feared or had even been advised. A fall in the dollar at that time could have scared off interested parties even further, due to the threat of currency losses. That could, in principle, explain the interventions in the gold and foreign exchange markets that week.

We want to illuminate the concatenations of this event further. Figure 23.2 shows the euro against the dollar, overlaid with the gold price (the percentage terms are equivalent to each other). This time the period encompasses the entire week, as well as two days of the preceding week and parts of the following Monday – altogether eight days. We see clearly that both ran more or less in parallel over the first three and a half days, as the euro and gold often do (the price of gold behaves like that of a currency, not like that of a commodity). Then the already shown interventions begin, abruptly in gold's case, relative to the behaviour of the euro. This apparent freefall in the price of gold is not owed to the metal's higher weight, but

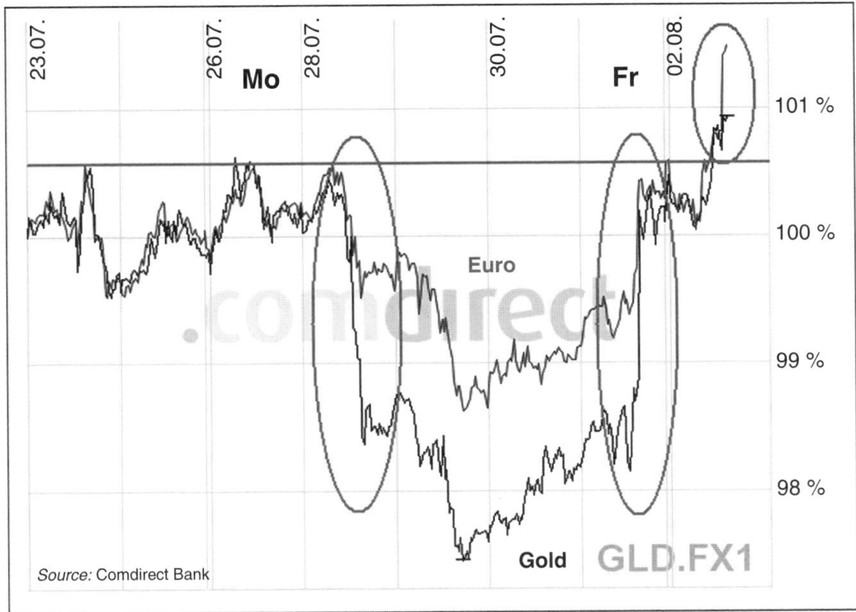

Figure 23.2 Gold and the euro from 23 July–2 August 2009, indexed

to the specific method of intervention in the precious metal (the foreign exchange market is too big for the central banks to intervene in the same manner as in the gold market). The comparison with the euro highlights the shock-like manner (marked by the big circle on the left-hand side).

The interventions were, however, only successful for a limited time period. By Friday afternoon, gold had shot up again in New York. The buying pressure was evidently too high. The deeper zone of intervention was abandoned. There is no other discernible reason for the sudden rise (important economic news for instance were already published hours earlier). After the auction was wrapped up, there was no longer any reason to make gold look especially unattractive in order to get better auction results. Thereafter, gold was intercepted at the higher intervention level of $955. The euro also rose commensurately, but less forcefully, as it had been put under less pressure previously. The euro and gold were back at the original intervention level after having been briefly walked down from there due to the auction. The adjustment process to the upside back to the previous intervention level was abrupt, but this time due to market forces (marked with right of the large circles of Figure 23.2).

We see that there can also be abrupt moves to the upside – in this case, apparently, as a result of the preceding intervention activity. Shock-like declines are, therefore, a strong indication of interventions. However, it cannot be concluded, conversely, that the existence of interventions means that there can be no fast moves to the upside. It is also not easily possible to analyse the abrupt moves numerically with the goal of a statistical intervention proof. Extent, type and duration of the shocks are individually quite different. Some shocks can last for many minutes and encompass a large decline, others take place much faster, whereby prices do not fall as far. In 2012, there were even declines in the precious metals sector that took place in the space of milliseconds. For instance, on 29 February 2012, at 10.47.21, the gold fund GLD fell by about 1 per cent in one third of a second.[76] The silver fund SLV suffered a lightning-fast decline on 20 March 2012 at 13.22.33, for a period of 25 milliseconds (a possibly record-breaking quote rate exceeding 75,000 prices per second was seen).[77] In gold itself there have been extremely fast price declines as well. On 27 June 2012, the gold price fell in late trading on the futures market within less than a second by $22.[78] To what extent a high-frequency decline is merely technology getting out of control or whether it is owed to new manipulation tricks is, in individual cases, difficult to decide from outside.

What must be considered, in addition, is that the downside shocks are only one intervention method of several, to which the braking of rising prices and the provision of physical gold through sales and lending belong as well. The market place is man-made and interventions are man-made too. There are, therefore, no static patterns, as would be the case in physical processes, but only anomalies that change over time and provide meaning only in a bigger-picture context. Figure 23.2 also shows several such braking activities, where the price was merely kept from surging further. For instance, on Friday, July 31, gold as well as the euro were intercepted at the upper intervention level after the lower level had been abandoned. That was around $957 per ounce, $1.43 per euro (marked by the line in Figure 23.2). This braking is also shown very nicely by the situation on the following Monday, when even the higher intervention level could not be held any more. After gold and the euro had broken out, gold could be intercepted again much earlier than the euro, which on account of the much larger size of the foreign exchange market rose immediately to above $1.44, where it was finally stopped. This discrepancy shows very nicely the (earlier) braking of a gold price rise (marked by the smaller circle on the right-hand side of Figure 23.2).

It is clear that the market wants to see the dollar lower here – not only versus other currencies such as the euro, but also against gold. The reasons range from the current account deficit, to the costs of the rescue and stimulus packages, to monetisation measures. The central banks pitted themselves against it. Central banks are not omnipotent, but they have decisive influence on the monetary, credit and real economy. They have this influence not only through determining the height of the base rate, which is held to be their classical instrument, but also through interventions in the foreign exchange and gold markets, through the handling of foreign exchange reserves (which in China, as a result of its incredible size, would have long ago deserved to be called by a different name), gold reserves, as well as by taking toxic securities on their own balance sheets (in order to avert a deflationary collapse) and through many other various measures. Here, they attempt to exercise their influence through interventions in the gold and foreign exchange markets.

We now want to examine the abrupt moves downward, a classical intervention pattern in gold, in terms of statistical frequencies. To this end, we first take a look at the shocks in table form, as they appeared per calendar year in the futures market. We choose quite extreme shocks, although not only those as strong as on 5 August 1993 (as that would produce too small a sample). We exemplarily select downside shocks of 2 per cent within 20 minutes. Figure 23.3 shows the number of days per calendar year with such downside shocks.[79]

We can, for instance, see that it didn't come to such strong intervention shocks from 1994 to 1998 (which was also the time when the gold market was sufficiently supplied by central banks with gold loans and sales). Primarily, we see that in 2008, in the course of the financial crisis, such interventions were engaged in fairly frequently. There were, altogether, 12 shocks of this type, 11 of which took place in the second half of the year that was marked by the financial crisis. Other reasons than interventions can be largely ruled out. The shock-like down moves have no correlation with weakness in the gold price that year, as gold rallied in the course of 2008, even if not by much. There were also years when the gold price fell and it didn't come to a single one of the shock-like, abrupt declines. These abrupt declines are not naturally appearing phenomena; they are the result of interventions (exceptions may confirm the rule).

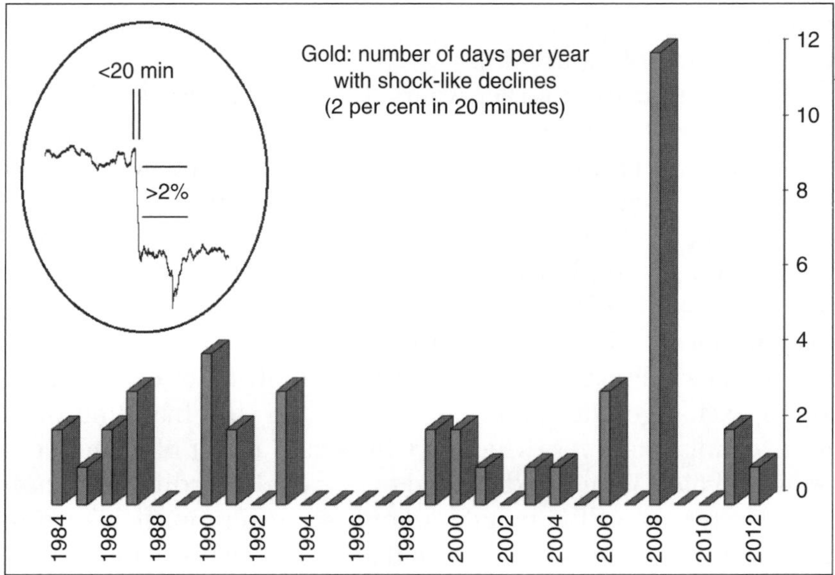

Figure 23.3 Gold: number of days per year with shock-like declines

The abrupt declines are also not a result of liquidity procurement, which existed in many other investment assets in the course of the financial crisis, even in gold (although rarely, as gold is a safe investment and functions as a safe haven currency). Such declines look different, not shock-like. In these cases, gold is simply steadily sold by market participants, because they require liquidity. Lastly, market participants don't coordinate their sales so that they all sell at once (to their own detriment!).

The first chart in Figure 23.4 shows one such steady sales process, which possibly came about due to the need to procure liquidity and which does not represent a shock. It is the intraday chart of 10 October 2008. On that day, the stock markets reached their first interim low in the course of the sell-off. It is, therefore, conceivable that this day was one of about half a dozen days when liquidity was more important than safety and liquidity procurement was, therefore, a reason for the decline in gold's price (but even this is to be seen in the context of the interventions, especially as gold was kept from rising only a day earlier).

One sees quite clearly a steady, accelerating price decline, of a perfectly normal type, as it can be observed in other markets as well. Nothing abrupt! For comparison purposes we also show the abrupt decline of 16 October, which was caused by intervention (second chart in Figure 23.4). As a complement, the last chart in Figure 23.4

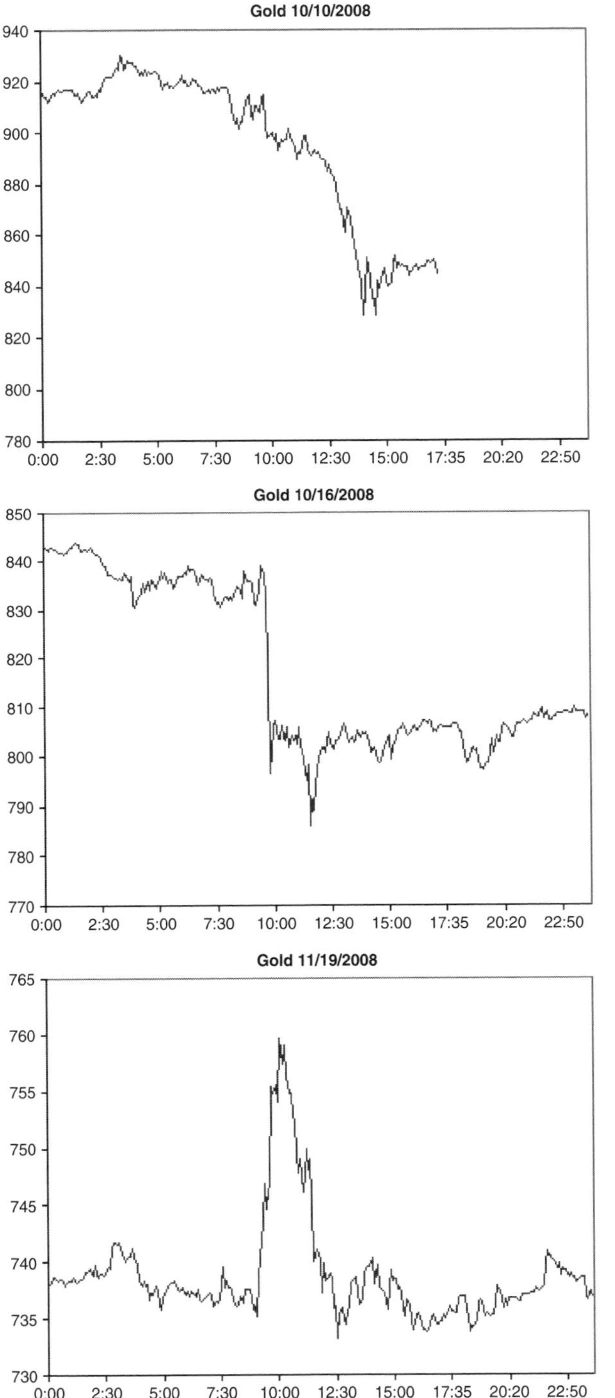

Figure 23.4 Intraday movements

shows the intraday movement on 19 November, which may make clear where gold really wanted to go in the course of the financial crisis. Apparently, there were temporary problems with the interventions on that day, and the gold price had to be roped in again after this strong increase.

The price shocks of 2008 are connected to interventions. Gold was not supposed to rise, so that it wouldn't signal a crisis that was about to get out of control. The intention was to contribute to a stabilisation of the markets. The standard behaviour, that gold as a safe store of value is in demand during times of crisis, was thus foiled.

Chapter 24

The Financial Market Crisis of 2008 and the Euro Crisis of 2011

Many people were surprised that gold didn't rise during the most severe stages of the financial market crisis of 2008, but actually fell between March 2008 and year end. After all, the complete collapse of the financial system loomed. The consequences would have been grave for the real economy as well. There was not only the threat that one would one day stand in front of an ATM which no longer released any money, but also that deposits in accounts would evaporate, that the payment system would no longer work and that, in the end, the finely spun latticework of our economy would have been rendered asunder.

As it happens, banking institutions are fundamentally different from other firms. If, for instance, one of ten car manufacturers were to go bankrupt, then the remaining nine would see their business increase. If, however, one of ten banks goes bankrupt, then the other nine are immediately in danger of insolvency as well, as they hold claims against each other. If some of those go into default, the threat of cascading defaults immediately looms. This can be averted by political means, via bailouts. This is exactly what was done in 2008. The aim is not to save allegedly systemically important banks or the bonus payments due to employees, but to guarantee the deposits and other payment promises an institution has made in order to avert defaults and follow-on defaults.

There are, however, drawbacks to this therapy – for example, an addition to government debt. Because they were ill-prepared and had such drawbacks in mind, politicians, both in the USA and internationally, hesitated (and then made a number of technical mistakes). In the case of investment bank Lehman Brothers, bankruptcy happened in mid-2008 and, by the end of September, the collapse of a number of banks and, with it, a chain reaction loomed large. For the first time in many decades, the imminent collapse of the global financial system threatened. The collapse

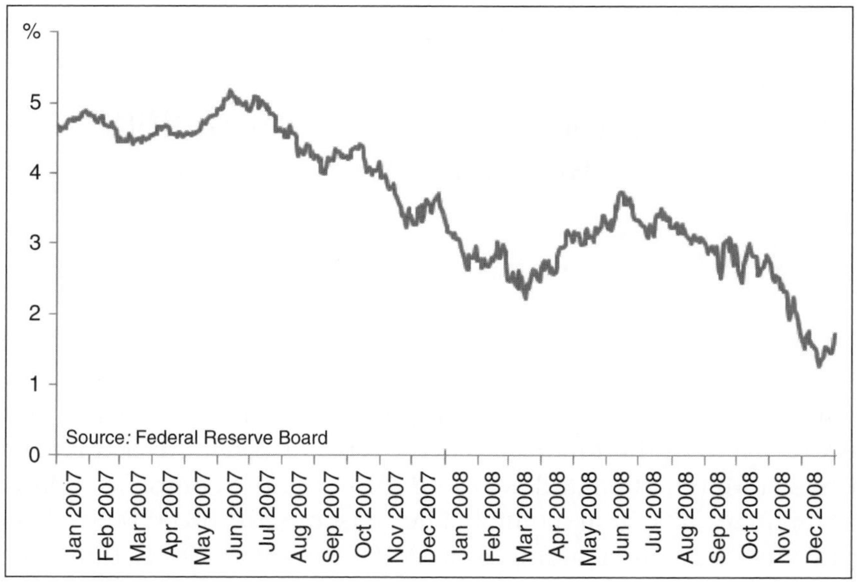

Figure 24.1 Five-Year Treasury Constant Maturity Rate

was now no longer merely the fear of a few crash prophets, but a concrete danger. A flight into safety at all cost ensued. Such a large number of government bonds (which were considered safe) was bought that their yields fell markedly (Figure 24.1). Safety was everything; return had become meaningless.

In the face of the threat of a collapse of the financial markets, gold was, of course, in demand as well, as it is absolutely safe from default. For weeks, gold coins could only be obtained under great difficulties and in small quantities worldwide. Private individuals paid large premiums in internet auctions. Coin dealers also offered above-average premiums in order to buy gold coins. Many dealers had to ration their sales, as their inventories were too small and they could barely keep up with demand. The US Mint said in a memo that it was temporarily suspending sales of American Buffalo 1 ounce gold bullion coins. 'Demand has exceeded supply', for the coin, it announced, and inventories 'have been depleted'.[80] The demand for coins was, however, only a part of the total demand. Demand for gold bars increased sharply as well. For instance, the German refiner Heraeus sold four times as many gold bars as normally.[81] One could have sold even more! Even though availability of gold bars was greater than that of coins, supply shortages developed. It was similar with funds that buy and hold physical gold for investors. Demand for them rose too. As a result, the gold holdings of the four largest ETFs in the world specialising in gold rose by 22 per cent in the crisis year of 2008.[82] Even at the peaks of the crisis, in the months of September and October, when stock markets fell precipitously and the US investment bank Lehman Brothers was forced into bankruptcy, their holdings rose by 13 per cent.

There can, therefore, be no doubt that a flight into gold ensued in the course of the financial crisis. Anything else would be rather astonishing, given that savers had to fear for their savings. It would be even more astonishing if the price didn't rise under the circumstances – but that is exactly what it didn't do. On the contrary, in the critical months of September and October, when physical demand was especially strong and shortages developed, the price of gold fell by 11 per cent! Contrary to what has been occasionally asserted, this was not due to additional supplies being offered as a result of the need to procure liquidity, as, in that event, there wouldn't have been such shortages on the physical market.

The reason why the gold price didn't rise was forceful interventions. In the course of these, sales were first executed in the 'paper market'. Only if the counterparty then insisted on delivery did it become necessary to actually provide the gold. Under such circumstances, only supply from central banks can explain the seeming mystery that gold was in a shortage in the physical market, while spot market prices fell (as ultimately the spot market is one involving immediate delivery). For the first time since 2001, additional gold was apparently provided to the market through gold lending, probably several hundred tons. Furthermore, massive sales of futures were executed, as the large number of abrupt price declines showed. The effort must have been enormous. By means of shocks and other price declines, buyers and interested parties were supposed to be scared off. The crisis barometer of gold was not allowed to emit a negative signal during the critical financial market crisis. Specifically, it was to be prevented from rising above the important round number of $1,000 per troy ounce (Figure 24.2).

The price of gold thus fell in the financial market crisis, just as it did on average in the smaller crises that have been examined statistically in Chapter 3. So what happened during the euro crisis? Before we examine this, we want to take a closer look at its evolution and causes. The euro crisis had already begun, in the wake of the financial market crisis, by late 2009. The measures to rescue the private sector in the course of the financial crisis had increased

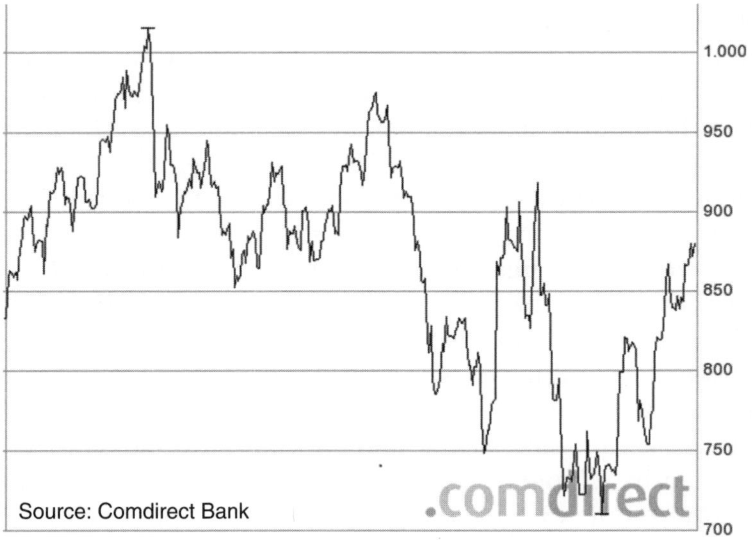

Figure 24.2 Gold in 2008

government indebtedness further all over the world. At that point, a number of nations experienced problems in refinancing themselves. Government bankruptcies and a global economic crisis threatened. However, why did this happen to countries like Greece and Spain, members of the euro area? After all, the public debt of Japan was far higher and the ongoing budget deficits of the USA and UK exceeded those of the euro area member nations. In Europe, theories made the rounds that asserted that there was a concerted move against the euro, similar to the 'attack' on the British pound in the course of the EMS crisis in 1992. However, we want to focus on the history of the euro and its structural weaknesses.

In the decades following World War II, the German Bundesbank established itself as a central bank that was more duty-bound than others to provide a stable currency and that didn't cave in to the demands of politicians, which was not only a thorn in the side of German politicians, but also foreign ones, especially the French. This meant that these politicians unable to order their central bank to run the printing press at will in order to boost the economy or finance the government's budget. Such an activity would have weakened their currency against the Deutschmark, which was seen as even less desirable. Thus, the German Bundesbank was able to impose limits on politicians in France. This limitation was not welcomed by the French elite, even though the Bundesbank's influence indirectly impacted the value of the French franc positively too. For these reasons, the German mark was to be absorbed into a European currency, which was conceptually akin to the mark, but would be administered by central bank committees with majorities from the nations pursuing a soft currency policy. Germany's reunification in 1990 was the catalyst that paved the way for the European currency union and with it the euro. For one thing, the French exerted pressure, indicating that they would stand in the way of reunification unless the euro was introduced.[83] However, this pressure would likely have had no effect if the Germans had refused to give in, as the Americans, the Russians and even the British agreed to reunification without this condition. What, then, was it that induced the Germans to relent? For one thing, the desire not to let any great disharmony with the French develop probably played a role. The general background and a later quote by then German chancellor Helmut Kohl on the introduction of the euro, however, suggest yet another motive: 'The path to unification of our continent has thus become irreversible.'[84] When Kohl pursued the unification of Germany, he apparently wanted to advance the unification of Europe as well. After the horrors of World War II, a unified Europe was supposed to make wars impossible. The idea of securing peace permanently by means of a currency union has actually had the opposite effect; by exacerbating economic differences between the member nations, it has aggravated political ones as well. It should also be mentioned here that a number of European politicians believe that the euro is more competitive with the US dollar than the individual national currencies.

The euro is more of a political than an economic project – however, whenever politicians elevate themselves above economic laws, the results are rarely good. Economically, the currency union was a linking-up of soft and hard currencies. In terms of economic effects, it is immaterial whether such a link is established by merely pegging exchange rates or introducing a unified currency. Accordingly, the consequences of the currency union were similar to those of other currency pegs, such as the pegging of Asian currencies to the US dollar prior to the Asian crisis. In the regions that were previously home to soft currencies, credit-induced bubbles ensued. Cheap credit was suddenly available in these countries, which could be used to purchase goods from abroad. As a result, enormous bubbles formed in the private sector (such as in the Spanish real estate market) or the public sector expanded out of all proportion (such as in Greece). These represented malinvestments on a grand scale, which are, for all intents and purposes, lost (as buildings were erected or additional civil servants were hired instead of building factories or creating business enterprises). Concurrent with these malinvestments that were not accompanied by rising productivity, a large increase in indebtedness occurred. In the process, the indebtedness of the private sector threatened to engulf governments as well, as they took these debts over in order to avert an economic crisis.

As if the tragedy were not already big enough, the common currency stood in the way of a rapid solution to the problematic situation: devaluation. Currency devaluation leads to more competitive wage levels, reduces the size of the public sector as well as that of savings relative to those of other countries and leads to a stop in unproductive borrowings and additional capital malinvestment. Devaluation was impossible and, for an exit from the currency union (which would have corresponded to it), there were neither mechanisms in place, nor was it politically desired. The mistrust of investors regarding the ability of the governments concerned to pay their debts couldn't express itself as pressure on the currency. However, it led to pressure on the bonds issued by these governments. Making things worse was the fact that there existed no preparations whatsoever as to how to deal with such a situation. As a result, the former soft currency countries of the euro area were the first nations that were actually threatened by national bankruptcy in the wake of the financial crisis.

This was further aggravated by the fact that monetary policy measures designed to avert bankruptcy and stimulate the economy are more problematic on account of the currency union. Such measures have to be viewed quite critically (as they threaten to subvert the currency), but in the USA the bond purchases by the central bank helped with keeping government bond yields at a low level. In a currency system comprised of independent nation states the situation is considerably more complicated. For a country like Greece, the euro is, from an economic point of view, largely equivalent to a foreign currency. For as long as Greece had its own currency, it was automatically punished by high inflation and currency devaluation if it pursued too loose a monetary policy. This intrinsic mechanism was abolished with the currency union. Whenever Greece now incurs more debt or 'prints money', the negative effects like inflation mainly affect other countries! The currency union has, thus, done away with every natural incentive to live within one's means or implement a responsible fiscal policy, especially in the smaller nations. In principle, it created incentives for nations to finance themselves at the expense of other nations. As a result, it was necessary to create a suitable body of regulations to counter the lack of this natural mechanism. However, these regulations were deficient or were simply ignored when crisis struck. Among these was the 'no bailout clause', which was supposed to prevent the financing of one state by the others. If not for giving support to individual states, a chain reaction threatened, with one state after another going bankrupt. Help for individual states, however, meant that the ban on financing oneself at the expense of others had to be suspended. New regulations had to be created to achieve both objectives – the 'rescue' of nations, as well as the prevention of future excesses. In principle, European politicians focused most of their efforts during the euro crisis on trying to resolve the problem of the artificial contradiction the currency union had created, between prevention of national bankruptcies and the misguided incentive to, once again, finance oneself at the expense of others in the future (a permanently sustainable solution failed to emerge). Interestingly, though, the situation led overall to European nations reducing their budget deficits markedly, contrary to what occurred in the USA. However, European politicians didn't do this out of judiciousness, but because the markets forced them to, by refusing to keep financing highly indebted governments (market participants, ultimately the conservative savers that invest in government bonds, were disparaged as speculators for this by politicians).[85]

The euro crisis was deflationary in nature, just as the preceding financial market crisis had been. This time, even the bankruptcy of states, the previous 'rescuers' of banks in the financial market crisis, loomed. A chain reaction threatened that had the potential to spread to other nations and the entire financial system. Investors, therefore, once again feared for their savings and once again a lot of gold was bought. There were also differences to the financial market crisis. The euro crisis did not develop abruptly, with a surprising bankruptcy, but dragged on over many months. Moreover, there was a political consensus during the euro crisis based on the experience with the financial market crisis, to avoid any major risks for the global economy. As a result, the euro crisis lasted longer, but was less severe (in terms of its effect on global economic output and share prices). Accordingly, the movements in the gold price developed differently as well. As signalled by the average intraday

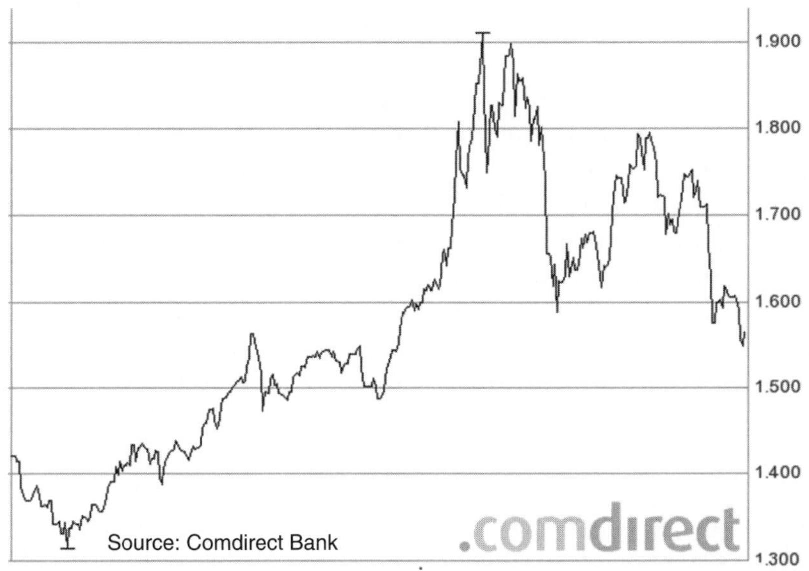

Figure 24.3 Gold in 2011

movements (see Appendix 1), there were manipulative interventions in the price movement between 2009 and 2011. However, they failed to suppress the gold price on a sustained basis, which managed to rise steadily during those years. Apparently, the interventions were, over long stretches, less intensive than the very heavy ones seen during the financial market crisis. The peak of the euro crisis in August and September 2011 also represented a peculiar anomaly. Figure 24.3 shows the price of gold in 2011 and makes the situation clear.

The crisis intensified markedly in August and September, which led to an accelerated rise in the gold price (and a strong stock market decline). In the process, it attempted to break out twice, targeting the $2,000 level. On both occasions it was abruptly stopped, which went hand in hand with price declines of 6.5 per cent and 8.5 per cent in the span of less than two days. The second decline, on 6 September, was characterised by a price shock in thin trading at 4 a.m. EST. In the middle of the euro crisis, the accelerating gold price abruptly turned around! Apparently, it was supposed to remain reliably below the $2,000 per ounce level, where it might have taken on a momentum of its own. That, in turn, could have been interpreted by market observers as a sign that it was barely possible to keep the euro crisis under control. The movement in the gold price in the second half of September is also notable. While the gold price rose strongly over several days in early August, in the course of the intensification of the crisis, it fell over several days, just as the crisis once again raged and threatened to spin out of control. There seemed to be a comprehensive effort underway to get a grip on the situation. On the whole, while there were interventions in the euro crisis just as in the financial market crisis, their effect on the gold price was less pronounced.

Chapter 25

Strong Dollar and Weak Mining Stocks

We now want to turn to two markets that are connected with the gold market interventions. In the context of the gold market interventions in the financial crisis year 2008 and the during the euro crisis in 2011, the main motive was clearly the combating of crises. At other times, however, it was the fight against inflation or support of the dollar. Support of the dollar deserves further examination. Since the mid-1990s, US politicians – deputy secretaries of the treasury, treasury secretaries and even presidents – have stressed time and again that they were pursuing a 'strong-dollar policy'. As they have never explained what the 'strong-dollar policy' actually consists of, it was suspected that this could only be the suppression of the gold price (for instance, on the part of GATA, which was founded to oppose gold market interventions). We want to examine whether there is any truth to the thesis that the 'strong-dollar policy' consists of gold market interventions in order to support the dollar indirectly.

What is it all about? In order to finance its current account and budget deficits, the USA needs inflows of money from abroad. If the dollar were weak, the willingness of foreign central banks to invest in treasury bonds would be diminished. With these inflows, the Americans can finance the current account and budget deficits at more favourable conditions than would be possible otherwise. In addition to that, today's entire monetary system is built upon the dollar as the main reserve currency, and a weak dollar is thus symptomatic of an overall loss of confidence. Alternatively, the USA could favour a weak dollar, in order to strengthen its own export industry, but the substance of the 'strong-dollar policy' is already clear, namely a declaration of intent not to pursue this path. US policy towards the outside world is strictly defined and makes investments more predictable, as a policy of devaluation doesn't have to be feared. But that is not all.

The beginning of the 'strong-dollar policy' is often dated to 1995, as then secretary of the treasury Robert Rubin began to propagate a strong dollar almost on a monthly basis. However, the first general statement by a politician of the time that a strong dollar was in the interest of the USA is found at an earlier date. It was issued by then deputy secretary of the treasury, Larry Summers, in August of 1993,[86] the same month in which the systematic gold price interventions began. Whether it was a coincidence or not, there is, of course, a connection. After all, support of the dollar was one of the motives for the gold market interventions. Moreover, Summers publicly announced (as already mentioned) the willingness of the USA to intervene in the foreign exchange market a few months earlier already, in April (which did occur, as evidenced by the Fed minutes and their appendixes). The gold interventions thus began in a similar environment of unwanted dollar weakness, just as the first formulations of a 'strong-dollar policy', and one of their motives was to support the dollar. In parallel, interventions in the foreign exchange markets were undertaken and 'talking the dollar up' commenced. The actors were, by and large, the same; Summers, for instance, was professionally entrusted with interventions and making public statements. Gold market interventions are therefore part of what 'strong-dollar policy' means, possibly they are the most important part.

Lastly, the 'strong-dollar policy' also consists of a mere 'talking up' of the dollar. In Fed meetings it was discussed in detail what words would have what effects, including how they would affect foreign exchange rates. It probably wasn't any different at the treasury. Ultimately, the mantra-like repetition of the 'strong-dollar policy' is what was mainly perceived by the public. It may also have had some effect. On the whole, the policy consisted of a declaration of intent not to want competitive devaluations, of the 'talking up' of the dollar in order to influence markets, as well as interventions in the foreign exchange markets and the gold market. It was not only a label, it was not only a bluff, but it also had specific, more or less important components. The 'strong-dollar policy' is also connected to the gold market interventions; gold market interventions, however, are only one item among several and have a variety of goals.

A market sector that is directly tied to the gold price is that of gold-mining stocks. Statistical proof of systematic interventions in gold-mining stocks does not exist to date. Market participants frequently report, however, that gold-mining stocks sometimes exhibit a lead relative to the gold price. Figure 25.1 shows the movement

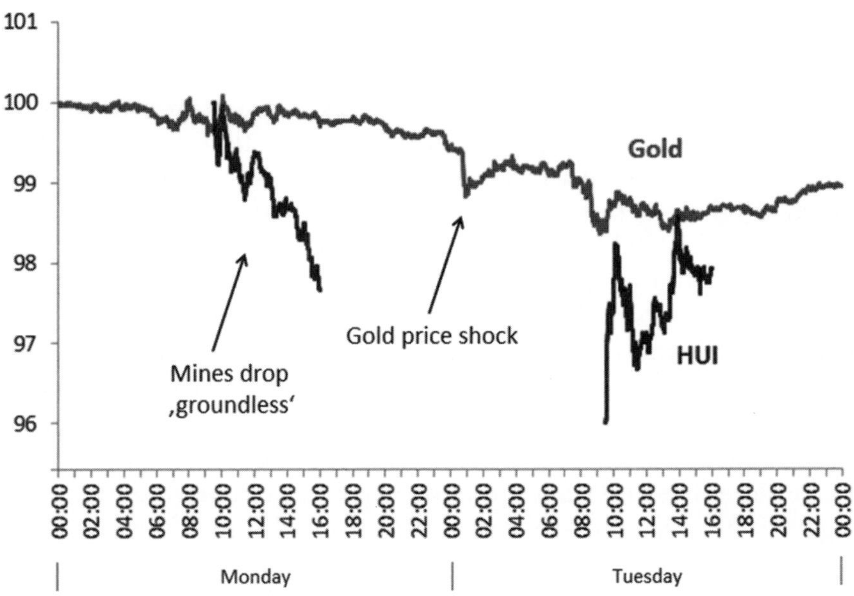

Figure 25.1 Gold mines and gold, 3 and 4 December 2012

in the gold price and in the gold-mining stock index HUI on 3 and 4 December 2012. One can clearly see that mining stocks were very weak on Monday, 3 December, losing 2.3 per cent. Gold, however, rose slightly (for reasons of comparability based on prices at the close of trading in the stock market). It was an entirely different situation on the following day, Tuesday, when gold came under great pressure, declining by 1 per cent, whereby two waterfall-like declines happened as well – apparently market interventions. However, the gold-mining stocks actually rose by 0.3 per cent that day! The mining stocks have, thus, led the decline in the gold price by one day. Obvious reasons for this 'premonition' of gold stockholders cannot be discerned; the influence of the stock market can be ruled out as a cause (it declined slightly on both days, by 0.5 and 0.3 per cent). Such leading moves by mining stocks can also be found to varying degrees (stronger, for instance, on 14 November 2012) or in different time windows (for instance, intraday on 4 August 2011, when the mining stocks began to plunge and gold followed an hour later). Due to the multitude of parameters, we want to refrain from a statistical examination in this instance and confine ourselves to individual examples.[87]

A possible cause for such leading moves in the gold-mining stocks in the context of gold price manipulation could be insider, or accompanying trades. The players could position themselves in such a way as to garner additional profits through front-running. The mining stocks lend themselves to this due to their correlation with the gold price, which would explain the leading moves. In the parallel market, additional profits can be obtained that could not be procured in the gold market alone (as the price decline in the mining stocks is due to an exogenous factor).

The explanation may vary on a case-by-case basis; as far as it is humanly possible to judge, it is improbable that there are interventions in the gold market over many years without individuals and institutions yielding to the temptation of making personal profits from them. That is a fundamental disadvantage of price manipulations, which is especially relevant when private institutions execute the interventions. These are – to phrase it cautiously – at the very least, on the edge of legality, which presumably lowers the threshold of inhibition towards engaging in such insider front-running trades. However, even the central banks are not beyond all suspicion. There were also anomalies in other cases prior to announcements of central bank measures – for instance, the leading move in the gold price prior to the WAG in 1999 or the foreign exchange trades of the spouse of the president of the Swiss National Bank prior to the raising of the exchange rate in 2011.[88] In addition to direct trades in the context of individual interventions, there is also the advantage of possessing the basic knowledge that can be exploited. Anyone who knew, in the 1990s, that the gold price wouldn't rise probably didn't buy any gold (or borrowed more of it).

Practically all of the profits that are generated as a result of price manipulations generate losses for other parties. Specifically, other investors are deprived of a part of their savings. What makes matters worse in the case of private institutions manipulating prices is that the profits remain with them and, contrary to interventions on the part of central banks, do not benefit society at large. It is immaterial, in this case, whether they act with the tacit approval of government agencies, as the profits remain with the private institutions. Among the many side effects of the gold market interventions there are, thus, also economically, morally and legally unjustifiable pecuniary advantages accruing to the perpetrators, which are concurrently detrimental to the wealth of innocent bystanders.

Chapter 26

Interventions in the Silver Market

When one examines the interventions in the gold market, the question arises what the situation with gold's 'little brother', silver, is. What is specifically of interest is whether there are independent price manipulations in silver, if silver is deliberately suppressed, or if there are only parallel price declines due to the high degree of correlation between gold and silver. In order to establish a better understanding of the situation, we will first take a look at the differences and commonalities between the two metals. Similar to gold, silver is a store of value. However, it is, to a larger extent, also a consumption good. Moreover, the above-ground stock of silver relative to annual mine supply and consumption is markedly smaller. The importance as a store of value is, thus, less pronounced in silver than in gold. From the point of view of a central bank it can, nevertheless, make sense to keep the silver price from rising. Similar to gold, this would scare additional investment demand off. It would prevent its use as a store of value increasing again. This would be even more problematic with silver than with gold, as the market's size is much too small to sensibly fulfil this role. The small market size plays another role too. It would make it easy for large participants to speculatively drive the market up It is the job of the regulatory agencies and, if need be, a matter of politics, not the job of the central bank (even less private financial institutions) to address this, as with other commodities. The situation would be akin to that in gold for such private financial institutions in the role of manipulators, as they could attempt to obtain profits by means of price suppression. In contrast to the case with gold, there are no known quotes by central bankers regarding silver stating that they would prefer a lower price or were thinking about interventions. Furthermore, lending cannot play a large role in silver price manipulation, as the official holdings of central banks are much smaller than their gold holdings.

These and other factors render the gathering of evidence much more difficult for silver than for gold. Nevertheless, in spite of the fact that it is a much smaller market and even though silver is less important nowadays as a monetary instrument, it appears as though silver manipulation attracts more public notoriety than gold manipulation (which can be seen from the number search results through the internet search portal Google or by dint of the fact that the US commodity market regulator CFTC concerns itself with the topic). One of the main proponents of the silver market manipulation thesis is Theodore Butler. The concentration of short positions in the futures market among commercial traders is at the centre of his deliberations.[89] A few commercial market participants, especially the large US banking house JP Morgan, hold a large portion of the short positions. This would, allegedly, only make sense if there were a systematic price suppression with the goal of procuring profits, whereby it is also alleged that they are backstopped by the US government. It is true that the extent of concentration is, indeed, extreme. It is higher than for gold and the next-placed platinum. It is difficult to exclude alternative reasons for this (especially given one cannot explain the reasons for various degrees of concentration in other, presumably not permanently manipulated markets). Most importantly, one cannot discern clearly differentiated phases in the course of events, such as is the case with gold.[90] The hints at manipulation can, thus, not be solidified. This is true also for some other attempts to provide statistical proof for silver manipulation.[91] Nevertheless, a lot speaks in favour of the existence of an independent manipulation of silver. Specifically, shock-like declines, independent of gold, can be frequently observed. In order to examine this statistically, we want to combine the prices of many days visually, as an average price movement, similar to previous figures we have produced for gold. Figure 26.1 shows the average intraday price movement in silver from August 1998, from whence intraday prices are available.[92]

It can be clearly seen that, at the time of the silver fixing in London – around 7 a.m. EST – sharp price declines occurred frequently. These price declines do not exist in the gold market (see, especially, Figure 7.2)! As is the case with gold, the cause for this clustering is presumably the importance of the London fixing as a reference price. A further sharp price decline can be seen at around 10 a.m. EST. The reason for this is the close correlation between silver and gold (as, at that time, the PM fixing for gold takes place, when the gold price is frequently pushed down). Altogether one can see marked differences to the situation for gold. Specifically, it is not possible to link the main price decline in silver at 7 a.m. EST with

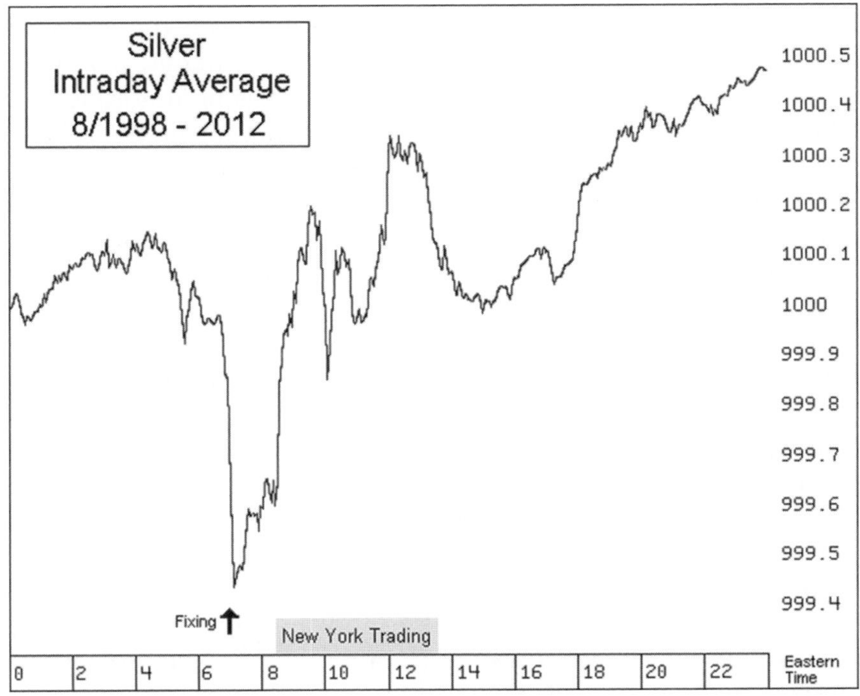

Figure 26.1 Average intraday price movement of silver, Aug. 1998–Dec. 2012

gold. Contrary to the situation at 10 a.m. EST, this decline cannot be ascribed to the high correlation with gold. The average intraday chart of silver shows that there are independent price interventions in silver that are not connected to gold.

Due to a lack of additional information (such as hints in Fed minutes), no further interpretation of the silver situation is provided here. Silver exhibits yet another distinctive feature, however, compared to gold. In the recent past, there was a phase when silver market interventions were apparently markedly reduced or even entirely abandoned. This can be seen both in the rally of the silver price and in the average intraday chart. Figure 26.2 shows the movement of the silver price from 2010 to 2012.

We can differentiate between two phases. First, silver rallied in a bull market until 1 May 2011, after which it fell, with two sharp price declines occurring. The rally phase is noteworthy, as there exist hints that interventions were abandoned. In September 2010, JP Morgan announced that they were 'in the process of winding down their proprietary trading operations'. Market observers suspected that the proprietary trading department at JP Morgan

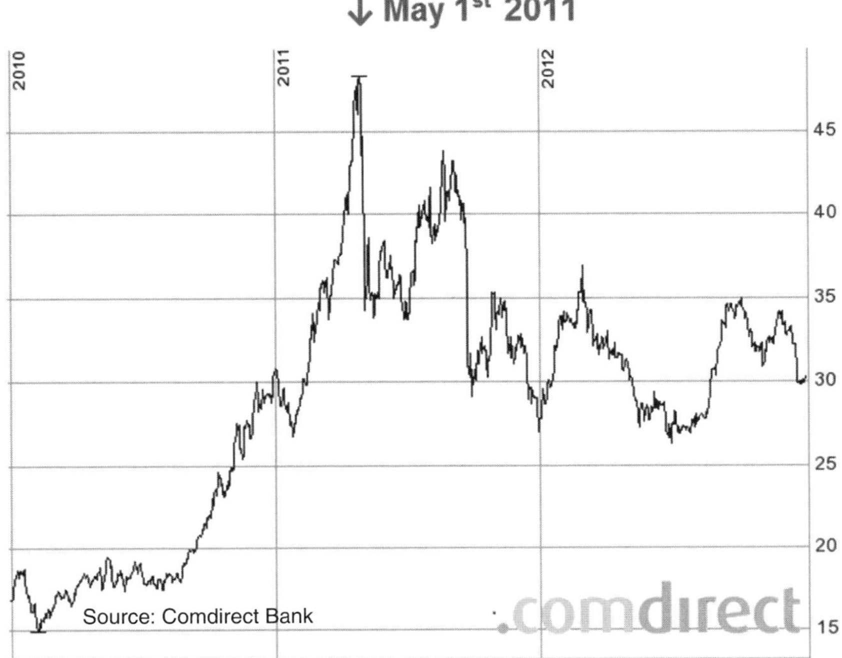

Figure 26.2 Silver price 2010–12, in US dollars per troy ounce (31.1g)

was responsible for the manipulation of silver. Accordingly, the National Inflation Association on 9 September 2010 – that is, on the eve the bull market – voiced the suspicion that the 'the silver manipulation could soon be over'.[93] The forecast appears to have come true – at least, the silver price more than doubled over the ensuing months. We now want to also examine whether the average intraday chart indicates a decrease in the price interventions during the bull market. Figure 26.3 shows the average intraday movement of silver over the 15 months until 1 May, during which the rally took place.

One can immediately see what seems a relatively inconspicuous progression. Specifically, there are no clusters of shocks around the silver fixing in evidence. This method finds no significant indications of price interventions at the designated time; they appear to have been stopped or reduced. But how did things evolve from there? On 1 May, the trend suddenly reversed and the bull market ended. Let us, first, look more closely at that day. It was a Sunday, but, due to the time difference, electronic trading had already begun. We are, therefore, talking about the first trading activity after the weekend, with only scant participation by European or

Figure 26.3 Average intraday price movement of silver Feb. 2010–April 2011

US-based traders. In about the first half-hour after opening at 6 p.m. EST, the market barely moved. As is usual at this early hour in Asian trade, trading activity was still calm. However, at 6.25 p.m., a price plunge began without a discernible catalyst, during which silver lost almost $6, or 12 per cent, within 11 minutes. It was one of the sharpest price declines in silver ever. There was no news item that could have triggered the sell-off, as market participants had apparently not viewed any event over the weekend as relevant for the silver price (in that case, silver would have started to fall immediately after the market opened).[94] Had the price manipulations begun again? To examine this further, we take a look at the 15 months after 1 May in terms of the average price movement (Figure 26.4).

It can be clearly seen that, at the time of the silver fixing, abrupt declines once again occur frequently; the interventions once again seemed to have resumed. Presumably, the preceding rally happened too quickly. During the rally there were no statistical anomalies at the time of the fixing; however, during the downward

Figure 26.4 Average intraday price movement of silver May 2011–July 2012

move they returned. The connection is quite clear: for some time there were no, or only very few, interventions and the price went up, then the interventions resumed and the price fell. In both phases this becomes evident in the intraday average! Similar to gold, it is shown here that price manipulations are often (not always) revealed in the average intraday price chart.

We can summarise at this point. In September 2010, JP Morgan decided to close its proprietary trading operation. Market observers subsequently forecast a rally in the price of silver, as this trading division was alleged to have been responsible for silver price suppression. In the following months, silver rose strongly, whereby the price more than doubled in a short time. Concurrently, there are no traces in the average intraday chart hinting at interventions that specifically target silver. But then the price threatened to move above the level of $50 per troy ounce. This level represents not only an important round number level; it marks also the historical record price of 1980. Apparently an uncontrollable breakout was feared at that point. This was to be prevented, which is why it was decided to resume the price interventions. Thus, a sharp price decline occurred on 1 May, in thin trading. This initiated the trend change, the silver price would subsequently fall for months. During this downward move, price declines at the time of the silver fixing are, once again, in evidence in the average intraday chart. These shocks attending the reference price are typical for price interventions. Their renewed appearance confirms that silver price suppression had resumed. The operation to keep silver from rising further had succeeded.

Chapter 27

Swapped Bundesbank Gold and Other Mysteries

We now turn to a theory that is probably only of interest well beyond German borders. For years it has been rumoured in the gold market that the Bundesbank has lent out about half of its gold, about 1,700 tons, via a swap with the USA (some people even say that all of the gold is gone). This assertion is a result of the fundamental mistrust of central banks due to their non-transparent information policy, the concealment of the size of gold loans and the interventions that have been kept secret for years. The dearth of information naturally encourages theories that attempt to fill in the blanks. For this purpose, sparse individual observations and individual hypotheses have to be combined to create an overall picture. In this type of exercise, one can, at times, overshoot the mark. We take a look at the individual theses that led to the assertion that the Bundesbank's gold is largely gone.

One such thesis is based on the fact that the gold vault in West Point in the USA has reclassified its gold inventory to 'custodial gold'. That is supposed to mean that the gold in the vault was transferred to someone else – namely the Bundesbank. The 1,700 tons of US gold were lent to the Bundesbank in the course of bilateral contracts (swaps), and the Bundesbank is said to have concurrently lent the same amount of its gold to the Americans. This has allegedly been done in order to be able to lend out the more easily disposable Bundesbank gold (customary good delivery bars) in the marketplace.

Although the reclassification is curious, the conclusion drawn from this is not sound, for the simple reason that it contradicts commercial custom. A swap agreement may encompass 50 or 100 tons (or rather, following the trade practice in gold loan contracts, a specific number of troy ounces), but not the precise amount held in a specific vault in the USA. That is absurd. Moreover, the amount of 1,700 tons is far too large (1994/95!).

Primarily, the alleged connection to the Bundesbank is not convincing. That has been asserted on the basis of the minutes of the

Fed meeting of January 1995. These minutes contain a remark that the ESF, which is charged with interventions, may enter into gold swaps. In addition, it is mentioned elsewhere in the minutes that it has a swap agreement with the Bundesbank. From that the conclusion was drawn that the swap agreement with the Bundesbank would concern gold (the aforesaid 1,700 tons).

This notion already falls short due to the alleged connection. However, it is questionable that the swap corresponds to one of the gold swaps. The people present are aware that the minutes are recorded and will as a rule (aside from spontaneous remarks, such as those on the ESF swap) avoid all hints concerning gold market interventions. Therefore, when they talk about swaps, they will simply have foreign exchange swaps in mind. It is also clear from the context that the swap with the Bundesbank must have been a foreign exchange swap: the topic of debate is whether, in the face of the tense liquidity situation at the ESF due to the support extended to Mexico, there exist still other obligations. These obligations can only encompass dollars, as dollars are what Mexico requires. The amount of dollars concerned (which has been mentioned earlier on), wouldn't be reduced if gold were swapped. Lastly, it is immediately evident from the wording that the topic has to be a foreign exchange swap, as shown by the following passage: 'if they wanted to advance dollars to the Bundesbank'. The debate, therefore, concerns a foreign exchange agreement (ultimately a swap line).[95] There is no reason to suppose that the Bundesbank has lent out half of its gold or used it in a swap.

Even if the interpretation overshoots the mark in this case, nothing changes with regard to the fact that central banks have lent out part of their gold and intervene in the market. In the face of years of secrecy on the part of the central banks, the temptation to read too much into things obtains as soon as one has realised that there are gold market interventions. This shouldn't be blamed primarily on those who attempt to make estimates and are eager to clear matters up, but rather on the non-transparency of the central banks. Already, Frank Veneroso had overestimated the amount of gold on loan, but at the same time he was the first person to point the problem out. The example highlights how a lack of information can lead to misinterpretations. No one is fully immune to making mistakes when putting together a picture from puzzle pieces. One can only try to proceed with as much precision as possible.

Three further examples highlight the danger of misinterpretation and should be mentioned on this occasion. One is about the export statistics: analysts recognize, time and again, the big amount of gold being exported from the USA. Over the last two decades, for instance, more than four thousand tons of gold have been exported above the amount that could be considered justified by production and other factors. The 'gap' in the amount is seen as evidence for gold that has been secretly brought from the vaults of the US government into foreign countries. The gold could have no other origin and was probably used to suppress its price. However, the amount can be explained with Gold that foreign central banks stored in the vaults of the New York FED: It is treated as export in the statistic when it leaves the USA. Such transports happened extensively in the last decades (for selling, lending and repatriation). Therefore, this 'mystery' is about the facts described in chapter 16.

The other two examples were cited, time and again, by market commentators as proof for gold swaps for the purpose of gold price manipulation. In both of them the word 'gold' is mentioned in connection with the word 'swap'. For one thing, the news service Bloomberg in 2005 reported a statement by then Bundesbank chief Axel Weber: '"We have been asked to negotiate with other central banks" about potential swap deals involving gold.'[96] Gold swaps are not what is meant here. Rather it emerges from the context that he refers to Germany's sales quota in the context of the WAG agreement. This agreement between central banks limited the amount of gold that each country was allowed to sell. Since Germany didn't sell any gold, it was able to cede its quota, in other words swap it (for instance, for a future quota, in the event that it wanted to sell at some point to come).

Another example is a statement by Fed governor Wayne Angell in March 1991: 'I would hesitate for us to have foreign currency holdings that have swap puts that just sit there, [which] is now becoming the case for our gold.'[97] Here too, gold swaps are not what is meant. Rather, it emerges from the context that the hedging of a foreign exchange position (via swapping of puts) would ultimately make it earn no interest, just as is the case with gold (which doesn't pay interest either).

In spite of these examples, there are hints that swap agreements between central banks play a role in making gold available for loans. Among these are mentions (e.g., in footnotes to book-keeping entries) regarding quality or location swaps, in which only gold of different quality or held in different locations is exchanged. Gold loans are likely the main reason for such swaps. In the next chapter we will also discuss the ESF gold swaps in greater detail.

Chapter 28

Who Intervenes?

The small amount of gold on loan and the lack of evidence regarding gold swaps confirm that the Bundesbank isn't a big player in the gold suppression scheme. That is actually not too surprising, as, due to the sub-optimal course of German monetary history, the Bundesbank is probably not very open-minded about such schemes. And yet, in spite of numerous monetary catastrophes (hyperinflation, deflation and currency reform), even in Germany forces from the realm of politics, from the media and even from within the Bundesbank itself frequently urged the sale of the Bundesbank's gold. However, they failed to hold sway. Things were different in the UK, for instance, where the central bank is also very conservative; in spite of that, the sale of gold happened. The reason is that the decision was not in the hands of the Bank of England, but in those of the Chancellor of the Exchequer – in short, the political establishment.

When considering the question of who intervenes, one must differentiate between institutions, and even within institutions, as not everyone is of the same opinion; moreover, potentially, positions are subject to change. It is, thus, possible that a central banker could have pleaded in favour of gold market intervention in 1993 in order to lower inflation expectations, but then been against further increases in the physical supply, which pressured the gold price from $400 per ounce to $250 per ounce in the second phase.

Originally, the initiative to intervene systematically must have emanated from the USA. Fed chief Alan Greenspan, after all, had pondered gold sales in May 1993 and Fed governor Wayne Angell spoke about holding the gold price in July 1993. Then, in August of that year, the interventions at the $400 level began. However, this was certainly not an institutional activity by the Fed. On the part of the US treasury, deputy treasury secretary Lawrence Summers was responsible, at the time, for foreign exchange interventions, and was lauded by Greenspan for his abilities in this context. A few years earlier, Summers, in his role as economic researcher, had conducted research into the relationship between gold prices and real interest rates.[98] It seems obvious that he must have seen more advantages than disadvantages in a gold price that no longer increased.

The above-mentioned persons may have belonged to the circle of people that made the initial decision to intervene against a further rally. On the UK side, Gordon Brown is conspicuous; he later pushed through the UK gold sales and announced them in advance, which pressured the price and increased the losses borne by British taxpayers. This apparent clumsiness was, by all appearances, rhetorical badmouthing of gold. But he was not yet in office in 1993. However, in 1993 British politicians may have been prepared, in principle, to agree to gold market interventions as a result of the EMS debacle a few months earlier.

The Fed itself cannot be the acting institution for legal reasons. The most likely institution to come into consideration in terms of the USA is the ESF, as Congress has little say over it and it doesn't publish minutes. There is strong circumstantial evidence for its de facto involvement. In the year 2000, Reginald Howe called attention to a balance sheet anomaly.[99] At the time the Fed's monthly statement included the treasury's gold holdings in one line (1.18), and in another line both those of the treasury and those of the ESF (3.12). Figure 28.1 shows the principle (the time periods are not identical).

From 1974 to 1995 the values were in most years identical. Later, there were frequently differences. Since gold is always disclosed at the same price in the balance sheet of the central banking system of the USA, the reason for the difference has to be due to gold trading activities. Repeated errors in the balance sheet can probably be ruled out (they should, if at all, only occur if there is a lot of activity in connection with the gold inventory). The Fed reacted extremely suspiciously after Howe published this anomaly and played it up in a lawsuit. Subsequently the ESF was simply dropped from the Fed's monthly balance sheet statements and the values were corrected.[100] The gold held by the ESF had been mentioned in Fed bulletins from the 1940s (Figure 28.2). A balance sheet tradition dating back more than 50 years, thus, was suddenly discarded.[101] When two central bank balance sheet items don't mesh, one would actually prefer to receive a cogent explanation.

A further indication that the ESF is the operational institution in the USA is given in the above mentioned quote regarding gold swaps. In the Fed meeting of January 1995, the topic was whether it was legally permissible for the ESF to extend a loan to crisis-stricken

3.12 U.S. RESERVE ASSETS
Millions of dollars, end of period

Asset	1997	1998	1999
1 **Total**	**69,954**	**81,755**	**71,516**
2 Gold stock, including Exchange Stabilization Fund[1]	11,050	11,041	11,089
3 Special drawing rights[2,3]	10,027	[illegible]	[illegible]
4 Reserve position in International Monetary			

1.18 FEDERAL RESERVE BANKS Condition and Federal Reserve Note Statements[1]
Millions of dollars

Account	Wednesday		
	2000		
	Sept. 27	Oct. 4	Oct. 11
ASSETS			
1 Gold certificate account	11,046	11,046	11,046
2 Special drawing rights certificate account	[illegible]	[illegible]	[illegible]

Figure 28.1 Excerpts from the Fed's monthly statement, January 2001

Mexico. This was confirmed in a number of ways. However, the participants wanted to make absolutely sure. At that point, legal counsel Virgil Mattingly joined the discussion and offered gold swaps as an example: 'It's pretty clear that these ESF operations are authorized… The statute is very broadly worded… it has covered things like the gold swaps.'[102]

Agreements covering the swapping of gold between central banks (already known under the term gold swaps at the time) have existed for many decades.[103] The question arises whether Mattingly meant those gold swaps which were customary at the time, including the supply of the market with gold (directly or through other central banks). The working environment suggests this (which would normally lead one to use contemporary examples), as does the fact that he mentions gold swaps at all: after all, it had been mentioned earlier that the ESF had loans and agreements with at least 37 countries. Harking back to times far in the past, he could have chosen from a multitude of examples concerning loans that would have suited the topic. However, he mentioned gold swaps, probably because they were ongoing, which is why they came to mind. This

January 2001

3.12 U.S. RESERVE ASSETS

Millions of dollars, end of period

Asset	1997	1998	1999
1 **Total**	**69,954**	**81,755**	**71,516**
2 Gold stock, including Exchange Stabilization Fund[1]	11,050	11,041	11,089
3 Special drawing rights[2,3]	10,027	10,603	10,336
4 Reserve position in International Monetary			

February 2001

3.12 U.S. RESERVE ASSETS

Millions of dollars, end of period

Asset	1997	1998	1999
1 **Total**	**69,954**	**81,761[c]**	**71,516**
2 Gold stock[1]	11,047[c]	11,046[c]	11,048[c]
3 Special drawing rights[2,3]	10,027	10,603	10,336
4 Reserve position in International Monetary			

Figure 28.2 Excerpts from Federal Reserve bulletins compared

idea is supported by the fact that he used the definite article: 'it has covered things like *the* gold swaps'. One employs a definite article when the subject matter is known to both the speaker and the listener. The people present appear to know which gold swaps he is referring to – at least, no one questioned him about them. There are, however, also arguments against this interpretation: the topic is a loan to Mexico, and previous gold swaps also represented loans (which were extended against gold collateral). However, six years later, when asked about this statement, Mattingly himself asserted not to know anything about gold swaps (and suspected that the transcript was faulty).[104] But if he was referring to gold swaps that had occurred decades in the past in 1995, he should not have forgotten about them a few years later. Moreover, loans collateralised with gold would have been quite unsuitable as an example, as the loan to Mexico wasn't going to be collateralised with gold. It would seem that Mattingly was referring to gold swaps outstanding at the time of the 1995 FOMC meeting. He probably simply gave an obvious example spontaneously, one which he assumed everyone knew about.

Another possible candidate for operational institution is the working group for financial markets, called the 'plunge protection team' in trader jargon. It was established after the stock market crash of 1987. Occasional meetings and reports are a matter of record. However, there are no hints about activities in the gold market. It may, nevertheless, have acted in a coordinating capacity.

In any case, the working group is important to the background, as it was supposed to favour solutions which would be implemented by private sector market participants,[105] a *modus operandi* that was put into practice during the market crash of 1987 – something that was, however, never officially confirmed. It is precisely this cooperation that occurred in 1987 that served as the model for the gold market interventions. This poses a special problem: if market interventions are implemented by the private sector, then private institutions must also make profits from them in the long run. But if they make profits, whether by carry trades, or in the futures markets by means of engineering abrupt declines, it follows that the temptation is quite great to pursue these interventions more or less on their own initiative and push for them. This manipulation of prices by private parties to their own advantage is definitely beyond the bounds of legality. However, it probably explains best why gold was pressured from $400 to $250 per ounce in the second phase of the gold market interventions from November 1996 to May 2001, in spite of the fact that it wasn't possible to sensibly connect this to inflation expectations or any other monetary policy goal. At the time, there was also an intense campaign against gold; among other things, moralising pressure was exerted against a number of central banks, such as that of Switzerland, in order to get them to sell gold. Such a course of action would be entirely atypical for a central bank, but it would be easy to explain if private sector interests were behind it.

Fundamentally, however, an institutional framework is not necessary for coordination. It can be implemented informally as well, as long as the interventions are profitable for the private parties and the central banks supply enough gold via gold loans. In principle, a limited cooperation suffices for this. On the part of the bullion banks it was sufficient to lobby the central banks in the second phase and motivate a large enough number of them to engage in sales and gold lending. Although central banks had no strong motive for the decline seen during the second phase, there may have been a few that pushed for the decline, be it out of hubris, out of habit, or as a favour to friends, or be it for other reasons (the introduction of the euro is sometimes mentioned, which would explain the sizable participation of many European central banks in sales and gold loans; however, conclusive evidence to that theses is not known). Apart from the US and UK central banks, the corresponding treasury departments which administer the gold must be mentioned as well.

With regard to private sector participants, the question arises whether, aside from the bullion banks, a few gold-mining firms were also involved in pushing for a concerted decline in the gold price. There were several among them that had borrowed an inordinate amount of gold relative to their production. A falling gold price served them well, as it created a competitive advantage for them due to their hedging. They were also mentioned as potential participants in the concerted gold price suppression based on the fact that some of them (similar to the bullion banks) had tight personal connections to politicians as well as access to extraordinarily long-term gold loans at extremely favourable conditions.[106] However, the share prices of the large gold hedgers (such as, e.g., Barrick Gold) didn't perform appreciably better than those of other gold-mining firms in the late 1990s.

One conspicuous fact is something Bill Murphy of GATA has often pointed out in the past, namely the nearly identical closing prices of gold in the years 1997–99. Gold closed in 1997 in New York at $288.80, in 1998 at $288 and in 1999 at $287.50 per ounce. The closing prices in the first three years of the second phase of the gold market interventions, thus, were within $1.30 of each other! All three were amounting almost precisely to $288. This simply cannot be a coincidence. The spread is even tighter if one looks at the annual closing prices of the relevant front month contract, the February contract, at the COMEX: in 1997 it closed at $289.90, in 1998 at $289.20 and in 1999 at $289.60 (Figure 28.3). The difference was a mere 70 cents at its widest! Day-in, day-out there is active trading and speculation over years, only to arrive at the same price time and again at the end of the year, as though these prices had been officially fixed. That cannot be a coincidence – and it is no coincidence, but rather the result of an agreement for reasons that have to do with annual financial statements. Therefore there must have been an agreement between at least two parties.

To be safe, we want, however, to briefly estimate the probability that a market price attains the same height in this manner on three

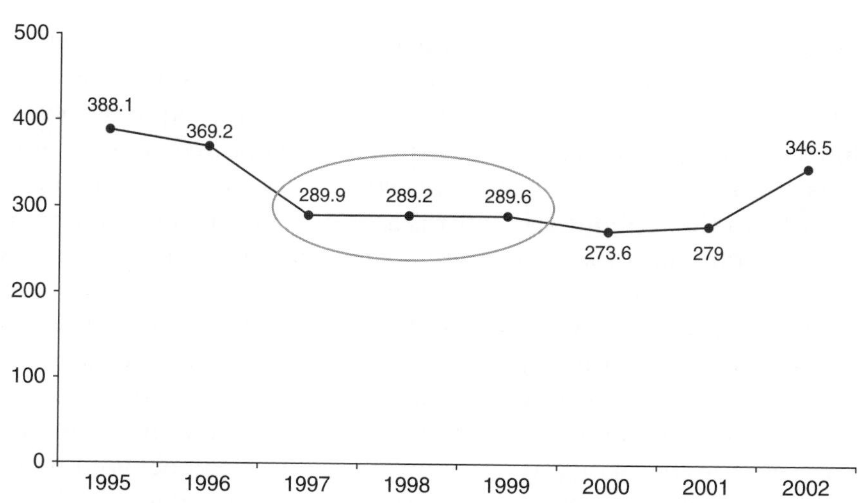

Figure 28.3 Closing prices of the front month contract at the New York COMEX for the years 1995–2002

consecutive occasions. Since there are deviations from normal distribution on the exchanges even without interventions, we are not calculating the probability theoretically. We rather measure it (to be precise: its frequency). For this purpose we take the longest available suitable time series, the afternoon fixing prices from the beginning of 1968 to the end of 2012 (the measurement thus refers to the spot price). The percentage spread within which the three closing prices of the years 1997 to 1999 are situated is calculated from the maximum range of $1.30 and the closing price of $288. It was, therefore, 1.3/288 (or 0.4513888 per cent). We now measure how many times it happened that three closing prices separated by exactly one year each (251 trading days) were situated within this range.

Out of 10,798 possible triples, there are only eight cases when three prices separated by one year were within this tight range. That corresponds to a probability of a mere 0.074 per cent. In short, the probability that three annual closing prices are this close to each other by coincidence is below one tenth of a per cent. The value is reduced even further if one considers the following. Of the eight cases when three prices separated by one year were that close to each other, six occurred in the time span 1994 to 1996, when the gold price was 'stuck' at a level of just below $400 due to interventions. At the time, it didn't move freely but rather was forced into a sideways movement (which in turn shows that the sideways movement of prices below $400 during phase one was not of a coincidental nature). This leaves just two real cases of a then reduced number of 9,900 possibilities overall, which results in a probability of 0.02 per cent. Even this marginal value would be reduced further if one were to employ the tighter range of $0.7 at the COMEX instead of the spot price range of $1.3! Anyway, mathematically and factually, the matter is already clear, what is at hand is not normal market behaviour (presumably the regulatory authorities could have easily investigated the precise circumstances based on these facts). The calculated value is generally quite robust. The probability that the closing prices of three consecutive years were as close to each other as they were in the years 1997–99 is at or below 0.02 per cent.

In the second phase of the gold market interventions, which began in November 1996 and lasted until May 2001, there was a regular target value to which the gold price was supposed to be pressured. It was no longer only the $400 level above which the gold price was not supposed to rise (for reasons such as the fight against inflation), but the $290 level in the futures contract gave a markedly lower target that was supposed to be reached by year end. Apparently, the overarching idea to remain below the $300 level led to picking the level of $290 just below in order to be safe, so as to prevent any buying that may have been set into motion if the $300 level was breached (analogous to how experienced traders don't place stops at round numbers). The target value was apparently agreed upon for the futures contract, as that was relevant for the balance sheets of the executing agents. Since no monetary policy goals can be discerned for this expansion of the gold market interventions, the goals could only be private ones. The existence of such a uniform level alone is a hint as to the importance private institutions had attained over the course of time, as central banks require no uniform annual closing price.

Due to the carry trade, there are private sector market participants that push for the suppression of the gold price out of self-interest. They are clearly part of the intervention practice; they are the private sector solution 'wherever possible', as it was analogously formulated in the remit of the working group for financial markets. They are, however, clearly also a force in their own right. They are the recipients of the gold that the central banks are willing to lend out in increasing amounts should its price rise, as Greenspan put it in 1998. There can, therefore, be no reasonable doubt as to their existence. They take a share of the work, but they also pursue their self-interest.

Influencing prices via the futures markets is, presumably, also part of the work that the private institutions are taking on, for pragmatic reasons, but also due to its profitability. The uniform annual closing price at $290 hints at that. But also the ESF, the treasury department or the central banks may be active in the futures market, indicated by the apparently often closely coordinated interventions in gold and foreign exchange. How the division of tasks in the futures market between private institutions and government institutions or institutions close to the government works, in detail, cannot be determined from the available information, or can at best be guessed at.

Even though the second phase of the gold market interventions only ended in 2001, forces that were against a further decline of the gold price had already gained the upper hand at the central banks in 1999. This became clear on 26 September 1999, when a number of important central banks holding about half of the world's gold reserves signed the already mentioned WAG, in which they limited their sales as well as their gold lending. In the subsequent days, this led to a sharp increase in the gold price by about 20 per cent (apparently, there was some insider buying ahead of the WAG announcement and if one accordingly takes the days prior to the announcement into account the rally was even stronger).

The participating central banks probably didn't expect such a strong rally. Nevertheless, a limitation of gold sales is, in principle, indicative of their intention; further price declines are no longer wanted. This appears to be quite harmless, but it raises important questions. Why are the central banks entering into such an extremely unusual and legally curious agreement? It is a declaration of intent, but also a message. The intention was to stop the decline of the gold price, and that is exactly what happened. The gold price made an initial low, and even though that was tested again two years later, gold has been in an uptrend since then. The message was actually not a new one, as many central bankers had previously made remarks on the topic individually. But they have now said, as a group, they do not want any further price declines, which ultimately means that from now on, the price will rise. However, this is an affront against the forces interested in a falling price. This lets the central banks off in terms of pressure to increase their sales, as an individual central bank can now always point to the common stance. Economically speaking, the participating central banks form a cartel, a counter-cartel against the existing cartel of gold price suppressors, to which they effectively belonged themselves. This is by no means a contradiction, as the differences are not only a thread running through the institutions, but are also visible in the historical evolution (a central bank may be in favour of interventions at a gold price of $400 in order to fight inflation expectations, but it can be against further price declines at $300 at a time of low inflation, as the value of its reserves otherwise dwindles alarmingly).

The message of the Washington Agreement must, however, be viewed primarily in the context of the preceding action by the UK. It was an open affront to announce the British gold sales in advance and thereby specifically exert pressure on the gold price. That openly showed that a lower gold price was the actual target. The forces that wanted to see no further gold price declines could and would not put up with this; they had to reply just as publicly. Once this had been set into motion, all the important central banks had to join, be it by joining the agreement itself or by means of later declarations, as otherwise there would have been questions as to why they were standing aside.

With that the end of the second phase of the gold interventions was initiated, with its strong private sector motivation, the lack of a monetary policy goal and the pressure against individual central banks (that at times bordered on blackmail) to get them to sell gold. The declaration of the central banks in the Washington Agreement was a 'commando operation' (French daily newspaper *Le Monde*),[107] on the initiative of the central banks of France and Germany. However, it was an operation that facilitated an orderly retreat for the enemy: by announcing simultaneously that they would continue with steady sales, they offered the bullion banks the possibility to cover the short positions resulting from the gold loans from central bank holdings (which then, in fact, happened). The private actors in the gold market interventions had overplayed their hand by pushing the gold price to $250 out of pure self-interest. But also their supporters, especially at the UK (and probably also the US) treasury department, lost all sympathies with their open announcement of Britain's sales. They had lost; the profits obtained from the price declines in the course of the gold carry trade were history. The carry trade, however, still had to be reversed.

With regard to the total amounts, apparent contradictions are only resolved if one includes the preceding gold loans. The Washington Agreement limited sales. In the ten years following the Agreement (and its successor), the central banks, however, sold more gold than in the preceding ten years. Nevertheless, the gold price rose markedly, while it had declined in the previous decade. The reason for this, as already explained, was that the supply of gold from central bank holdings fell in real terms. In the ten preceding years a lot of gold entered the market through gold loans; in the subsequent decade gold was taken off the market by the repayment of gold loans. The central banks had evidently realised that they had altogether lent so much gold to the bullion banks that the latter were unable to deliver it back in a regular manner. Only the central banks themselves could supply the gold. They had to sell gold from their own holdings in order to enable the bullion banks to repay the gold they had borrowed.

That is what the central banks then did; they increased their overall sales and reversed the loans, transforming previous loans into front-loaded sales. As an aside, at the latest from the moment when the total gold on loan exceeded an amount that could be repaid in a regular manner, the central banks could no longer disclose their loans, as that would have revealed the situation into which they had manoeuvred themselves. From that perspective, the WAG was an announcement to the bullion banks that the gold-lending business would be reversed but also that the central banks themselves would make the gold for this purpose available.

The events surrounding the Washington Agreement were not aimed against the US Federal Reserve (if anything, against the US treasury department, which administers the US gold). It may well be the case that the Europeans were not entirely in agreement with US monetary policy, and it may also be the case that the preparations for the Washington Agreement initially took place without the Fed's participation. One must, however, note that the Fed was materially involved in the most important precursor activity – because there had already been such an activity and it was evidently coordinated too. After the British treasury had announced its gold sales in advance on 7 May 1999, and thereby caused the affront, the governor of the Bank of France, Jean-Claude Trichet – speaking on 19 May in the name of four central banks, among them the US Fed – said in a clear statement that these central banks did not want to sell any gold. Only one day later, on 20 May, Alan Greenspan weighed in with relatively strong words in support of holding gold as a central bank reserve, such as 'Germany in 1944 could buy... not with fiat money, paper. And gold is always accepted and is the ultimate means of payment'.[108]

This action in favour of gold as a component of central bank reserves was undoubtedly arranged, not only on account of its temporal proximity, but also because Trichet spoke on behalf of four central banks (which he would surely not have done without an agreement). The four central banks that hold the biggest gold reserves (USA, Germany, France and Italy) had already expressed their opposition to gold sales in a coordinated manner on 19 May 1999. They did so immediately after the British announcement of 7 May and, just as was the case with the Washington Agreement later, so was this precursor campaign a reaction to it, and the Fed participated. The four central banks had already expressed clearly that they were against a further decline in the gold price, even if the desired effect had not yet materialised, which then made the Washington Agreement necessary. Only then the success was clearly signalled, as the gold price exploded in its wake (probably a little bit too much, even for the central banks that caused it – one or two may have lent a helping hand in roping the price in again).

Greenspan's position as one of the presumed main initiators of the gold market interventions can be reconciled with his weighing in against central bank gold sales. He was, initially, in favour of gold market interventions, but in the first phase the objectives were monetary policy goals such as the fight against inflation. He didn't back the second phase, in which other motives, such as the profits of private institutions, were the driving force. There is still the question of why the US central bank didn't take on an offensive role in the Washington Agreement, although it had done so in the precursor campaign. Since Greenspan probably had the Fed at his back for the most part, one explanation that suggests itself would be that parts of the US treasury department didn't agree with his position. Contrary to the first phase of the gold market interventions, when monetary policy motives dominated and persons associated with the Fed were the driving force and provided the ideas, it appears that, in the second phase, persons from the political establishment in the treasury departments of the USA and UK were the driving force (on the part of the private sector, the main incentives were profits). US president Bill Clinton, treasury secretary Bill Rubin and also French president Jacques Chirac were consequently among those who urged, in March 1999, in close succession that the IMF should sell its gold. Politics, not monetary policy, was the driving force at that point.

In the second, profit-driven phase, it was the bullion banks, as well as politicians – especially in the UK and the USA – that desired a lower gold price. In both countries politicians, not monetary policy-makers are administering the gold. In the USA, it is, as a rule, also the political establishment that triggers foreign exchange interventions. Moreover, it is the US administration, not the Fed, that controls the ESF, which apparently engages in gold market interventions. If, therefore (as is often the case in this book), gold market interventions by central banks are spoken about, then this represents a semantic simplification (to be more precise, one would have to speak of 'gold administering government institutions' or something similar). Indeed, it was actually the central banks, including that of the USA, that took the steps in 1999 that slowly but surely ended the systematic gold market interventions.

The assignment of roles between the UK and US administrations requires a bit of additional illumination. When the British announced their gold sales, this led to a number of conjectures. Specifically, the British opposition suspected that the government sold gold in order to enable the central bank to buy more euros in order to support the European currency union. This thesis is not tenable, however, in light of what is known regarding the imperatives that resulted from the gold-lending business. The gold sales were announced in such a manner as to lower the gold price, so that the proceeds for the buying of euros would have been lower as well. The advance announcement was conspicuous, but no explanation for it could be found. In reality, the reason was to either create profits or prevent losses in favour of the bullion banks, or perhaps also the American ESF. The British gold sales were executed – and announced in advance – in order to create a price decline, and thereby served to generate profits elsewhere. A motive may also have been to prevent the ESF from making losses akin to those it may have suffered in interventions. The ESF cannot cover losses easily through alternative funding sources, and it may have come to the attention of Congress (one argument against this theory, though, is Greenspan's statement against gold sales after the British announcement, which would have been a strong affront by the Fed against the treasury). Precisely who was supposed to profit from the British gold sales remains unexplained to this day.

The second phase of the gold market interventions raises the most questions. We, therefore, want to perform another statistical analysis which is directly connected with the findings concerning the first phase. In the first phase, from August 1993 to November 1996, the gold price was supposed to be held below the level of $400, meaning it was frequently clustered just below that round number. We therefore make a frequency analysis, to see how many times the price of gold is just below a round number. Since the central banks (and other price manipulators) at the time used round numbers as guideposts, this must be evident in a frequency analysis.

In order to measure how often the price remains in relatively close proximity to levels just below a round number, we count how often the gold price traded in the upper quartile below round numbers. We thus determine the prices between 175 and 200 or between 275 and 300 or between 375 and 400, and so forth. Next, we apply an annual smoothing in order to obtain a less volatile curve. This measurement has certain weaknesses (specifically the percentage spread between 75 and 100 is a lot different from that between 975 and 1,000). However, in view of the fact that the intervening central banks use round numbers for orientation, it is quite useful for our purpose. Figure 28.4 shows the frequency with which the gold price was just below round hundred marks and the corresponding gold price.

As only every fourth price is in the upper quartile, the line should, over the years, level off at 0.25 (see the horizontal line). Until the beginning of the interventions, it actually fluctuates around this mean and spends most of the time between 0 and 0.5. Then the frequency measure vaults almost to 1, as the price was held below $400 in the first phase. One can easily see in Figure 28.4 how the price clustered below this level (first circle). In this first phase there was a clear intervention level, an agreement between various central banks not to let the gold price rise above $400. The motives were the aforementioned monetary policy-related ones ('thermometer').

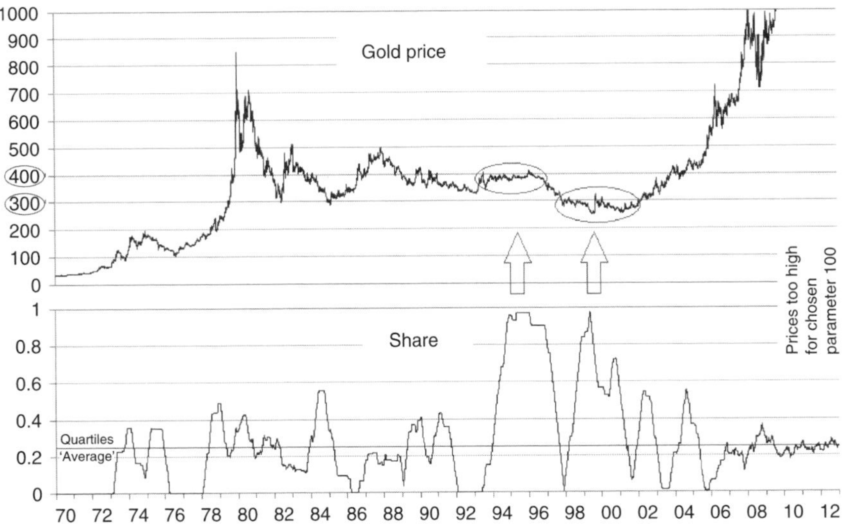

Figure 28.4 Gold and share of prices in quartiles below round hundred numbers (x75–x00), smoothed

The frequency measure signals, however, that there must have been a second level as well. In the second phase the frequency once again rises almost to 1. One can also see in Figure 28.4 how the price is stuck below the new level of $300 (left-hand half of the second circle). The intervention level of $300 must have existed as well! The frequency measurement, thus, shows us something that one recognises in the price chart of Figure 28.4 itself only at a second glance: a new price level had been agreed upon. The new level was $300; the price was supposed to remain below it (the agreed-upon annual closing price of $290 at the COMEX is part of the *modus operandi* with regard to this level). There is no further information, either about the level itself or about the reasons to strive for this lower level; apparently, any talks were strictly 'off the record'.

The frequency measure, however, reveals this second level to us (and, as an aside, confirms the first one). The existence of such a level suggests itself; after one had used $400 as a guidepost, the next target was attacked. The new level didn't last as long, however. After the price had remained below $300 for a little less than a year, the British treasury arranged for a further price decline (middle of the second circle), which then led to the opposition of the majority of central banks. With the Washington Agreement they succeeded in getting their way, which then led to a sharp rally (the vertical line in the middle of the second circle). This is actually the beginning of the slow end of the systematic gold interventions. Although the price was pushed down to almost $250 in 2001 once more, it has risen since then. The second phase is the least uniform one, exhibiting the most contradictions. It also raises the most questions: why was a lower level agreed upon and the price pressured from the $400 level to the new level of $300? And why did the British then want an even lower gold price? For both questions, the main issue is why a lower price of gold was the aim and not only the prevention of a rally, which could be explained by monetary policy-related motives.

The level of $300 was probably decisive for the timing of the proposed IMF sales and those of the British, as they were announced as gold was about to rise back above $300 (see Figure 9.2). The level was still informally relevant, however, even after the British had broken ranks and gold fell even further. From that point onward, it is no longer as easily discernible in the price chart of Figure 28.4 as the $400 level (but $250 is 'below $300' as well). The level continued to be maintained until early 2002, although it was only defended halfheartedly by then. Ferdinand Lips points out in his book[109] that the first three announcements by then Bundesbank president Ernst

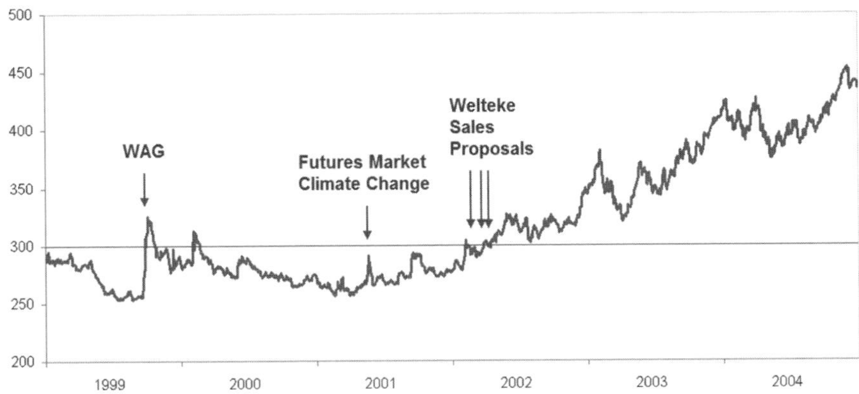

Figure 28.5 Gold: defence and abandonment of the $300 level

Welteke that he was pondering gold sales occurred whenever gold appeared close to breaking through the $300 level. The timing constitutes a kind of official confirmation of the importance of the $300 level, in the face of the lack of transparency. The level couldn't be held; the price only made a few brief countertrend moves.

The brief, spectacular and embarrassing phase of gold price suppression by means of advance notices of sales was, anyway, coming to an end. There were also no gold sales by the Bundesbank (as we have seen, it succeeded later in getting its leased-out gold back, without having to supply any from its own holdings). Two years later there was, apparently, another attempt to hold the gold price at the previous level of $400. Figure 28.5 shows the rally following the WAG and the Welteke sales proposals are indicated, as well as a sharp advance in mid-May of 2001 (which, in anticipation of the following chapter, is referred to as 'futures market climate change').

Chapter 29

The Mystery of 18 May 2001, 12.31

With 5 August 1993 we have found the day when the modern-day systematic interventions began – first, against a rising gold price and, from 21 November 1996 even in favour of a declining one. We now want to identify the day when the tide turned. Twice, in 1999 and 2001, the gold price put in a low in the vicinity of $250 per ounce. The year 1999 was, in addition, marked by the WAG, with which the central banks announced a change in their views regarding gold, and which led to a brief price spike. Nevertheless, it is a day in the year 2001 when the third phase, and with it the first stage of the termination of the gold market interventions, began. The interventions since then are no longer dominated by physical supply from gold lending, but are mainly focused on the futures markets. Due to the lack of additional central bank gold supply, moreover, the gold price is rising. Since then the price is no longer held, its rise is merely slowed down. If the main focus is now on the futures markets, it is obvious that one should look there for further traces left behind by interventions.

In the USA there is a reporting requirement for positions in the futures markets that exceed a certain threshold. Market participants thereby have to assign themselves to a specific group of traders. One of these groups are the 'commercials'. Commercial market participants are, by and large, differentiated from the remaining two groups by the fact that they don't have a purely 'speculative' interest in price movements, but that of a commercial enterprise. Commercials include, for instance, mining companies that sell their production forward in the futures market, or jewellers that buy the metal they require for future delivery. Market commentators have suspected for a long time that interventions at the COMEX are visible in the data on commercial positions.

Once a week the US regulatory authority CFTC publishes extensive statistics about the positions entered into by the different groups of traders. In these statistics one can see what positions

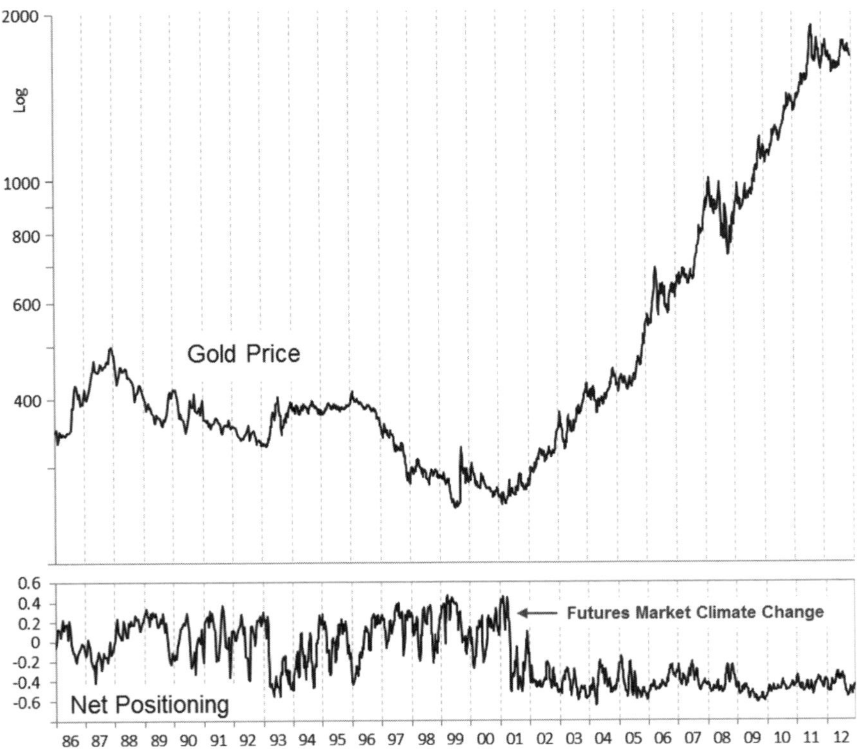

Figure 29.1 Gold: net positioning of commercial hedgers (proportion of total open interest)

the commercials, behind which the intervention forces may be concealed, have adopted. Figure 29.1 shows the positioning of the commercial hedgers over the entire available time period from 1986 onward, together with the price of gold. For this purpose, the number of contracts they are long is subtracted from the number of contracts they are short in order to discern their net position. This number is then divided by the total open interest so as to identify the net proportion of the commercial positions. Values below zero thus mean that the commercials are betting on falling prices.

We can clearly see that there was a sharp decline in the week to 22 May 2001. Since then, the value has almost always been below −0.2, often even markedly lower. In the many years before, it oscillated around the zero line! This is a significant difference, which coincides approximately with the beginning of the gold bull market. The value markedly below zero means that the commercials overall bet, to a large extent, on falling prices. They are in a loss-making position in the course of the entire rally.

We know from the earnings reports of gold-mining firms that they have reduced their hedging against falling prices notably during the gold bull market. To the extent that they have used the COMEX for hedging purposes, the closing out of their hedging positions would have had to result in an analogous rise in the above line. That is not the case. The positioning in the futures market, however, corresponds roughly to what one would expect in the context of futures market sales for the purpose of interventions. Since May 2001, the forces of intervention have been apparently barely able to cover their short positions and that is why the value remains below −0.2.

However, we don't want to overestimate the evidential value of this statistic. It is indirect and we don't know for certain which group the forces of intervention are formally attached to. Moreover, prior to beginning of the interventions in August 1993, there were also decreases in the line of the commercials in Figure 29.1, which is equivalent to increases in their net short position (possibly because the mines, for instance, sold into price rallies for hedging purposes). These decreases may have been systematically widened in the bull market since 2001 (but this would not mesh with the decline in mine hedging since then). Generally, we can see that the positioning structure in the futures market has fundamentally changed since 2001. Moreover, the week to 22 May 2001 is conspicuous by the large decrease in the positioning oscillator.

We expand our examination by an additional statistic published by the US regulatory authority, making information on the concentration of positions available. Concentration refers to the size of the market represented by the largest market participants. The idea behind this is that interventions are only executed by very few or perhaps even only a single institution, while normal market participants are widely spread across many institutions. Concentration should, therefore, increase when numerous interventions take place. Interventions for the purpose of suppressing the price, which are executed by only a few firms at the COMEX, must lead to an increase in concentration (provided the positions cannot be covered again). That is then visible in the statistic. Figure 29.2 shows how big the share of the four largest institutions in the total net short position (bets on falling prices) has been since 1986.

We once again discern a shift in the level. While the short-side concentration until 1993 was, on average, at the 15 per cent level, it rose thereafter to about 20 per cent, often fluctuating. Since the week to 22 May 2001, however, it has been at about 30 per cent,

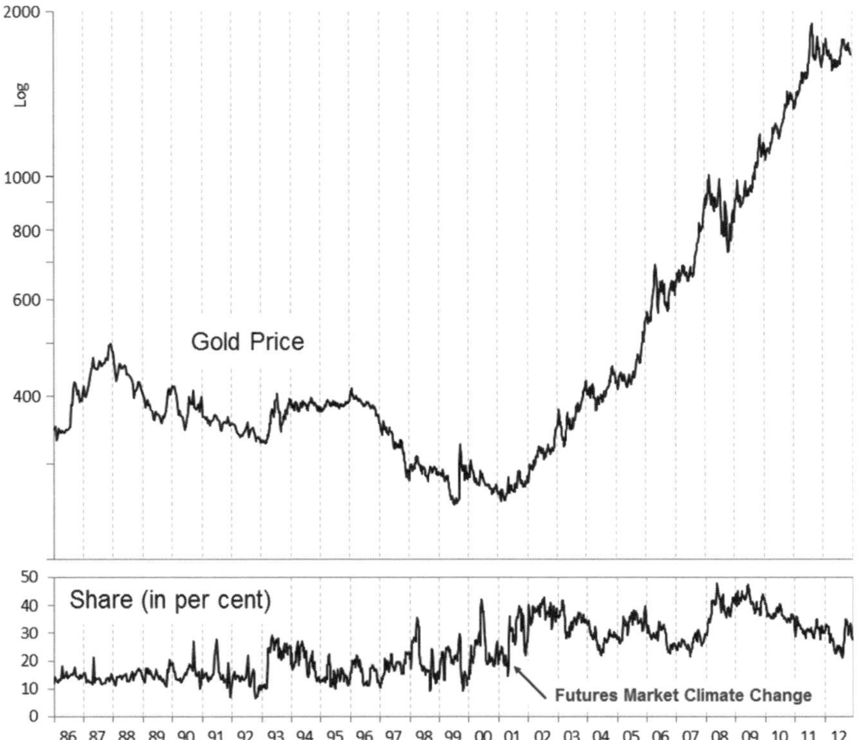

Figure 29.2 Gold: share of the four largest traders of the total net short position (in percentages)

a level that in the earlier years was only briefly reached at peaks. Often, the share of the short positions held by the four largest traders reached even 40 per cent and more! Once again, a marked shift in the level is discernible since the week to 22 May 2001. But we don't want to overestimate the evidential value of this statistic. It is indirect, and there were large concentrations in other commodities in the past as well.

However, it fits well with the interpretation that the structure of the futures markets has been altered due to the change in intervention activities since 2001. Furthermore, the week to 22 May 2001 is once again conspicuous, this time by dint of a strong increase in concentrations to a higher level, in addition to drawing attention to itself already due to the notable and also permanent increase in short positions held by commercials. What exactly happened in the week to 22 May 2001? We take a look at the intraday price movement over the weekend, more precisely an amalgamation of the two half trading days of Friday, 18 May and Sunday, 20 May 2001.[110]

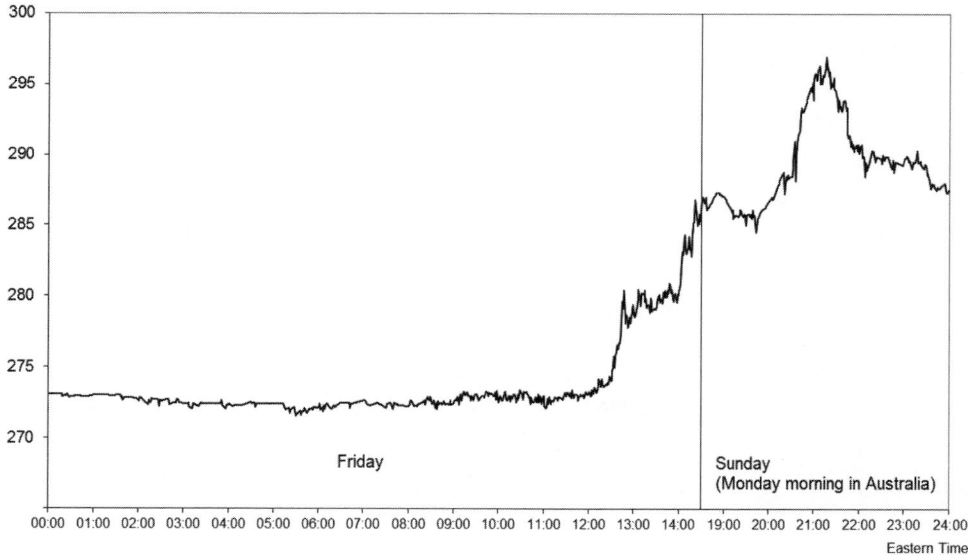

Figure 29.3 Intraday movement of gold from 18–20 May 2001

Figure 29.3 merges the close of trading in New York on Friday afternoon and the first few hours of trading on Monday morning in Sidney (which is equivalent to Sunday evening in New York).

Friday, 18 May 2001 started out quietly; there were only small fluctuations. At 12.31 the front month gold price suddenly went through the $275 level (in the spot market, shown here, it happened slightly later). It then continued to rise to almost $300 in the morning hours of the next trading day on Monday morning in Asia. This happened in thin trading over the weekend. The rally started without a catalyst. It amounted to almost 10 per cent within a few hours of trading. At the same time, it marked a structural change in the futures markets; since then, the commercials have been unable to extricate themselves from the short-side, and concentration has reached an elevated level. In addition, lease rates are since then at a very low level (even if the move to this level didn't start exactly in May). Although prices thereafter came down again one more time, 18 May 2001 marks a turning point.

We want to take a closer look at the situation back then in terms of press reports published at the time. The first thing that is conspicuous is that lease rates had risen noticeably in the preceding weeks, without a corresponding rise in prices. Central banks, therefore, didn't offer enough gold for gold-lending purposes; they had possibly changed their policy. Moreover, this time was also characterised by activities in public, in political circles and before the courts that were initiated by the organisation fighting against gold interventions, GATA. The background can be illuminated in detail with the help of an unofficial statement, which is shown here as an exception to the rule in order to clarify said background. This is because the statement gains a lot of credibility by means of the exact forecast it contains and its strong congruence with the (only later) discernible overall context of an altered structure of both the gold-lending business and the futures market.

On Monday, 14 May 2001, five days prior to the remarkable price increase, it was precisely forecast in an announcement. Bill Murphy of GATA wrote, in his information service, that Bob Chapman, the editor of another information service, had given him an advance excerpt from his market newsletter. In it he says:

> Our intelligence sources have informed us that Alan Greenspan has given the bullion banks until the end of May to clear up their hedging and outstanding gold derivative positions... They also said they thought that gold would break out over $275.00 an ounce by Friday.[111]

It is, therefore, not merely a price forecast, but an exact prediction of an extremely unusual event. The price would break out on Friday and accelerate at the $275 level (as Figure 29.3 shows). The rally occurred in thin trading, without a trigger and was exceptionally strong. The background it discusses, namely that the bullion banks should prepare for changes in terms of gold lending and futures trades, can later be discerned quite well in the statistics. This is why an unofficial statement is admitted into the book here as an exception. Moreover, proof of gold market interventions is not what this is about (which is exclusively proffered with the aid of verifiable sources), but the illumination of the background of one aspect.[112]

But who triggered the rally? At the time, a report appeared that at first glance looks like a 'penny dreadful', which, however, explains the events best. It was reported that a group had formed that wanted to force a short squeeze (i.e., a covering of the short positions held by bullion banks at markedly higher prices). George Soros was mentioned (who already 'broke' the Bank of England), as well as an Arab and a Chinese name. The executing houses on the buy side were said to be Refco and Moore Capital, on the side of the sellers were Goldman Sachs and Chase Manhattan. Whoever it was, it suggests that a concerted action for this purpose existed. It would basically have been a counter-cartel to the cartel of central banks and bullion banks – for the purpose of putting an end to the interventions. As a side effect, a sizable profit may have been obtained as well. Many things point to such a concerted action: the preceding leak of the rally (including the day and the price level), the point in time of 12.30, which looked like it was prearranged (similar to apparently 8.30 a.m. in 1993 at the beginning), the great strength of the rally, the lack of a catalyst and the capitalising on thin trading conditions over the weekend. In addition, there is a plausible background: a forced short squeeze could have been very profitable in view of the outstanding amount of gold on loan. There was, thus, an intense struggle behind the scenes. The bullion banks involved won one more time, with the help of several central banks. However, the structure of the futures market was permanently altered from that point in time onward. Furthermore, it appears that the structure of the gold-lending market has also changed since approximately that time.

To summarise: the central banks involved recognised that they wouldn't be able to hold the gold price at this level on a sustainable basis, and told the bullion banks that had bet on falling prices that they should prepare for rising prices. As the deadline, the end of May 2001 was specified, but this deadline was probably postponed one more time from May to the end of the year (until then the gold price would be held below $300 and only rise thereafter). The end of the second phase characterised by the carry trade was, thus, initiated; the interventions that have been ongoing since 5 August 1993 were converted to a new mode, which solely aimed to limit advances. At the same time, the beginning of the end of the gold market interventions was initiated, in the sense that the original main goal of preventing a gold price increase could no longer be achieved.

As additional gold that came to the market through gold lending fell away as an instrument of price suppression, the futures markets have been, increasingly, employed for interventions . The change started abruptly around noon of 18 May 2001. A group of well-informed large investors, who took issue with the gold interventions and wanted to make money at the same time, had undertaken to break the cartel of bullion banks and central banks and force them to give up their positions. Apparently, 12.30 was the agreed-upon time to begin buying; a minute later the agreed-upon level of $275 was breached in the futures contract, with the goal of producing a rapid rise in thin trading. This was supposed to entice others to hop aboard, forcing them to cover and thereby create an upward push. The bullion banks, presumably with the direct support of several central banks, stemmed themselves against it and were able to intercept the price below $300 and bring it down again over the coming days. To do so, they had to take on large short positions, which they have been unable to reduce ever since, as evident in the statistics published by the regulatory authority. Moreover, they were given more time, until the end of 2001, to be able to better prepare for a rising price. Since then, the price has risen, representing an orderly but slow retreat of the interventionists. In order to minimise potential losses on the part of the bullion banks, the central banks have, since then, reduced the lease rate to near zero.

Just as 5 August 1993 initiated the beginning of the systematic interventions in the gold market, so 18 May 2001 ended the time when gold could be prevented from rising by means of leasing out additional gold. Interventions in the futures markets have been the dominant feature since then, and the price rise could only be slowed down. It is this change in the *modus operandi* on the futures market, together with the conjectured demand of Greenspan with regard to gold loans, which makes 18 May 2011 for the upward move in the gold market what 5 August 1993 is for the downward move: a decisive date for an overarching trend in the gold market, but also for the effects on the other financial markets and the real economy connected with it. With the former, the impetus for the financial market bubble, which had been begun concurrently with the gold market interventions on 5 August 1993, also expired. Although the trend change in the stock market had begun earlier – technology stocks, in particular, had already declined – it is still remarkable that on the following Monday, 21 May 2001, the Dow Jones Industrial Average made an important high (it was often suspected at the time that there were interventions in the stock markets as well, especially in the Dow) (see Figure 29.4). In the overarching picture, the stock markets put in a multi-year peak around the turn of the millennium, and gold a multi-year low. Whether it is coincidence or there is a connection (and if so, of what kind), the suppression of gold is never solely about the gold market, but also about its antagonist, the world of credit and credit money. It should also be mentioned here that the beginning of the end, on 18 May 2001, was no longer directed by the central banks, but by the market – specifically, a number of market participants (similar to the end of the pegging of the pound at the beginning of the EMS crisis).

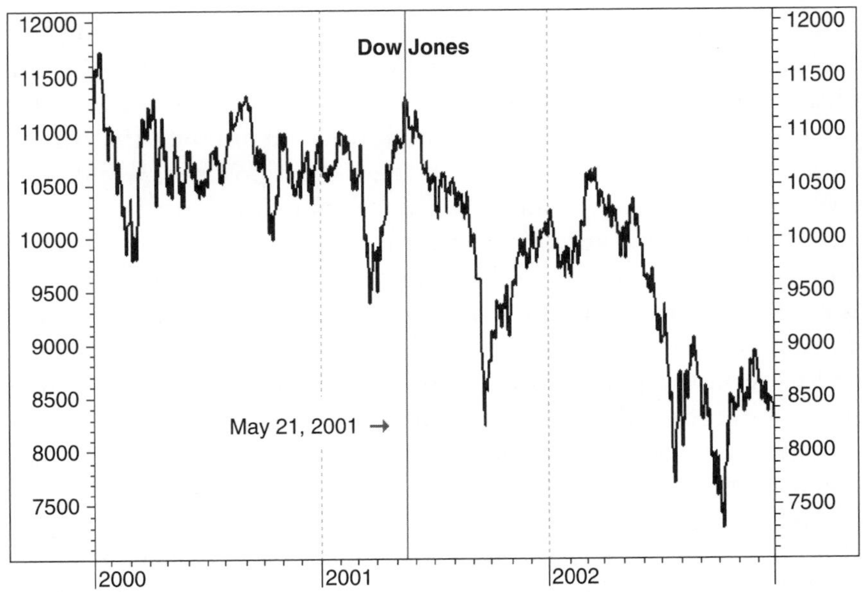

Figure 29.4 Dow Jones Industrial Average, 2000–02

Traces left in the market and in documents have helped us to gain an understanding regarding the motives, actors and actions connected with the systematic interventions that shape the gold market since 5 August 1993. Many things, however, remain unexplained for now. Among them is the specific motive of the UK administration for its advance announcements, the motives on the part of governments in favour of falling prices in Phase II since 1996, the names of the institutions in charge in both the public and private sectors, the profits of private sector participants as well as their potential later losses and, of course, many details, ranging from the split within the institutions at the turning point in 1999 to the precise circumstances of May 2001 to the specific *modus operandi* employed in shock-like interventions and the covering of short positions. We have seen motives that are understandable, such as the fighting of crises, and suspect that were also questionable ones, such as the profits of the gold carry traders (and on the part of central banks – the responsiveness to their lobbying).

Among the monetary policy motives of central banks there was the fight against rising inflation expectations, with the goal of lowering inflation rates and capital market yields. The question arises whether this medication has worked, but also what its side effects were. Have gold market interventions contributed to the financial market architecture of the late 1990s? Did they add to the stock market bubble, the later real estate bubble, the current account deficit of the USA and the rise in debt everywhere? And hasn't, perhaps, all of humanity lived in a giant financial bubble for years – a bubble which, among other things, has been blown up even further with the help of the gold price suppression?

Chapter 30

The Effects of Gold Price Suppression

Many trails point to interventions in the precious metals market and make it possible to analyse the causes. Now, we want to turn to the question of what the consequences of these persistent interventions were. What is further of interest are the fundamental facts concerning the two antagonists in the realm of liquid stores of value: the difficult–to-duplicate, debtor-free commodity money gold, on the one hand, and the easy-to-multiply-at-will, default-prone credit and credit money on the other.

Let us, first, look at the magnitude of the amounts involved in the gold market interventions. If one assumes a total of 170,000 tons of gold that have been mined so far, then a mere price movement of $200 per ounce, which was surely achieved by price interventions, represents a financial loss of $1,093 billion. Not all the gold is actually available any more, so one would have to assume a smaller total. However, the assumption that gold would have at least intermittently traded at a more than $200 higher level despite the interventions seems realistic. The estimate of a roughly $1 trillion financial loss suffered by gold holders is, thus, a reference amount for the size of the intervention. It would probably rank as the biggest instance of financial damage in history, and, if one were to regard it as fraudulent, the biggest fraud ever! The damage is quite real, even if for example, an individual owner of a wedding ring doesn't realise it, and even if it is only of a temporary nature (assuming that the interventions will ultimately fail). There are, of course, also tangibly affected parties, be it investors holding gold, people forced to sell family heirlooms in an emergency, mine workers that have lost wages, or commodity-producing countries that have lost tax revenues.

When judging the damage, one must differentiate whether the interventions are pursued by private parties with a view to profit or by government in the interest of a better monetary policy. Naturally, the damage is put into perspective if it is juxtaposed with intended positive effects of gold market interventions, such as the lowering of inflation expectations and inflation. However, these effects have to be put into the context, not only of their intended short-term positive outcomes, but also their possibly negative long-term consequences. Often interventions in the markets have short-term positive effects, but quite negative long-term ones! This is widely recognised in connection with the real economy, but in the realm of money and credit these concatenations often remain misunderstood.

We want to divide the effects of gold price suppression into two groups: on the one hand, those that concern mainly the dollar; on the other hand, those that concern money and credit more generally. The gold price suppression was supposed to support the dollar. It was designed to motivate foreign investors, especially foreign central banks, to invest in dollars. Moreover, it was supposed to help with financing the US trade deficit. Since the 1950s, the USA has had an external deficit, spending more output and capital overseas than it earns. The temptation to do this was initially considerable, given that it called the greatest gold treasure on earth its own. However, as so often happens, small deficits add up after a while and the gold holdings diminished ever more, leading to the collapse of the gold exchange standard in 1971. Since then, a pure paper money system has been in force worldwide for the first time.

The cutting of the tie to gold, however, actually began several years earlier. Germany, as one of the most important dollar-holding countries, passed on exchanging dollars for gold in the 1960s. This was explicitly confirmed in the already mentioned 1967 letter written by Karl Blessing. More than 40 years ago, a system was thus introduced that, in principle, still works in the same manner today and shapes the political and economic state of the world. We want to take a closer look at what happened back then and what people were thinking.

The Americans had military bases in Germany. In 1967, they wanted Germany to share more of the costs. Germany only wanted to participate to a limited extent, but it also didn't want to risk the protection provided by US troops. Even the defence alliance hung in the balance. As a result, it was decided to employ a trick: with the government's backing, then Bundesbank president Karl Blessing pledged to no longer exchange dollars for gold, but to be satisfied with US treasury paper instead. The Americans left their troops in place. In the face of the massed forces of the Eastern Bloc the Germans didn't have the courage to join the French, who continued to demand gold from the USA. The underlying mechanism of financing public debt by international central banks has been of fundamental importance to the political and economic order since then.

The extent to which today's monetary order was already created at the time is made clear by a contemporary report to the US president. It explains the mechanism quite well. It describes the German agreement not to exchange dollars for gold in 1967:

> In effect it will put the Germans on a dollar standard. And it is an enormous first step toward getting the other Europeans (ex-France) to agree to the same kind of rules. If we succeed... we will no longer need to worry about reasonable balance of payments deficits.[113]

American troops needed to be financed. Countries like Germany only had a limited willingness to share in the costs directly. Instead, they financed the troops by means of their central banks buying US debt. US interest costs were reduced and external economic effects were neutralised. Foreign central banks have financed the US external deficit since then. The USA can, thus, pay abroad on credit in its own currency. Previously, gold stood in the way, and it would be standing in the way today as well. Should foreign central banks demand the supra-national currency gold, this system would break down. That is as true today as it was in 1967. However, different countries are involved today; Germany's importance in terms of foreign exchange reserves has declined. Over time, more or less all central banks have participated in this financing.

They did so as a result of other motives as well, including the subsidisation of their own export industries. Moreover, they prefer the dollar due to the market's size, its importance in trade and on account of the relatively small political and military risks dollar investments entail. These reasons, however, don't suffice to explain that the dollar often represents a share of up to 75 per cent of the foreign exchange reserves of central banks.[114] They could invest their reserves in all sorts of currencies, but haven't done so for decades. The central banks of the world thereby finance the US military presence overseas. They do that even if their countries are against US decisions about wars in specific instances, or if they belong to a different cultural and political sphere – and even if (such as the Chinese) they sometimes are touted as potential future wartime enemies. Certainly, foreign central banks are given incentives to buy US treasury paper – and one of the means to this end is gold price suppression, which plays a role regarding the fact that the share of financing of the US public debt by foreign central banks has increased from less than 10 per cent to approximately 25 per cent. These countries are not threatened; at most, they could suffer the revocation of protection. Apart from Germany in the 1960s, this has probably been true for countries like Japan or Taiwan, with their pronounced security dependence on the US. However, even for other countries this military motive may play a role, in the sense of a 'Pax Americana', which delivers a predictable measure of safe trade, investment security and raw material supply – and of general security.

An overarching power, even if it is imperfect, limits conflict. This is so in preschool, in the schoolyard, in civilian life, between tribes and also between states. The big wars in Europe in the first half of the 20th century, or the legion of religious conflicts in the Muslim world since time immemorial, demonstrate the high level of peace that has prevailed over recent decades. It was the precondition for the enormous global economic upswing during these years. The fact that the Americans didn't do it out of altruism, that they didn't act militarily as an impartial judge and that they didn't grasp the opportunity offered by the end of the East–West conflict to further develop international law, doesn't alter the fundamental principle.

It doesn't matter what criteria precisely the central banks of the world use to decide on the composition of their reserves. The connection to security policy is well documented for Germany in the 1960s; for other countries similar reasons may have been applicable – the others should at least have been aware that they were partly also financing the military. In the end, it doesn't matter whether they actively participated in financing the 'Pax Americana' or whether a status quo has emerged as a result of a historical process. In their totality, the nations of the world willingly financed the existing order. The decisive building block was indirectly via their central banks, where the international US debt piled up (the settlement of international trade in US dollars – the 'petrodollar' – only played an indirect role, because foreign claims against the USA are essential).

In the assessment undertaken here, in the sense of a 'Pax Americana', which the other nations voluntarily supported in order to maintain the status quo, the voluntary nature of the decision-making process with regard to foreign exchange reserves plays a role. Although this only applied to a limited extent due to the gold price interventions, it was definitely significant in the context of the more important question whether and how much is to be invested in the dollar. Voluntariness presupposes the possibility of being informed. That was a given, at least in expert circles, even though the tenor of public information was different ('the US consumer strengthens the global economy'). The true state of affairs, how the abandonment of gold convertibility and the creation of dollar reserves served to finance the US military, has been prominently publicised since the 1970s.[115] But a one-sided evaluation via imperialism falls short, as the financing was not the result of a military threat (at least, there is no evidence that the Americans would, for instance, have bombed China if the Chinese had put a billion less into financing the US current account deficit). One must picture the whole situation as a process of successive decisions.

Independent of the (also variable) motives, the ending of the dollar's tie to gold (formally in the early 1970s) and the build-up of dollar reserves at foreign central banks are closely connected with the financing of the US military. Not only was it carried out from abroad, but also in individual currencies (which could be devalued). The Americans, nevertheless, gradually paid a price internally, as they could ultimately not avert the drawbacks of a current account deficit. The constantly overvalued dollar exchange rate weakened their own industry, and the eager buying of debt instruments by foreign central banks furthered the growth in indebtedness.

The gold price suppression since August 1993 is part of a system that has existed since the late 1960s to finance the external deficit and the 'Pax Americana', to support the dollar and make the unbacked dollar in foreign trade what gold (or silver) was previously. We want to spell out what magnitudes are involved nowadays. Figure 30.1 shows the foreign exchange reserves of the central banks of Japan and China ('foreign exchange reserves' is actually a misleading term, as a fraction of these amounts would suffice as a reserve; it has long ago become a global financing mechanism). The rise in the curve after 1993 is notable, when the systematic gold market interventions began.

The immediate main motive of the countries involved is the subsidisation of their own export industries. It is a costly subsidisation, as the amounts are so immense that they themselves determine the exchange rate. China's central bank alone has reserves worth $3,000 billion, which are mostly held in US dollars. If it tried to use them for anything, it would have to put up with marked exchange rate losses. These losses (i.e., the difference between the current exchange rate and that which would have resulted without

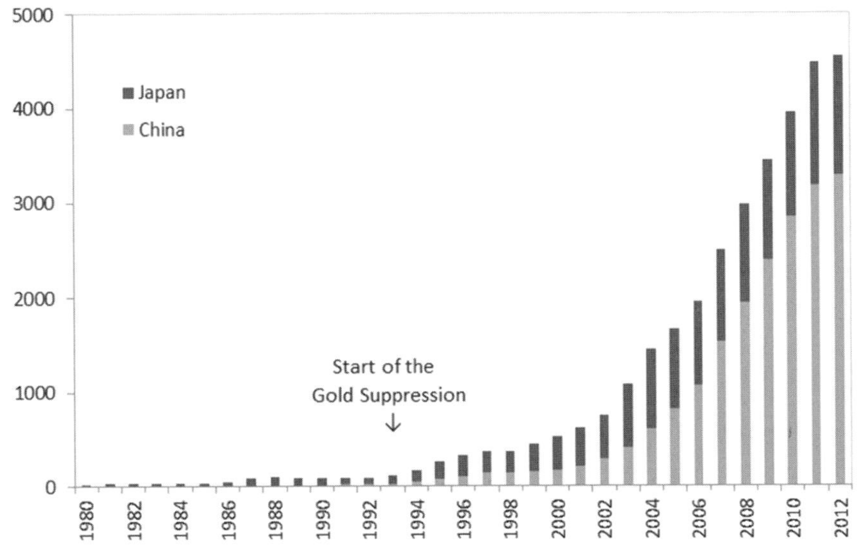

Figure 30.1 Foreign exchange reserves of Japan and China

these foreign exchange interventions) are, in effect, the subsidy and should effectively be written off. They are not visible in the central bank's balance sheet because it determines the exchange rate itself. In view of this one-sided arrangement, China has recently increasingly attempted to reduce the share of the dollar in its reserves.

By buying the dollar, a foreign central bank not only subsidises its own export industry, but also the US consumer. Moreover, it supports the US government, which can refinance itself at favourable terms and which can afford its international deficits only because other central banks are willing to finance them. These events have to be seen in the context of the global credit and money creation process, in which especially China has manoeuvred itself into a dilemma, as it is a creditor depending on a debtor whom it must continue to finance so that its debt instruments don't lose value. The Americans, in turn, are dependent on China buying treasury debt, which is why they have been unable to take any steps against China's subsidisation of exports, which harms US industry (for instance, by imposing tariffs). What has attained such incredible proportions nowadays began almost casually with the pledge of Germany's Bundesbank president in 1967! Figure 30.2 makes the increasing willingness of foreign countries to finance the US public debt clear.

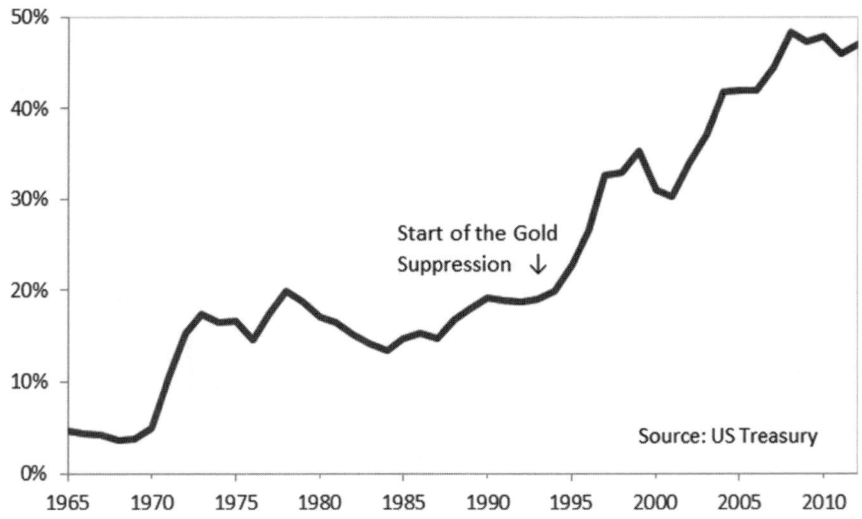

Figure 30.2 Share of foreign holders of US federal debt

One can see how big the share of foreigners (i.e., central banks, in particular) among holders of US treasury debt is. In the 1960s it was marginal, but it rose markedly with the cutting of the dollar's tie to gold in the early 1970s. While the foreign share was below 20 per cent for the following 20 years, it quickly rose during the mid-90s to about 50 per cent. Both increases are connected with gold. The first one was set into motion by the fact that foreign central banks could no longer exchange dollars for gold. In the course of the second one, the artificially suppressed gold price apparently contributed to dollar investments being favoured. Foreigners, especially central banks, bought US treasuries as a result of the gold policy in the 1970s, as they needed to build up foreign exchange reserves due to the abolition of gold convertibility and, in the 1990s, as foreign exchange appeared more attractive to them than it really was due to the low gold price. The two phases that began in 1971 and 1993, thus, are determined politically (by monetary policy), in that the importance of gold was reduced (not by the development of the gold price, which went up in the former period and down in the latter). We now want to see what importance gold has for central banks and to this end take a look at gold's share of global central bank reserves (Figure 30.3).

At the end of the 19th century, after gold had superseded silver and a gold exchange standard was only in the process of being established, gold's share of all central bank reserves stood at about

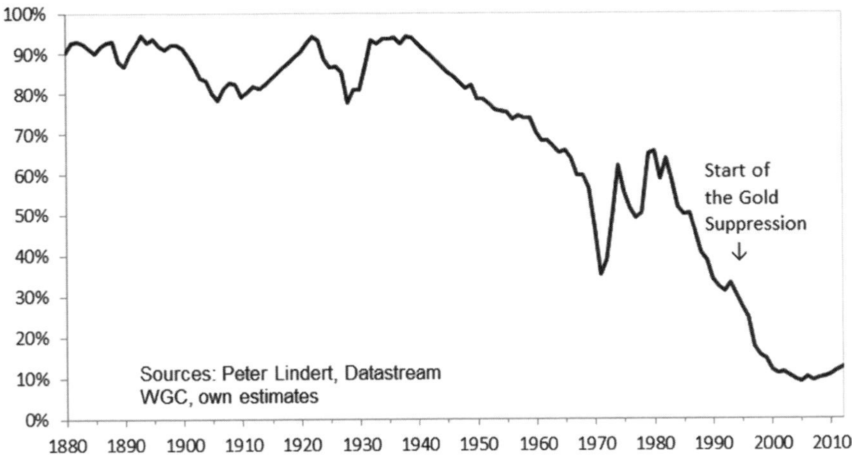

Figure 30.3 Gold's share of total central bank reserves

90 per cent. Until 1950 it was above 80 per cent most of the time; since then it has been falling amid fluctuations (it fluctuated especially in the 1970s due to the end of gold convertibility and the subsequent strong increase in the gold price). In 1993, as the systematic gold market interventions began, the share was still above 33 per cent (the small spike in Figure 30.3). Within a few years it fell by two-thirds to about 10 per cent! This strong decline was also a consequence of the gold market interventions, as holdings declined (due to sales), prices declined as well and currencies were favoured as an alternative.

Since the 1970s, central banks have not used gold for their payments; however, it has been an alternative reserve asset. Due to their tasks, the importance of gold is greater in the world of central banks than among other investors (few liquid alternatives, no domestic investments, etc.). Consequently the share of reserves held in the form of gold, is in most cases, greater than among private investors. Central banks are, thereby, subject to a natural dichotomy, as a suppressed gold price affects them in two directions: it makes gold less attractive and thus increases the allure of dollar-denominated investments, but at the same time it erodes the value of existing reserves.

The USA values gold differently for balance sheet purposes than the European nations, at a very low price, so it is less sensitive in this regard (which is perhaps an additional explanation for why the Washington Agreement was initiated primarily by Europe). The share of gold in reserves is actually much higher in the

USA and many European nations than in other, especially Asian nations. In the USA, Germany, France and Italy it amounts to about 75 per cent. It is, perhaps, no coincidence that other central banks invest predominantly in foreign exchange issued by countries that have a large share of gold reserves (at least, it follows the tradition of the gold exchange standard, in which the currencies of countries with gold-backed money are held as reserves). The Asian nations are large reserve holders, for instance, but their currencies are held by almost no one (Japan's currency is considered for to a small extent). There are, however, more important reasons why the central banks don't bid adieu to their gold. Greenspan already said it: gold is always accepted, but currencies can become worthless due to political, financial or military events. Central banks, as the ultimate money and credit authorities, possess an inviolable reserve with gold. Who, if not they, should hold the ultimate means of payment? And among them, in turn, primarily whose currencies are held as a reserve? However, gold creates confidence even in normal times. It is important as an investment as it tends to move inversely to the dollar.

One real economic consequence of the exceptionally large accumulation of currency reserves was the growing current account deficit of the USA (Figure 30.4). It is primarily due to an excess of imports over exports. In this context a parallel exists to the period beginning with the late 1960s, when gold's importance was reduced with the definite intention of pushing through an ongoing external deficit. From the mid-1990s, making gold unattractive by means of systematic interventions helped with the financing of the deficit by foreign central banks and with strengthening the dollar. The dollar's exchange rate tended to be too high for US industry. The consequence of the strong dollar policy was a sated US consumer who didn't produce enough in his role as producer. One can easily see that the US current account deficit has risen to a level since the mid-1990s that has probably never before been seen in such a great nation.

The main difference to other countries is, however, the special role of the USA in the specific financial architecture since the mid-1990s, with a suppressed gold price, a higher dollar and higher demand for treasury bonds (especially among central banks), low interest rates, financial market bubbles, overconsumption and a current account deficit. A current account deficit of this size is, however, not historically unique, by a long shot – only its cause is. In the

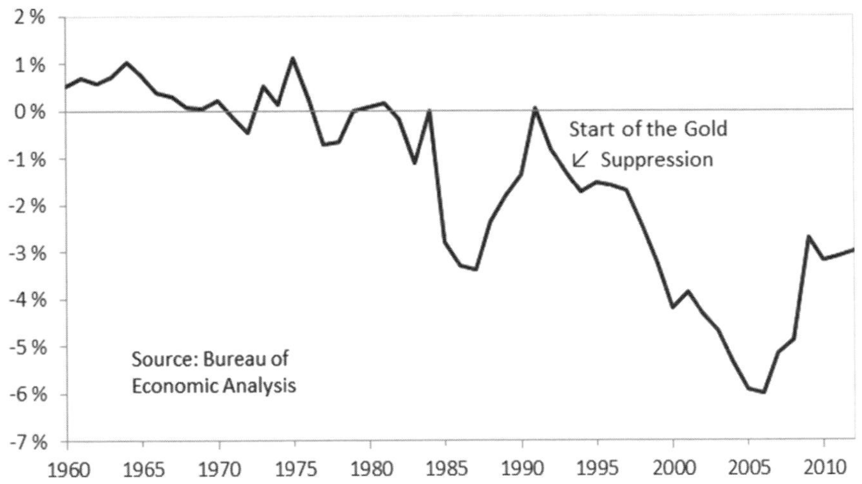

Figure 30.4 US current account deficit

case of the US the position of the dollar as the reserve currency artificially influences the exchange rate, whereas in other cases it is mostly currency pegs (without the balancing mechanism of a gold standard) that create current account deficits (such as in the case of the affected nations prior to the Asian crisis or the euro crisis). The mechanisms are comparable; the USA has had a chronically overvalued currency for years as well as artificially low interest rates. The result is a consumer sector bloated by credit financing to the detriment of the competitiveness of domestic industry. The political decision for this wasn't taken for the first time with the systematic gold market interventions from 1993, but earlier, in 1967, when the tie to gold was increasingly abandoned in favour of steady deficits, which other central banks financed. Due to their purchases of US treasury bonds, the dollar's exchange rate tended to be raised, and interest rates were reduced. As often happens, politicians only gave thought to a comfortable means of financing the budget deficit, not to the long-term consequences for the nation as a whole. Since then the USA has moved on from its once strong position as a creditor nation and has built up large debts with foreign nations. Now it is forced to deal with the contradictory situation of requiring a strong dollar for reasons of financing, which, however, damages domestic industry, which, in turn, is needed to be healthy from a real economic standpoint. Other countries that had a comparable current account deficit have usually corrected it, most of the time after having been forced to do so by a crisis. The market is always in motion; it also seeks to attain equilibrium, though, and corrects previous incorrect political decisions and undesirable socio-economic developments. Even the US current account deficit has lately decreased somewhat (Figure 30.4), especially due to the financial market crisis of 2008. However, the USA remains far from a neutral position, not to mention surpluses which would be needed to reduce the debt position that has been built up with foreign nations over many years.

Chapter 31

The Wonderful World of Bubbles

In the 1960s, one was probably barely able to imagine these developments, but they began at the time when what are, from today's perspective, minimal aberrations were not corrected. The largest negative development was, however, not in foreign trade, but the steadily increasing level of indebtedness. It, too, is connected with the abandonment of gold. Although gold cannot prevent credit excesses, it still works as a brake. In the already mentioned 1967 report to the US president on the occasion of Germany's waiving of its right to exchange dollars against gold, the following remarkable sentence can be found: 'This arrangement will not give us an unlimited printing press. But as long as we run our economy as responsibly as in the past few years, it will permit us to live with moderate deficits indefinitely.'[116] It was known, at the time, that cutting the tie to gold would make 'unlimited' deficits possible – it was even the goal! From the perspective of government, it is convenient to get funding as easily as possible. However, is indebtedness in perpetuity desirable for a nation?

We want to turn to credit now. Debt is always only one side of the coin; every debt has as its counterpart an asset, a credit claim. The credit claim is the obverse of the debt. Debt, credit claim and the neutral term credit all concern the same thing, but each of them describes a different side of it. When one speaks of indebtedness, one also emphasises the effort of servicing the debt. Ministers of finance complain when the public debt increases, as they have to raise more funds in the following year to service interest costs. The effort of servicing a debt can represent a great burden and, in terms of personal fates, can lead to great misery, while macro-economically the potential problems on the side of credit claims are immeasurably larger.

This is because every credit claim contains a power, the potential to demand goods in the market and set inflation into motion, but also a kind of powerlessness, the risk of default, which can create a chain reaction of plummeting demand and trigger a deflationary collapse. Both the threat of inflationary devaluation and the threat of a deflationary collapse are the shadows that accompany every economy in which credit claims exist. Ever since credit claims have appeared on the scene in macro-economically relevant sizes, these problems have existed. All over the world and throughout history there have been thousands of cases in which these shadows unfolded their effects. Credit-driven bubbles emerged and then burst. There were recessions, crises and utter collapses. Of all problems related to money and credit, the bubble is the only one that has hitherto not been resolved. It is also the only one that is fundamentally not solvable. One can, however, handle it better. It is, therefore, one of the most important things in economics to understand credit claim-driven bubbles.

When Greenspan took over the chairmanship of the Fed in 1987, it was he, of all people, who, as a staunch proponent of a free market economy, presided over the supreme regulatory authority. When Greenspan took over the chairmanship of the Fed in 1987, he even became leader of an institution the existence of which he had previously – as evidenced by an essay that was published in 1966 – strongly opposed.[117] Life is always good for surprises. In 1966, he was in favour of reducing excessive credit growth by subsequent recessions. Now, he led the very institution that was supposed to prevent precisely those recessions and thus boosted credit growth. By providing sufficient liquidity in every crisis (which was later referred to as the 'Greenspan put'), he energetically pursued the opposite of what had once been his conviction. Once he had arrived in political practice, he looked towards short-term solutions.

In the beginning, as Greenspan took over the chairmanship of the Fed, he was still in favour of a tight monetary policy. He was the only one who realised that a bubble had developed in the stock market. His colleagues and 200-strong staff of advisers were clueless. Greenspan noticed that the increase in asset values made people feel richer and enticed them to increase their spending, which led to an overheating of the economy and threatened a devaluation of money. Greenspan, therefore, pushed through the first hike in the discount rate in three years in September 1987, as well as a sharp increase in the federal funds rate, in order to brake a further increase in share prices. Shortly thereafter, the stock market crash occurred. Recalling the global economic crisis of the 1930s, which followed on the heels of the stock market crash of 1929, people feared the worst. Possibly, the crash was a formative experience and the cause for abstaining from a restrictive monetary policy henceforth.

When Greenspan became Fed chairman in 1987, the USA had situation in which, on an economy-wide basis, debt relative to real economic magnitudes such as GDP was historically high, and at best an effort to reduce it borne by all relevant forces would still have been of avail. He couldn't have achieved a reduction in the level of credit as defined in his 1966 essay all by himself.

When Greenspan became Fed chairman in 1987, he became part of an institution that had the legally mandated goals of preserving price stability and ensuring sustainable economic growth, not of limiting the amount of outstanding credit. Perhaps he had such a limitation in mind, perhaps he was still thinking of the necessity of reducing too generously granted loans as per his deliberations of 1966, when he was the only one who argued for an increase in the discount rate in 1987 and then pushed it through. His statements, however, revolved around the threat of inflation. His priorities were the stability of the purchasing power of money, economic growth and, perhaps, the reduction of government debt, but the reduction of debt in the other sectors of the economy was no longer priority.

When Greenspan became Fed chairman in 1987, he may still have been favourably disposed to the gold standard. This is supported by the clarity and thoughtfulness of his theses in his 1966 essay, as well as the fact that he sympathised with the gold standard in 1981 and even in 1998 (but over the years he appears to have shifted his focus from the amount of credit outstanding to price stability).[118] Such a strongly held stance is not something one simply abandons within just a few years. He would, however, not have been in a position to push the gold standard through against the political establishment.

When Greenspan became Fed chairman in 1987, a bubble was already in evidence, an overhang of credit claims on a society-wide basis, and Greenspan was part of an institution the power of which would not have been sufficient to limit the totality of credit claims and even less to decrease it. It was actually almost the other way around. If one rigorously implements the goals of the Fed, namely price stability and sustainable economic growth, but not a limitation of credit claims, this leads to the perfect bubble. For these goals lead to growth by means of the steady expansion of the amount of credit claims, which (at first) doesn't affect prices. That is what happened in the 1990s: the economy grew, the employment rate was high, prices were stable, asset values increased. It was paradise. Was it an illusory paradise? The amount of claims or rather debts or rather credits increased. That could contain the seed of future problems. Let us, first, look at how a bubble actually works.

Credit-financed bubbles result from credit-financed purchases. Let us take a closer look at such a purchase. You have $100,000 in an account and want to buy a house that costs $200,000. Both parties together – you, as the prospective buyer, and the later seller possess wealth of $300,000. You go to your bank, borrow $100,000 and buy the house. Now the balance sheet of the two parties looks as follows: you own the house worth $200,000 and have a debt of $100,000, after deducting the debt your wealth thus amounts to $100,000. The seller has the $200,000 in his account. The total wealth of both parties therefore once again amounts to $300,000 – to be expected, since no value was created.

So much for the static consideration of an individual case. The real world is, however, dynamic and there are many individual cases. Let us examine the credit-financed purchase again: the credit financing has made the purchase possible in the first place; without it, it wouldn't have taken place. The credit financing itself has, therefore, created demand. According to the law of supply and demand, additional demand also increases prices. Although, if one considers the individual case in a static manner, the total wealth of the two parties is the same before and after the purchase, it is different in a dynamic world with numerous credit-financed purchases. In actual fact, credit-financed purchases lead to an increase in the level of prices. If, therefore, many people in a region take out loans to buy houses, house prices will rise. They do so although nothing has changed in real terms. Credit financing is the only reason for the price increase.

What does the price increase mean for financial statements? Let us assume that, on account of many credit-financed purchases in the region concerned, the value of the house increases from $200,000 to, say, $300,000. After subtracting your debt you now have a fortune amounting to $200,000, while the seller continues to have $200,000 in his account.[119] The total wealth of both parties now amounts to $400,000! The additional purchases that were enabled by additional credit creation lead, in the example, to an increase in wealth of $100,000, without anyone having lifted a finger to produce anything tangible. In a credit-financed bubble, additional credit-financed purchases thus lead to a rising price level of assets. The totality of all credit-financed purchases leads, in a dynamic process, to the participants booking profits without anything having been created. They feel richer although in reality nothing has changed.[120]

We are confronted with a decision-making problem: the books do not reflect the real world! Simply by way of financial transactions, a total fortune of $300,000 became one of $400,000. In the real economy something would have to be produced for that – for instance, the house expanded by half. The problem is not that nothing has been created as such, as profits made in the financial economy can make macro-economic and micro-economic sense as well. The problem of the credit-financed bubble is that all participants have become more wealthy, that there was no loss while a profit emerged elsewhere. When all participants become wealthier by means of nothing but accounting procedures, essential decision-making fundamentals are influenced. The profits from price increases are booked, but they have no basis in real changes in the economic situation. Their only basis are the credit-financed purchases themselves.

Since, in bubbles, credit-financed purchases lift the level of prices and, thus, simulate an increase in wealth that exists only on the books but not in reality, they suspend the short-term regulative forces of the market. A marketplace cannot be efficient when mere accounting activities lead to similar changes in decision-making processes as real production activity. The credit-financed purchase, that has this 'self-induced' profitability, is by its nature the creator of a mirage. It is only justifiable if, somewhere else in the system, a loan of commensurate size is paid back, so that by its repayment the total amount of credit isn't increased (or only increases in line with economic growth).

The failure of market efficiency due to the pretence of profit makes credit-financed bubbles into processes that are not immediately corrected, but, similar to chain letter systems, only at a later stage. Economic history is full of examples of credit-financed bubbles that, at first, led to a boom that was later corrected by painful price declines and recessions. In terms of timing, the correction may occur one year after the bubble starts, but often it takes several years and sometimes even decades to take effect. Historically, the correction always happened, unless it was prevented by government intervention.

Such a correction is marked by the reversal of all the activities that previously accompanied the emergence of the bubble. The elevated level of prices deflates and the amount of credit outstanding is likewise reduced. The latter happens by means of defaults – that is, the bankruptcy of debtors. Just as during the formation of a bubble additional purchases made possible by credit creation raised prices, the bursting of a bubble leads to sales due to credit defaults and, with them, prices are lowered (there are, however, other mechanisms in play as well, which is why the price level begins to decline before there are defaults). The bursting of the bubble also destroys the wealth that was previously booked, but not created. It disappears from financial statements, but also from people's minds. They now feel poorer again. It is, ultimately, the desire of human beings to become rich that leads to the emergence of bubbles and that makes it so difficult to accept their bursting.

It is not the laws of the market that fail, but their efficiency. Economic laws assert themselves in bubble periods as well, but they do so with a lag (whereby it generally holds that the closer money is tied to gold, the earlier; the more government intervention there is, the later). During bubbles, a multitude of aberrations occur. Credit-financed bubbles, as a rule, are not sensible. While they can accelerate trends, their cost is, nevertheless, higher than their benefit, as a great many undesirable developments occur on account of them (details on this below). There are only very few cases in which credit-financed bubbles make sense – for example, if they anticipate a local price increase (for instance, in the case of real estate in an enclosed bay, which is opened for tourism by a new road). However, this is also only the case if the increase in credit at that location is accompanied by a reduction in credit elsewhere, so that it amounts to a shift, or if it is supported by economic growth. Otherwise, the entire economy will ultimately be affected by it.

Whenever a credit-financed bubble increases the amount of outstanding credit claims in an entire economy, it has the character of a credit-creation process that pays for itself. It doesn't matter where the bubble occurs. Often, there are bubbles in real estate, but also in stock markets (i.e., in enterprises). There were, however, historical bubbles that are quite astonishing in hindsight, such as the tulipomania of the 17th century. Bubbles can also jump from one item to another, such as the bubble in technology stocks in the USA at the end of the 1990s, which, at the turn of the millennium, was replaced by one in real estate. Credit-financed bubbles, however, can also encompass several asset classes at once, such as real estate and stocks in Japan in the late 80s, or can finally broaden to include the entire economy.

Credit-financed bubbles are characterised by self-induced profitability. This brings forth the typical bubble phenomenon that bubbles reinforce themselves. The movement often accelerates in the late stages of the bubble. The backdrop to this is that the increase in values leads to a reduction in debts – at least in accounting terms. In the example above, the property was worth $200,000 in the beginning and a $100,000 mortgage loan was taken out on it. After prices had risen, the value of the house stood at $300,000, but the mortgage debt still only amounted to $100,000. So the loan on the property initially amounted to 50 per cent of its value, but later only to 33.33 per cent. At a similar loan-to-value level of 50 per cent, a new buyer of this or a similar property now could borrow $150,000 and thereby contribute to further increases in prices. This leads to a feedback loop in which purchases that pay for themselves through credit creation reinforce each other and push the price level ever higher. Figure 31.1 illustrates this self-propelling feedback loop in a credit-financed stock market bubble. Since the mechanism only increases wealth in terms of an accounting fiction, but not in reality, credit-financed bubbles, as a rule, burst after some time.

At this point, permit us to briefly hark back to the gold carry trade as a parenthesis: it has led to the first inverted bubble in history! The bubble feedback loop of the carry trade was precisely inverse to the typical bubble feedback loop: gold was borrowed and sold – in the conventional bubble, money is borrowed and something else (like real estate) is bought. The additional supply led to a decline in prices – in a conventional bubble the additional demand leads to price increases. The decline in prices resulted in a profit for the gold borrowers solely by means of selling the borrowed gold – in a conventional bubble the rise in prices leads to profits for the borrowers of money. These profits in turn created the opportunity to borrow even more gold and set the bubble feedback loop into motion – in a conventional bubble, correspondingly, more money is borrowed.

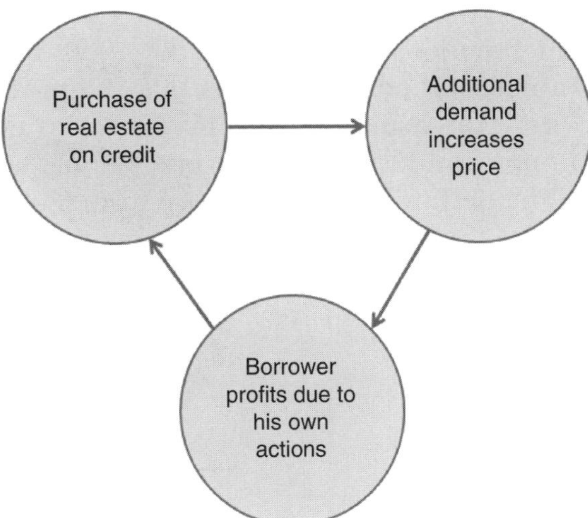

Figure 31.1 Conventional credit bubble

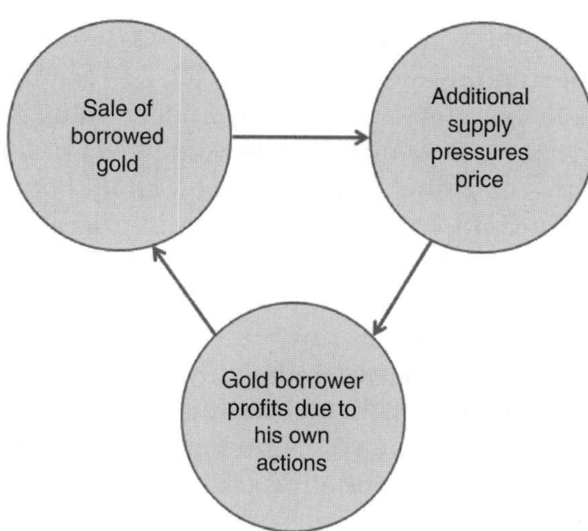

Figure 31.2 The inverse bubble of the gold carry trade

An inverse bubble is, thus, the exact mirror image of a conventional bubble. Due to the gold carry trade (and, more generally, the gold-lending business) the first inverse bubble in history was created in the 1990s (insofar as one relates bubbles, as is usually done, to the prices of goods and not to currencies or a single stock). The precondition was the easy availability of goods, as it is given only with gold due to its inventories exceeding annual consumption many times. Another precondition was the introduction of the gold-lending business from the early 1980s in the wake of the end of the gold exchange standard. Although the causes of the second phase of the interventions at the end of the 1990s are only partly known, we can make an educated guess that the profits of private bullion banks were the main motive. This process is even easier to understand if one considers that an inverse bubble was occurring (Figure 31.2). The decline in the gold price from $400 to $250 per ounce at the end of the 1990s was the 'top point' – and viewed from the perspective of the price movement the 'low point' – of the first inverse bubble in history.

Chapter 32

Have Many Mini-Bubbles Created a Mega-Bubble?

A conventional, credit-financed bubble is, thus, a self-reinforcing feedback loop. In a credit bubble – with, for instance, purchases of stocks or real estate on credit – a buyer profits from rising prices, concurrently creating additional demand and so generating rising prices, by means of which he himself makes purchases on credit profitable – until the bubble bursts. Economic history is full of such bubbles: in 1635 there was a bubble in tulip bulbs in Holland; in 1720 the Mississippi and concurrently the South Sea bubble took place; around 1760 there was a boom in Prussia; around 1835 there was a land boom in the USA; and, one decade later, there was a railway boom in Germany. One could arbitrarily continue the enumeration – there were bubbles even in antiquity or in ancient China. Bubbles emerge as soon as there are developed markets in which payments are made with promises to pay. Early forms existed even in societies without developed markets (for instance, North American Indian tribes gave ever more copious gifts to each other, until they couldn't be increased any more and the bubble burst. These bubbles weren't based on credit claims but on their predecessor, the tradition of the time-delayed return present).

Bubbles exist in societies with precious-metal money, in those under a gold standard and in those where payment is made in paper money. Bubbles need, for their formation, only the human desire for wealth in connection with payment by credit claims. Even though government often plays a big role in their emergence, they are, at their core, an economic phenomenon; they don't even require state-administered money.

One example illustrates especially well that credit-financed bubbles emerge only on the basis of promises to pay. In the early 1980s, the former camel market in Kuwait, the Souk al-Manekh, advanced due to new regulations (not a rare phenomenon) to a trading place for stocks, apart from the main stock exchange. What was traded there were the secondary stocks of the region, in a global context utterly insignificant companies. In 1982, a spectacular bubble developed. It had become customary to buy stocks with predated cheques. The sellers of shares, thus, didn't deposit them in banks – instead traders trusted each other. Conduct that works well in individual cases and is understandable between friends and business partners, becomes, when many practice it, a dynamic process with ever faster rising prices.

That was exactly what happened: ever more cheques were issued but not deposited, and stock prices rose. The buyers were, therefore, sitting on profits and could buy even more stocks by issuing ever more cheques. Stocks rose at such blinding speed that the implied yield on the cheques increased to about 100 per cent per year (as the sellers of shares expected appropriate compensation for the profits they were missing out on). At the peak of the bubble, the former camel market, measured by the market capitalisation of all these small companies, had become the third largest stock market in the world after New York and Tokyo. Then the bubble burst (it was actually no real bursting, as trading was simply suspended due to a lack of demand), the stock exchange disappeared and Kuwait fell into recession. This example not only illustrates how bubbles solely emerge due to purchases on the basis of promises to pay, but also the possibility of a complete collapse in a chain reaction once confidence evaporates (something similar threatened in the financial markets in 2008 on a global basis).

Bubbles, however, also exist in more developed markets. There was, for instance, a credit-financed bubble in both the stock and real estate markets in Japan in the 1980s from which Japan has still not recovered to this day (2013!). One of the first bubbles the progression of which is historically well documented as exchange listed stocks were involved, is the South Sea bubble in the UK in 1720. It also shows nicely how the state (and the king) supported the bubble. Prior to its emergence, there was even perceptive talk in parliament about 'imaginary riches' that would ruin the country, and in the wake of the bubble a recession promptly ensued (nowadays, almost 300 years later, it was also known in advance in the context of the most recent bubble how financial instruments like loan securitisations would inflate real estate prices). The state's interest in bubbles, as well as bubble formation by means of state intervention, will be discussed later. For now, we want to discuss the economic process. Figure 32.1 shows the movement of a daily stock index calculated from three British stocks.[121]

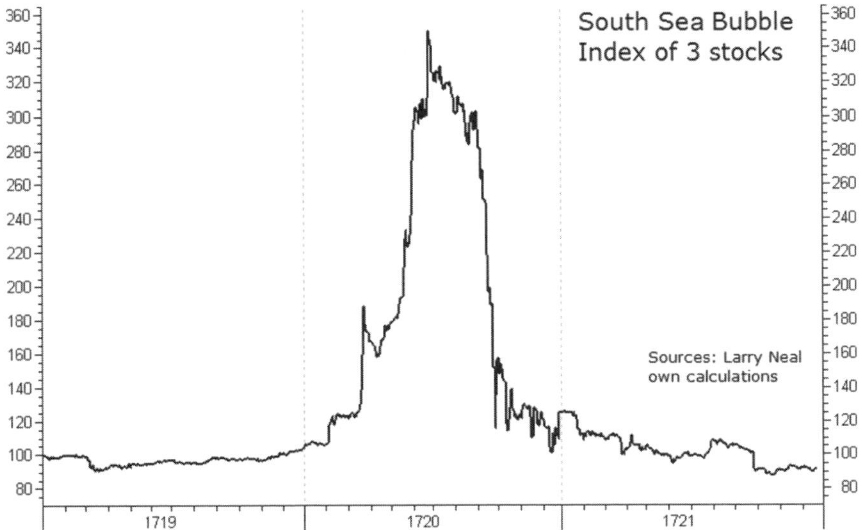

Figure 32.1 South Sea Bubble

Credit-financed bubbles create wealth on the books. While they develop, there are seemingly only winners among all participants. As a rule, the necessary actions are only taken once a bubble has burst. This is because, when bubbles burst, recessions usually follow. Although they have their origin in accounting activities, bubbles have an effect on the real world. After bubbles burst, the lessons are typically learned that are supposed to prevent comparable bubbles (in the example of the bubble in Kuwait in 1982, which was created by means of predated cheques, a ban on predating cheques suggests itself). There is quite a multitude of regulations that are supposed to prevent the formation of bubbles. In spite of that, bubbles recur again and again for a variety of reasons.

Therefore instead of avoiding the causes the idea came up to avoid the consequences. Much deliberation has been targeted towards what could be done to prevent the typical crises and recessions that follow in the wake of a bubble's bursting or, at least, how to soften them. Economists like John Law (1671–1729) and John Maynard Keynes (1883–1946) considered fighting the price declines after the bursting of bubbles with countervailing measures. This entails the provision of credit, increasing the money supply and generating government demand. The idea is, therefore, to prevent price declines of consumer goods (deflation) or, at least, to attenuate them. Primarily, however, a chain reaction of debt defaults is to be averted, thus preventing, or at least mitigating, recessions.

State-owned institutions can, for instance, take delinquent loans onto their own books to prevent a chain reaction, they can provide liquidity or they can engage in spending and thereby stimulate demand. The measures affect the demand side; demand is supposed not to fall away. The price level that has been increased by the bubble is supposed not to decline too much, and under no circumstances should there be large-scale defaults. The measures even work. Ever since this policy has been systematically employed (about the 1950s), the number of recessions in such countries as the USA has declined. However, the measures have a 'construction problem': they ultimately employ the same means that created the bubble in the first place – credit and liquidity. Is this an attempt to extinguish a fire with petrol?

Credit crises in the wake of bubbles bursting are among the crises in the course of which a previous, at times long-lived, misguided development is corrected. They are not among the crises in which only current influences or decisions have an effect. Measures that fight credit crises with credit, however, aim only at the present, they don't take the consequences of the past (in the form of accumulated credit claims) into account. They focus on flows or variable magnitudes (such as the increase or decline in outstanding credit), and not on stock magnitudes (such as the amount of outstanding credit).

With regard to bubbles, there exist two fundamentally different economic conceptions. One, just described, focuses on the present and changes in flows. It regards state intervention, which prevents a recession by means of taking on debt, as possible without any great drawbacks for the future. This view is currently clearly predominant. The other conception regards the intervention as arresting the corrective process, which can only be expected to lead to a future, even worse crisis, as the volume of credit increases even further. This view was, among others, propagated by representatives of the 'Austrian School' (which owes its name to the fact that it was founded by Austrian economists).

Even Alan Greenspan, before he became Fed chairman was of this opinion. In his 1966 essay (see note 118), he writes about economic development under the gold standard prior to the founding of the Fed in 1913 and prior to the beginning of World War I in 1914:

> The readjustment periods were short and the economies quickly reestablished a sound basis to resume expansion. But the process of cure was misdiagnosed as the disease: if shortage of bank

> reserves was causing a business decline – argued economic interventionists – why not find a way of supplying increased reserves to the banks so they never need be short!

If a bubble has emerged, one should allow the correction to take place, which also doesn't last long if one always proceeds in this manner so that no large-scale bubble emerges. The recession, which the interventionists want to avert, is a 'process of cure'. Thereafter, with the undesirable developments corrected, things should pick up again. According to his essay, it is an important goal to prevent too much credit creation (i.e., the emergence of credit-financed bubbles). Primarily for this purpose, Greenspan proposes an (improved) gold standard, about the effects of which he writes: 'This tends to restrict the financing of new ventures and requires the existing borrowers to improve their profitability before they can obtain credit for further expansion.' Credit growth is, thus, supposed to occur in lock-step with real economic development, and not exceed it. Greenspan clearly pleads for a strict limitation of credit growth in his essay, and in the event this occasionally fails, for a swift and forceful reduction.[122]

However, where do things stand today, 40 years after the link to gold was abandoned – many decades after we have begun to fight recessions with the help of credit and liquidity; many decades, also, in which governments themselves took on debts? We want to, first, look at the money supply – that is, the amount of financial claims in a tight delimitation. In this way, only claims are considered that are typically used for payment (i.e., claims that are available on demand ['money']). Figure 32.2 shows the US monetary aggregate M2 relative to GDP since 1908.

Actually, the relationship has developed in a fairly stable manner. This time period includes two world wars, the likewise quite expensive Cold War, the global economic crisis of the 1930s (with its severe economic contraction) and the strong inflation of the 1970s. Naturally, there were fluctuations in the curve, primarily in the economic crisis and during the two world wars, but the fluctuations are generally fairly small. Even the end of the link to gold didn't result in great fluctuations. All in all, there was a strong devaluation of money in these hundred years and also phases of higher inflation rates. Thereafter, however, there were periods of low inflation rates; stabilisation was, therefore, possible. The economy also grew quite well and recessions weren't overly severe. On the whole, one could

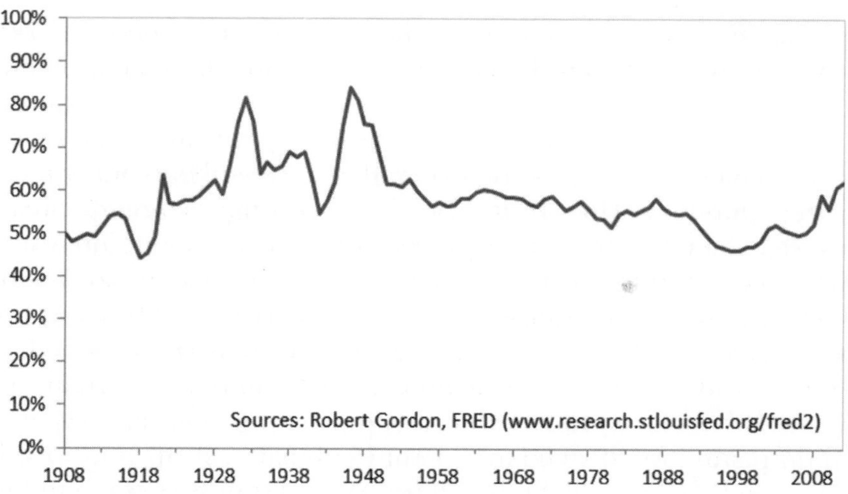

Figure 32.2 US monetary aggregate M2 relative to GDP

be quite satisfied. In spite of intermittent inflationary phases, the ratio of the money supply to the real economic reference magnitude GDP remains at about the same level as a hundred years ago.

Based on this, one could simply continue in the same stable manner, as though the past century hadn't happened. The mechanisms to limit the money supply work only passably in terms of absolute numbers, but sufficiently well relative to nominal economic output. One of the reasons for this is the relative independence of the central bank, which makes it more difficult for the government to pay for its spending directly via the 'printing' of money – without a doubt, one of the most important innovations of today's paper money standard compared to its predecessor in ancient China. The paper money standard there, which was for the first time described in the West by Marco Polo, dissolved in the 14th century in galloping inflation, as the 'money printing press' financed many government expenditures, although the theorists of the time were well aware of the problem. Thus far, we can observe progress.

However, the question arises whether it is enough to pay attention to the money supply. This is because financial claims that are not circulating (i.e., that are saved) are potentially money and can, therefore, potentially exercise demand in the market. In practice, they only have to be transformed into standard money in the short term. Moreover, many of these claims have been used to buy things in the market when they were created (often investment assets like real estate) and have raised the level of prices. They also have to

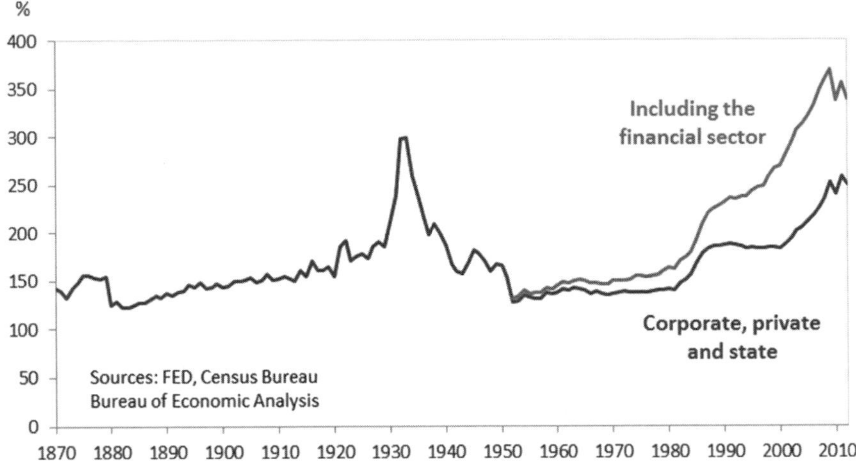

Figure 32.3 USA: total debt relative to GDP

be serviced, since the financial claims of one party are the debts of another. We, therefore, pay attention to the level of credit claims. The method of reacting to credit crises by issuing credit, and the frequent taking on of debt by the state itself, have resulted in an increase in credit outstanding. Figure 32.3 shows the total amount of credit market debt from 1870, which is owed by the sectors of the US economy – government, households and corporations – once again relative to economic output, as well as separately the same magnitude, including the financial sector. Unfortunately, there are no precise official data; especially in connection with the credit claims of the financial sector, there is a degree of double-counting, which cannot be easily resolved. The actual value, therefore, probably lies somewhere between the two lines (presumably close to the lower one).[123]

We can see a kind of limit at the 150 per cent level. Up to this limit, it was apparently almost possible to keep the level stable (but even below it slight increases were always discernible, so that the level of 150 per cent is probably too high to be regarded as a permanently stable limit). This limit was exceeded twice, once with the beginning of World War I up to the global economic crisis, and again from the 1970s and, in accelerated fashion, since the early 80s, as the Cold War was escalated, until today.

At the peak of the bubble in the late 20s, the total amount of credit claims was at 190 per cent of GDP (the increase after the bursting of the bubble is owed to the massive decline in the denominator, GDP).

In the 30s, the level of credit claims was ruthlessly reduced worldwide, with many defaults occurring. This large decline in accounting wealth went hand in hand with a considerable decline in economic activity. The decline was so powerful that it strongly furthered the spread of radical political ideologies (such as National Socialism in Germany, ultimately laying the foundation for the outbreak of World War II).

Today, the sum of outstanding credit claims is even higher than in the late 20s, at 336 per cent of economic output, a historically extremely high value (it has decreased somewhat as a result of the financial crisis; however, the value excluding the financial sector continues to increase and is at a very high 249 per cent). This puts the relatively positive image that we perceived in terms of the money supply, economic growth and the small number of recessions into perspective. After all, if there are, today, twice as many credit claims than in the 1960s, then the quality of these claims must have declined. Today's savers have twice as many claims relative to the economy's output than their grandparents. It is, at times, argued that the number of credit claims is irrelevant in this case, as the debts were incurred in domestic currency. It is, allegedly, possible simply to inflate the debts away. If that were so simple, then why hasn't already at least enough inflation been generated to keep the level steady at a lower level? At least by the end of the Cold War, one would have expected to see such a stabilisation or a reversal. On the contrary, the level of credit claims outstanding has continued to grow. Evidently the existing debt (and the interest on it) is serviced by issuing additional debt; obviously new credit keeps being created at a rate exceeding the nominal growth (including inflation) of the economy. Are we in a series of successive credit-financed bubbles? Are we in the middle of a mega-bubble?

We want to take a closer look at the phase of excessive credit expansion of the recent two decades plus. We want to examine the backdrop, the circumstances and the consequences of the excessive credit expansion. The relative increase of credit is, of course, a result of the policy to fight credit crises by issuing more credit. It is, however, also a result of government taking on debt for all sorts of purposes. The term 'mega-bubble' denotes that the bubble not only concerns a limited market, such as the Souk al-Manekh in Kuwait, but the lion's share of the most important markets in the world. Above all, it means an especially high level of outstanding credit.

The characteristics of bubble formation should, by and large, apply to a mega-bubble as well. The growing amount of credit in recent decades is evident in the case of the USA. Other countries also exhibit an increase, even though not always quite as excessive (still at or above a level that went, in the past, hand in hand with bubbles). The loans were used to buy something, at least during the expansion phase of credit-financed bubble formation – that is, after all the purpose of credit (later, the main aim is increasingly to simply replace existing credit). The increase in asset prices is, therefore, the second important characteristic of bubble formation. The most important asset prices are those of real estate and corporations. A guide for the development of the values of corporations is the total market capitalisation, the value of all stocks. Figure 32.4 shows the market capitalisation of US corporations relative to GDP from 1885 onward.

We can see three phases during which corporations were valued above average relative to national economic output. One occurred in the 1960s, when the US economy was highly productive and also flourished internationally. The other two are connected with bubbles: one at the end of the 20s (with an echo in the 30s), the other from the mid-90s. Measured relative to economic output, the level of stock prices at its peak in the current mega-bubble

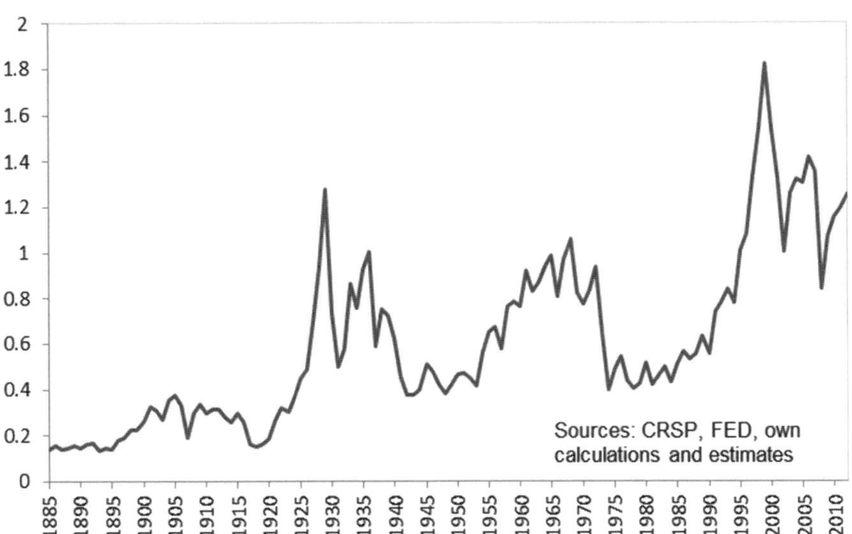

Figure 32.4 Market capitalisation of US corporations relative to GDP, partly estimated

markedly exceeded the level seen at the end of the 20s! But not only the market capitalisation of US stocks increased; the market capitalisation of stocks has also more than doubled relative to economic output worldwide between 1990 and 2000. Although stocks corrected thereafter, there were strong advances in real estate prices. Generally, the recent past is characterised by markedly higher asset prices. In stocks and partly also in real estate, the developments were similar in most parts of the world. Exceptionally high asset prices worldwide, in conjunction with the high level of outstanding credit, show clearly that we are in a global mega-bubble.

When something 'happens' there is always the question of who benefited from it. In principle, the seeming benefit appears to predominate in the expansion phase of a bubble, as wealth is accumulating on balance sheets – many winners and strong forces advocate bubble-blowing. The profiteers in a bubble are all those whose balance sheet wealth increases – that is, the buyers and holders of the affected items. There are no obvious losers; only if one looks closer it is possible (as we will show further below) to spot losers in the process of a bubble's formation, and not only once the bubble bursts. Since, on the whole, it is an increase in balance sheet wealth, the profits of the winners are generally higher than the losses of the losers. The holders of assets, real estate, stocks – or even flowers – are thus the direct profiteers during the formation of the bubble. Once the bubble bursts, they, of course, suffer commensurate losses.

In the economy, forces form around the booming sectors that profit from the bubble as well. First of all, there is the financial sector (banks, brokers, insurance companies and similar firms); as the bubble needs to be financed, the additional credit must be extended and the associated fortunes must be managed. The financial sector typically grows while the bubble expands. This is also true in the current mega-bubble. The financial sector's share of the economy is markedly higher than, for instance, in 1980. If one looks at the salaries of employees in the financial sector compared to those of all employees, the market capitalisation of financial enterprises compared to all other companies, the profits of the financial sector relative to all other sectors, it is discernible that the share of the financial sector at the peak of the current mega-bubble was markedly higher than previously. The profits of the US financial sector, for instance, rose at the peak to about twice the long-term level that pertained prior to 1980. It is, therefore, clear that the financial sector has great interest in a bubble. However, it is also interested in preventing its bursting. This is because it is the sector with the most to lose, both in absolute and relative terms. For this reason, but also because it is most directly involved, the financial sector was historically the first sector that attempted to keep bubbles from bursting – for instance, by means of coordinated support purchases or the creation of a central bank (which historically, as the 'top layer' of the banking system, expands the tighter limits of money and credit creation under a precious metals standard).

However, there are also winners in the real economy. In the case of a real estate bubble, more buildings are erected, so that, for instance, artisans, building materials producers and real estate brokers all profit. But also state agencies, the media and researchers that are involved with the booming sector profit (so that their views undergo change). The formation of a bubble, therefore, causes investment in certain sectors of the economy purely on the basis of accounting profits ('misallocation'). At this point, it also becomes clear that at the time in which a bubble that increases overall wealth on balance sheets forms, there are already relative losers: namely all other sectors of the economy.

Bubbles, however, also create a structural detriment in terms of income distribution. Just as the time period of the late 1920s, the current time is characterised by a considerable widening of the gap between rich and poor. Relative to the 60s, for instance, the distribution of income is more extreme. This can be easily explained. The amount of credit outstanding relative to GDP (i.e., economic output) is more than twice as high today as in the 60s, meaning that the profits resulting from it (interest) tend to be higher as well. The same holds for the remaining fortunes, which have also increased in value and the profits they produce. To this one must add the increase in asset values. But wealth is unevenly distributed. Due to the mega-bubble, the profits from wealth have increased and, due to the uneven distribution thereof, so has the gap between rich and poor. There may, in particular cases, also be other reasons for the widening gap; the increase in outstanding credit is, however, the main cause.

It must be pointed out here that it makes economic sense that wealth is unevenly distributed: it provides an incentive; it ensures the owner looks after it; and leads to people deciding responsibly, based on market requirements, in what to invest. Moreover, only when wealth is unevenly distributed will there be a sufficient level of investment – when a millionaire earns another million, he will invest almost all of it; if one distributes the million among 1,000 persons, almost all of it will be spent (therefore socialism wasn't really a redistribution from rich to poor, but rather from substance to consumption, which became obvious in crumbling buildings and backward factories; too little was invested). However, the artificial increase of the gap between rich and poor due to a credit-driven bubble is not economically justifiable.

The same causal connection that leads to the widening spread between rich and poor also causes a structural shift to the detriment of profits from production. When incomes from wealth grow, the profits of manufacturing enterprises and the people employed in them fall in relative terms. One could even state more generally that incomes from entrepreneurial activity and labour are weakened relative to incomes from wealth. If one takes into account further misallocations (such as the growth of the financial sector, perhaps also higher unemployment), the bubble must be judged to be a cause of lower industrial growth in the developed nations. There are, of course, additional reasons – such as the smaller incomes in emerging countries or, in the case of the USA, a mispricing of the currency in the context of the current account deficit. The lower profitability of production has motivated a number of industrial corporations to become active in financial businesses ('bank with a car factory tacked on').

Indications show that unemployment rises due to factors such as the widening gap between rich and poor, the weakening of income from production and the misallocations, even if the associated causal relations are more complex. It is, in all likelihood, yet another paradoxical lagged effect of the bubble, that credit-financed stimulus of the economy causes permanent unemployment in the medium term – the opposite of what was intended (but could only be achieved in the short term).

If bubbles generate only illusory profits and harbour great disadvantages both when they form and especially when they burst, the question arises as to why they come into being, but also why the government cannot or doesn't want to prevent them – or why it may possibly support them or even create them. The primary reason for the emergence of bubbles is found at the moment of the decision. Since the advantages initially prevail, while the disadvantages only come later (when it bursts), or are not immediately visible (at the remaining sectors that lose out), there is a preference to decide in favour of bubble formation. Strictly speaking, if one looks only at the moment of decision, there are no losers at all, since the moment the amount of credit is first expanded there are only profiteers and people that are unaffected. Only later do the drawbacks (i.e., the losers) become detectable, as the amount of credit outstanding has increased (there is, therefore, a connection with the magnitudes of both stocks and flows). Since the benefits are in the present, but the drawbacks in the future, decisions are biased in favour of bubble formation.

This bias is relevant for all participants, including the state. The state is the only entity that can, by means of regulations (such as the ban of predated cheques) prevent this distortion and with it the emergence of a bubble. However, it profits as an institution from bubbles as well, or it creates them as participant in the economy for reasons of its own. How does the state profit from bubbles in the economy? For one thing, it receives higher tax revenues. Economic activity and the price level are initially furthered by the bubble, which increases tax revenues. The government can, moreover, tax the blown-up book values – in the USA, for instance, by means of capital gains taxes. The state profits (e.g., in elections) from the fact that citizens are more satisfied with the economy and due to their rising wealth. The lobbying by sectors that profit from bubbles, such as the financial sector, comes in addition to that. All of this leads to the government tolerating or even supporting bubbles in the private sector of the economy.

One example is the stock market bubble from the mid-1990s in the USA (among other things furthered by the gold market interventions), which led to higher tax receipts and lowered the government's borrowings. Another example is the real estate bubble that followed thereafter, which preceded the financial market crisis of 2008. It was desired, in terms of social policy in the USA, that income strata that, up to that point, had rarely owned homes should attain home-ownership. The government, therefore, saw to it that mortgage loans were extended to people who could not really service them, and could at best profit from the increase in house prices, which, in turn, was a consequence of the loans themselves. The government did this with the help of state-owned mortgage credit agencies (which furthered the credit growth directly and indirectly) and also by approving credit-expanding financial instruments.

One example for such instruments can be seen in credit securitisations, in which many loans are bundled in a security and sold to investors. Shifting credit claims is, as such, not objectionable in principle. However, in contrast to covered bonds, the mediating credit institution is, in the case of these securities, from the beginning no longer liable. This means that those who decide whether a loan is extended are, by contrast to a normal banker, only interested in sales and have no interest of their own in ensuring the creditworthiness of borrowers. Such securitisations are, therefore, bubble-blowers of the first order.

The state was, thus, materially involved in bubble formation in the private sector of the economy. In the course of the financial market crisis of 2008, many of these securitised mortgages went into default. Central banks and governments took the loans that were initially created by the private sector during the bubble onto their own balance sheets in order to prevent a deflationary collapse. Even though most politicians today pretend that it was a 'market failure', it was primarily a political failure. (Ultimately, there is no such thing as a market failure. An aeroplane crash isn't caused by a failure of physics either, but human beings can err. They move within the framework of economic laws, such as that of supply and demand.) It is, however, also a failure of the citizenry, as citizens were in favour of the bubble. It is an interplay, in which the government failed to fulfil its duty to prevent a bubble. In addition, there was widespread failure of the media, as the media, by and large, uncritically accepted the misrepresentations of the political establishment. Economic science also joined in and busied itself with sugarcoating the complex of problems surrounding the level of credit in ahistorical narrow-mindedness.

However, the state tolerates or supports not only credit bubbles that are emerging in the private sector, but also creates them itself. This is because the state is an economic agent as well and must finance its expenditures. As such, it is subject to the laws of economics, and its decision-makers and administrators are subject to the laws of human nature and its flaws. Historically, wars have taken place at the beginning of most of the big bubbles. Over the centuries it has transpired that states that finance their wars by issuing bonds are more likely to be victorious than those that rely solely on tax revenues. As a result the financing of wars via bonds has become customary, even though thereafter government finances were regularly devastated and national bankruptcies, strong inflation and currency reforms often followed.

Government credit doesn't create a conventional bubble, as it is used to pay for consumption goods instead of investment assets. Nevertheless, loans exist thereafter and the level of outstanding credit is increased. As an example, let us mention the War of the Spanish Succession (1701–14), which subsequently gave John Law the idea to bring large amounts of paper money into circulation in Europe for the first time ever. It was a similar situation with the first paper money in China, which was used in the 11th century to finance a war. Even today's financial system is a consequence of earlier wars, as, after them, the debts remained in place.

Many people don't realise it, but the history of the 20th century is, in large part, connected with the level of outstanding credit. World War I devoured vast amounts of funds, and those were largely financed by means of government bond issues. The gold standard was suspended, as it would have made it impossible to finance the war. After the war, the debts remained in place, including those of the victorious nations. While Germany suffered hyperinflation and a new currency was subsequently introduced, the victors had credit-related problems of their own. These led to the bubble of the 1920s, in which new loans in the private sector of the economy increased the level of credit further. In 1929 the stock market crash occurred, followed by the global economic crisis that brought Hitler to power. In the 30s unemployment was fought with a government spending programme (also laying the foundations for today's economic theories). The still-too-high level of debt couldn't be adequately reduced; only the hyperinflation events and currency reforms after World War II, in Germany in 1948, finally removed the debt overhang that had begun in 1914! It is, therefore, anything but an easy task to reduce high levels of outstanding credit, and it can not only lead to economic, but also to political, societal and military cataclysms.

One radical change after World War II was the spread of socialism, which led to the Cold War, including armed conflict such as that in Vietnam. The East–West conflict began to ruin government finances in the 1960s, which was the reason for abandoning the gold exchange standard in 1971. However, only in its final phase, in the 'decisive for the outcome of the war' arms build-up of the 1980s, did the level of credit rise markedly. After the end of the Cold War, there were severe economic crises and strong inflations in the former nations of the Eastern Bloc. In the West, the high level of debt not only remained in place, it was expanded even further. In the process, a bubble in the private sector emerged in the 90s, on the basis of the expanded level of credit claims due to government debt increases, while government finances remained relatively stable. This is very similar to the situation after World War I, when, after the government debt orgy of the war and the abandonment of the gold standard, a bubble emerged in the private sector as well.

Today's mega-bubble, therefore, has its historical precursors – only we have come farther, and the bubble is bigger.

The state not only creates bubbles by increased spending in the special case of war, but also by means of its ongoing spending, today especially in the welfare sector. The state has a tendency to find it difficult to economise, as politicians and civil servants spend other people's money. In the welfare state, bribing the citizenry (in democracies: voters) is an additional factor. The government promises higher pensions, higher social spending and similar things; however, it glosses over the fact that it must also take the sums involved from the citizenry.

This is where the state itself likes to make use of the trick of financing by credit. It pretends that the additional expenses won't burden the citizen, and finances them with debt. In order to hide the burden on the citizenry, it relies on a characteristic of debt financing of the state, namely that the individual citizen doesn't add his share of the commonwealth's debt to his personal balance sheet. Citizens thus feel wealthier than they really are.

A schematic example will illustrate how the state hoodwinks the citizenry by taking on debt: if the state raises pensions by $100, it would consequently have to burden the disposable income of families by the same $100. This would lead to a reconciliation of the interests of various groups on the basis of real numbers. Instead, the state takes on debt of $100 and gives the money to the pensioner. The family wasn't burdened according to its own books, but the pensioner still gets an additional $100! The liability of $100 is in the government's books, where is doesn't bother anyone personally. As the state can, however, only take on debt, but cannot conjure up real resources, the family was still burdened in real terms by $100 through price increases (possibly the effect is, in the short term, lowered by additional imports or economic growth, but in principle this is the schematic outline of what occurs).

In order to avoid misunderstandings, it is not the individual measure that is the bone of contention, but full transparency with respect to the basis for decision-making – perhaps pensions would be, as an end result, even higher than they are now (while transparency would prevent the decision-making process from being distorted by taking on additional debt, it should also help to avoid nonsensical expenditures elsewhere). What has been demonstrated here for the largest item of expenditure, the welfare state, holds true for other areas of spending as well – for instance, for the preferred clientele of political parties or specific sectors of the economy. They, too, are subject to a multitude of subsidies, which have to be taken in again from somewhere else (often from the same persons or corporations). Fundamentally, government debt leads to more frivolous expenditure, as it allows for the pretence that the expenses won't really have to be paid for. But, since it doesn't create any resources, as it is a pure accounting activity, these have to be taken from the citizenry at some other point. Thus, government debt forcibly sets a cascade of redistributive measures into motion, in which the actual political purpose is often completely defeated in the final analysis. In any event it creates a lot of costs for both the authorities and the economy and causes damage by its intended or unintended exertion of influence.

However, the citizen also wants to be hoodwinked. Consider the enormous society-wide opposition when the topic of raising the very low retirement age in some European countries was discussed. Citizens simply want to feel more wealthy, even if nothing can be created by accounting games. Often, basic economic knowledge is lacking (this holds true for politicians and unionists as well). Let us seize upon a few of the standard ideas that are widespread. For instance, many are not bothered about where the state gets the means for additional spending; they think it is their right to demand something from the state. Paradoxically, that often also holds for those who pay for it all in real terms, for instance families (and future recipients of pensions), to hark back to the previous example. This widespread basic stance *vis-à-vis* the state is deeply rooted in human nature, as though the 'father' state were a separate person that can produce something on its own, analogous to how one's father once provided food in one's childhood, without the child having to do anything. Psychologically, this basic stance is understandable – after all, we were well-cared for children for many years – but it is completely misguided. If one asks where the payments are supposed to actually come from, credit is often mentioned. If one reminds people that no additional resources can be created that way, redistributionist ideas often come to the fore, either within the government budget or within society. There is often also an interplay between citizenry and state with regard to government debt. Financing by means of government debt is nothing but a deception manoeuvre – self-deception, if you will.

The welfare state is also a difficult topic insofar as the argumentation is often irrational, emotional or moralising. Man wants to be good (or thought of as good) and sometimes finds it difficult to make a seemingly tough, but long-term positive decision (what is discussed here in the context of the welfare state is also true for widely adopted global subsidies). What this is about is the question of transparency of the decision-making process; it is about not letting oneself and others be deceived by the trick of financing the state with debt. Without government debt, would there be a completely nonsensical redistribution apparatus that (depending on the data-gathering method) makes large parts of the population into receivers of social benefits, which they largely pay themselves at some other point again? Would social welfare aid have mutated from an instrument that softens individual blows of fate into an all-encompassing fount of money that produces wrong-headed incentives, if citizens had been squarely informed about its burden? Would Europe have allowed the immigration of persons that are burdening its welfare state (but not that of the country of origin), who aren't participating in productive economic life, if European wage earners and consumers had been forced to finance them openly through tax increases? This is not about passing judgement on individual measures; it is transparency that is the issue. Decision-making processes can only work properly if the fundamental basis for making decisions is correct. Government debt deceives the citizenry.

Government debt doesn't lead directly to a bubble in asset markets, as it is mainly used for buying consumption goods. It is, rather, a price driver for consumer goods, the consumer is 'taxed'. However, it increases the amount of credit outstanding. Historically, it can be observed with some regularity (as is the case also in the current bubble) that, following a marked expansion of government debt, a credit-financed bubble in the private sector tends to emerge in subsequent years, so that coincidence can probably be ruled out (the causes probably have to do with the interplay between stocks and flows – i.e., circulating money and money that has been saved, between consumption goods and means of production).

With regard to the welfare state, debt financing produces the exact opposite of what is intended from a socio-political perspective. This is because it leads, with a lag, to a bubble and a bubble, in turn, leads to a widening gap between rich and poor, as we can currently observe. The debt-financed social beneficence of 30 years ago brings about poverty today. It is absurd or shortsighted when politicians or unionists demand an expansion of credit in order to widen the welfare state, for instance, or to stimulate the economy in order to create employment. In the medium term, they thereby only foster another bubble and bring about a widening of the gap between rich and poor – that is, the opposite of what is ostensibly intended. Politicians, like all people, prefer success in the here and now, even if there is a high price to pay in the future. It is conspicuous that the welfare state is, today, much larger in most Western nations than it used to be decades ago, and yet the social problems are greater too. A fire was put out by pouring petrol on it.

A further aspect of bubble formation should be mentioned – somewhat vague in nature, but notable. It is the effect on morals. Bubbles and government debt suggest an easier way of financing than exists in reality, as the price to be paid isn't immediately visible in the present. That influences behaviours and attitudes of private persons, corporations and government authorities. Everything seems easy to pay for. This promotes wastefulness in all areas. However, it also promotes the stance that the state is responsible for things that have traditionally been the province of private individuals. Government debt, thus, has apparently also contributed to fundamental social phenomena, such as the weakening of the family (as its relative economic importance has been weakened). Other demoralising factors include loss of the value of savings and bubble-induced too-low incomes from productive work.

The fundamental question is whether the formation of bubbles leads all in all to more or less real production. The fact that credit expansion stimulates the economy is empirically well supported. This is simply due to the additional demand and the higher profitability reflected in balance sheets due to rising asset prices during the formation of a bubble. This real-world effect of the bubble is classically reversed in the subsequent recession, where, conversely, repayment of loans and defaults lead to a decline in real economic activity. Today, the state intervenes at that juncture and prevents such recessions, but it also prevents the reduction of the outstanding debt. One must, perhaps, await the end of the current mega-bubble cycle (i.e., the time when credit outstanding is actually reduced) to be able to make a well-founded assessment. However, it can already be stated that the 'wriggle room' for stimulating the economy by means of additional credit becomes ever smaller due to the already attained level of outstanding debt. Additional loans barely reach the real economy, as they must service already existing debt.

It is fundamentally questionable whether it is possible to create sustainable wealth through the accounting profits attained in bubbles. If one considers, in addition, the misallocations, the solely bubble-induced enlargement of specific sectors such as the financial sector to the detriment of other sectors, one should all in all expect a diminution of wealth. There are, moreover, examples for a stagnating or even shrinking level of credit (the UK after World War II), which sometimes went hand in hand with quite strong economic growth. Ultimately, it is the freely thriving human mind that creates wealth – living before the invention of the wheel is not the same as living thereafter – not credit. Presumably, factors like misallocations in the economy, government and society result in the short-term boon credit creation brings (in the form of additional production) being transformed into a drawback overall (both in terms of its size and in terms of its benefit, which is naturally smaller in misallocations, even though it shows up in the macro-economic aggregates). The finiteness of the effect of additional credit-based stimulus measures, as well as their reversal when credit is reduced, argues – in conjunction with misallocations – that real wealth, as measured over the duration between two mega-bubbles, will be higher if the emergence of a mega-bubble is prevented – by not letting any bubbles form or creating them on purpose, or by letting smaller bubbles intermittently burst in due time, as was customary in times of the gold standard.[124]

In describing the formation and demise of bubbles, it was assumed that, in parallel with the increase in the amount of outstanding credit, asset prices rise and that both later decline when the bubble bursts. In the face of government intervention, this no longer holds true. Due to state intervention nowadays, bubbles no longer burst completely, but only in terms of the partial aspect of asset prices. The stock of existing credit claims remains in place and is not removed by debtor defaults. If one speaks of the 'bursting of a bubble' today, it is usually the decline in asset prices that is referred to. Since the credit claims continue to exist, the bursting is, however, incomplete. The bubble has only disappeared at a superficial glance (prices have declined); its cause (in the form of a higher amount of credit outstanding) remains in place. Of the two most important characteristics of credit-financed bubbles, credit and increased prices, the elevated level of credit is preserved.

The still extant credit claims form the basis of the (today global) series of partial bubbles. The increased level of financial claims, the original reason for the rise in asset prices during the preceding partial bubble, expedites, soon after its bursting, the formation of a new partial bubble. The financial claims continue to exert an effect on demand in the world, and raise specific asset prices (until they begin to have an inflationary effect on consumer prices, possibly at the end of a mega-bubble). One example is the bursting of a partial bubble in stock markets after 2000, in which the level of financial claims was preserved. Thereupon, the next partial bubble formed in real estate. The temporary decline in asset prices in a partial bubble, thus, doesn't alter the fact that a mega-bubble exists. For these reasons, it can make sense to speak of a bubble even if only one of its characteristic features (such as an increased level of credit claims) is given.[125]

We can schematically differentiate between three types of credit-financed bubbles, without distinguishing between them too sharply. There are those that emerge only in the private sector, and which the government tolerates and which are difficult to prevent. They are usually of brief duration. Then there are those that the government supports, which, however, also emerge in the private sector. Furthermore, there are those that the government itself creates. If the government intervenes, bubbles can become very large. All types of bubbles lead to illusory prosperity; people feel wealthier, without anything real having been produced. This is visible in the increase of the total amount of financial claims relative to GDP. Government debt is a special case as it is also a unique instrument of deception – the individual doesn't feel personally responsible for the debt of the community.

Bubbles emerge because, at the time the decisions are initially taken, the benefits appear to predominate. This distortion of the basis of decision-making concerns all participants: households, entrepreneurs, the financial sector and the state. Only later, when the bubble bursts, is the illusory prosperity removed from the books. This bursting usually involves a recession. The economic contraction in the course of such recessions can, in the wake of bigger bubbles, easily amount to a quarter of economic output or more. Only once the amount of outstanding credit claims has reached a lower and stable level is the bubble fully worked off, which can take many years and encompass several financial crises. If the recession is severe, political upheaval can bring radical ideologues (socialists, fascists, bureaucratic planners, religious fanatics) to power and can – by means of defence spending, for example – sow the seeds of future indebtedness and bubbles. However, even during the bubble there is a multitude of distortions, including misallocations, which favour certain sectors of the economy, the state and society to the detriment of others. Spending in the financial sector, the bubble sector (such as, e.g., real estate), as well as defence and welfare is inflated.

The drawbacks of bubbles are considerable. Man is imbued with reason; perhaps it will be possible, based on sufficient knowledge, to prevent the formation of bubbles in the future, or to limit them or make them rarer, in spite of the formidable forces that are arrayed in support of such formation. It is, therefore, worth taking a closer look at the Janus face of the carriers of value. That will provide us with a better basis on which to develop scenarios for the possible outcomes of the current mega-bubble.

Chapter 33
Money or Credit?

'Your money or your life!' the bank robber shouts and still only gets credit. This is because today's money is credit. This is also why it is called 'credit money'. It has always two sides: someone who owes it and someone who holds the credit claim. There are very few exceptions (involving insignificant amounts – such as a profit disbursement by a central bank in the case of an upward revaluation of gold) in which money is created 'net' – that is, without there being a corresponding debt. Other than that, our money is, today, nothing but a credit claim that is associated with a debt of the same amount.

Let us look once more at the example of a real estate purchase on credit, which we used to illustrate the emergence of a bubble. In this example you took out a loan of $100,000 in order to pay for a house. After the purchase you have a debt of $100,000, while the seller has received a deposit of $100,000. In this manner this $100,000 has been additionally created. It is held by the seller of the property in the form of a deposit as a claim against the bank, and the bank in turn as a claim against you, the buyer of the house. The entire process is by no means neutral, although there exists a debt as the obverse to every claim. The positions do not simply cancel each other out – one cannot simply ignore them macro-economically, it is not a zero-sum game – as these claims can exert effects in the market. He who holds a deposit can effect payment, can exercise demand in the market, by means of which he (slightly) affects prices and raises them.

The $100,000 constitutes an additional claim in the system, it is additional 'money'. In this way and no other, is money created today. It is not the case (as one might assume in terms of a concrete conception of money) that the $100,000 that the bank lends out has been paid in by someone else and simply transferred.[126] It is created *ex nihilo*. Only if debt is repaid somewhere else in the system (really repaid, out of income or real wealth, not by taking on new debt) the total level of debt doesn't increase.

This system strikes one as absurd, as the claims are not conveying any right except the right to receive a claim of the same type. They do not convey the right to redeem them for a commodity like gold or silver. However, the system still functions, as there are rules governing the banking system and central banks which limit the creation of new credit claims (otherwise they would lose their value quite fast). Moreover, these claims also have a market value by dint of being legal tender.

One can visualise this in greatly simplified form as follows: in the past silver was, for instance, used for payments. It was, however, equivalent to pay with warehouse receipts for silver that was stored at a bank. It was, likewise, equivalent to pay by transferring a deposit (per 'remittance' or 'cheque') held at a reputable bank. Later, '1 gram of silver' was renamed as '1 dollar' and, still later, the connection to the precious metal was omitted altogether, as it was anyway just lying around at a bank. Hey presto, today's credit system was complete. Since then, there is (almost) only money that represents a claim, and for every claim there exists a debt. Even cash such as a bank note represents a claim; it was merely made anonymous by the banking system and made safe from default as well as more transferable.

At issue are financial claims, their amount and their value. Secondarily, there are also the questions of maturity, interest, fitness for circulation, creditworthiness, type and character of the debtor and the like. We will also look at these things, as soon as they are of importance. We try, however, to focus on those things that are material to the current financial situation, for the mega-bubble, but also to past and putative future bubbles. In addition, we want to examine the effects on the real economy and monetary stability. We abstain from an extensive description of the history of money, the origin of money, the definition of money, specifically a definition by concrete or legal categorisation, and we abstain from praising earlier monetary systems. We are simply trying to focus on what is economically relevant, on what has an effect on the market, on what can create demand there – on financial claims.

The customary criterion for evaluating the quality of a unit of a financial claim (such as the dollar or the euro) is price stability. If a saver can still buy approximately the same amount of goods with his savings today as, for example, a year ago, the money concerned is held to be 'stable'. A small loss in purchasing power is regarded as tolerable – after all, the saver also earns interest. From this perspective everything seems to be in order. However, doesn't the coin have another side as well? What about the amount of outstanding credit claims? As we have seen, the amount of credit claims relative to economic output has nearly doubled in the USA since the 1960s and now stands (including the liabilities of the financial sector) at approximately 350 per cent of GDP.

However, if there are more than twice as many credit claims, doesn't it follow that their quality must have declined? This refers not only to the devaluation of money over time (which has markedly reduced the value of money over the past 40 years), but also to the total amount of credit claims. Forty years ago one could use a definite amount of financial claims to buy a definite amount of goods; today one can use a markedly larger amount of claims to buy the same amount of goods. In addition, however, the amount of credit claims has doubled relative to economic output! In addition to the devaluation of money, something has considerably changed in the realm of financial claims. The customary criterion of evaluating the quality of a unit of a claim, price stability, only concerns individual savings, the value of a single claim. It ignores the fact that the entirety of savers holds twice as many financial claims today! This is adjusted for price changes and economic growth, therefore substantial change has taken place in the realm of financial claims.

Credit claims cannot be of the same quality if there are twice as many of them, even if that is not mirrored in measurements of the depreciation of money. Although the individual saver can purchase the same amount of goods with his financial claims regardless of whether their total amount is at 100 per cent or 200 per cent of GDP, the same doesn't hold true for all savers in the aggregate. The value of their claims relative to the real economic output has halved. There is, therefore, a big difference, even if it doesn't necessarily become manifest, as all savers won't suddenly liquidate their savings. There can be no doubt that the risks have increased when twice as many credit claims are outstanding.

However, what has actually changed? How can there be twice as many financial claims without prices (in addition to the normal inflation) doubling? Why was the devaluation of money so small relative to the increase in credit claims, which grew much more strongly? In order to answer this question, one must consider what the owner of an existing claim can use it for. Formally, the difference between stocks and flows is at issue – in concrete terms, the difference between financial claims that are used on an ongoing basis for payments and those that have been put aside for the purpose of saving.

We want to set forth the difference in more detail. The $100,000 which the seller of the house has received as a deposit, he can spend (for instance, to buy a car), or save. In the first instance, demand will result, affecting the real economy; in the second instance, it will not (for the moment). Due to the (slightly) higher demand, prices will (slightly) rise in the first instance, but not in the second. If existing claims are not spent (transferred), they have no effect on the level of prices.

A carrier of value (to employ a general term, since, apart from financial claims, it can also take the form of commodity money like gold or silver), therefore, has two aspects. First, one can spend it, in which case it is called 'money'. The associated process is referred to as an 'exchange' (or 'payment' if one regards only one half of the exchange). Second, it can be put aside for future expenses, in which case it is commonly referred to as a 'store of value'. The associated process is 'saving'. It is one and the same carrier of value which is used for different purposes.

It is, therefore, not a concrete feature of a carrier of value whether it is 'money' or a 'store of value', but it depends on how it is used. If a carrier of value is used for payment on an ongoing basis – if we, for instance, use it to exchange our labour for food – it is part of the circular flow of the economy. If we put it aside for our children, for example, then it is potentially part of the economic circuit in the future, but has no effect on demand in the present, and thus the level of prices in the present.

We use the generic term 'carrier of value', which encompasses both 'money' and long-term claims, in order to avoid artificial delimitation. Of the three most important functions of money – means of payment, store of value and measure of value – we don't refer to the measure of value, for the simple reason that money is not demanded because of it. Although the measure of value function is useful, no one acquires money because of it. That is only done to either purchase something in the near future (means of payment) or to store it for later use (store of value). These are the primary functions of money. Money is only demanded in order to carry value (over the multitude of goods/services ['exchange'] or over time ['saving']), but not to measure anything.

We don't focus on maturity, as one can leave one's savings for years in a demand deposit, or, conversely, one can use a ten-year bond for payment by exchanging it for money in one's current account (whereby, from a macro-economic perspective, an investment demand of the same magnitude emerges on the part of the counterparty, if all other parameters remain the same). We focus only on what has an immediate economic effect, the process of payment.

A financial claim of whatever type that is used for payment is fundamentally different from one that is saved, as it exercises a demand for goods in the present. For this reason, we focus on the overall turnover rate (respectively 'velocity of circulation'),[127] not one that is limited by maturities of claims or similar things. Since all financial claims can be potentially used to exercise demand, it makes no sense in an overall examination to refer in connection with the rate of turnover, the measure that connects stocks and flows, to less than the totality. Therefore, the rate of turnover of all financial claims is of importance, and not that of a limited volume of money.

For instance, most of a monthly salary will be turned over once a month; a part, however, will, say, be saved until year end (Christmas), thus being turned over less often, and so forth. The obverse of the turnover rate is the duration of investment. Figure 33.1 demonstrates schematically the two facets of carriers of value, exchange (payment) and saving.

It is these two facets of carriers of value (in today's monetary system they consist, as mentioned, of financial claims) that are primarily of economic relevance. They are at the centre of the question whether there is buying or not, whether there is or isn't economic activity, whether prices are rising or not. This depends on whether a claim is in circulation or whether it is saved. Many other aspects,

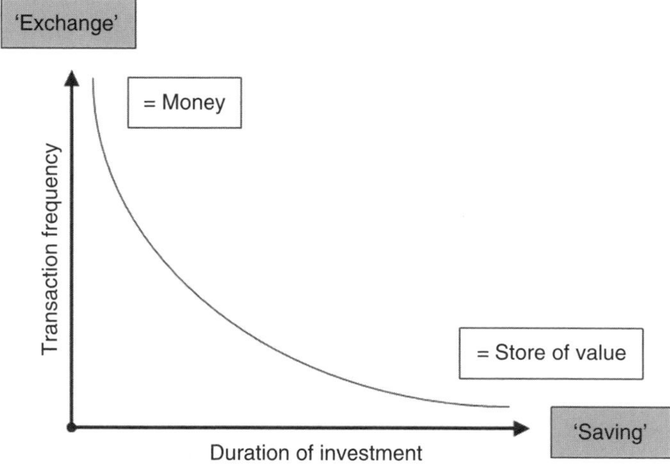

Figure 33.1 The two facets of carriers of value

from maturity to interest to creditworthiness and many more are, by comparison, secondary. In addition there is only payment with newly created credit claims, as described in connection with the formation of bubbles. This is similar to gold in times of yore; one could pay with gold that had been in circulation for centuries just as well as with gold that had just been mined. There are, therefore, today, two possibilities with regard to payment: one can transfer an existing claim, or pay with a newly created one.

Since payment is connected with demand and demand with inflation, the trend of prices is a process which is determined by the position of a carrier of value in this interval between the two facets 'payment (exchange)' and 'saving' and not only by its existing amount. When carriers of value change over from the area of circulation ('money') to the area of investment ('store of value'), demand declines and inflationary pressure eases. The opposite process is the changeover from the investment area to the circulation area, which has the effect of raising prices (the other price-driving process is the already described purchase financed by credit).

The development of inflation based on inflation expectations is, thus, a real concern, as human beings decide where, in this interval, they hold their carriers of value, whether they spend them or whether they save them. Accordingly, the mechanism which the Fed relied on from August 1993, when it fought inflation by lowering inflation expectations by means of gold market interventions, could be an effective procedure. It prevented inflation by encouraging saving (and presumably pushing inflation out into the future – 'damming it up' , so to speak). The opposite process can be best observed in the case of hyperinflation, in which all efforts of people are directed towards spending their money without delay, even buying things which are actually not needed. Due to strong monetary debasement, there is no longer any saving. In addition to this it should be mentioned that, in the case of non-durable consumer goods, actual requirements are a factor as well, as one doesn't eat twice as much or only half as much solely because one expects rising or falling prices.

In the course of the formation of the current mega-bubble, which has been emerging since the 1960s but especially since the 80s, there has not only been an increase in the level of outstanding financial claims, but, in parallel with that, their turnover rate has also decreased. Only in this way was it possible for the amount of credit claims to rise relative to economic output. The change in the turnover rate explains why prices are not simply moving in proportion to the number of outstanding claims. We now want to demonstrate how changes in the turnover frequency are connected to the relative increase in credit claims since the 60s.

The following illustration divides claims into different groups: those that are used for payment on an ongoing basis (i.e., flow magnitudes) and those which can be associated with saving (i.e., stock magnitudes). It is merely a schematic diagram for illustration purposes, as it isn't precisely known when a claim is used to effect payment. The starting point was the total amount of outstanding claims relative to GDP of approximately 150 per cent in 1965. For 1965, the claims are in the following illustration distributed equally among the different groups of turnover frequency (conversely investment duration).

The first group of claims of one standardised month corresponds approximately to salaries (cash, current account), the second group of three months to the cash management of enterprises. Both are largely in the area of flows, to be counted predominantly among ongoing payments. The one-year group relates to household purchases, and five-year group to purchases of big ticket items, such as a car. Then follow the final two groups, which are predominantly related to savings, with 15 years for such purposes as saving for retirement or for the education of children and, lastly, temporally unlimited permanent savings without a definite purpose, or as reserve for emergencies.

This is contrasted with the current total level of credit claims of about 350 per cent of GDP. In terms of the distribution, it is assumed that the flows of claims must have remained basically constant relative to GDP in accordance with the deliberations up to this point, something that is also suggested by the relatively constant ratio of the monetary aggregate M2 to GDP. The first 50 per cent are, therefore, distributed among the first two groups, analogous to 1965. The remaining 300 per cent of credit claims are increasingly attributed to savings-related groups in the illustration (with a long investment duration and low turnover rate). Figure 33.2 is merely a schematic that is meant to demonstrate how, in the course of the emergence of the current mega-bubble, the stock of financial claims has increased relative to their circulation.

There are good reasons to pay attention to the entire amount of financial claims, not just parts such as government debt or a tightly limited monetary aggregate (and, therefore, also to examine the turnover rate of all credit claims, not only that of the volume of money). This holds already in the phase of credit expansion during

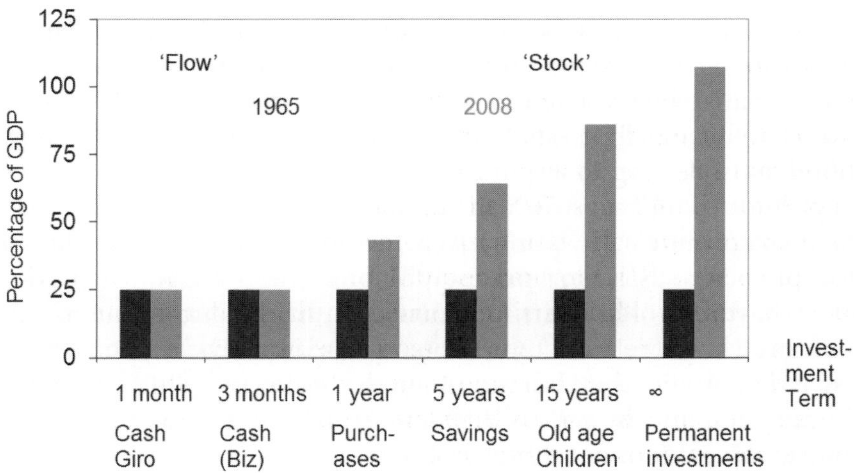

Figure 33.2 Investment duration of financial claims: amount relative to GDP

bubble formation, as every credit can be used to effect payment, independent of its type, when it is created. Later, considerable economic changes increasingly occur (such as misallocations and the widening gap between rich and poor). In addition, the structure of financial markets is altered, insofar as more existing loans must be serviced; newly created loans, thus, serve increasingly to service existing loans and don't reach the real economy. It is also sensible to examine all financial claims in the context of the phase of the peaking of a bubble and its bursting or dissolution (as well as, fundamentally, for the analysis of the effects exerted by the level of credit claims).

When there are more credit claims, the risk in financial markets grows automatically, since there is more debt that can be defaulted upon. The probability of default rises, as there is less real economic output per unit of financial claims, which ultimately must service the debt. Moreover, the debt-attenuating effects of the bubble formation recede and the servicing of existing debt becomes increasingly difficult. Obviously, in the event of a chain reaction of cascading defaults the number of affected loans would be far greater. The fourth area in which the level of claims plays a role is its inherent demand potential. If there are more financial claims, potential demand is necessarily higher.

Just as during the bubble formation inflation was avoided by means of claims shifting from circulation to savings, the increased level of credit claims harbours the potential that claims are removed from the stock and returned to the flow, where they exert demand and price effects. This type of bubble dissolution would simply be the reversal of the processes during the formation of the bubble and, thus, not a classical bursting of the bubble, as the claims would not become worthless on account of bankruptcies of debtors. Rather, the emergence of the bubble would be reversed in such a manner that, as a result of rising inflation expectations, saved financial claims would begin to circulate again and create strong inflation (Figure 33.3).

There are, therefore, good reasons to engage in research on the effects of the total stock of financial claims. Current economic research has given scant attention to the total stock of financial claims. In industrial countries, the focus is mainly on examining government debt. The total level of financial claims plays only a subordinate role, although it has been rising relative to GDP for many years and the process can, therefore, not be regarded as stable. The level of debt in credit crises of emerging countries, as well as in historical bubbles, is often examined. However, most of the time only a part of the outstanding credit, such as external foreign exchange-denominated debt, is considered in these cases as well.

Sometimes, it is argued that if debt was taken on in domestic currency, the total level of debt poses no problem, as it can be easily 'inflated away'. This is not as easy as it might seem, as, throughout the world, an effective disencumbering via inflation has obviously not occurred in recent decades, although debt relative to GDP has

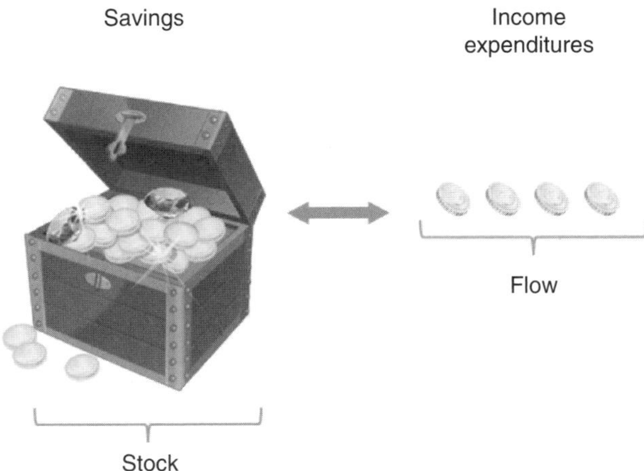

Figure 33.3 Stocks and flows

increased in the majority of countries. In addition, there are the many other effects of a high level of total debt (ranging from misallocations to default risks) which are of considerable importance and would, therefore, be worthy topics of research.

Just as it is usually only the stock of claims of individual sectors (such as that of the state *vis-à-vis* foreign countries denominated in foreign exchange) that is analysed by researchers, there are, elsewhere, restrictions to the claims contained in more tightly limited magnitudes such as M2, which are regarded as money. Even though, in this manner, an amount and the size of a stock is rightly examined, the main stock of credit claims, savings of longer investment duration, is still ignored. To include only one limited monetary aggregate and not all saved financial claims misses the central point, namely the shifting of financial claims between stocks and flows.

By focusing on a limited monetary aggregate instead of the totality of all financial claims, one can formally examine the size of a stock ('volume of money M2'); in practice, however, one examines then the size of a flow, as the stock of M2 is much more constant relative to GDP than the total amount of credit claims, which has grown much more. This leads to the stock being finally ignored, as a limited amount that correlates strongly with flows has been focused on. A monetary and credit policy that takes the money supply into account (as is customary in the tradition of the Bundesbank), thus, pursues the correct idea, but it cannot achieve sustainable stability as long as the total amount of outstanding credit is ignored.

Price stability is usually regarded as the measure of a money's quality, focusing primarily on inflation rather than the level of all outstanding credit claims, and with it the extent of potential purchasing power. Using this approach, however, the effects of credit-financed bubbles are completely ignored, skewing consideration in favour of devaluation of money, a periodic value, instead of the size of a stock.

Generally, there seems to be a tendency in the examination of money and credit to focus on the change of values (credit growth) and to ignore the stock (the total amount of credit outstanding). This holds also for politics and the public debate. Such a perspective is, however, incomplete. One must pay attention to both, flows as well as the total stock – just as one doesn't only pay attention to how much water is released by a dammed lake, but also how much it actually contains. And, just as the total amount of water in a dammed lake is of importance and not just that in a specific area of it, so the total amount of credit claims is relevant. Although it is more complicated in economics, one must not ignore the stock. Both exist after all, stocks and flows, and they are mutually interdependent and generate additional effects.

Chapter 34

Possible Scenarios for the Future

The problems that humanity has burdened itself with in recent decades due to the growing amount of debt are considerable and not easily solvable. The excess of financial claims built up in World War I was only reduced after World War II, which gives an idea of the temporal dimension. In the decades in between, there were inflation periods, deflation periods, economic crises, social upheaval, wars and currency reforms, which were all connected with the amount of credit outstanding. Today's overhang of credit claims is larger. The future is as yet unwritten, however; there is no need to shoot at each other just because there are many credit claims outstanding!

The economic outcome remains open as well. If it were otherwise, stock market forecasts would be child's play and we would all be rich. Is deflation in the offing, inflation, or will it be business as usual? The basis for further deliberations is the level of financial claims, the amount of household, corporate and government debt relative to GDP.[128] The more credit claims there are, the higher is the potential for a deflationary collapse, a default by debtors and with it the destruction of the associated credit claims. Conversely, the potential for inflation is also elevated, as these claims represent potential demand. Moreover, should there be success in holding the level of prices halfway steady, the effort involved in reducing the amount of financial claims to a low level is once again reached, and the duration of the task, will be commensurately greater.

We have established that there is a very high level of financial claims in the USA, where there also has been a high current account deficit for many years. In this, the USA is similar to the typical crisis countries of recent history, such as the countries affected by the Asian crisis or the Southern European countries affected by the euro crisis. In these countries, the crisis was also preceded by a high current account deficit and large credit growth. The USA is a special case, however, as it has taken on debt in its own currency. Furthermore, foreign central banks make the financing of the deficit easier for the USA, due to their investment decisions in favour of dollar-denominated reserves, but this does not alter the fact that the fundamental problem exists.

The course for the imbalances was set in the 1960s, when a decision in favour of unbridled credit growth and a permanent external deficit was made, a decision that was never fully corrected. Although an economy can accumulate large debts without an external deficit, the two often go hand in hand. Such a deficit denotes that more is consumed than is produced. The associated difference must be financed, which typically is done by means of incurring additional debt.

There are, however, also countries that have no current account deficit and necessarily also countries that have a surplus. In their case, there is no reason for a mispriced currency to serve as an encouragement to take on more debt, and as a result their indebtedness could be smaller (as long as no mistakes were made in other areas). A mispriced currency, together with an ongoing external deficit, is only one reason for the chronic build-up of debt. Historically (as well as currently), Germany is one of the most important surplus and export nations. We, therefore, want to take a look at how the stock of credit claims relative to GDP has developed in Germany since 1950 (Figure 34.1). To this end, the debts of households, corporations and the government are, once again, examined, this time without those of the financial sector.[129]

We can see that the current level, at 222 per cent, is smaller, but close to the US magnitude (249 per cent without the financial

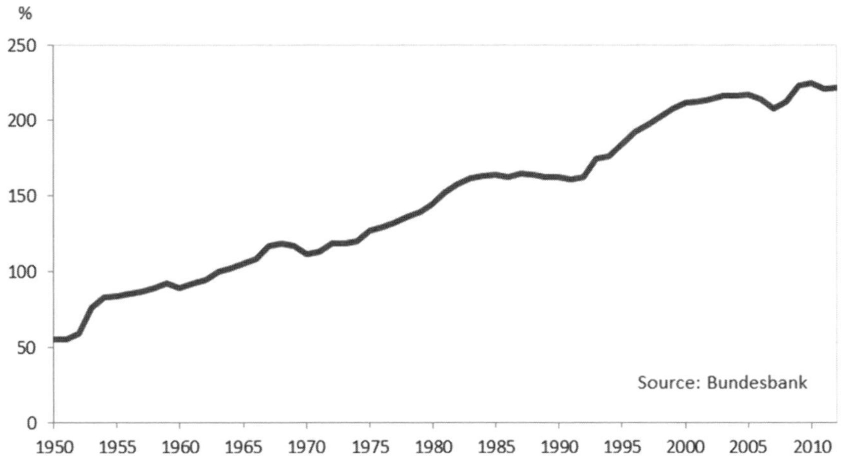

Figure 34.1 Germany: total debt relative to GDP

sector). In Germany too, the current level is markedly higher than the levels that were plateaus in the past, and which one might call well balanced for an economy (of, perhaps, 100–150 per cent). Moreover, in Germany the long-term trend of the relative amount of credit steadily increasing is in evidence too, a development that can certainly not be called stable. As important as it is to avoid credit excesses due to an overvalued currency, it becomes clear from this example that it is far from sufficient. Interestingly, the charts of Germany and the USA differ in the details. The strongest increase occurred in Germany from the early 1990s, which is mainly connected with the credit financing of the post-reunification build-up of the part of Germany that had been economically devastated by socialism. Similar to the USA, there were phases when the relative amount of outstanding credit didn't grow or only grew slightly. One can discern four such phases, with a duration of seven to nine years, in the 50s, around 1970, in the 80s and since 2000.

That is remarkable, insofar as it shows that a stabilisation at a high level, even with low economic growth (as in the past several years), is possible, even if this could only be achieved for limited time periods. This stabilisation, in turn, is an indication that a catastrophic outcome – in the form of deflation similar to the 30s or a hyperinflation such as in Germany in the 20s – which some people fear, is not mandatory. However, a substantial reduction was not achieved either, so it is not easy to afford a more comfortable method of deflating the current mega-bubble a high probability. Even Canada, which managed a slight reduction of the total debt from the mid-1990s (Figure 34.2), does not disprove this. Because of its raw material deposits, Canada is not representative and, furthermore, could not change the long-term trend.

Let us look at the scenarios that have historically resulted from a phase in which the stock of credit was excessive. The classical outcome that dominated economic history until the global economic crisis of the 1930s was deflation. Falling prices and defaulting debtors, and with them claims that become worthless, are what historically typically followed in the wake of bubbles. The underlying mechanism is the complete reversal of the bubble formation process. The formation of a bubble is based on purchases financed with new credit, which pushes up the prices of the purchased investment assets (real estate, stocks and so forth), so that these can be used as collateral for even more loans, which leads to further credit-financed purchases, and so forth. The bubble must burst, as the flow values (rents, dividends, etc.) do not keep pace with the growth in

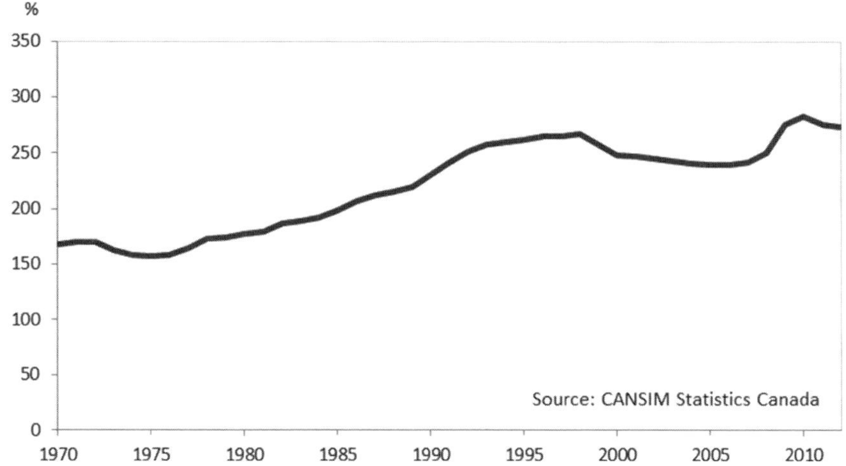

Figure 34.2 Canada: total debt relative to GDP

the stock of credit (as the devaluation of money is, in relative terms, too small, not too high). This opens up gaps, both in terms of flows and stocks; increasingly widening spreads are generated. In terms of flows, the proceeds (rents, dividends, etc.) decline ever more relative to the nominally fixed interest rates. In terms of stocks the additional credit-financed purchases have less and less effect on the already elevated level of prices.

Beginning with the least creditworthy debtors, a chain reaction is now set into motion. In the threshold range of the bubble peak the smaller increase in prices per unit of credit created, in conjunction with the reduced yields, is no longer sufficient to service the debts on the liabilities side. The first debtors default, concurrently fewer new borrowers enter the scene. The process reinforces itself, as the falling price level pushes ever more debtors below their lending limit. At the same time, fewer and fewer new loans are granted, as the defaulting debtors represent a loss of wealth for creditors and they notice that prices are falling as well. The artificial prosperity and the artificial accounting profits disappear, at first gradually, which begins to exert an influence on the real economy, leading to lower values of periodic flows (rents, dividends, earnings, etc.), thus attacking the ability to service debt from that side. The falling price trend, moreover, lessens the attractiveness of purchases. Prices retreat completely, the amount of outstanding credit falls back to its initial size, artificial prosperity disappears from financial statements and the economy collapses. This is how the classical bubble formation and bubble collapse develop, as we could see, for instance, in the case of the South Sea bubble, but also in many other examples.

Often a bubble was preceded by government taking on debt (or it was accompanied by it). Furthermore, there were often changes in financial market regulations, in which the goal of preventing the formation of bubbles wasn't sufficiently provided for.[130] The state was often a participant, even an important co-creator of bubbles (that makes it so difficult to prevent bubbles, as there is no power that limits the state and can bring it to its senses, although the state can limit the emergence and magnitude of bubbles that form in the markets). The fact that there exists a great number of parallels between bubbles, despite the fact that they have occurred in various time periods and under very different circumstances, is quite remarkable.

Such a deflationary scenario threatened after the stock market crash of 1987, but also in the financial market crisis of 2008.[131] In both cases a decline in prices (on the stock and real estate markets, respectively) was limited, but not avoided. However, what was definitely avoided was debt default. This prevented a deflationary collapse due to a chain reaction of cascading cross-defaults, which, in view of the level of financial claims outstanding in 2008, could have resulted in a recessionary contraction of perhaps 25–50 per cent – instead of about 5 per cent as actually happened. The government can always avert deflation if it wants to. What it ultimately depends on is that the credit amount that has grown excessively during the bubble doesn't shrink in an abrupt collapse.

The government can, for instance, take defaulting debts onto its own balance sheet, thereby preventing a decline in the amount of outstanding financial claims. This is what it did in 2008 in great amounts, as many real estate buyers in the USA stopped servicing their mortgages and central banks took bad debts in the billions onto their own books. The balance sheet of the Fed expanded almost explosively as a result of these actions. Similar actions happened all over the world.[132]

The state can, however, also simply issue guarantees and prevent loans from defaulting that way, concurrently furthering the creation of new credit. This happened in 2008 – for instance, Germany's chancellor guaranteed all bank deposits. This instrument is remarkable insofar as it can increase both credit creation and the level of prices, thereby making the guarantees themselves superfluous again (possibly at the price of another partial bubble and a further expansion of the mega-bubble). Hyperbolically speaking, the state could guarantee mortgages extended to homeless people, which they would, of course, immediately use to buy real estate financed with credit, which would raise the price level in bubble fashion.

The state itself can take on debt and transfer funds to the citizenry in the form of tax breaks or subsidies – another feature of 2008, for instance, in the USA, where the buying of cars was sweetened with the 'cash for clunkers' programme. Government debt can not only indirectly, but also directly create demand in the marketplace. The government can take on debt and use it to finance its own expenditures, such as direct or indirect measures of job creation (this method probably wasn't employed in 2008 because both the method and the government apparatus were too slow in the face of the fast progression of the financial market crisis). Government measures against deflation are often summarised under the term 'reflation' and tend to go hand in hand with an increase of both government indebtedness and the state's share in total economic activity.

With this multitude of measures the state can prevent deflation. For many decades most nations have decided against deflationary developments; there are only a few and (in terms of magnitude) minor exceptions (however, a number of nations suffered large-scale inflation in the 20th century). Although this doesn't mean that a future deflationary collapse that contracts the level of outstanding credit claims of the current mega-bubble can be ruled out, it would be rather atypical. Ultimately, it is a political decision. A deflation could, for instance, occur if the political establishment wants to avoid further growth in government debt or if it doesn't intervene quickly and forcefully enough (2008 was, indeed, a close shave, and the main impetus was provided by only a handful of people, such as Fed chief Bernanke, who had studied the collapse of the early 1930s extensively). The advantage of a deflationary collapse would be a sudden, complete adjustment. The drawback would be unemployment on a scale that no one can seriously take responsibility for.

There are, however, still other methods to push the price level up. Among these is the classical (i.e., the real one, not the metaphorical) 'printing press', the net creation of new money, without debt being created concurrently such as in the credit-creation process, where, in addition to a credit claim, a debt comes into being concurrently. There are several methods available for this. Since the 'printing press' was historically associated with inflation, it will be discussed in this context. It can, however, also be used for fighting deflation.

Apart from these two points, which take aim at the amount, the increase in credit and the net creation of money, there is an additional method. The emergence of the current bubble was accompanied by measures that had an effect on both forms that financial claims can take: circulation and saving. The original main purpose of the gold market interventions was to lower inflation expectations, in order to motivate savers to leave their money in their accounts and not spend it out of fear of inflation. This process can, of course, be reversed. Claims that are currently saved can come into circulation and create demand. Such an increase in the turnover rate would also have the effect of raising the price level.

Specifically, one can also achieve this by the opposite of what was done in the price-suppressing gold market interventions: a rising gold price raises inflation expectations and gives savers an incentive to spend their money more quickly. A rising gold price, therefore, could well be in the interest of central banks, in order to raise the level of prices and counter a deflationary development, without having to hazard the negative consequences of measures in the realm of credit.

Aside from this exertion of influence via the gold price, an administrative method of getting saved financial claims into circulation has also been discussed. It involves, effectively, punishing saving. Among these measures are negative interest rates, taxes on holdings of credit claims ('circulation fees') and regular declarations that a part of the value of the means of payment is no longer valid (this was done in early medieval times in the form of a kind of coin tax). Such measures have their disadvantages and can be easily circumvented (which is why no state is doing it, although it would be a comfortable source of revenue). Moreover, it is questionable how many claims would indeed circulate instead of simply being shifted into stocks or real estate (this question arises with all measures that aim at the rate of turnover, when inflation expectations are fanned by a rising gold price). There are means of fighting deflation that are not aimed at stock (the amount of outstanding credit), but at flows (the frequency of turnover). Similar to the two previously described methods, these are, conversely, also important when examining a possible inflation.

A second possible consequence of the mega-bubble is inflation, possibly even very strong inflation – that is, paradoxically, the exact opposite of the classical deflationary outcome. The reason for this is the measures taken to counter the threat of deflation, as these by their nature necessarily have inflationary effects. One could suppose that a balance can be struck, that measures against deflation can be limited, so that, at a later stage, the opposite effect can be achieved. For this purpose, the central banks 'take liquidity out of the market' again, subsequent to enacting the support measures. This can be done in the case of smaller bubbles, as has been shown in the past. However, is it always possible? Or does the high level of existing financial claims in the mega-bubble threaten a slide into stronger inflation?

The claims are, after all, potential demand and this potential demand is at the current level of financial claims in the USA. Let us, for the sake of convenience, simply round it to 300 per cent of GDP, about twice as high as in the 1960s, when it amounted to 150 per cent. We want to take another look at the question of how demand in the market can be generated and how this can push up inflation specifically under the aspect of an inflation threat. Methods include credit creation and 'money printing' (net, without a debtor), and the shifting of saved financial claims into the area of flows (the increase of the turnover rate of all financial claims).

Regarding loans, one can observe, in the course of the mega-bubble, that when a partial bubble bursts there is initially less credit creation in the free market and that debts are defaulted upon. As discussed above, the government compensates for this process with a multitude of measures, such as taking delinquent credit onto its own books (a delayed write-off of defaulted debt by the private banking sector has a comparable effect). That, however, only represents an exchange of claims, market participants now have solid credit claims on their balance sheets and no longer go bankrupt, and the government has the bad debts on its books. No new credit has been created. In the context of the partial bubble that burst in 2008, it can, however, be observed that the decline in credit creation in favour of households and corporations has been compensated for by additional credit creation in favour of the government, so that, overall, credit growth continues. In addition, the government is trying to fight a credit crunch in the non-state sector in order to get households and, especially, corporations to take on new debt as well, or at least not to reduce their existing level of debt too much. What is important is only how much new credit is created in the economy as a whole. This scenario holds in most countries since the financial market crisis, which tells us, primarily, that no deflationary collapse via debt defaults is in train at present. However, the statement that the amount of credit is currently growing concerns only the flow variable. It ignores the important magnitude of the stock, the level of financial claims and its feedback effects. However, before we get to that, we take a look at the classic method of inflation, the net creation of money, culminating in 'money printing'.

In the case of the net creation of money, only the carrier of value comes into existence, but, in contrast to the credit-creation process, no debt. It is either difficult (mining) or easy (simple printing of paper money) to accomplish. We look at net money creation sequenced by the degree of difficulty involved. The more difficult it is, the more stable the value of money usually is. We begin, therefore, with classical commodity money. The creation of commodity money (gold, silver (today only to a small extent), at one time also sea-shells and similar things) is historically the first form of net creation of money – accomplished by mining, in the case of precious metals (sometimes also by robbery...). It was usually strictly limited (apart from exceptions such as the conquest of America), as the extraction involves a lot of effort. Therefore, commodity money is a very stable carrier of value in the long term. The often criticised high costs involved in the creation of commodity money enforce its scarcity and thus make it superior to credit money, the scarcity of which must be achieved by artificial means. Commodity money cannot be made to disappear, in spite of countless attempts by usually deficit-laden governments, as, viewed historically, their money sooner or later always became problematic.

Aside from mining, however, there is an additional form of net money creation in the commodity arena. It is also of a limited nature, if to a smaller extent, and brings us promptly to the present time. It pertains to the distribution of gains from the revaluation of gold reserves held by central banks. When the gold price rises or is officially raised, an accounting profit is booked, which the central banks can distribute to the government (or use for other purposes). Although such a revaluation is easier to accomplish than the difficult mining of new gold, it comes in second place in this enumeration. The revaluation of central bank gold could soon play a role – for example, if the central banks want to get rid of the bad debts they have taken onto their own books since the financial market crisis. Such a gain from net money creation via the revaluation of gold reserves is, thus, one of the possible reasons why central banks could be interested in a rising gold price in the near future.[133]

Let us now discuss the types of net money creation that could occur in largely unrestricted fashion in earlier times and in entirely unrestricted fashion nowadays. Historically, seignorage is important for the state; it is earned when the precious metals content in precious metal coins, which bear the name of a currency unit (such as 'dollar' today), is reduced. A precondition for the success of this trick is simply that the currency unit, not its precious metals content, is established as the measure of value (the transition to using currency units and the dilution of the metal content are historically necessary precursors of today's completely precious metal-free money). The government finances its ongoing deficit with the debasement of the coinage. Such a debasement of the coinage was a constant feature of the Roman Empire, up to the collapse of the Roman financial system in the middle of the 3rd century. It took two generations to establish a new currency that wasn't plagued by the earlier mistakes and which remained stable for centuries. We know quite a few things about the Roman Empire – for instance, that there was a high level of debt – but we have practically no data regarding its economic output or the total level of credit claims.

The terminal point of the debasement of coinage is the omission of valuable precious metal. Historically, however, the development often didn't occur directly via the debasement of coinage, but via warehouse receipts ('notes'), the coverage ratio of which was reduced. The bank notes used in Europe for 400 years were initially fully backed by precious metal. But, as they circulated, it was possible to reduce the backing, eventually making possible the repeal of the redemption obligation entirely. The classical 'printing press' is, thus, the plain minting of worthless coins or printing of paper notes (without accompaniment by a credit-creation process, such as with today's money, which can also, if less effectively, limit money-supply expansion).

The debasement of coinage leads to inflation. In antiquity it was only limited by the costs of minting the coins and those of the raw materials. Since everything was done manually, the costs limited even the minting of simple bronze coins, which restricted the devaluation of money. That is why hyperinflation periods first occurred in the modern era, as only then the costs of minting coins no longer limited government's free-spending habits. The costs of money creation were already largely eliminated in China in the first half of the second millennium, in the first paper money system. The level of information regarding ancient China provides (just as in the Roman Empire's case) little by way of macro-economic data. However, not only have the monetary theorists of the time bequeathed us their ideas, but also the numbers they were familiar with, specifically concerning the size of the government's deficit – which was, at times, about half as big as its total expenditures. The deficit was financed by issuing paper money. This led to a strong devaluation of money and, by the mid-14th century, to the complete worthlessness of money and the breakdown of China's financial system. Once again, it took more than two generations to re-establish a currency based on precious metals. Intermittent attempts to reintroduce paper money failed, in spite of various accompanying measures, such as the threat of punishment or the liability to pay taxes with paper money. The real problem, the government deficit, remained unsolved and financing via the printing press (or, rather, its Chinese precursor) continued. By accepting only precious-metal money, the market as the economic policy agent of the people, ultimately forced the government to rein in its spending, which it wouldn't have done voluntarily.

To an extent, the paper money system of ancient China is useful as a model for today's system (among other things in the several hundred year-long history of its origin). There are differences, however; a degree of progress is discernible today. For one thing, the deficits of today's governments are smaller. If it was possible to succeed, in modern industrialised nations with modern administrations, in bringing the deficit from up to 50 per cent down to a level of less than 5 per cent, then bringing it down to 0 per cent might be accomplished in the next cycle or a subsequent one. After all, one thing is strongly suggested by a multitude of historical examples: stable money, economic development free of mega-bubbles and a monetary basis for a society that is free and transparent in its decision-making processes are only possible if governments permanently neither run a deficit nor have a public debt.

What then is the modern-day equivalent of the earlier 'printing press'? In this context, we pay attention to accounting processes as well, as the images from hyperinflation events with their copious amounts of cash bearing values in the trillions – such as in Germany in the 1920s or, most recently, in Zimbabwe – are deceptive: physical printing is secondary for the modern-day printing press, today's money is credit money. The modern-day printing press is based on accounting processes, it no longer depends on the multiplication of cash such as in Rome (coins) or in China (paper money). As the starting point of the deliberation, one need only imagine a world without cash, in which payments are effected solely by wire transfers, by cheque or with credit cards. How, then, is money 'printed' today via accounting procedures?

As an example for net money creation, we have already mentioned the revaluation of a central bank's gold holdings, which then distributes the accounting profit that this generates. This occurs, but is largely harmless, as gold cannot be duplicated (however, it is not entirely harmless, because a revaluation could happen often, without limit). Instead of revaluing its gold reserves, the central bank can also revalue something not sufficiently valuable – let us say, a piece of cheese (although it could be anything of little value) – raise its worth to hundreds of billions and distribute that amount (in this fundamental examination, legal aspects are, for now, put aside).

When I decided on cheese as an example in the German language forerunner of this book, I did it because, in the German language, cheese stands metaphorically for nonsense. Nevertheless, this trick has been seriously debated in the USA in the context of making use of a legal loophole. The idea was to mint a platinum coin with a denomination of $1 trillion, so that the treasury could 'pay' the Fed for its debts. This would clearly be a net creation of money, money without an offsetting debt. By contrast to customary circulating coins (which are usually also 'net' money), net accounting money would be created, since the coin wouldn't circulate. A liability would be booked without an offsetting asset! So, in the meantime, the isolated creation of net money within the central banking system via fictitious accounting processes (i.e., without a revaluation of gold holdings or the issuance of coins) has been seriously debated in a Western industrialised nation.[134] What is also interesting in this context is that not all the participants in the debate seemed to be aware of the economic difference to a debenture (or to a customary circulating coin).

Of course, one could just as well omit the piece of cheese or the platinum coin altogether and leave the balance sheet in debit. In customary practice, the central bank employs a piece of paper, usually some type of credit claim. *Et voilà*, the money 'printed' via accounting procedures has come into being. Such money is, historically, mainly created in dictatorships, such as the bureaucratic socialist nations, in which always more money than goods could be produced. Why is money mainly 'printed' in this manner in totalitarianist systems? This is simply due to the immense power of a dictator, many autocrats don't want to let a central bank (if there even is one) dictate to them how much they may spend. In democratic republics this is countered institutionally by the (more or less extensive) independence of the central bank. However, even complete independence is no guarantee that the central bank won't 'print' money. It can be prompted by the need to prevent a deflationary collapse by creating 'net' money via accounting processes, which is what has happened, in a rudimentary manner, since 2008, as central banks brought mortgage-backed paper onto their balance sheets that was worth less than the central bank paper they issued for them. The difference, the amount that hasn't been written off, is the net addition to the money supply. The process is not critical, at first, with regard to inflationary pressures due to the creation of new financial claims, since it merely amounts to an exchange of claims. However, this raises the question whether we see a mechanism here that, in view of the high level of credit claims in the economy as a whole, could lead to the large number of financial claims that are saved being shifted into circulation, to become 'money'. In this way the fight against a deflationary collapse could, due to the large stock of financial claims, lead to strong inflation. Before we turn to this key question, we want to try to differentiate the net creation of money via accounting processes from normal government debt from two perspectives.

We are faced with quite a problem of differentiation. The core characteristic, namely whether it represents 'money printing' (i.e., net money creation), or credit (i.e., whether there exists a debtor), cannot be definitively decided in the case of accounting processes, in contrast to the case of printing physical bank notes. How would we know whether a liability at the central bank won't be paid back later (i.e., become a genuine government debt)? And how do we know whether a government debt that has been incurred conventionally will be serviced? Promises to pay that are not going to be serviced are no different from simple money printing. If the state doesn't service its debts out of taxation, but only by issuing ever more debt, its promises to pay don't become worthless, as would be the case with a private debtor at some point, but initially retain value. The difference to a note printed 'net' disappears. The state is no normal debtor, after all, as no citizen or corporation regards itself personally liable for servicing its debt, with no citizen or corporation taking the associated liability onto their balance sheet on a pro rata basis. No one can force it to limit its debt expansion. If the minister of finance only attempts to reduce the deficit, then one can only speak of a restricted debtor, who – in contrast to most debtors, such as the head of a family – most of the time doesn't repay his debts. The state may perform interest payments and redemptions for many years, but no one can keep it from taking on new debts all the time and using them to service existing debt; and no one can make it continue increasingly – up to the point when money becomes utterly worthless. It, therefore, depends solely on the willingness of the state and the choices available to it (which depend on the environment), if and to what extent the state debt has to be regarded as 'net' money creation. In the end every government debt harbours the danger that it boils down to 'money printing'. Although, in terms of government debt, there is formally a debtor, there is a relation to 'money printing', as both debt and money can be issued without limit. One could summarise the differences as follows. When money is 'printed', there is no debtor, but when government debt is issued, there is a debtor, albeit one who is negligent with regard to successive debt issuance. In household and corporate credit, by contrast, there is a debtor who is prepared to look after servicing his debt – or is forced to service it. Furthermore, 'money printing' tends to quickly lead to inflation, government debt harbours systemic risk and household and corporate credit harbour individual risk.

The second aspect of the differentiation of government debt to 'net money' in terms of accounting processes leads us to the key question, namely the different effects in the marketplace. When they are created, both have the same effect: whether the government pays with freshly 'printed' money or with newly created credit, in both instances demand is generated and the price level is raised (provided the government pays for something in the market and doesn't merely service old debt). Subsequently, both creation processes have a different effect. While 'printed' money tends to continue to circulate, the financial claims that are created in the form of government debt mostly tend to be saved. The difference is, therefore, that one carrier of value tends to be situated in the realm of circulation, the other in the realm of saving.

The main instrument to move government debt from circulation to savings is the interest it pays. It is the incentive that is designed to encourage saving, as it makes government debt competitive with other investments that also yield a return. By being shifted from the realm of circulation into the realm of saving, government credit has less of an inflationary effect after its creation than interest-free, 'printed' money. At the same time, it increases the stock of credit claims in the economy. We are, once again, confronted with the question of where, in the area between 'circulation' and 'savings', a carrier of value is situated. Whether the central bank monetises (creates money by transformation of investment assets) or sterilises (transforms money into long-term assets), the question is, ultimately, where financial claims are situated, in the realm of circulation or savings; at issue is the rate of turnover of all financial claims. The key question is now whether the central bank is able to control this at will if there is a very high level of financial claims outstanding and it wants to prevent a deflationary collapse at the same time.

If in, the course of the final phase of the mega-bubble, strong inflation were to emerge, then it would be due to the shift of financial claims from the realm of savings into circulation. Will a sufficiently large number of people decide to spend their savings? There are twice as many savings relative to economic output than in the 1960s. Potential demand is, therefore, also twice as high, and so is its potential effect on prices. One can picture this as a dynamic process, since once prices begin to rise, more and more people may decide to spend their savings, a large enough amount of which would still exist to exercise further demand.

In addition, the 'marginal area' is presumably greater. If only a part of the savings, say one tenth, is soon going to be spent (i.e., shifted into circulation), then it amounts to 15 per cent of economic output if the level of financial claims stands at 150 per cent of GDP; if it is at 300 per cent, however, it will be 30 per cent that effects demand. Finally, the shift into circulation must be related to a marginal area.

The question in a mega-bubble is, thus, whether large amounts of financial claims shift from stocks to flows. Outwardly, it would appear as though the central bank were creating money and as if it were acting ineptly. However, what would its alternatives be? Ultimately, it (or indirectly the government) must bring bad debts which are on the books of the private sector onto its own books if it wants to prevent a deflationary collapse. Given the high level of credit claims outstanding, there would be the threat of such a collapse; the breakdown of interbank trading during the financial market crisis of 2008, in spite of massive government rescue measures, demonstrated the risk.

A further question arises in the context of long-term investments, especially bonds. Their turnover rate is usually very low. However, even they can be used relatively quickly for purchases, even for purchasing consumer goods. Although no one actually pays for a car with a ten-year treasury note, in principle, it could be done – the process would simply involve a transfer of the note to the car dealer at the current price. In practice, the note would have to be sold by the car buyer and be bought by the dealer after the money has been transferred. From a macro-economic perspective, there is no reason why the prices of bonds should suffer from such processes. Theoretically, only a keystroke is required. In practice, there may be pressure on prices due to the supply. Primarily, though, the bond market would be under pressure from rising inflation expectations (after all the bonds would make additional purchases, such as that of the car, possible). In that case, the question would arise whether central banks would have to act as buyers if they wanted to prevent a rise in yields, as otherwise, in view of the high level of outstanding credit claims, debtors, especially the government, would have to make high interest payments (central banks have already become buyers of bonds, but for different reasons such as to make the financing of government debt easier or to help low-quality debtors). Be that as it may, the long maturity of bonds protects the debtor from frequent refinancing, but it doesn't tie up the bondholder. Bondholders can transfer long-term bonds as many times as they want, and use them to buy both capital and consumer goods.

Neither creditworthiness nor maturities are a compelling reason, in the case of a mega-bubble, as to why financial claims that are part of the stock cannot shift into circulation. The question to which it all boils down, in the context of a mega-bubble, is, therefore, whether the turnover rate of all financial claims increases and the level of prices begins to rise. During the emergence of the mega-bubble, the shift of financial claims from circulation to saving played the decisive role. This shift explains only the increase in the relative level of financial claims. It was achieved by a multitude of processes, from government credit to gold price suppression. In the final phase of a mega-bubble that doesn't collapse in a deflationary cascade of defaults, the opposite can happen – a shift from savings into circulation – which would cause strong inflation. This would reverse the preceding prevention of inflation. Inflation, thus, wouldn't emerge by a simple increase in the level of financial claims, but through the influence of the stock variables, the volume of financial claims, on the flow variables, the circulation.

There were numerous strong inflation periods in the 20th century, with varying backdrops. However, inflation cannot be regarded as a comfortable solution to an excessive level of financial claims. For one thing, it is by no means the case that a rising price level reduces the level of financial claims. In parallel with rising inflation, interest rates and the amount of newly created money and claims usually rise as well. This is why the actual solution to an excessive level of credit claims often consists of debt forgiveness, currency reform, taxes or other compulsory measures and partial or complete bankruptcies. In the process, savers will lose part or all of their savings, which is something they don't want and which demoralises them. Moreover, one must be able to stop an inflation that has been set into motion, as otherwise all financial claims become worthless. In addition, other problems emerge during inflation, from day-to-day worries (like having to get rid of money quickly in hyperinflation) to a contraction of the real economy (which can be very pronounced and even existence-threatening).

The high level of financial claims represents potentially high demand and, with it, potential inflation. In contrast to a classical pent-up inflation (such as in socialism), there isn't too small an amount of goods relative to the money supply at fixed prices, but too large an amount of saved financial claims relative to those in circulation. Should an inflation begin, a flight into real assets could ensue. This would be sufficiently fed from the stock of financial claims via feedback effects, as savers would be eager to get their claims to safety before they lose in value. The question would arise, in this case, which types of goods would be subjected to rising prices and when, as there are two types of goods: consumer goods, which relate to the flow variable, and investment goods, which relate to the stock variable. The transmission mechanism, how precisely the stock of financial claims would bring about price increases of consumer goods, remains an open question at this time. Presumably, inflation expectations would spread gradually, and increasingly affect the consumer goods area. Historical examples suggest that this goes hand in hand with extensive government financing by the central bank (in the wake of the financial crisis there have been more and more bond purchases by central banks worldwide). Should an inflation eventuate, the mechanism by which financial claims move from the stock into circulation should become clear. But does there have to be a strong inflation at the end of a mega-bubble, if one wants to avert a deflationary collapse, or are there other alternatives?

In order to make a judgement, it pays to take another look at history. A country that had a very high level of financial claims outstanding, without a deflationary collapse or an excessive inflation resulting, was the UK after World War II. At its peak, government debt amounted to 250 per cent of GDP, added to which there was the, albeit relatively small, indebtedness of households and corporations. The level of all financial claims combined was even higher than that of the USA today. The UK was, in subsequent years, able to reduce this level markedly and exhibited economic growth at the same time. It managed the feat of debt liquidation with concurrent economic growth – it, basically, grew out of its debt. The example of the UK after World War II shows that a high level of financial claims does not necessarily have to be followed by negative outcomes such as deflation or excessive inflation. It shows that even economic growth is achievable (though it was weaker in the UK than in comparable countries). This is rather atypical for economies that are liquidating a high level of debt. The UK, however, found itself in a special situation after World War II – in terms of the restructuring of its public economy, the structure of its debts and the high economic growth of neighbouring countries (which following currency reforms started fresh and debt free). It was, therefore, not a classical bubble in asset prices. Nevertheless, it is certainly a remarkable example; exceptions from the rule can be especially helpful in gaining a better understanding of an issue. Figure 34.3 shows the development of debt levels in the UK from 1940, broken down into groups (households and corporations on the one hand and government on the other), as well as the total level (excluding the financial sector). Unfortunately, it also becomes obvious that the laboriously achieved reduction in debt was once again gambled away, and that the record highs of World War II have almost been reached again today.

A more suitable comparison to today's situation in the USA may be provided by the mega-bubble in Japan in the late 1980s.

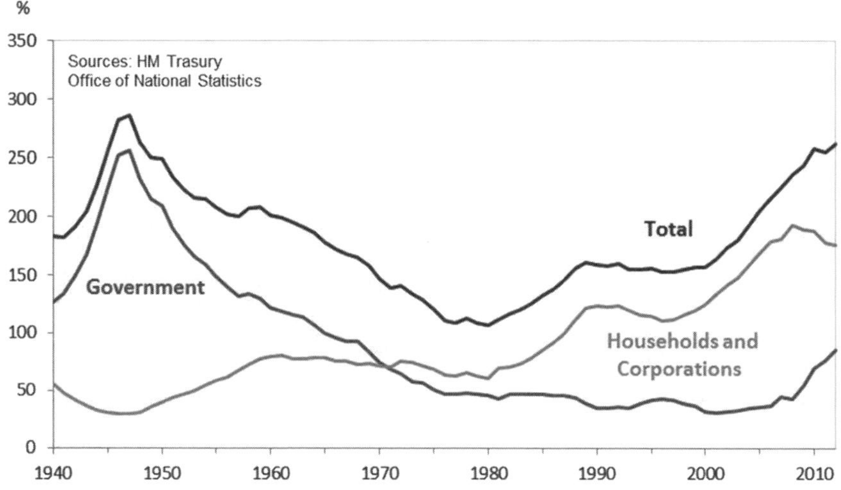

Figure 34.3 UK: total debt relative to GDP

It was preceded by credit-financed support of the economy by the government in the 70s, as the spirit of the times and economic orthodoxy demanded then. That raised the level of credit and laid the basis for subsequent developments. Egged on by this credit expansion, the indebtedness of households and corporations rose strongly from the early 80s. As a result of this credit growth and the associated increase in the level of financial claims, credit-financed bubbles emerged in the 80s in both the stock and real estate markets, characterised by markedly excessive prices. It was said that the emperor's palace in Tokyo was worth as much as all of California. The goal was economic growth at almost any price; the means was the credit-financed bubble, supported by a special financing system courtesy of Japan's banks. While this happened, the government managed to reduce its debt in the short term; total indebtedness, however, continued to increase (the bottom line was that the private sector took over the debts of the government).

Other than that, it was a classical mega-bubble; at the end, households and corporations were strongly indebted, while the government's debt level was relatively small by comparison. When the bubble burst in 1990, the total amount of credit claims was at more than 250 per cent of GDP, similar to that of the USA today. From then onward, the state increasingly took over the debts of the corporate sector, which the latter could no longer service, in order to prevent a deflationary collapse, leading to a strong increase in government debt, which continues to this day. The total level of debt has been above a possibly record-breaking 350 per cent of GDP since a few years. So far there hasn't been a severe crisis. Nevertheless, economic growth has been very low over this long time period; stock and real estate prices have been mired in a bear market lasting decades, yields on government bonds have been extremely low. A lowering of the level of financial claims has not been achieved. The paralysis following the mega-bubble is likely to last a lot longer than the phase of elevated growth in the 1970s and 80s that caused it.

Japan's mega-bubble shows many parallels with that in the USA today, from the very high level of financial claims to the large share of debt of households and corporations to the taking over of bad debts by the public sector. There are, however, also differences, such as the structure of financial markets, the current account, the net debt position *vis-à-vis* foreigners and the importance of the currency as a reserve asset for central banks. Figure 34.4 shows Japan's debt level relative to GDP since 1964, broken down into

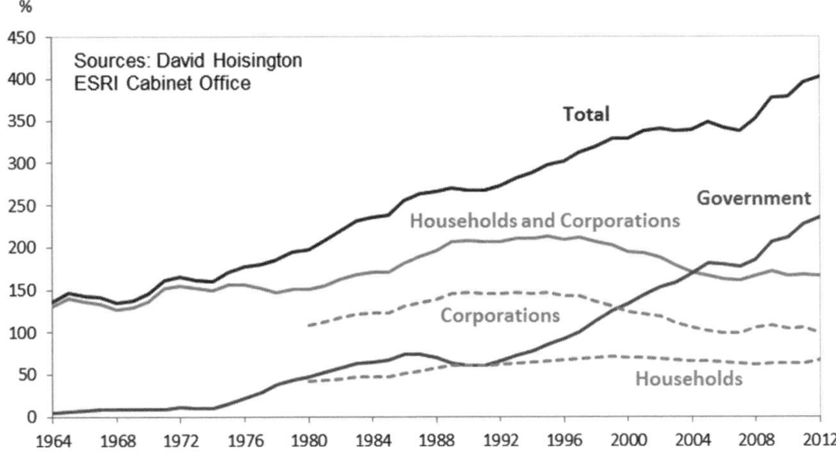

Figure 34.4 Japan: total debt relative to GDP

sectors (households, corporations and government) as well as the total (excluding the financial sector).

How is it possible that the bursting of a mega-bubble didn't lead to a major crisis in Japan, be it deflationary or strongly inflationary? How did Japan manage to escape the fate of most historical bubbles (at least so far, as there hasn't been any reduction in debt yet)? For one thing, it should be noted that Japan hasn't succeeded in escaping its fate altogether. It seems rather that Japan has succeeded in transforming the possible sudden deflationary collapse or strong inflation (up to hyperinflation and subsequent currency reform) into a slow-motion collapse. The economy didn't contract by 25–50 per cent all at once (coupled with the associated massive social and other problems); instead it has remained below the potential it could attain, if the level of financial claims were not excessively large, for many years. The gains made in the bubble have not been given back abruptly, but gradually; the illusory prosperity in financial statements has not been abruptly wiped out, but reduced steadily; the mega-bubble has not been followed by a mega-crisis, but by permanent paralysis. In Japan, it also seems to be the case that the gains in terms of real economic output (higher economic growth) that emerged during the formation of the mega-bubble, due to steadily increasing credit growth, have been given back entirely (due to misallocations probably even more than that). There is merely a prolonged extension of the process instead of an abrupt crisis.

But how has Japan succeeded in preventing a more negative outcome so far? Let us take a look at the flow and stock variables, both in the real economy as well as in the financial sector. In the real economy, the flow variables relate to consumption goods (such as bread) and the stock variables to profit-producing capital or investment goods (such as a bakery). There are also goods that lie in between and change their position (such as the baker's car, which he uses both for picking up wheat and going on jaunts). In the financial sector, the flow variable is the turnover rate of financial claims; the stock variable is the level of financial claims. Due to Japan's mega-bubble, excessively high asset prices manifested themselves in the real economy. Real estate prices were extremely high relative to rents and incomes, the prices of stocks likewise relative to dividends and earnings. These mispricings have since then been reduced. The stock market, for instance, trades almost three-quarters below the peak reached 23 years ago. There is, thus, a prolongation of the adjustment process underway in this area as well. In Japan, asset prices have declined steadily and not in a big crash. It is one of the biggest bear markets in history, but lacking an abrupt progression. The necessary adjustments in the real economy are, thus, taking place in Japan. The stock variables, the prices of assets, have been reduced in relation to the flow variables, profits and incomes. However, in Japan this adjustment process has taken place in a temporally stretched-out manner.

The actual mechanisms that have so far prevented an abrupt collapse in Japan are, however, in the financial sector. Let us also look at the flow and stock variables there. Japan has had an extremely low level of interest rates for many years. One consequence of a low level of interest rates is that a higher outstanding level of debt can be serviced by the same level of economic output. It amounts to the same thing for an economy whether it pays 6 per cent interest on a debt amounting to 150 per cent of GDP or 3 per cent interest on a debt amounting to 300 per cent of GDP. In both cases, 9 per cent of the recurring economic output must be produced to pay the interest. But that doesn't reduce the level of debt: that requires debt repayment as well. Japan hasn't (as evidenced by the data) reduced its indebtedness. The UK did it after World War II, if under different circumstances. Assuming that Japan has succeeded in retiring 6 per cent of its debt per year, then the debt service, according to our calculation example, would, together with the 9 per cent of GDP to be paid for interest, amount to 15 per cent per year (in reality, interest rates are even lower in Japan).

The repayment must be financed out of ongoing economic output, which is already reflected in the total level of financial claims relative to GDP. If, say, a debt retirement amounting to 5 per cent of GDP per year is undertaken, then a reduction (all other parameters remaining equal) from 350 per cent to, for instance, 150 per cent of GDP will take 40 years (200/5), one from 200 to 150 per cent, however, only ten years (50/5). In addition, there is the problem of interest payments, which are higher as well.

However, even if it seems easy mathematically, in practice one cannot simply halve interest rate levels; moreover, the remaining parameters can change. Specifically, it is important that savers don't take their savings and shift them into circulation in spite of very low interest rates, as that would bring about inflation. That has so far been achieved in Japan. One of the reasons was the lack in attractiveness of important alternative investment assets, as both real estate and stocks barely produced any yields on account of the bursting of the mega-bubble and didn't rise in price (often even declining). That alone, however, is not enough, as there were of course many high-yielding and accessible investments abroad. What seems more important is who the holders of the financial claims are. State-owned pension funds, central banks and well-heeled, often elderly gentlemen don't spend their money lightly – for example, on another pair of shoes – just because the money barely earns them interest; often they no longer make major investment decisions. The precondition for a prolonged extension, the stabilisation of a mega-bubble as per the Japanese model, or even its downsizing, as per the British model, is therefore that the portion of financial claims that enters into circulation is not so large as to engender inflation, and that the portion of financial claims that seeks out alternative investments is not so large that it results in too big an outflow from government bonds. Both are strongly connected with who the holders of financial claims are and what decisions they make, and are thus not easily graspable mathematically. A further precondition is that the low level of interest rates, as is customary in Japan, doesn't lead to new credit creation and with it to a new partial bubble. There are several reasons for this, among them the bubble itself, as falling asset values provide no encouragement to invest.

A prolonged extension of adjustment processes has historically seldom been observed. A stable situation over many years, such as in Japan, or even growing out from over-indebtedness such occurred in the UK after World War II, is possible, if a number of parameters behave appropriately. For one thing, the supply of money and credit must remain stable relative to economic output or even decline. Moreover, the rate of turnover must not change abruptly – that is, not too many savings must enter circulation. Typical characteristics of a prolonged extension are low nominal interest rates (possibly in combination with a tax on deposits), as well as government measures that steer money into credit claims and ensure that it remains there (these measures are summarised under the term 'financial repression'). In addition, there is marked, but not excessive inflation (for example, of 5 per cent), that renders real interest rates negative. Favouring credit repayment as opposed to credit-creation processes (including fiscal discipline) is necessary, to prevent an increase in the level of debt due to new credit creation. In addition, real economic growth as strong as possible is required, so that economic output, which is needed to service the debt, increases.

Policies globally appear to be aimed at such a temporal extension of the adjustment processes (and at a creeping dispossession of creditors, but without an economic or a currency collapse). In a best-case scenario, a real credit reduction and a 'growing out' from the debt as in the UK after World War II ensues. In the worst case, one simply loses one or two decades, which then are nevertheless followed by a negative outcome in the form of deflation or strong inflation. Should a reduction of the debt level by means of a temporal extension be possible, the duration is likely to be at least ten to 30 years. The problems on this path are many, ranging from the difficulty of keeping inflation under control to the danger that societies become less free and petrify, to the difficulty of correcting, if possible, all the undesirable social, governmental and economic developments which the mega-bubble has engendered.

A classical post-bubble process is, thus, deflation, in which debts are defaulted upon and a recession is abruptly triggered. Moreover, there can be strong inflation, in which these deflationary defaults are prevented by government-sponsored credit and money creation. The reduction occurs, in this case, first by means of negative real interest rates and then through subsequent currency devaluations or other state interventions. They can sometimes not be clearly differentiated from the third process: with the prolonged extension of the adjustment processes we have seen a further variant of what can follow in the wake of an excessive level of credit claims. Instead of an abrupt correction process, a temporally extended one takes place, in which the mismatch between stocks and flows is gradually rectified, in small steps, over successive time periods. Altogether there is either a downward adjustment (deflation), an upward adjustment (inflation) or a sideways adjustment (a prolonged extension). These three post-bubble processes are characterised by a change in the total level of credit claims.

There is, however, also the possibility of an administrative measure in the form of a 'currency reform'. This does not entail a confiscatory deflation, or a simple debt jubilee, or a suspension of debt repayments, or compulsory bond issue, or the introduction of a parallel currency or anything similar, but a direct intervention in the correlation between stocks and flows. In it, the total level of credit claims is reduced in such a manner that payment streams (salaries, rents, etc.) continue as before, but there are no bankruptcies due to excess indebtedness thereafter (liabilities and assets are, for instance, considered on an individual basis).

Such a currency reform is, in principle, possible, as credit claims are contracts between individuals and as such the possibility of altering them exists. In this way, the level of credit claims could, from an abstract perspective, almost be perfectly reduced, as it would neither lead to a deflationary collapse, nor strong inflation, nor to a long-winded tedious working off of debt with an uncertain outcome. Such a currency reform would, however, directly interfere with the wealth of savers, it would amount to a partial expropriation (whereby in other post-bubble processes savers would lose their savings as well, the illusory prosperity may even be reduced more radically). Its effect would, however, be extremely demoralising. It would prevent mistakes that had been made in state and society in the course of the formation of the mega-bubble being compulsorily reversed. Such a measure would also have a demoralising effect on the state, as it would be tempted to use the measure frequently and would be even more inclined to take on further debt in the future. The question would arise from what level of credit claims one would be allowed to take this measure and what level of credit claims should be the goal. Usually, currency reforms (including other types of them) only occur after wars, revolutions and strong inflationary periods. One such currency reform happened in war-torn and financially devastated Germany in 1948, with an adjustment factor of more than 10:1. In the USA and many other countries, there is currently an excess of credit claims of perhaps 2:1 (if the goal is a level of debt relative to GDP in the range of 100–150 per cent).

These four paths (deflation, inflation, prolonged extension and currency reform) are the options for an economy that finds itself at the end of a mega-bubble. Theoretically, there would, of course, be others, such as the abolition of the financial system (followed by human beings continuing to exist as autarkic self-supporters at a bare subsistence level) or the introduction of a planned economy, in whatever form (which would also promise a low standard of living and, moreover, bondage). The introduction of a parallel currency, even if it were backed by gold, would not solve the underlying problem, as the financial claims represent balance sheet prosperity, in whatever currency they are denominated. Also other proposed solutions will likely fail due to this fact, as the bottom line is that, at the end of the cycle, when the level of credit claims is reduced, less such 'booked' prosperity will exist. Apart from the four paths, mixed forms are also conceivable, such as the already discussed combination of 'inflation' and 'temporal extension'. A mixture is also possible in successive periods – for instance, initial deflation, followed by inflation. It would be possible to attempt to limit the level of credit claims or its effects by means of a partial debt cancellation, special taxes and other interventions, which would threaten substantial side effects.

Of these four paths at the end of a mega-bubble, deflation has become atypical in recent history, and it would, at the current level of credit claims, probably also be disastrous. A currency reform of whatever kind would be atypical as well, if there is no preceding trigger event (such as inflation). A typical outcome for a mega-bubble, as it prevails today in the USA and many other countries in the modern era, would be a period of strong inflation. It exists in various forms, such as abrupt, accelerating, with or without 'net' money. The other typical, if historically hitherto rare, path would be the temporal extension of the adjustment process. This raises the question whether the USA and other countries are able to go down the path that Japan has taken since the mid-1990s or even that of the UK after World War II.[135] The journey has already begun down this path (as can be seen from negative real interest rates). The many difficult preconditions make the outcome hard to predict. One must also pay attention to other macro-economic factors, such as the importance of other countries in an economically interdependent world. The cases of both the UK and Japan were isolated, while concurrently the rest of the world grew in conjunction with its amount of outstanding credit. This time around, ultimately, the whole world is concerned. What will matter, is that the global level of credit claims will be reduced. But over the past several decades it has steadily increased (Figure 34.5), pointing to a lack of political will and also a lack of opportunity.

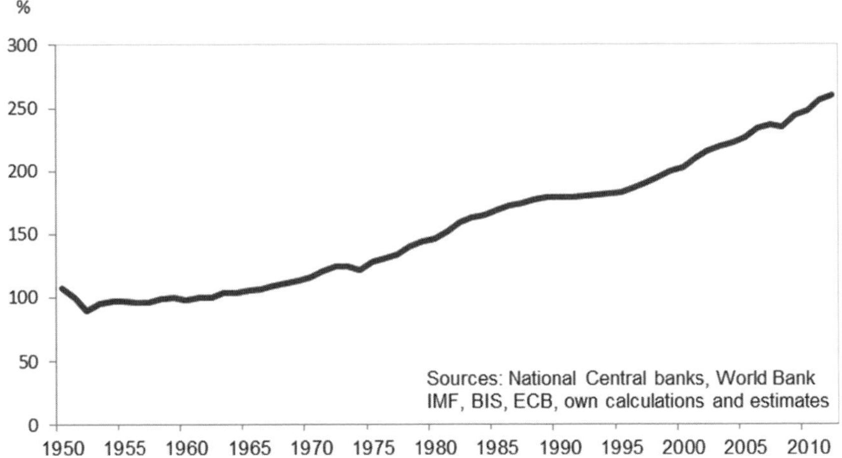

Figure 34.5 World: total debt relative to GDP

In connection with the end of the mega-bubble, the question of timing arises. After all, it may well continue for many more years, during which time the amount of credit outstanding will continue to grow worldwide, before the turning point is reached. Japan's example seems to suggest that modern nations with suitable financial market techniques are able to drive a mega-bubble to a level at which the size of the total stock of credit claims amounts to 350 per cent of GDP. However, this number is not carved in stone. Perhaps 500 per cent is possible as well? In other economies, the end of the line could be already reached at 200 per cent. Some countries other than the USA have a lower level of debt, and additional borrowing would be possible for them even if one were to regard the level of debt in the USA as a turning point already. Both, the unknown level of the turning point and the possible wriggle room enjoyed by other countries with regard to adding more debt means that, on a global basis, the worldwide mega-bubble could still continue to grow for years. This could be combined with a stabilisation of the level of credit claims in the USA, while concurrently debts could continue to grow elsewhere, with new partial bubbles emerging there. Other scenarios are also conceivable, among them a rapid devaluation in one region, without a comparable development taking place elsewhere (an especially fast example of which occurred in Argentina in 2002). The USA thereby plays, in many respects, a special role, due to its current account deficit, its economic importance and the reserve currency status of its currency. This special role can be

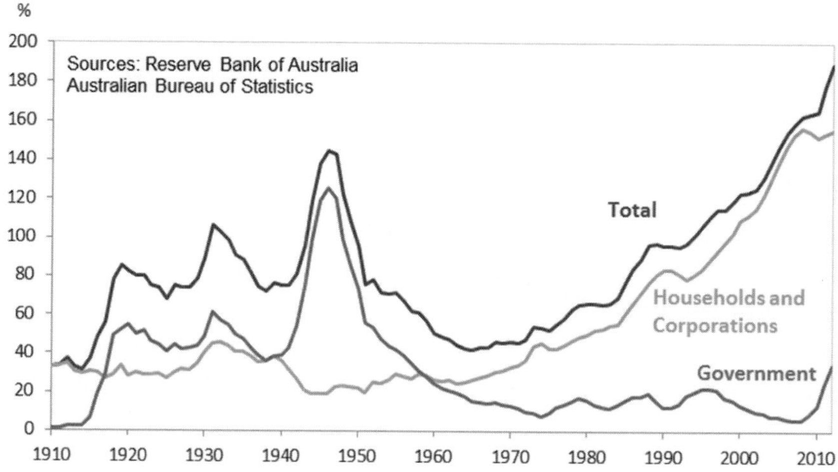

Figure 34.6 Australia: total debt relative to GDP

expected to be important for the final phase of the worldwide mega-bubble.

Basically, indebtedness is a worldwide problem. However, although almost all countries have a too high level of debt, differences should occur in the future process. As shown above, Canada succeeded to reduce its debt level temporarily, as did the UK after World War II. Another example is Australia (Figure 34.6), which also reduced its debt level after World War II (although from a lower base level). But Australia is interesting because there has been a strong increase in the debt of the private sector in recent decades without preceding extensive public debt, as is usually the case. Thus, as the public sector can create excess indebtedness, also the private sector can do so all alone. In Australia, this resulted mainly from credit excesses in the real estate sector. It would have been easy to prevent this bubble from arising.

The foundation for the present and future situation was put in place at the end of the 1960s and in the 70s, as a decision in favour of an external deficit and the taking on of public debt in order to combat recessions was made – and a decision against the gold exchange standard, which represented an obstacle to these plans. Everything that has happened since has been based on that. The increased level of debt furthered new partial bubbles, which have formed since the 80s everywhere. They were already based on an excessive level of debt. Occasionally, asset prices were corrected, but not the level of credit claims, which in turn created the preconditions for the next partial bubble. The correction of the excessive level of credit claims has yet to happen. It is the main task. Political mistakes that lead to credit growth have repercussions, which can at times only become obvious after decades – the drawbacks of which outweigh the previously enjoyed benefits.

The theoretical foundation for this development has been put in place before. Money and credit were simply not sufficiently well understood – perhaps the lack of understanding was deliberate. In principle, this is true to this day. The focus has been almost exclusively on the quality of a single monetary unit, the value that the individual saver can obtain and the stability of purchasing power. The total level of credit claims has been completely neglected, as well as the level of all debt relative to economic output and the demand that savers could potentially exercise with it. The flow, the changes, credit growth and inflation were studied, but the stock of financial claims in relation to economic output was ignored. This may have been encouraged by looking at history, as the classical bursting of bubbles was deflationary and involved severe recessions, which was precisely what one wanted to prevent. Why worry about the level of debt? The incentive was very small, since everything went well for decades. It doesn't correspond to one's day-to-day experience of life that something that has worked well for decades perhaps cannot work permanently. It can, therefore, be very difficult to swim against the tide. Even Alan Greenspan apparently gave in to the spirit of the times, although he was well aware of the core problem of the level of debt in his younger years. In a speech he delivered in 2002, he mentioned the low inflation of the past two decades, which allegedly raised hopes that the paper money system could be responsibly managed. He didn't mention the level of debt.[136]

This one-dimensional perspective cannot be maintained. Too much speaks against ignoring the stock of outstanding credit claims. One can either confront the observations and arguments, or one can wait for the future to deliver definite proof. However, one can already state today that the relative level of debt is not a stable magnitude, but instead grows steadily, a clear indication that something of fundamental importance urgently needs to be considered.

A long-term-oriented monetary, credit and economic policy won't solely pay attention to flow variables, but also to the size of the stock. That is uncomfortable, as it requires consideration of future consequences and is an obstacle to solutions which are aimed solely at the present. In this, the society-wide level of credit claims is similar to a private loan. Everyone knows that taking on such a loan means one has to forego something because of it. A high level of debt, measured against a flow variable such as GDP, is in many respects disadvantageous. Moreover, the aftermath of a bubble is problematic, risky and bad for growth. The small benefits in terms of growth in its build-up stage – for instance, in Japan in the 1970s and 80s – is followed by considerable detriments, which can also be clearly seen in Japan. Somewhere between 100 and 150 per cent of GDP appears to be a threshold, beyond which no permanent stabilisation (thus also one lasting over many decades) is possible any more.

The problem is not only a mathematical or economic one, but also a human one. A linear stabilisation for about ten years is possible in today's societal, political and economic reality as the examples of the USA and Germany show. In reality, it then comes to increases that one would have to reduce afterwards in order to get back to previous levels. For a variety of reasons this becomes ever more difficult the higher the level of outstanding credit claims is, among other things because more accounting prosperity must be reduced.

In principle, economic growth without excessive credit growth is possible, as it is ultimately the result of the freely flowering human mind, which can flourish in a positive environment. Problems with the level of credit claims have accompanied economies for thousands of years, but nothing better has been found to replace financial claims. Ideological concepts – from a ban on interest to circulation fees up to the socialist command economy – only offer pseudo-solutions. Even a precious-metal currency or a currency

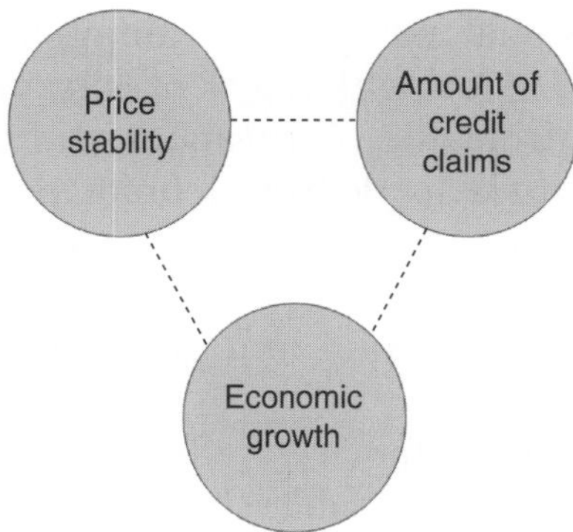

Figure 34.7 The golden triangle of monetary and credit policy

backed by precious metals merely attenuates the problem, but cannot be a comprehensive solution per se.

A monetary, credit and economic policy that is not only aimed at short term successes, but also keeps long-term consequences in mind, will, by means of what government does and doesn't do, not only pay attention to price stability and economic growth, but also to the total amount of outstanding credit claims (Figure 34.7). Given that the gold standard was an instrument for this purpose, as there exist terms like the 'golden rule', and this book is about gold, we want to call these three goals the 'golden triangle of monetary and credit policy'. Price stability is already a goal of monetary policy. The volume of credit replaces the volume of money, which is part of the former (and which continues to be of importance, among other things due to the turnover rate). Economic growth is addressed as a reference value in this context; it is not about a credit-financed spending policy, but generally about an environment that fosters growth.

Chapter 35

Back to Gold

And how does gold relate to all of this? It doesn't. Not at all. That is the point: gold is independent from the merry creation of credit and making of money. That is what makes gold interesting for private investors and economies, but also for governments and central banks. As a commodity money its supply cannot be increased at will; it must be mined at great effort and sacrifice. That is a disadvantage, but also an advantage, as its supply is limited. Figure 35.1 shows the extant stock of gold relative to global GDP. In recent decades the stock of gold has increased considerably due to technological progress. However, real global GDP grew strongly as well; economic output grew even more strongly than the stock of gold. Both, however, pale compared to growth in the stock of credit claims (we refrain from including it in Figure 35.1 as it would be 'off the scale').

For the first time in history we have a paper money system all over the world, and, after the forerunner in ancient China more than 500 years ago, it is the second time that a large economic region is affected by it. In contrast to back then, the mistake to simply 'print' money 'net' in large amounts in order to finance government budgets has been avoided (at least so far). However, a creeping deficit has been financed with credit, and subsequently the formation of a bubble and credit creation in the private sector ensued. In contrast to ancient China, there is not simply too much 'money' circulating, but too many saved credit claims, which can either be defaulted upon (resulting in deflation) or be activated (resulting in inflation). The volume of credit claims has been growing for years.

In recent decades there has been a multitude of currency crises – although they have, at least, been regional and limited in extent. This time it looks as though, with the USA, the centre is affected as well. The too high level of credit is a worldwide phenomenon, which only a few smaller countries have managed to sidestep. Given that the very high volume of credit claims has created (illusory) prosperity of immense magnitude on balance sheets, a simple solution

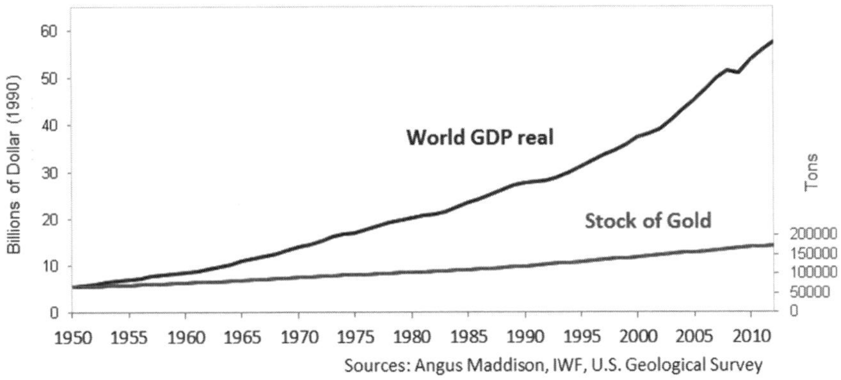

Figure 35.1 World GDP and the global stock of gold

can be ruled out. What path history will take to correct this unstable condition will be known in five or perhaps 50 years; a course cannot be determined at present, as there are several options, with future events bound to affect participants' reactions. The cycle will probably only end once the volume of credit claims has declined and is somewhere between 100 and 150 per cent of GDP (or at 0 per cent in the event of a complete destruction of money's value).

The advantage of gold is its limited supply. Scenarios are conceivable in which this advantage comes to the fore, such as in the event of inflation. The latter will probably be different from that in the 1970s, as it would proceed from a much higher volume of credit claims. However, similar to back then, gold would be a stable alternative currency. During periods of inflation, parallel market structures with stable money develop. In the Mediterranean countries, the German mark was in demand in the inflationary 1970s, in the socialist countries it was Western currencies, in the hyperinflation countries of Germany in 1923 and, most recently, Zimbabwe it was the US dollar. What happens, however, when the senior currency is affected and the others are not much better?

In ancient China precious metals were reintroduced in the end – it is unlikely that sea-shells would be used today. It is conceivable that, similar to ancient China, the ownership of precious metals will be proscribed or at least taxed. However, governments would do well not to stand in the way of an emerging parallel currency, as that would also undermine its benefits. That is best illustrated by the extreme case of hyperinflation, in which it is simply not practical to run through the streets with bundles of bank notes, buying useless things for the mere sake of getting rid of the money as quickly as possible. If market participants in an inflationary environment force the adoption of a stable money like gold, it makes no economic sense to try to thwart that. Moreover, the question arises by what right the state could bar citizens from owning a liquid store of value.

The price of gold has, in addition, an indicator function with regard to the stability of the system of credit claims. It simply makes no sense to ban an indicator. Thus, the rising price of gold in the 1970s signalled to politicians that there were problems at the time, even if not all the necessary steps – especially a permanent limitation of indebtedness – were taken. Instead of blaming the bearer of the message, one should take the message seriously and try to take appropriate measures.

Alan Greenspan used the nice metaphor of the 'thermometer'. This would alter the 'psychology' if it were to rise. When he stopped the 'thermometer' in its tracks, lowered the indication of the 'thermometer' by means of gold market interventions, the patient was already ill (to stay with the metaphor). There were already too many credit claims. A lowered thermometer indication, however, doesn't lower the fever. The patient may perhaps feel a bit better in the short term if his physician encourages him in this manner, but he remains ill if he isn't treated properly. The suppressed gold price signalled that the system of credit claims was healthy, even though that was no longer true. As a result, the second half of the 1990s could be seen as an economic success. There was low unemployment, good growth and stable prices. However, the gold price would, if it had not been kept from rising, have pointed to the barely noticed rising level of credit.

But there were also recognisable inconsistencies, such as strongly rising asset prices. Another partial bubble was on hand. It was part of the mega-bubble, which originated from steps taken already in the 1960s. Above all, however, the foundation for an excessive level of credit claims was laid by the government debt increase in the 70s. In the early 80s it may still have been possible to achieve a stabilisation fairly easily, but instead increasing government indebtedness ensued, as well as the constant formation of partial bubbles.

The actual causes are older, however; they are due to theories that sugarcoat indebtedness, but also due to human nature and human forms of organisation. Later repairs were attempts to treat symptoms; the volume of credit claims was not reduced. The gold market interventions since 5 August 1993 were part of this misguided cure. They initially actually imitated a gold standard, in that they 'fixed' the price of gold. However, only a part of the function of

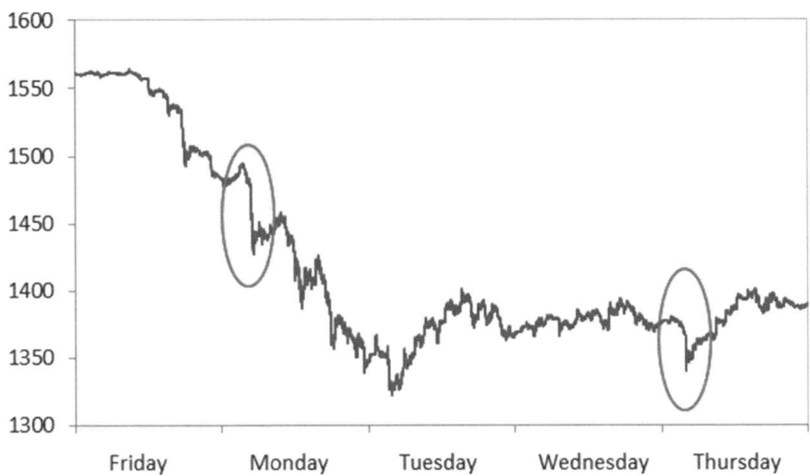

Figure 35.2 Gold 12–18 April 2013 – the 'Gold Crash'

a gold standard was fulfilled, specifically the fight against inflation. Other functions were neglected – for instance, the current account deficit was not only not reduced, but even increased. Yet other functions, such as the reduction of the volume of credit claims, were undermined, as the artificially suppressed gold price signalled low inflation.

This made it possible to hold interest rates at too low a level, resulting in excessive credit expansion. Saving was made artificially attractive, not least among foreign central banks. They willingly financed the US government's debt directly. The main problem, however, is the excessive level of credit claims. It was created on the part of governments as well as the private sector worldwide, due to a failure to enact the necessary reductions and limitations. The excessive level of credit, in turn, is the actual cause of the financial market crisis of 2008 and all subsequent crises.

Figure P.2, depicted in the preface, showed how the price of gold fell like a stone in a very short time, in keeping with the typical intervention pattern. These sharp declines still occur even today (2013). Interventions are still taking place on a regular basis. An especially strong decline occurred over the weekend from Friday, April 12 to Monday, April 15 2013. The two day slump of almost 14 per cent was the strongest in three decades and was to enter the history books as the 'Gold Crash'. While other crashes, like the one in the stock market in 1987 or the one in gold in 1980 were preceded by strong rallies, prices barely rose in advance of the event this time. The gold price was only slightly higher than two years earlier, so it was not a case of an overheated market. On Thursday, one day before the first strong decline, gold mining stocks fell while the gold price was unchanged, as so often happens prior to interventions. Typical for an intervention was the shock-like plunge in early trading on Monday in Asia, as the gold price broke down by $20 on two separate occasions in a row within a few minutes. While sellers intending to make profits split big orders in small parcels and prefer liquid markets in order not to influence prices to their disadvantage by their own orders, a thin market can be advantageous for interventions. When most market participants are absent, an order can achieve the biggest effect in terms of influencing prices. The following illustration shows the intraday movement of the gold price during the five days of the crash from 12 April to 18 April 2013 (for a clear exposition, basis Eastern Standard Time plus seven hours). The circle on the left hand side highlights the above mentioned decline on Monday. It helped to trigger sales by other futures market participants in the further course of the trading day. The circle on the right hand side highlights another lightning-fast decline in thin market conditions three days later. Since prices had already been lower earlier, this decline cannot have been the result of forced selling by other market participants.

Even though the interventions have yet to be confirmed officially, there has been a little bit of movement among central banks regarding gold. The biggest change occurred in Germany. In 2012, strong public, institutional and political pressure built up. In its wake a secret report by the Court of Auditors concerning a gold audit was leaked to the press. The distribution of the Bundesbank's gold in different storage locations could be inferred from it; foreseeing that the matter of the distribution of its gold would become public, the Bundesbank decided to take the initiative and published the information. However, the matter didn't rest there, and one thing led to another. In December 2012, the biggest German television station, ZDF, made a film about the Bundesbank's gold. In the course thereof, I had the opportunity, as a critic of the hitherto existing information and storage policy, to conduct a lengthy conversation about the Bundesbank's gold and its storage locations on camera with the Bundesbank board member in charge, Carl-Ludwig Thiele. In agreeing to this conversation in such a public forum, the Bundesbank signalled clearly that it would henceforth attach greater importance to transparency and face up to criticism regarding the high share of its gold holdings stored abroad. The signal was followed by deeds. Shortly thereafter, German news magazine

Der Spiegel published an article about the history of the storage locations, based on information it had received from the Bundesbank. In mid-January 2013, Thiele announced that the distribution of storage locations had been examined on the basis of objective criteria. Henceforth, half of the gold would be stored domestically. To complete the picture, the Bundesbank shortly thereafter published further details on the history of Bundesbank's gold, listing many transactions. After years of silence, these events were nothing short of sensational. The Bundesbank faced up to the public's well-founded need for information. It remains to be seen whether other central banks will follow the Bundesbank's example and decide in favour of transparency with regard to gold. In terms of gold's antagonist, credit and the money based on it, developments are not as positive. The indebtedness of most nations continues to be at historical record levels. The consequences of this problem are fought with legally and economically questionable monetisation actions. One of the most bizarre proposals in this context was the idea to create $1 trillion by placing that value on a platinum coin. That would indeed be possible. Comparable amounts of money have already been created by other methods. One thing continues to be impossible, however: no government can create 1,000,000,000,000 grams of gold by decree.

Appendices

Appendix 1

Figure A.1A Intraday charts of gold to 4 August 1993

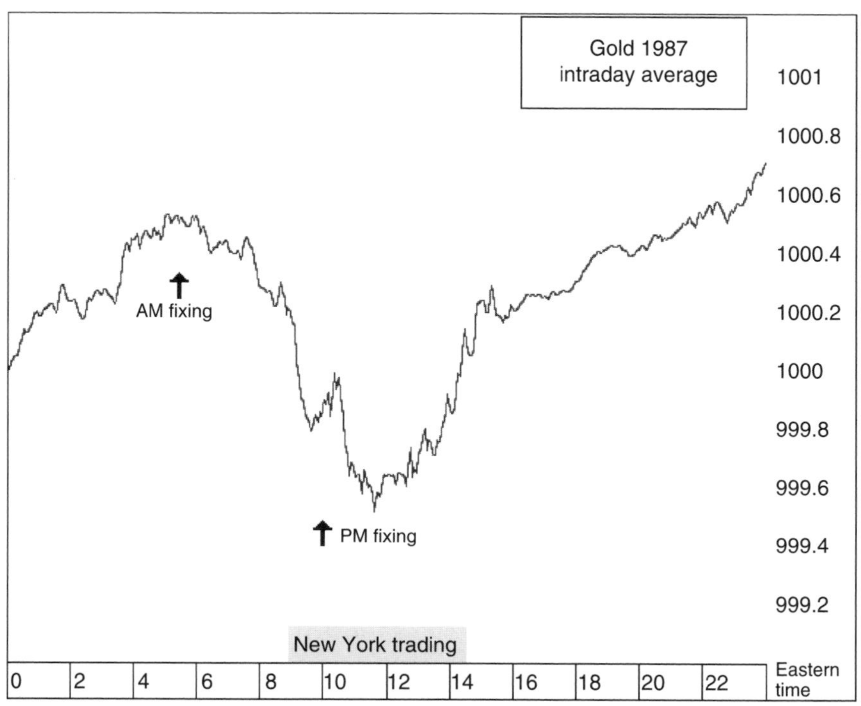

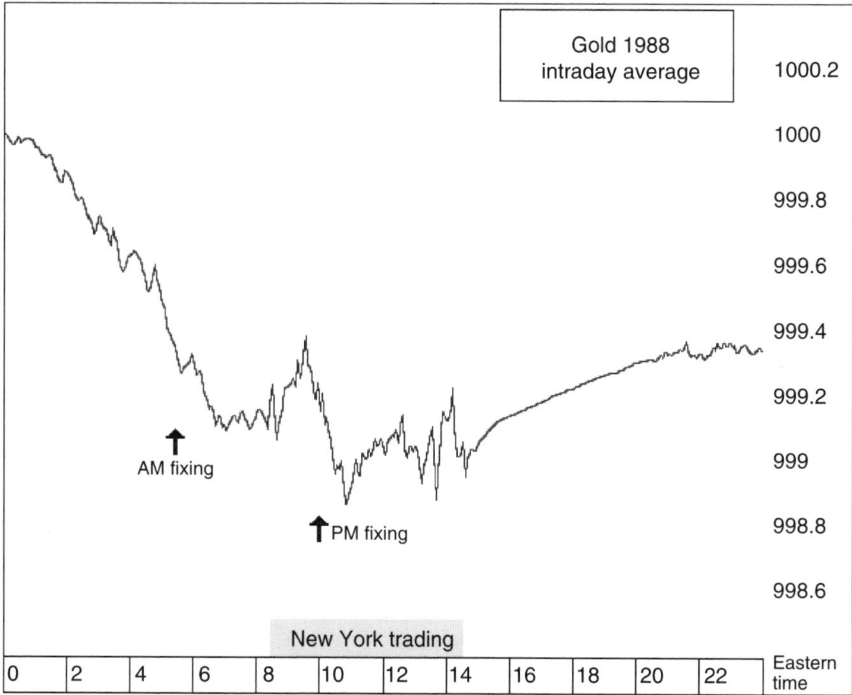

Figure A.1A (Continued)

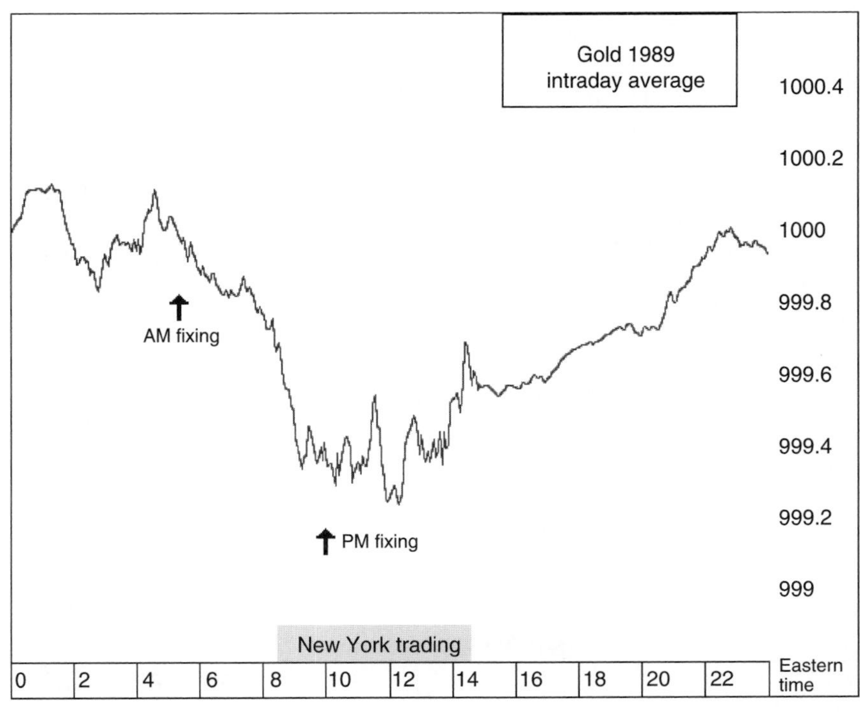

Figure A.1A (Continued)

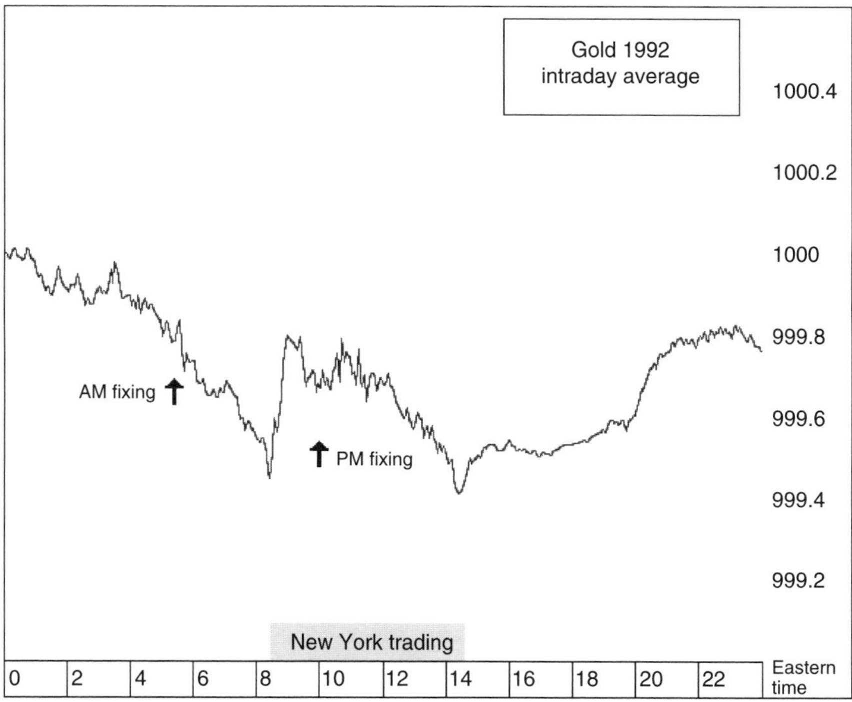

Figure A.1A (Continued)

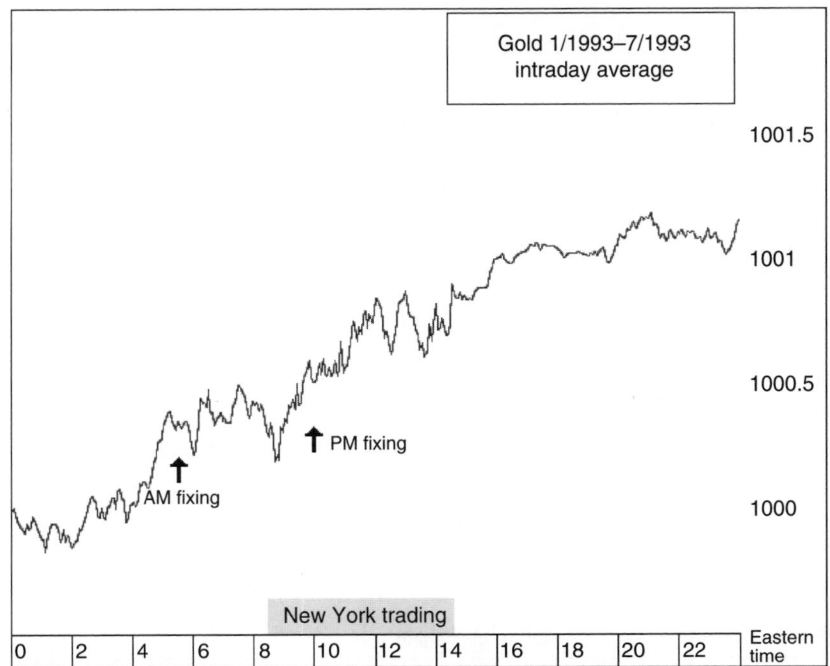

Figure A.1A (Continued)

Figure A.1B Intraday charts of gold from 5 August 1993

Figure A.1B (Continued)

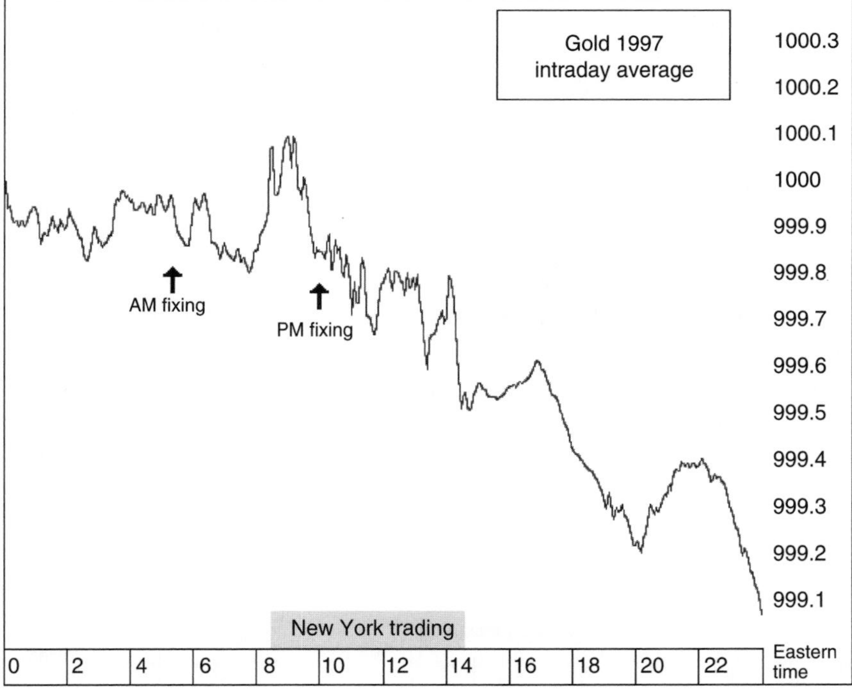

Figure A.1B (Continued)

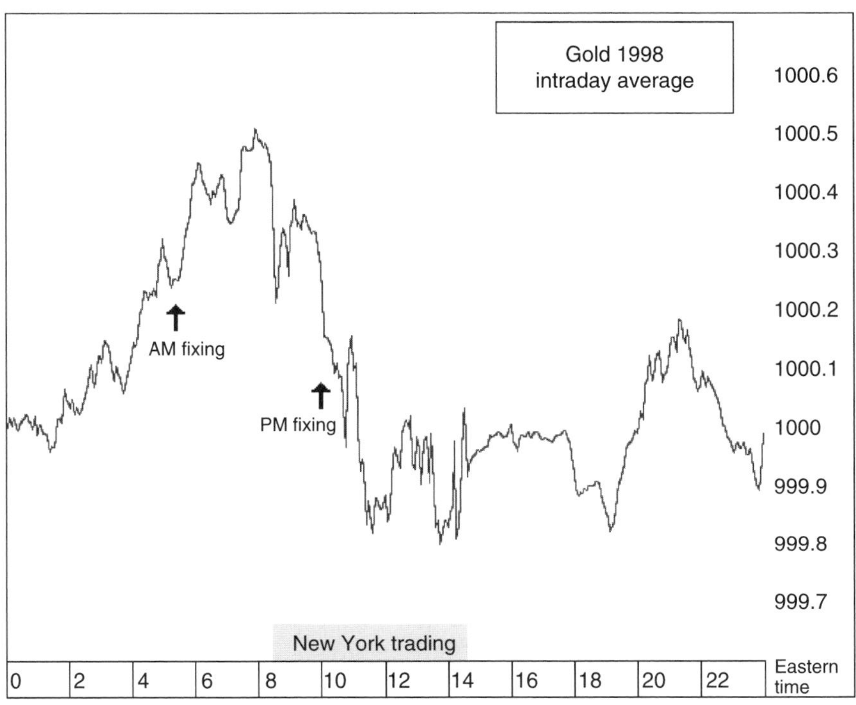

Figure A.1B (Continued)

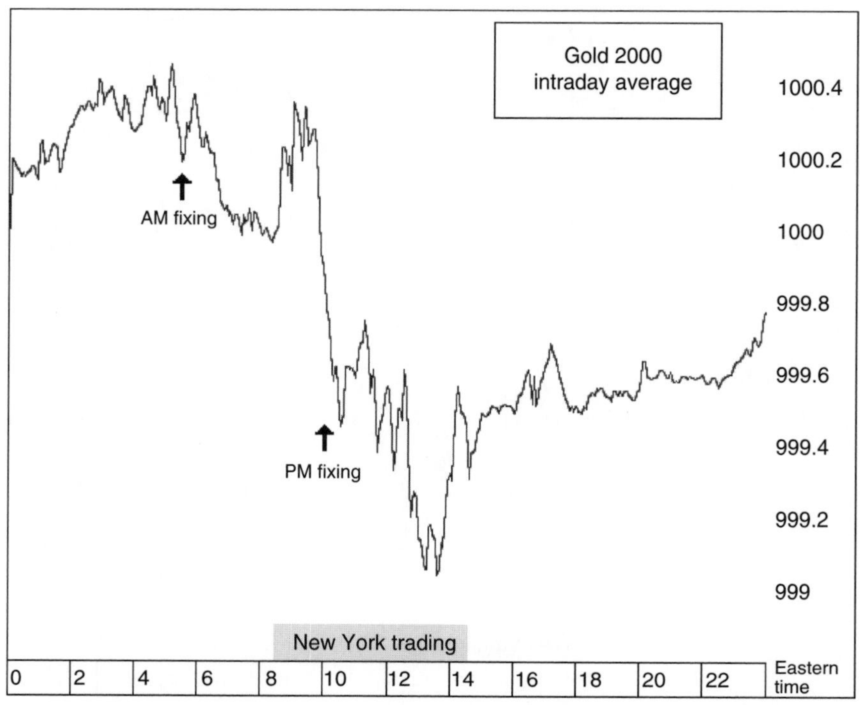

Figure A.1B (Continued)

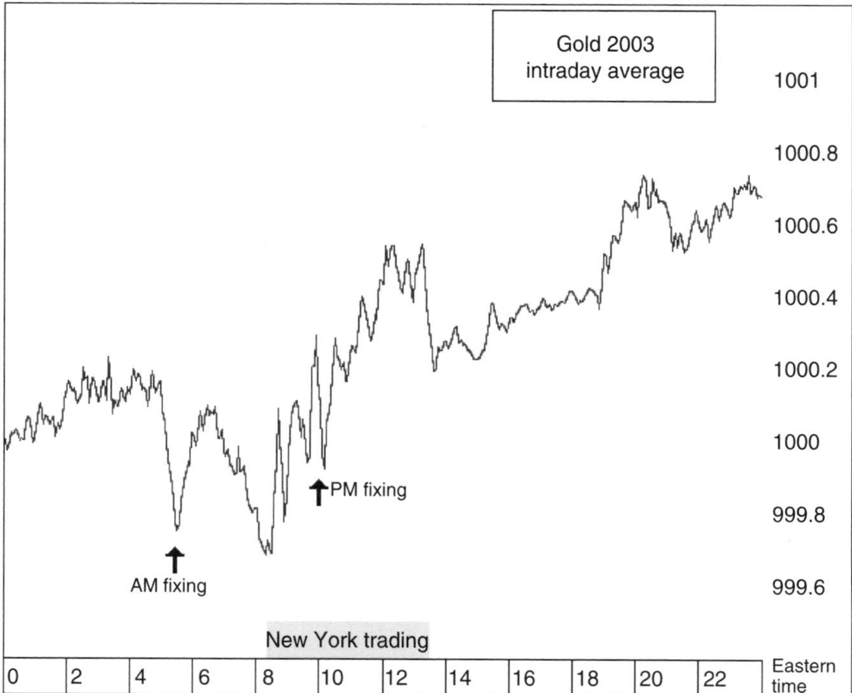

Figure A.1B (Continued)

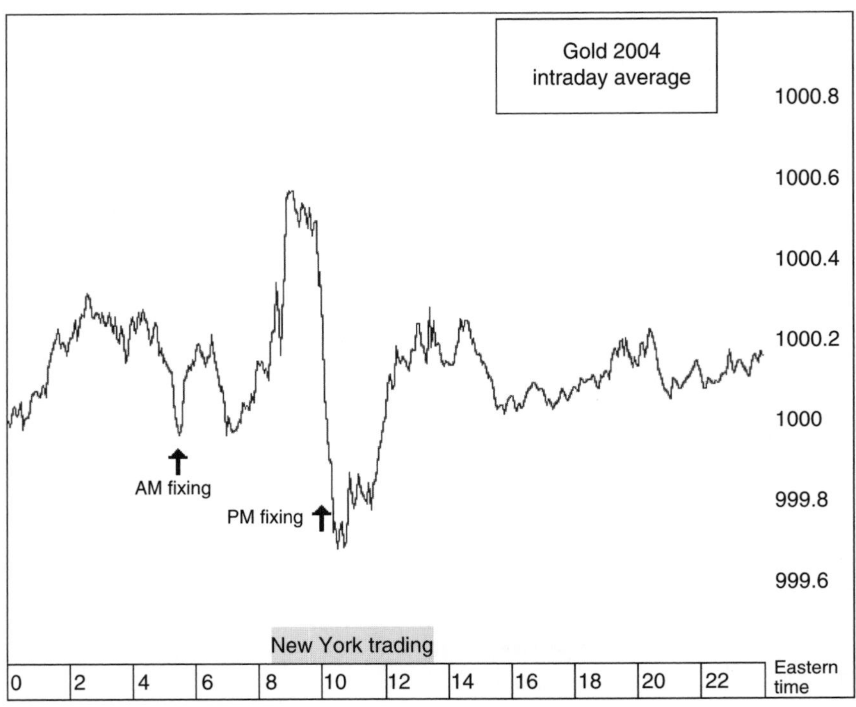

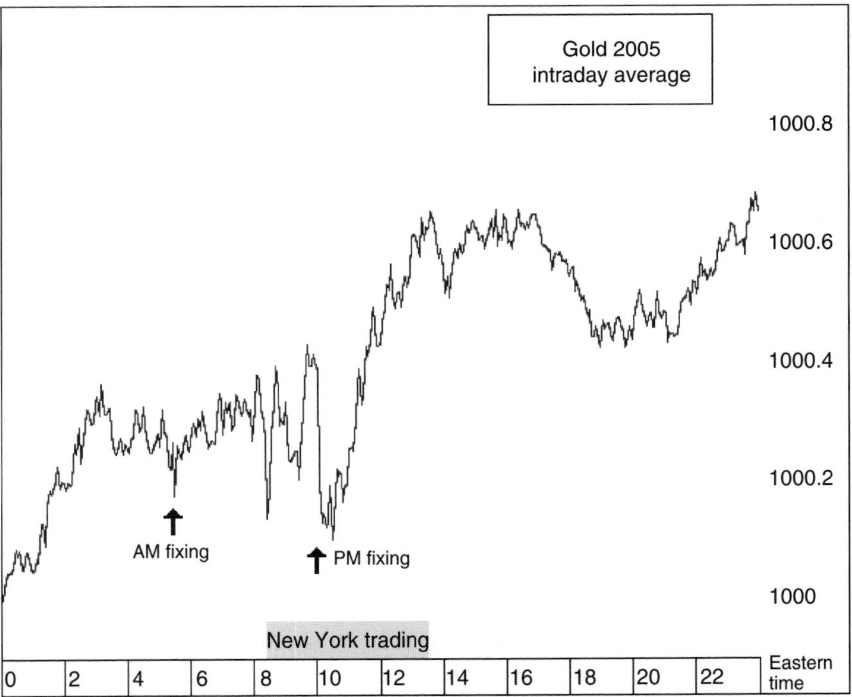

Figure A.1B (Continued)

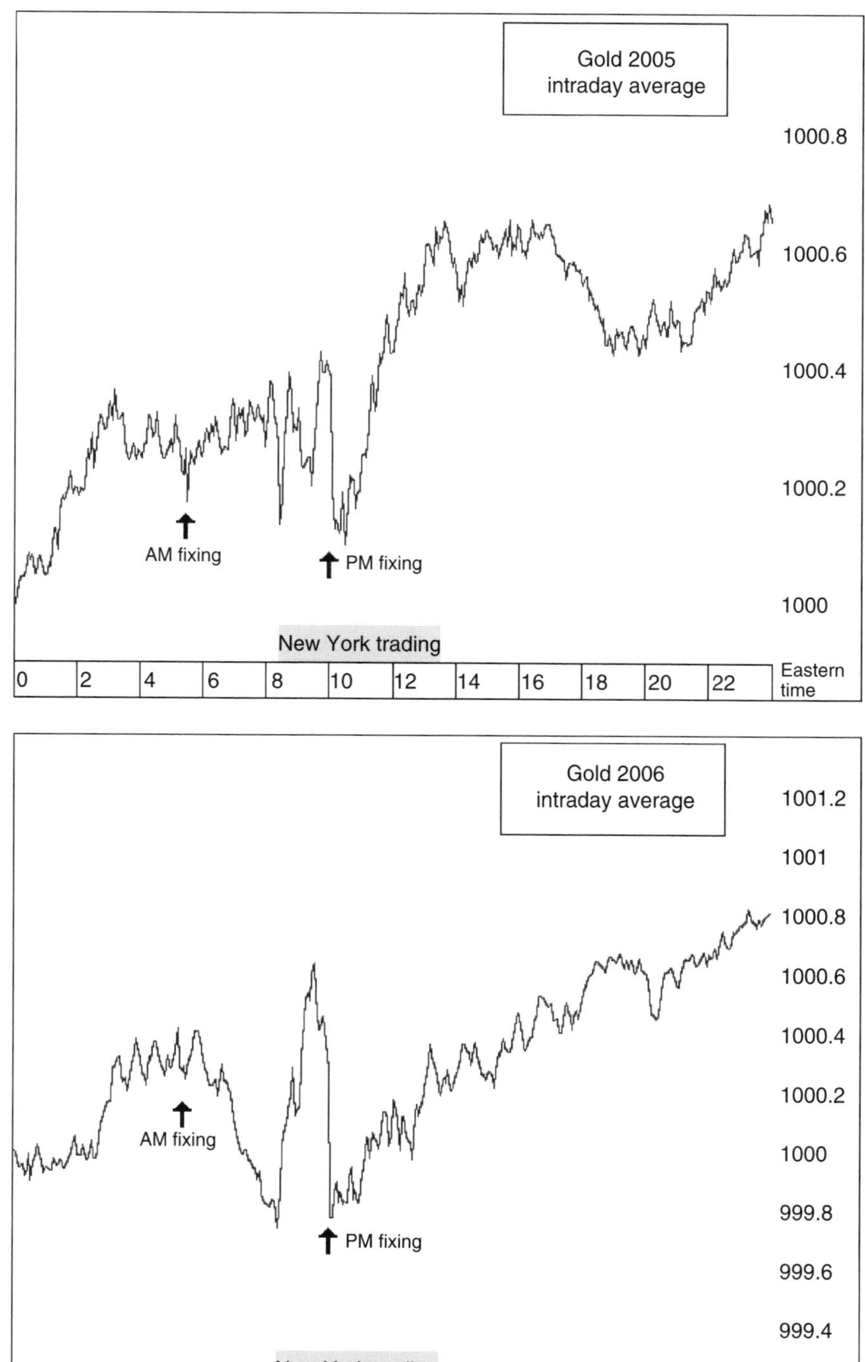

Figure A.1B (Continued)

Figure A.1B (Continued)

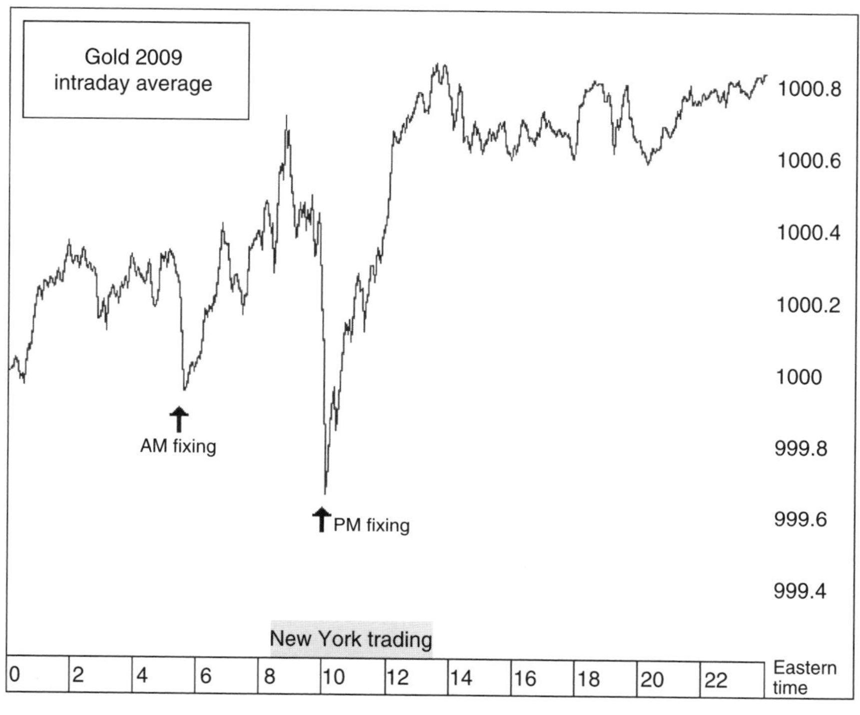

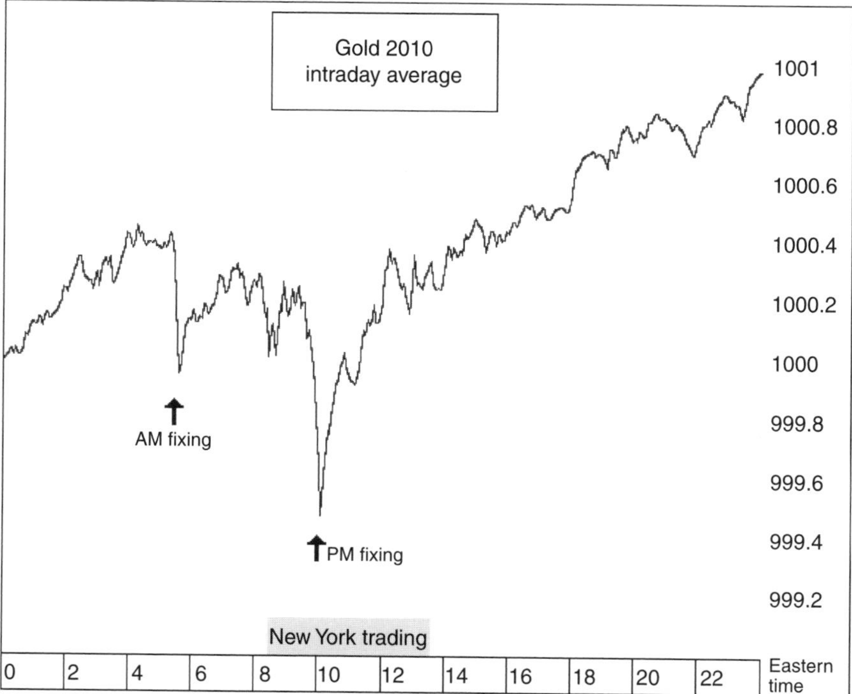

Figure A.1B (Continued)

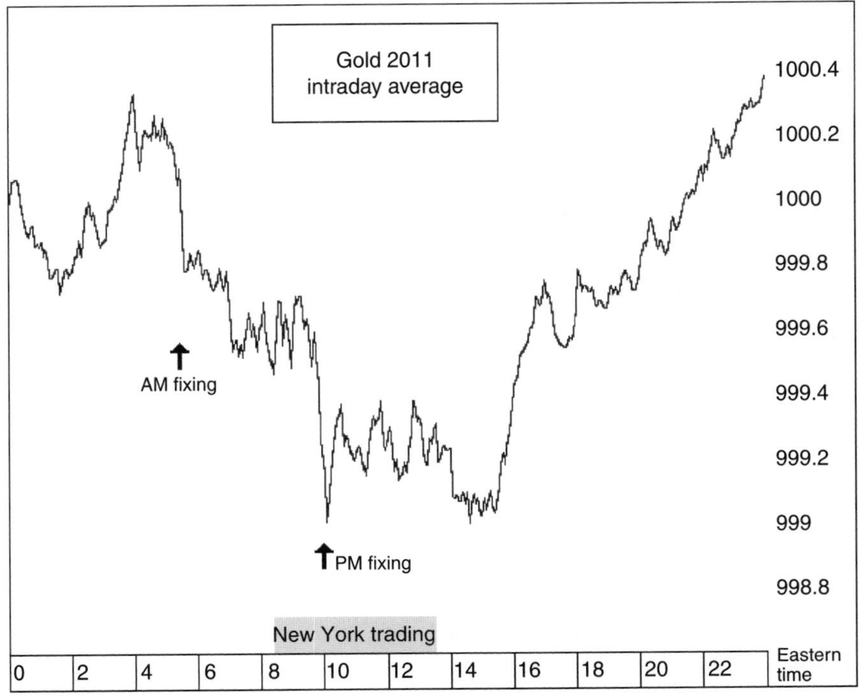

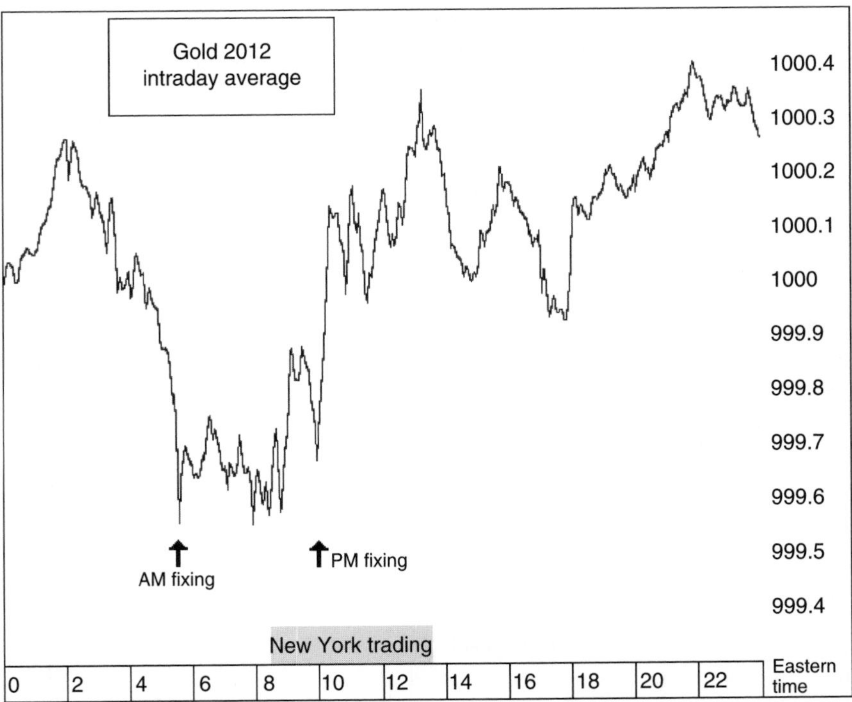

Figure A.1B (Continued)

Appendix 2

Details regarding the measurement of the intraday anomaly

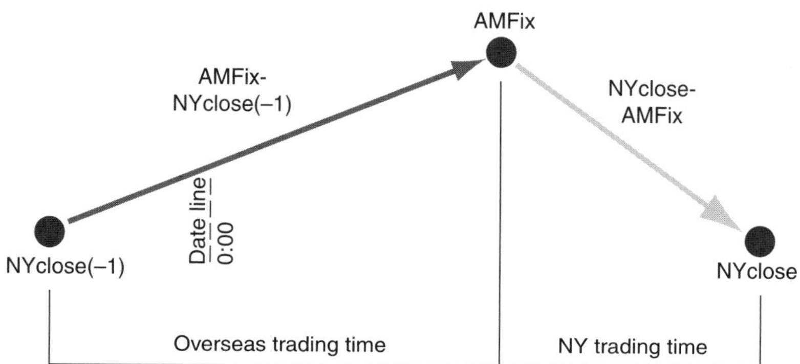

Figure A.2 Illustration: gold intraday intervention pattern (schematic)

Clawar considered the difference between the closing price in New York and the AM fixing in London as an approximation of the price movement during New York trading hours (mathematically formulated as NYclose – AMfixing). The price movements in the trading hours of the rest of the world can correspondingly be depicted as the AM fixing in London minus the closing price in New York on the preceding day (AMfixing – NYprecedingclose). If one now subtracts one term from the other, one obtains the relative price movement during these trading hours ((NYclose – AMfixing) – (AMfixing – NYprecedingclose)). What is calculated is therefore the difference between the price movement in New York and that in the rest of the trading day. If, similar to the example, gold rises by $1 in New York, while it adds $10 in the rest of the world, the price falls by $9 in New York in relative terms ($-9 = 1 - 10$). A negative term thus expresses that the price has declined in New York relative to the rest of the world. This is also clearly the case in the example, as it only rose by $1 in New York, while it rose by $10 in the remaining time. The move in New York was therefore weaker. In an April 2000 article, Clawar came close to a comparable approach, as he planned to exploit the anomaly for trading.[137]

Appendix 3

Details regarding gold leased out by the Bundesbank

On 2 January, the Bundesbank surprisingly conveyed the amount of gold it had lent out to me by email. Previously, I had estimated the amount of gold on loan for the German-language forerunner of this book based on other data.[138] This presented me with an excellent opportunity to check an estimate. One can get an idea of the effort that has to be expended for the best possible estimate and the range within which it is accurate. As an aside, it appears that the statements published by the Bundesbank over the years are internally consistent. We therefore want to take a look at the estimate (in a compressed version).

The estimate of the amount of Bundesbank gold that was lent out was based on the data on the returns from gold lending. Although the returns are not stated precisely in the balance sheet, it was possible to enhance the precision of balance sheet line items with the aid of an iterative method. These data were then correlated with additional information. Only this quite elaborate method made an estimate of the amount of gold lent out by the Bundesbank (the second-largest holder of gold in the world) possible. Let us look at the relevant item in the 2008 annual report.

Interest income

	2008	2007	Year-on-year change	
Item	€ million	€ million	€ million	%
Interest income in foreign currency Gold	0	1	–1	–56.0

Figure A.3 Illustration: excerpt from the balance sheet of the German Bundesbank

Below 'Interest income in foreign currency' in '€ m.' we find under 'gold' the number '0'. Based on the rounding rules 0 million means that the Bundesbank earned between €0.- and €500,000 in interest income. At the same time, it states that the change was -56 per cent. This means that it must still have received interest income in 2008, otherwise it would say -100 per cent there. With the statement denoting the change, we get additional information.

By using both the stated interest income and the precise statement regarding the year-on-year changes in income it is possible to calculate quite precisely what the interest income from gold lending actually amounted to because the change relative to the prior year narrows the upper and lower limits for subsequent years. The numbers were first published in 2003 (in 2002 they were submerged in the 'other' category). Interest income of €7 million in 2003 indicates, due to rounding, that between €6.5 million (lower limit) and €7.5 million (upper limit) was earned. For the following year 2004, the Bundesbank states €6 million, from which a lower limit of €5.5 million and an upper limit of €6.5 million follows. In addition, it states that the change was -19.4 per cent. From this, a more precise upper limit for 2004 can be gleaned, since in the preceding year, the maximum was €7.5 million (upper limit in 2003), which cannot have become more than €6.045 million if 19.4 per cent are deducted. Since €6.045 million is less than € 6.5 million, we have found a precise value for the upper limit! For the lower limit in 2004, it is not possible to arrive at a more precise value than € 5.5 million, based on the second boundary condition (as 6.5 – 19.4 per cent is 5.239; in order to be able to raise the lower limit value we require a number greater than 5.5). By means of this iterative limiting procedure, the spread between upper and lower limits can be reduced year after year. This allows an ever more precise calculation of the values, even if they jump around a lot. Table A.1 illustrates the method.

For instance in 2008, the Bundesbank earned interest income of between €0.442 and €0.443 million from gold lending. This spread results if one calculates

Table A.1 Interest income of the Bundesbank from gold lending (in millions of euro)

	2003	2004	2005	2006	2007	2008
Interest income	7	6	6	0	1	0
Change (in per cent)		−19.4	−8.7	−94.3	220.2	−56.0
Upper limit	7.5	6.045	5.519	0.315	1.007	0.443
Lower limit	6.5	5.5	5.5	0.314	1.004	0.442

to three decimal places as in Table A.1. If one calculates with higher precision to within one euro, €441,684 is the result for the lower limit and €443,216 for the upper limit. Thus, the Bundesbank earned interest income from gold lending amounting to €442,450 in 2008 (which can be stated with a precision of +/−€776).

Based on the interest income and the known lease rates it was, therefore, possible to estimate the amount of gold lent out by the Bundesbank. Unfortunately, the lease rate fluctuated widely and its height also depended on maturities. Shifts must be taken into account as well, as the interest income earned in one year may only have been received in the following year. Other statements made by the Bundesbank over the years helped only marginally with determining the value. The estimate resulting from this could, therefore, only be a rough one. It amounted to 350 tons at the peak.

In reality, it was 250 tons that the Bundesbank had maximally lent out. The decline in gold lending occurred markedly faster in the beginning and subsequently more slowly than I had estimated. If one considers that, at the time (and even still today), many market observers believed that a large part of the gold holdings (for example, 1,700 tons and more) were lent out, the precision of the estimate with a deviation of 100 tons from the peak value is quite good (it would mean, for instance, that the Bundesbank earned 0.7 per cent in interest instead of the estimated 0.5 per cent). In the face of excessive speculation about the amount of gold on loan, it is gratifying that the Bundesbank has now disclosed the amount. Gold lending, which the Bundesbank first decided to pursue in 1996, has meanwhile been discontinued.

Appendix 4

Details regarding gold lent out worldwide

Figure 16.3 shows two lines, one reflecting the directly calculated values and one based on values that have been corrected by additional factors. The direct method is solely based on the amounts stored in New York (from 2005 onward those stored in London are taken into account as well). The known values of the central banks of Switzerland, Germany and Portugal, and the overall environment, however, suggest a more pronounced decline. By incorporating additional factors, we adjust the curve accordingly. To this end, we, first, compare the values of specific years with the results of other estimates. Apart from estimates that must be considered as too extreme with regard to the size of the carry trade in one or other direction, there are, luckily, estimates for two points in time based on different methods. For year end 1993, an estimate can be made based on a survey by the Bank of England. It didn't encompass the entire market, but can be extrapolated to values of between 3,000 and 4,700 tons.[139] Our 'New York method' arrives at just under 4,000 tons for 1993, which is situated within the boundaries of this estimate (however, it is higher than the more realistic lower value). For the turn of the millennium, there exist further estimates that don't deviate too much in one or the other direction. They amount to 7,000 and 6,000 tons. One of these estimates was presented by Dinsa Mehta (Chase Manhattan) in April of 2000.[140] The other one, published at around the same time by Jessica Cross (Virtualmetals), is based on a survey; Andy Smith (Mitsui) arrived at a similar value.[141] The method based solely on the quantities in storage gives a peak value of 8,000 tons, close to these estimates (but once again a little too high).

Apart from these anchor points, we also pay attention to the progression. In the method based on the amounts stored in New York, a constant ratio between different vaults was assumed. However, in the years immediately preceding 1980, there was a small reduction in the quantity stored in New York, with no corresponding decline in the total quantity. There are a number of possible reasons for this (for instance, a withdrawal, as the importance of this storage facility declined after the end of gold convertibility in 1971). It is conceivable that this trend persisted after 1980 too, which would result in a slight exaggeration of the amount of leased-out gold. An escalation of this effect could become noticeable from 2001 in the course of gold loan reductions, as possibly a disproportionately lower amount of gold is returned to New York.

Conversely, there is yet another big unknown, the amount of US gold on loan. There are hints that US gold was lent out via the ESF (see Chapter 28). If US gold was lent from US vaults (not, for instance, by means of swaps via other countries), this would naturally not be captured by a method that is based on movements of foreign gold. There are, therefore, a number of possible distortions which are only known in terms of their direction, and which are partly opposed, and thus perhaps cancel each other out. For this reason – and because the mentioned anchor points are anything but precise and, therefore, cannot provide any clarification – the curve calculated from the quantities stored in New York can be regarded as a reasonably precise representation, if it consistently also encompasses US gold (there is no reliable evidence regarding the amount of directly lent-out US gold). *Nota bene*: it is a method that doesn't even attempt to directly capture the amounts lent out!

In the adjusted curve, we attempt to integrate these (uncertain) factors. If one considers the anchor points and the altered progression, a somewhat lower-lying curve results. The first anchor point is given by the lower value of the enhanced Bank of England estimate (3,000 tons). It corresponds with the skew imparted to our method on account of the trend of gold withdrawals from New York that was already in evidence prior to 1980. For the turn of the millennium, we assume 7,000 tons (whereby we continue to assume that this maximum value was reached in 2001).

From 2005 onward, the values for the Bank of England's storage facility are available to us as well (unfortunately, no longer history is available). The changes in the quantities stored there are incorporated in both curves. For 2012, the estimate for the adjusted curve is 3,000 tons. This magnitude is consistent with the marked decline of known gold loan amounts (Bundesbank and Swiss National Bank), coupled with continuing gold lending by other central banks. It must be considered that purchases by central banks out of ongoing production do not lead to changes in the amount of gold on loan (but are interpreted as such by the direct method).

In fact, the most up-to-date value theoretically harbours the greatest lack of precision. The reasons for this are that the method leads to a compounding of errors over the years, and that no reasonably solid foundation – based on surveys, for instance – is available. Conventional estimates arrive at just under 2,000 tons. There are, however, still estimates circulating in the market that assume an amount of more than 15,000 tons of gold on loan, a multiple of the 3,000 ton estimate used here. Based on available information, it is however very difficult to determine how many carry trades still exist in an environment of rising prices and how difficult it was, indeed still is, to close them out.

The values employed for the anchor points of the adjusted curve in 1993 and 2001 are each, by about 1,000 tons, lower than the values that have been calculated directly from the quantities stored in New York. The current value is strongly influenced by the amount of gold stored in London. With these benchmark values, the second, adjusted curve is constructed. The path between them is commensurately adapted.

Appendix 5

First mention of the gold intervention

It was probably Frank Veneroso who mentioned for the first time the systematic gold interventions. In the article ‘What’s holding gold down’, published in Forbes Magazine in 5 June 1995, he wrote: ‘Again, the gold price has met resistance at $400 an ounce. The markets are abuzz with rumors that central banks have capped the price.’

Notes

1. Estimates regarding fundamental data relating to gold are, as a matter of principle, quite uncertain. Only vague estimates are possible regarding historical production, how much is produced 'off balance sheets', how much is actually traded in this opaque market and how much private persons and institutions actually hold.
2. However, this had, in fact, happened already in the 1930s. See Michael Bordo, Owen Humpage and Anna Schwartz, 'The Historical Origins of US Exchange Market Intervention Policy' (NBER Working Paper 12662), 2006, http://michael.bordo.googlepages.com/w12662.pdf, S. 20.
3. Roy Jastram, *The Golden Constant: The English and American Experience, 1560–1976* (New York: John Wiley, 1977).
4. With regard to gold, the LTCM crisis is also of importance because there were rumours that LTCM was short 300 tons of gold. These rumours were never officially confirmed and could not be proved, which is why there is no further mention of them here. However, they prompted many market participants to suspect that central banks are active in the gold market behind the scenes.
5. A manual method is suitable enough in this case and avoids the potential problems of automated techniques, such as may occur in the measuring of specific percentage declines in specific time periods (which could lead to somewhat weaker crises being overlooked, while double-counting could happen in the case of a crisis that progresses in several distinct waves).
6. See Appendix 5.
7. Disk Trading, Iavor Kindekov, http://disktrading.is99.com/disktrading.
8. Harry Clawar, 'A New Gold War?', www.gold eagle.com/editorials_00/clawar031300.html.
9. The start date ('99') is apparently erroneous.
10. Front month prices (i.e., those of the respective nearest futures contract), in trader jargon, also referred to as 'spot prices', which, however, only approximate actual spot prices. This appears not to have appreciably impaired the results of his study. Michael Bolser, 'Evidence of Gold Manipulation on the COMEX', www.goldensextant.com/commentaryBA.html#anchor51667.
11. For details of the calculation, see Appendix 2.
12. Dimitri Speck, 'Tracks in the Trading: When Did the Gold Price Manipulation Begin?', www.gold-eagle.com/editorials_01/speck022301.html.
13. Commodity Research Bureau, Chicago, www.crbtrader.com; while the data series employed, 'GC', includes prices prior to 1991, the actual New York closing prices are no longer contained in them.
14. Olsen Financial Technologies, Zurich, www.olsendata.com.
15. Systrade, Neuville de Poitou, www.tickdatamarket.com.
16. Even though the central banks as a result triggered a rise in the gold price in this case, it does not necessarily follow that no central banks are involved

in gold price suppression. For one thing, they may not necessarily have expected such a price increase. Moreover, central banks are not a monolithic bloc; the central banks that were primarily involved in proposing the WAG were not the same financial institutions that wanted to see a low gold price at the time.

17. The average intraday movements of all years for which data are available can be found in Appendix 1.
18. See Ferdinand Lips, *Gold Wars* (New York: FAME, 2001), pp. 177ff.
19. April 1999, February 2005, April 2007 and April 2009. See Michael Kosares, 'The Gordon Brown Gold Rally Indicator Flashes Buy Signal', www.usagold.com/amk/abcs-gold-rally-indicator.html. See, also, John Embry and Andrew Hepburn, 'Not Free, Not Fair: The Long-Term Manipulation of the Gold Price', 24 August 2004, p. 36, www.sprott.com/media/105296/not-free-not-fair.pdf.
20. Alex Hämmerli, 'Wo liegt das Schweizer Volksvermögen?', *20 Minuten*, 31 March 2012, www.20min.ch/finance/news/story/Wo-liegt-das-Schweizer-Volksvermoegen–22947306.
21. John Garret, 'Monetary Policy and Expectations: Market-Control Techniques and the Bank of England, 1925–1931', *The Journal of Economic History*, 55(03), September 1995, p. 618. Found by Tyler Durden (pen name).
22. Bob Woodward, *Maestro: Greenspan's Fed and the American Boom* (New York: Simon & Schuster, 2000), p. 46. Woodward describes the events as a possibility, since such a cooperation may have been illegal. However, he mentions this reason in such an open manner as if this 'possibility' would correspond to the actual facts.
23. Executive Order 12631, www.archives.gov/federal-register/codification/executive-order/12631.html.
24. John Crudele, 'Fix Was In: Bloomberg Mag Seconds a Scoop', *New York Post*, 8 December 2011, www.nypost.com/p/news/business/fix_was_in_bloomberg_mag_seconds_t0MKHkjTB8AMZGGj8tAbtJ#ixzz2CCXVxyej.
25. Angela Monaghan, 'Barclays' Libor Scandal Hits Bank of England Governor Race', *Telegraph*, 3 July 2012, www.telegraph.co.uk/finance/newsbysector/banksandfinance/9373641/Barclays-Libor-scandal-hits-Bank-of-England-governor-race.html. There are further parallels to the situation on the gold market. Many people were aware of what was going on (and yet only a few spoke out); something always escaped to the outside world (and yet the case wasn't cleared up); the manipulations went on for well over a decade (www.businessinsider.com/the-federal-reserve-was-worried-about-libor-manipulation-as-early-as-1998-2012-7).
26. US Congress, Senate, Hearing before the Committee on Agriculture, Nutrition and Forestry. Testimony by Alan Greenspan, Chairman of the Board of Governors of the Federal Reserve. 105th Congress, 2nd Session, 30 July 1998, http://agriculture.senate.gov/Hearings/Hearings_1998/gspan.htm. The quote is often cited by GATA (the organisation that tries to end gold market interventions).
27. Annual Report 2011 of the German Bundesbank, p. 134, www.bundesbank.de/Redaktion/EN/Downloads/Publications/Annual_Report/2011_annual_report.pdf.
28. §266 HGB, §26,2 in connection with §3 Bundesbankgesetz. There is no exception allowed in this context.

29. 144 central banks (as of September 2012) report to the IMF in this manner. International Monetary Fund, 'Currency Composition of Official Foreign Exchange Reserves (COFER)', www.imf.org/external/np/sta/cofer/eng/index.htm.
30. Annual report of the Bank of Portugal 2011, p. 144, www.bportugal.pt/en-US/PublicacoeseIntervencoes/Banco/RelatConselhoAdministracao/Publications/RelCA_11_e.pdf (its gold swap quota, once 50 per cent, has been completely eliminated). Annual report of the Swiss National Bank 2011, p. 122, www.snb.ch/de/mmr/reference/annrep_2011_komplett/source; BIS 82nd Annual Report, BIS 2012, www.bis.org/publ/arpdf/ar2012e7.pdf. Sight and term deposits are, for reasons of simplification, added to gold loans, although it is not indicated if and how much of the sight deposits ('collective custody') is actually lent out in the market.
31. Belgium (37 per cent at the end of 2011, http://derstandard.at/1350259138672/Oesterreichs-Gold-ist-unzulaenglich-geprueft) and Germany (stopped lending in 2008) have recently begun to publish more information.
32. Quoted from Bruno Bandulet, 'Where is the Gold?', International Precious Metals and Commodities Show, Munich, 18–19 November 2005, p. 66. See also www.goldseiten.de/content/kolumnen/artikel.php?storyid=4.
33. For example, Anne Y. Kester, 'International Reserves and Foreign Currency Liquidity: Guidelines for a Data Template', Washington 2001, points 72, 99 *et al.*, http://dsbb.imf.org/vgn/images/pdfs/opguide.pdf.
34. Email sent by the Bundesbank to the author, 2 January 2013. For details regarding the calculation of the amount lent based on the published lease revenues, see Appendix 3.
35. The subject-matter is different, as with the central banks, which include gold receivables with their disclosed gold holdings. Carry traders can disclose gold liabilities together with other liabilities.
36. In reality gold is not consumed – like oil, for instance – but reshaped. The term 'consumption' to describe the flow is, however, commonly used and thus employed here.
37. Frank Veneroso, *The 1998 Gold Book Annual* (Los Angeles: Jefferson, 1998).
38. The mining companies, for instance, wouldn't demand more gold just because an expansion of the loan supply would lead to a decline in the lease rate from 0.1 to 0 percent. Speculators can also be excluded, as they could only make use of the gold if it is subsequently sold (as borrowed gold stored in a vault cannot participate in price changes); if that was the case, the speculator would come into possession of investable proceeds and would himself become a carry trader.
39. An 'official' mention of the gold carry trade can be found in the 'Reserve Bank of Australia Bulletin' of November 1999, p. 28. An early reference of (modern) gold lending by central banks and the possiblility of a carry trade (he talks about arbitrage) can be found in Edward Jay Epstein, 'Ruling the World of Money', *Harper's Magazine*, November 1983, p. 45, www.edwardjayepstein.com/archived/moneyclub2.htm.
40. Frank Veneroso, 'Facts, Evidence and Logical Inference', 2001, www.gata.org/node/5275.
41. Reginald Howe and Michael Bolser, 'Gold Derivatives: Moving towards Checkmate', 2002, www.goldensextant.com/commentary23.html#anchor19855.

42. James Turk, 'More Proof', 2003, www.gata.org/node/4247.
43. Reginald Howe and Elwood: 'The Fed: Up to its Earmarks in Gold Price Manipulation?', 15 May 2000, www.goldensextant.com/commentary11.html; the stored gold can be found in the Federal Reserve Bulletins as 'earmarked gold' under 3.13 (currently: 'Foreign official assets held at Federal Reserve Banks'), p. 3.
44. Details to this follow, and are also in Appendix 4.
45. Details to this follow, and are also in Appendix 4.
46. For details of the calculation, see Appendix 4.
47. For instance: 'Tomorrow's price must be high relative to today's in order to induce private above ground stock owners to hold gold.' Dale Henderson, John Irons, Stephen Salant and Sebastian Thomas, 'Can Government Gold Be Put To Better Use?: Qualitative And Quantitative Effects Of Alternative Government Policies', International Finance Discussion Paper 582, 1997, p. 12, http://papers.ssrn.com/sol3/papers.cfm?abstract_id=38760.
48. 'Au vom Thron', *Der Spiegel*, 22 January 1968, p. 70; 'What a Blessing', *Der Spiegel*, 4 December 1967, p. 152. The latter article mentions a secret meeting of leading international central bankers, where even the menus at the hotel were destroyed. The FOMC (Federal Open Market Committee) minutes of the time often have the gold outflows as a topic and allow one to recognise the details and background.
49. Letter by Karl Blessing to Mr William M. Martin Jr, no reference, unclassified, 30 March 1967, in Lyndon B. Johnson Library, NSF, NSCH: TTNAN, Box 50, 1966–67, Book 2, Tabs 72–98 [1 of 2], www.larsschall.com/2011/01/29/der-mysteriose-brief-in-austin-texas. The letter isn't about the immobility of Germany's gold reserves, as is sometimes alleged.
50. These assertions were made by Francis Bator, deputy national security adviser to Lyndon B. Johnson. Thomas A. Schwartz, 'Lyndon Johnson and Europe', in H.W. Brands (ed.), *The Foreign Policies of Lyndon Johnson: Beyond Vietnam* (Texas: A&M University Press, 1999), p. 53; Hubert Zimmermann, *Money and Security* (New York: Cambridge University Press, 2002), p. 229.
51. 'Shrinking Role for US Money', *Time*, 15 October 1979, www.time.com/time/magazine/article/0,9171,916948,00.html. We owe this find to Eric Janszen.
52. 'Former Federal Reserve Chairman William McChesney Martin says that if he were still in office, the US would sell gold only "over my dead body".' *Ibid*.
53. Paul Volcker, 'From Dollar Float to Inflation Fight', *Nikkei Weekly English*, 15 November 2004 (Part 2 of an excerpt in three parts from the memoirs published in Nihon Keizai Shimbun, *My Personal History* [Tokyo: Nihon Keizai Shimbun-sha, 1980]). We owe the find to John Brimelow. The reason why a decision by central banks to prevent a rise in the gold price by means of coordinated sales wasn't taken was that France was against it.
54. For those interested, there are publications on the topic of interventions by, for instance, Michael Bordo, Owen Humpage, Anna Schwartz, William Osterberg, Kathryn Dominguez, David Sondermann, Bernd Wilfling, Mark Trede, Michael Frenkel and Georg Stadtmann.
55. Board of Governors of the Federal Reserve System, Transcript of the FOMC meeting, www.federalreserve.gov/monetarypolicy/files/FOMC19870429confcall.pdf.

56. Kenneth Gilpin, 'Currency Markets', *New York Times*, 28 April 1987, www.nytimes.com/1987/04/28/business/currency-markets-dollar-ends-hectic-day-with-rally.html?scp=1&sq=gold&st=nyt.
57. 'Well, Frank, what are you going to do when the dollar is falling and the price of gold is soaring?', www.federalreserve.gov/monetarypolicy/files/FOMC19880630meeting.pdf, p. 61.
58. 'A Blitz of Selling', *Wall Street Journal Europe*, 6/7 August 1993, p. 9.
59. 'Erste Zweifel an der Goldhausse' ['First Doubts about Gold Rally'], *Süddeutsche Zeitung*, 8 June 1993, p. 27.
60. Two likely data errors in the high/low differential of the one-minute intervals, which made the move look even more volatile were removed manually.
61. FOMC19930707meeting.pdf. The picture shows the scanned version, which was available in January 2003 at www.federalreserve.gov/FOMC/transcripts/1993/930706Meeting.PDF (in the meantime the data have apparently been processed with OCR software, to make them searchable for strings). Note: although these are verbatim minutes, they are in many ways incomplete. On this topic see Robert Auerbach, 'That Shreddin' Fed: Just 18 Minutes of Watergate Tapes were Erased, While the Fed's 'Edits' Veil Years of Historic Record', Barron's, 10 December 2001, http://groups.yahoo.com/group/gata/message/940.
62. www.federalreserve.gov/monetarypolicy/files/FOMC19930707meeting.pdf, p. 40. For quotes from Angell (in this chapter) see Figure 20.2.
63. FOMC19930817meeting.pdf, p. 41.
64. FOMC19930518meeting.pdf, pp. 32f.
65. Greenspan mentions the treasury, as, in the US, it is the treasury and not the central bank that holds the gold reserves. 19930518meeting.pdf, pp. 40f.
66. www.federalreserve.gov/monetarypolicy/files/FOMC19930518material.pdf, pp. 3f.
67. 19930518meeting.pdf, p. 4.
68. Ibid., p. 6.
69. Ibid., p. 8.
70. Ibid., p. 21.
71. Ibid., p. 25.
72. Ibid., pp. 35f.
73. 19930707meeting.pdf, p. 71.
74. See Lips, *Gold Wars*, p. 188.
75. Dennis Gartman, 'The Gartman Letter', 29 July 2009, pp. 2f., www.thegartmanletter.co; excerpts included from www.gata.org/node/7637.
76. www.nanex.net/aqck/2924.html.
77. www.nanex.net/aqck/2967.html.
78. www.financialsense.com/contributors/dimitri-speck/a-high-frequency-attack-on-gold; even after 23 emails the question of whether there were data errors in the official Time and Sales report (published on the CME website), which could have provided an alternative explanation of the at the same time observed ups and downs, couldn't be cleared up.
79. On the basis of closing prices of one-minute intervals of the COMEX intraday data of the front month in the normalised time period from 8.20 to 13.30. The prices can, due to their high number (1.5 million), only be checked for mistakes to a limited extent. One apparent shock turned out to be an

erroneous data point, which was isolated and not confirmed by the spot price data bank with one-minute frequency (11 March 1988). Missing data points can, naturally, not lead to wrongly identified shocks. It could be, however, that shocks that existed in reality were not identified due to gaps. Most gaps are not very extended (one to three minutes), so , the probability of low-balling appears to be small. The distribution of gaps relative to calendar years is not conspicuous in its importance for the result. The data vendor apparently doesn't use some of the methods that occasionally falsify results, such as filling gaps with previous values.

80. Moming Zhou, 'More Gold Coins Halted as Investors Seek Haven', *MarketWatch*, 7 October 2008, http://articles.marketwatch.com/2008-10-07/news/30735650_1_gold-coins-south-african-krugerrand-bullion-coins.
81. Handelsblatt, 25 October 2008, 'Goldbarren gehen weg wie nichts' ['Gold Bars are Selling Like Hot Cakes'], www.handelsblatt.com/unternehmen/industrie/zwei-farben-gold;2068770.
82. The sum of the holdings of SPDR Gold Shares, Gold Bullion Securities (LSE), Gold Bullion Securities (ASX) and New Gold (JSE); www.exchangetradedgold.com.
83. A detailed account can be found in Philipp Bagus, 'The Tragedy of the Euro', 2010, http://mises.org/books/bagus_tragedy_of_euro.pdf, p. 51 *et passim*.
84. Helmut Kohl, 'Wir haben das für die Zukunft Notwendige getan' ['We Have Done What was Necessary for the Future'], *Frankfurter Allgemeine Zeitung*, 31 December 2001, p. 14, www.seiten.faz-archiv.de/faz/20011231/fd3200112311234709.html.
85. The creation of this scapegoat was pursued by, among others, French president Nicolas Sarkozy, German chancellor Angela Merkel and euro-group chief Jean-Claude Juncker. This distraction from political mistakes is nothing new; for instance, US president Richard Nixon also badmouthed speculators in 1971 when he failed to get a grip on the deficit and had to abandon the dollar's tie to gold. Such distraction manoeuvres still work relatively well with parts of the population, as economic concatenations are often not sufficiently well understood. In other situations in life, by contrast, no one would entertain the notion that, if a bridge collapses, for example, a minority ethnic group should be held responsible rather than its builder.
86. Bradford DeLong and Barry Eichengreen, 'Between Meltdown and Moral Hazard: The International Monetary and Financial Policies of the Clinton Administration', 2001 NBER Working Paper 8443, p. 13, footnote 21, http://emlab.berkeley.edu/users/eichengr/research/clintonfinancialpolicies9.pdf.
87. Numerous parameters have an unfavourable effect on the significance and thus the informative value of a statistical analysis. The price movement of gold stocks is strongly correlated with the stock market (since they are stocks) and at the same time with the gold price (as the earnings of mines depend on the gold price). One therefore has to correlate the price movements of three items. Since also the forerun is not static, it too has to be regarded as a variable.
88. She entered into a foreign exchange position on 15 August 2011. Shortly thereafter, the Swiss National Bank, under the leadership of her husband, announced that it was planning to intervene in the foreign exchange market.

89. Theodore Butler, 'A Manipulation Timeline', 26 November 2012, www.silverseek.com/commentary/manipulation-timeline-7831.
90. See also Chapter 29.
91. An interesting approach has been developed by Adrian Douglas. He examined the correlation of silver and gold and concludes the high values could be only the result of manipulation, as the two metals are fundamentally too different. However, the result cannot be confirmed when methodically correct correlation of returns instead of prices is measured. Adrian Douglas, 'More Forensic Evidence of Gold and Silver Price Manipulation', 21 September 2010, http://marketforceanalysis.com/article/latest_article092110.html.
92. Disk Trading, Iavor Kindekov, http://disktrading.is99.com/disktrading. Intraday prices that go back further are costly, which is why we passed up an examination of these time periods. The original study, including an average gold intraday chart covering the identical time period, can be found in Dimitri Speck, 'Price Irregularities in the Silver Market', 9 November 2011, www.gold-eagle.com/editorials_08/speck110911.html.
93. National Inflation Association, 'Is JP Morgan's Silver Manipulation Over?', 9 September 2010, www.inflation.us/jpmorgansilver.html.
94. News of the killing of terrorist leader Osama bin Laden came over the wires hours later. The raising of margins for silver futures could not have triggered the decline alone (since long positions were well in the money due to the strong rally); they can, at most, have intensified the decline.
95. FOMC19950201meeting.pdf, p. 125: 'It is obligated only in the sense that they have one other swap arrangement with the Bundesbank. So, in some sense if they wanted to advance dollars to the Bundesbank, they would use some of the dollars for that. But nothing is obligated in a current commitment.' William Osterberg and James Thomson, 'The Exchange Stabilization Fund: How It Works' (Cleveland: Federal Reserve Bank of Cleveland, 1999), footnote 13. www.clevelandfed.org/Research/commentary/1999/1201.pdf, where the swap with the Bundesbank is mentioned. The 1,700 ton hypothesis is, for instance, found in James Turk, 'Behind Closed Doors', www.fgmr.com/behind-closed-doors.html, combined with James Turk, 'More Evidence From 1995', www.fgmr.com/more-evidence-from-1995.html, both in 'Free Gold Money Report', 2001.
96. Simon Kennedy, 'Bundesbank's Weber Comments on Central Bank Gold Reserves', Bloomberg 2006-10-05 10:00 (New York).
97. www.federalreserve.gov/monetarypolicy/files/FOMC19910326meeting.pdf, p. 19.
98. Lawrence Summers and Robert Barsky, 'Gibson's Paradox and the Gold Standard', *The Journal of Political Economy* 96(3), Chicago 1988, pp. 528ff., NBER Working Paper 1680; contrary to what the title may lead one to surmise, the time after the gold standard is included. Greenspan's lauding of Summer can be found in www.federalreserve.gov/monetarypolicy/files/FOMC19930518meeting.pdf, p. 5.
99. Complaint Howe vs Bank for International Settlements *et al.*, US District Court for the District of Massachusetts Civil Action No. 00-CV-12485-RCL, www.goldensextant.com/Complaint.html, points 62ff.; www.goldensextant.com/P'sSecondAffidavit.html, points 6ff. www.goldensextant.

com/commentary18.html; www.goldensextant.com/SecondAffidavitExhibits.html.

100. That central banks are deliberately altering balance sheets in order to conceal information is evidently not to be easily proved with documentation. A proposal to this effect can, for instance, be found in a working paper lacking any further identification, 'US Foreign Exchange Operations: Needs and Methods', dated 5 April 1961, from the documents archive of then Fed chief William McChesney Martin, p. 9. http://fraser.stlouisfed.org/docs/historical/martin/23_06_19610405.pdf. We owe this find to Elaine Supkis. As already mentioned, the Bank of England falsified data in the 1920s in order to manipulate interest rates (see note 21).
101. Federal Reserve Bulletins can be found online at http://fraser.stlouisfed.org/publications/FRB.
102. www.federalreserve.gov/monetarypolicy/files/FOMC19950201meeting.pdf, p. 69.
103. The last reported gold swap of the ESF was a gold–foreign exchange swap with the Bank of Portugal in 1978. www.treasury.gov/resource-center/international/ESF/Pages/history-index.aspx, footnote 3. However, an agreement over a swap of gold for gold in 1981 has become public, in which the US treasury, which is tightly connected with the ESF, participated: http://treaties.un.org/doc/Publication/UNTS/Volume%201267/volume-1267-I-20864-English.pdf. We thank Ronan Manley for the find.
104. Memorandum dated 8 June 2001, from J. Virgil Mattingly to Alan Greenspan; letter dated 25 June 2001, from Alan Greenspan to Senator Jim Bunning, Complaint Reginald H. Howe, Plaintiff, vs Bank for International Settlements, *et al.*, District of Massachusetts, Civil Action No. 00-CV-12485-RCL, exhibit 5B, www.goldensextant.com/SecondAffidavitExhibits.html.
105. 'The Working Group shall consult, as appropriate, with representatives of the various exchanges, clearing houses, self-regulatory bodies, and with major market participants to determine private sector solutions wherever possible.' Presidential Executive Order 12631 – Working Group on Financial Markets, 18 March 1988, www.archives.gov/federal-register/codification/executive-order/12631.html.
106. For instance, Dieter Siebholz, 'Barrick Gold und seine Derivate – Chancen und Risiken am Goldmarkt' ['Barrick Gold and its Derivatives – Chances and Risks in the Gold Market'] 7 August 2003, www.goldseiten.de/artikel/144–Barrick-Gold-und-seine-Derivate—Chancen-und-Risiken-am-Goldmarkt.html.
107. *Le Monde*, 30 September 1999.
108. 'This issue was debated, incidentally, in the United States in 1976, and the conclusion was that we should hold our gold, and the reason is that gold still represents the ultimate form of payment in the world. It is interesting that Germany in 1944 could buy materials during the war only with gold, not with fiat, money paper. And gold is always accepted and is the ultimate means of payment and is perceived to be an element of stability in the currency and in the ultimate value of the currency and that historically has always been the reason why governments hold gold.' On 20 May 1999, before the banking committee of the Senate, http://commdocs.house.gov/committees/bank/hba57053.000/hba57053_0.htm. Trichet, according to a secondary source

(debate in the UK House of Commons on 16 June 1999), www.publications.parliament.uk/pa/cm199899/cmhansrd/vo990616/debtext/90616-02.htm .

109. Ferdinand Lips, 'Die Goldverschwörung' [literally, 'The Gold Conspiracy'] (Rottenburg: Kopp, 2003), p. 303. (in the English-language edition of the book ('Gold Wars'), this passage is missing. Lips, at one point, mentions 8 February 2002; he must have meant 18 February). Welteke later repeatedly made proposals for sales with alternating justifications. Apparently, the government had recommended him for the job of Bundesbank president because it expected him to push gold sales through. According to press reports, he initially didn't have a majority of the Bundesbank's board backing him. He could only gain the required majority if the money were not to be allotted to the government budget (that, at least, was what he then proposed). Later, he had to resign because of an affair. Members of the opposition suspected at the time that there was a intrigue to push the gold sales through in favour of the budget. Christian Reiermann, 'Und ewig lockt das Gold', *Der Spiegel*, April 2004, S. 75, www.spiegel.de/spiegel/print/d-29725583.html; 'Kauder: Eichel will Bundesbank-Gold für Wahlkampf nutzen', *Frankfurter Allgemeine Zeitung*, 15 April 2004 S.2, www.faz.net/aktuell/politik/inland/adlon-affaere-kauder-eichel-will-bundesbank-gold-fuer-wahlkampf-nutzen-1159801.html.
110. The data had to be corrected manually, as they contained too many errors. According to market reports published at the time, the peak price had even reached $298.
111. http://groups.yahoo.com/group/gata/message/769. The dating of the Tuesday prior to the Friday is beyond question, due to the publication at an independent web service. Sources for further information on the topic: www.lemetropolecafe.com 14. Mai 2001 ff. (closed circle of users).
112. There exists unverified evidence of gold interventions, which is disseminated over the internet, but is not mentioned here even if it appears credible.
113. Quoted from Thomas Holderegger, 'Die trilateralen Verhandlungen 1966/1967' ['The Trilateral Negotiations 1966/1967'], in Andreas Wenger (ed.), *Zürcher Beiträge zur Sicherheitspolitik und Konfliktforschung*, 76, Zürich 2006, p. 235, http://e-collection.ethbib.ethz.ch/eserv/eth:28459/eth-28459-01.pdf.
114. The IMF's statistics appear to show a slightly smaller share, but they also contain a position with currencies that are not specified. These currency positions, which haven't been reported to the IMF, however contain a similarly large share of dollars (this is evident from later reporting of past amounts), so that a commensurately larger dollar share results.
115. Michael Hudson, *Super Imperialism: The Economic Strategy of American Empire* (New York: Holt, Rinehart and Winston, 1972).
116. Quoted in Holderegger, 'Die trilateralen Verhandlungen 1966/1967', loc.cit. p. 235.
117. Alan Greenspan, 'Gold and Economic Freedom', in Ayn Rand, *The Objectivist*, 5(7), 1966, www.gold-eagle.com/greenspan041998.html.
118. 'All That Talk About Gold', *Time* magazine, 5 October 1981, www.time.com/time/magazine/article/0,9171,921073,00.htm; United States Congress, House Committee on Banking and Financial Services, Subcommittee on Domestic and International Monetary Policy: 'Conduct of Monetary Policy: Report

of the Federal Reserve Board pursuant to the Full Employment and Balanced Growth Act of 1978, p. l. 95-523; 'The State of The Economy: Hearing before the Subcommittee on Domestic and International Monetary Policy of the Committee on Banking and Financial Services, US House of Representatives, One Hundred Fifth Congress, Second Session, July 22, 1998', Washington 1998, p. 24. Greenspan said: 'I am one of the rare people who have still some nostalgic view about the old gold standard, as you know, but I must tell you, I am in a very small minority among my colleagues on that issue', http://fraser.stlouisfed.org/historicaldocs/679/download/17593/CMP_105HR_07221998.pdf.

119. For the determination of the cause–effect mechanisms of bubbles, things are simplified as far as possible here. Interest for instance, which seems to suggest itself ('exponential function'), only has secondary importance with regard to the bubble phenomenon.
120. There are also non-credit financed bubbles, set in motion by purchases not financed on credit, but by shifting funds – if, for instance, due to a fad, there is a run on certain goods. They are not the topic here, as their financial consequences also consist merely of shifts.
121. Equal-weighted chained index with daily rebalancing of the Bank of England, the East India Company and the South Sea Company.
122. At the same time his proposal inadvertently makes clear that, with respect to the level of credit outstanding, there is no market equilibrium, but that it depends on the political framework (such as the detailed rules for a gold standard he proposes). Whether the total amount of credit in an economy should be at 100 per cent or 150 per cent of GDP is down to the price effect of credit – not a market question, but one of political determination. Greenspan, 'Gold and Economic Freedom', loc.cit.
123. There are credit claims that show up in the statistics of both the financial and non-financial sectors. If a corporation, for instance, takes out a loan with a bank and the bank refinances itself, then this liability can show up both in the corporate and the financial sector, although it is in terms of the amount involved – as if the corporation had financed itself directly in the capital markets. Conversely, there are also independent liabilities of the financial sector – for instance, for real estate investments – so that the financial sector can also not simply be excluded.
124. To blame the gold standard for the global economic crisis of the 1930s is misleading, as it was already abandoned in 1914, making the credit excesses possible in the first place. It was only later reintroduced amid already existing imbalances (high level of indebtedness, external imbalances), which amplified the then stronger deflationary reaction.
125. This holds also if there is only the feature of 'rising asset prices' in evidence – for instance, through a fad-induced shift into a popular sector; bubbles that are not financed with credit are, however, only a side topic here.
126. A depositor's money continues to exist as an additional (and transferable) deposit at the bank.
127. The term 'velocity of circulation' is misleading as the matter concerns a frequency.
128. This real economic reference value is especially well suited as a yardstick, as the credit claims must be serviced out of it. It is, moreover, a flow value and is,

unlike stock values such as the total value of an economy, as such not directly influenced by the amount of outstanding financial claims.

129. The relative debts of the financial sector in Germany are much higher than in the USA, as bank financings which could lead to double-counting are far more prevalent than in the USA. If one were to add financial debt, one would create an exaggerated picture relative to the USA. The actual level of debt in Germany is, however, still higher than the illustration shows, as the financial sector also has debts for its own account, not only as an intermediary.
130. Paradoxically, even new rules that are designed to increase security often lead to more uncertainty elsewhere and overall. That happened in Kuwait in 1982, where new stock exchange regulations made the camel market into the alternate marketplace, and it also holds for the financial crisis of 2008, as the demand for more safety in banking furthered the shedding of risk in the form of dangerous securitisations. That bubbles can literally be created by the introduction of new laws could, however, can already be observed in the case of the South Sea bubble.
131. It also threatened in the euro crisis of 2011. Due to the preceding financial market crisis, the political and central bank establishment was, however, more willing to act (even though the cacophony of voices in European politics may have made it look otherwise).
132. In the course of this, however, the banks were saved, and not the credit claims directly. Saving entire institutions prevents small institutions from growing in their place that would perhaps be better and would pay smaller bonuses.
133. Other reasons are the increase in value of investments and the creation of higher inflation expectations in a deflationary environment (i.e., the opposite of one of the main justifications employed at the beginning of the interventions). Net money creation via a revaluation of gold was thought of at the Fed (back then with disapproval) in 1995. www.federalreserve.gov/monetarypolicy/files/FOMC19950706meeting.pdf, a find of Goldthumb (pen name).
134. Already 2001, I raised the possibility of such money creation without credit in a post to a forum in 2001. 'Should once a "real asset be created *ex nihilo*", in order to avert deflation, an international organization like the IMF could theoretically create this "artificial gold" in a specific quantity (i.e., declare its existence) and distribute it to national central banks according to a key. They could then, in turn, issue "debt-free" money. Compared to a (just as arbitrary) revaluation of gold, this wouldn't set superfluous additional gold mining into motion. Compared to a national "money creation from thin air", this would create the mutual assurance that the respective other national currencies wouldn't be created from thin air at will.' www.dasgelbeforum.de.org/ewf2000/forum_entry.php?id=76284; www.washingtonpost.com/blogs/wonkblog/post/can-a-giant-platinum-coin-save-our-credit/2011/07/11/gIQA2VAPjI_blog.html; www.thomhartmann.com/blog/2008/12/transcript-ellen-hodgson-brown-09-december-2008.
135. Japan was once criticised by a number of US economists for the path it took; now the USA may well be glad if it succeeds in pursuing a similar path. These economists tended not to pay attention to the total level of credit claims; instead, they were focused on variable magnitudes.

136. However, one certainly gets the impression that there is a hint of doubt: 'Central bankers' success, however, in containing inflation during the past two decades raises hopes that fiat money can be managed in a responsible way... If the evident recent success of fiat money regimes falters, we may have to go back to seashells or oxen as our medium of exchange. In that unlikely event, I trust, the discount window of the Federal Reserve Bank of New York will have an adequate inventory of oxen.' Alan Greenspan, 'The History of Money', opening speech at the exhibition of the American Numismatic Society, Federal Reserve Bank of New York, New York, 16 January 2002, www.federalreserve.gov/boarddocs/speeches/2002/200201163/default.htm.
137. However, he didn't calculate the difference of the differences, and didn't interpret the approach as a means to achieve a precise dating to the day independent of the overarching market trend. Harry Clawar, 'Making Money with Manipulators', www.gold-eagle.com/editorials_00/clawar040300.html. The idea of earning money with gold intraday movements is even sometimes embraced today, for example, 'Revisiting Our Proposal for an Overnight Gold Fund', www.skoptionstrading.com/updates/2012/1/14/revisiting-our-proposal-for-an-overnight-gold-fund.html.
138. Dimitri Speck, 'Geheime Goldpolitik' (Munich: FinanzBuch, 2010), pp. 80ff.
139. See Veneroso, *The 1998 Gold Book Annual*, p. 34 (3,000 tons) and p. 49 (4,700 tons = [5,200 – 500 from private sector gold lending]); the latter figure seems too large.
140. www.goldensextant.com/Complaint.html.
141. www.gata.org/files/GDBC_Report.pdf.

Index

Australia, 42, 258
Austrian School of Economics, 202
Angell, Wayne D., 90, 99f., 154
Asian crisis, 6, 135, 189

Bank of England, xvi, 5, 40, 47f., 82, 154, 286
Bernanke, Ben, 237
Blessing, Karl, 83, 181
Bretton Woods, 66
British pound, 5, 92, 132, 134
Brown, Gordon, 39f., 155
bubble, 135, 179, 191f., 198
bull market, 70f., 78, 92, 94f., 146, 171f.
bullion banks, 41f., 118, 159, 164f., 175f.
Bundesbank, 52f., 57f., 134f., 151f., 181, 185

Canada, 234f.
cancellation of debts, 38, 256
carry trade, 43f., 61f., 92, 117f., 163, 197f., 290
CFTC (Commodity Futures Trading Commission), 90, 123, 145, 170
Chapman, Bob, 175
Chase Manhattan, 175, 286
China, 100, 127, 184f., 199, 204, 213, 241f., 263
Chirac, Jacques, 165
Clawar, Harry, xix, 19f., 283
Clinton, Bill, 39, 114, 165
Cold War, 59, 183, 203, 206, 213
COMEX (Commodity Exchange), 16, 22, 25, 77, 89f., 116, 159f., 168, 172
credit bubble, 135, 179, 191f., 198
credit financing, 189, 194, 234
credit securitisation, 211
currency crisis, 6, 262
currency reform, 154, 212f., 232, 247f., 255
current account deficit, 105, 184, 188f., 232

debt level, 249f., 258
deflation, xvii, 121, 137, 154, 191f., 212, 232f.
Dow Jones, 9f., 177f.

EMS (European Monetary System), 5f., 91f., 134, 177
ESF (Exchange Stabilization Fund), 6, 89, 152f., 166, 286
Euro, 40, 124f., 134f., 166
Euro crisis, 5f, 133f., 189
European currency union, 5, 88, 135f., 166
exchange rate, 5f., 88, 110, 135, 184, 189

Fed (Federal Reserve Bank), 8, 50, 65f., 86f., 99f., 108f., 141, 152f., 164f., 192f., 236
Federal Reserve Bank of New York, 65f., 153
financial market crisis, 119, 131f., 211, 236f., 265
flow variable, 239, 247f., 252, 259f.
FOMC (Federal Open Market Committee), 88, 99f., 158
Forbes, xix
foreign currency, 6, 89, 153
foreign exchange reserves, xv, 53f., 102, 127, 182, 184f., 290
foreign exchange swap, 152
futures market, 18f., 45f., 76f., 87f., 119f., 161, 169f.
futures market climate change, 169f.

Gartman, Dennis, 122
GATA (Gold Anti-Trust Committee), xix, 16, 140, 159, 175

Germany, 5, 52f., 58f., 135, 153, 164, 181f., 233f., 266
GFMS (Gold Fields Mineral Service), 37, 62f.
global economic crisis, 88, 134, 192, 203, 213, 234, 297
gold carry trade, 44f., 52, 63, 118, 197
gold crash, 265
gold ETF (exchange-traded funds), 133
gold lending, 41f., 52f., 61f., 119, 162, 170, 198
gold standard, 1, 59, 82, 189, 193, 199, 203, 264, 297
gold storage, 59, 64f., 285f.
gold swap, 152f., 295
Green, Gretchen, 110
Greenspan, Alan, 50f., 63, 88, 99f., 107f., 154, 164f., 188, 192f., 203, 259
Greenspan put, 161

hedge fund, 5, 8, 37
high-frequency trading, 126
Howe, Reg, 64, 155, 295
Humphrey–Hawkins meeting, 101
hyperinflation, 213, 226, 241f., 263

IMF (International Monetary Fund), 6, 38f., 53f., 165
inflation, 3, 34, 88, 99f., 203, 229f., 238f.
intraday anomaly, 19, 32, 283
intraday chart, 16f., 268f.
intraday movement, 16f., 27f., 95, 129, 148, 174

Japan, 44, 63, 110f., 185, 250f.

Keynes, John Maynard, 201
Kohl, Helmut, 135
Kuwait, 200

Law, John, 201, 212
Le Monde, 163
Lehman Brothers, xiv, 131, 133
Louvre accord, 88
LTCM (Long-Term Capital Management), xiv, 8

market anomaly, 29, 32, 283
McChesney Martin, William, 86, 295
McTeer, William, 112
Mexico, 6, 152, 156f.
misallocation, 7, 209f., 217f.
Moore Capital, 175
Murphy, Bill, xix, 159, 175

New York Times, 89
Nixon, Richard, 84, 293

Omnibus Budget Reconciliation Act, 115

Paris agreement, 88
Pax Americana, 183f.
petrodollar, 183
Plaza agreement, 88
plunge protection team, 158
precious metals, xiv, 1, 37, 74, 82, 89f., 126, 180, 222, 240f., 260f.

real estate, 8, 196f., 208f., 221f., 250f.
real estate bubble, 179, 209
recession, 84, 114, 192, 201f., 219, 254, 259
Refco, 175
Russia, 6, 8, 14

short squeeze, 64, 175f.
socialism, 210, 234
Soros, George, 5f., 92, 175
stock market bubble, 88, 179, 197, 211
stock market crash, 48, 87, 158, 192
stock variable, 247f., 252
strong dollar policy, 140f., 188
silver market interventions, 144f.
Souk al-Manekh, 199, 206
South Africa, 40
South Sea Bubble, 199, 201, 236
Süddeutsche Zeitung, 94
Summers, Larry, 110, 141, 154
swap, 152f., 295
Swiss National Bank, 47, 54, 118f., 143, 287

Tequila crisis, 6
Thiele, Carl-Ludwig, 266
Time magazine, 86, 296
Turk, James, 64, 294
turnover rate, 225f., 238f., 246, 252

United Kingdom, 5, 39f., 52, 107, 155, 163f., 248f.
USA, 39, 52, 65f., 82f., 111, 140f., 181f, 189f., 205f., 232
  US treasury, 47, 52, 109f., 140f., 154f., 163f.
  US treasuries, 83, 111, 124, 186

velocity, 225
Veneroso, Frank, xix, 62f., 152, 287
Volcker, Paul, 86f., 111
Vietnam War, 82, 213

WAG (Washington Agreement on Gold), 25, 143, 153, 163, 165, 170
Wall Street Journal, 94
Weber, Axel, 153
Woodward, Bob, 48
World War(s), 38, 65, 135, 203, 213, 232